T0247793

Praise for *Miss May Does Not Exist*

"What an upbeat, positive, and perceptive take Carrie Courogen has given us on one of our funniest and most interesting film artists, the extraordinarily elusive and talented Elaine May! Her research has followed her subject's 'factual fiction' crumb-trails to hell and back with great love to elucidate on May's truth, even if it means she's going to get an excoriating tongue-lashing for giving a younger generation a story it needs to know if they want to be half as smart as May. We get the feeling that Carrie Courogen understands Elaine May really well. Their intelligence has no gender."

—Tina Weymouth, of Tom Tom Club and Talking Heads

"Don't miss *Miss May Does Not Exist* by Carrie Courogen, a brilliant mix of stalker-thriller, quest-saga, and awe-inspiring biography. Drop-dead talented, funny, singular, gorgeous, and imperious, Elaine May is a figure both elusive yet professionally impossible to overlook for women interested in stand-up, in humor, in comedy, in film, in theater, in writing—and in the world. Spotlighting the grueling, finally triumphant trajectory of May's inimitable career and strewn with new insights and commentaries from May's friends and colleagues, Courogen's well-researched book is at once hilarious and very, very important. In *Miss May Does Not Exist*, Elaine May is finally, wonderfully, and delightfully captured by Carrie Courogen."

—Gina Barreca, Ph.D., Board of Trustees Distinguished Professor of English Literature at the University of Connecticut, author of *They Used to Call Me Snow White . . . But I Drifted* and *It's Not That I'm Bitter*

Miss May
Does Not Exist

Miss May

DOES NOT EXIST

The Life and Work of
ELAINE MAY,
Hollywood's Hidden Genius

Carrie Courogen

ST. MARTIN'S PRESS
NEW YORK

First published in the United States by St. Martin's Press, an imprint of
St. Martin's Publishing Group

www.stmartins.com

The Library of Congress Cataloging-in-Publication Data is available upon request.

ISBN 978-1-250-27922-4 (hardcover)
ISBN 978-1-250-27923-1 (ebook)

Our books may be purchased in bulk for promotional, educational, or business
use. Please contact your local bookseller or the Macmillan Corporate and
Premium Sales Department at 1-800-221-7945, extension 5442, or by email at
MacmillanSpecialMarkets@macmillan.com.

First Edition: 2024

10 9 8 7 6 5 4 3 2 1

"Elaine is a very talented girl. Elaine is a very difficult girl.
I have found that the two are synonymous."

    —Fred Coe, 1962

"People would leave me saying, 'She's a nice girl. What is this big
thing about? She's a nice girl.' And the thing is, of course, I wasn't
a nice girl. And when they found this out, they hated me all the
more."

    —Elaine May, 2006

For difficult girls

CONTENTS

PROLOGUE: A Few Thoughts from a Bench Across the
Street from Elaine May's Apartment   1

CHAPTER 1. I Will Tell You Anything, but I Warn You Now,
It's a Lie   7

CHAPTER 2. When in Doubt, Seduce (1952–1957)   21

CHAPTER 3. Nichols and May Take Manhattan (1957–1961)   50

CHAPTER 4. What the Hell Happened to Elaine May?
(1961–1967)   80

CHAPTER 5. You Make the Crew Nervous: *Adaptation/Next*
and *A New Leaf* (1968–1971)   112

CHAPTER 6. Laugh and Laugh and Laugh and Shudder Later:
The Heartbreak Kid (1972)   132

CHAPTER 7. Two Stolen Reels and a Clown Car: *Mikey and
Nicky* (1976)   152

CHAPTER 8. Nothing Was a Straight Line: *Heaven Can Wait,
Reds,* and *Tootsie* (1976–1985)   180

CHAPTER 9. Dangerous Business: *Ishtar* (1987)   210

CHAPTER 10. There's No Prize, Just a Smaller Size (1988–1996)   239

CHAPTER 11. Don't Call It a Comeback: *The Birdcage* (1996)
and *Primary Colors* (1998)   255

CHAPTER 12. We Adapt Very Quickly (1998–2014)   275

CHAPTER 13. What Is Important in Life and Art? (2015–2023)   307

Acknowledgments   329
Notes   332
Index   377

A Few Thoughts from a Bench Across the Street from Elaine May's Apartment

It's a crisp Tuesday evening in September, and as I sit on a bench on Central Park West across the street from Elaine May's apartment, the thought occurs to me that I have absolutely lost my mind. This isn't the first time I've felt close to insanity; the feeling has hit me several times over the past three years that I've spent working on this biography. But as I try to subtly adjust the too-tight long blond wig on my head—you see, I'm just as scared of being recognized by Elaine as she maybe is of me—that looks every bit the $25 it cost, I think: This simply has to be the nuttiest I could possibly get. Why am I doing this? What could I possibly gain from it, except a fleeting glance of a recluse? Stakeouts, I realize, are not for the excessively nervous.

For the vast majority of the time I spent writing this book, I lived two blocks from Elaine on the Upper West Side of New York. The location wasn't intentional, I promise. But every morning when I woke up and opened my curtains to a view of the San Remo's twin towers, I had to admit that it was deeply, darkly funny. And I liked to think, if she had known, she would have thought so, too. I had long fantasized about seeing Elaine on the street someday, had played out every hypothetical of what I would do if I ever did. Would I dare speak to her, tell her politely that I was a fan or thank her for her work? Or would I just watch from afar and let her live in near-total anonymity the way she wants? I never knew. But once I embarked on this bizarre journey of writing about her, I began to see her everywhere. Knowing we were neighbors only made it worse. There she was: standing on the corner, waiting for the light to change; walking through Central Park; in every grocery store within spitting distance I walked into, browsing the produce or waiting in line. Countless anonymous women became victims of my anxious sneaking sideways glances and curious double takes. Statistically, at least one of them had to have been her, but I'll never know for certain. I never had the guts to say anything—because, really, what would I even say?

"You would tell her the truth," Phil Rosenthal, creator of *Everybody Loves Raymond* and one of Elaine's good friends, tells me when I reveal this predicament to him. "That you are the one who's been bothering her about the book. And she would be completely sweet. She would."

"I would hope so," I reply, anything but optimistic.

"It's just a defense that she's got. It's not you," he says.

"That's reassuring," I say, still wary.

"It is. It's everyone." He's got me there. *That* I know.

Still, I remained unconvinced that she wouldn't say something that would send me wading straight into the Hudson River with pockets full of rocks. So anytime I had a potential sighting, I kept quiet, sent frantic texts to friends, then spent the next several hours overthinking every moment of the failed interaction. Again and again and again and again. Which brings us back to the park bench, the disguise, the sitting and waiting and hoping for just a sight—just confirmation that she was real, that she existed somewhere outside the confines of my own mind.

I had tried everything to reach Elaine: mailed her postcards, messengered her cookies, established regular contact with her de facto consigliere, talked to some of her best friends. I spent $200 printing and mailing her 341 pages of museum scans of old family documents she hadn't known existed, sent emails that bounced, cold-called numbers that rang endlessly, walked by her building hoping I'd happen see her coming out of it, attended events she RSVP'd to, then ghosted at the last possible moment. And yet: crickets. At one point, a friend suggested sending her an entire smoked whitefish from Zabar's. In hindsight, I kind of wish I had. Maybe then I wouldn't be sitting on this park bench.

I'm kidding, of course. If there's one thing to know about

Elaine May, it's this: No one, and nothing, can convince her to do anything she doesn't want to do. The woman is an indomitable force, an immovable steel rod disguised in the body of a fragile old woman.

Full disclosure: At one point, I did hear from Elaine. Sort of. After years of chasing, she finally agreed, through a close confidant, to answer four questions in writing. Agreed, of course, in her characteristically controlling fashion, hinging the arrangement on a non-negotiable stipulation that our brief Q&A be printed in its entirety. And then, just when I thought she was within grasp, she was gone. When I objected to her confidant's edits of my questions, the offer was withdrawn. I didn't have to like the decision, but one thing's for sure: I had to accept it.

YEARS AGO, ELAINE explained the difference between romance and comedy: Comedy, she said, was more like real life. This story isn't a romance. This story, like life, is a comedy, one entirely of Elaine's own making, not dissimilar from the ones she wrote, where trust is withheld and betrayal seems a given, where the truth is buried under a million little lies and aspirations fall short. Elaine was never going to go on the record honestly about her life; she'd always find a way out, while still trying to have things on her terms. Always directing, even in absentia.

"A romance means it can't happen," Elaine insisted. "It *never* happens that way." She was right. It would have been romantic if Elaine had agreed to talk after all, but it wouldn't have been truthful. *Truthful,* that one word on which all of Elaine's work had always been predicated, was what mattered more than anything. You sort of can't help but love her for remaining silent; speaking would change the narrative, would go against everything she appears to be. (And even if she did, how much could we really trust what she told us?) Her voluntary absence, her unwillingness to alter her behavior, isn't just perfectly her, isn't just truthful. It's comedy.

This book is not a romance, but it is a love story. I should tell you that now. Because to like Elaine, as you will come to see, is to love her—but it's to be frustrated or infuriated or bewildered by her, too. It is also in part a love story about relentless creativity, about caring for your work so fiercely you'll do anything to protect it, whether that's stealing reels of film or continuing to blaze on after every devastating setback. It's a love story about the kind of Hollywood that doesn't exist anymore, one that valued original storytellers more than existing intellectual property (although it's also a love story about the countless women left behind by that version of Hollywood, the ones who were probably just as talented as Elaine but not as lucky). It's a love story about the concept of genius, those we allow into the club and those who are allowed to stay. Mostly it's a love story about difficult women, the prickly broads who are not always easy to work with or easy to love, but inhabit their full humanity anyway.

When we deify people like Elaine May, genius though they may be, and deny them the acknowledgment of their real fallibility, we forget that they're still human and thus still one of us. "They don't make them like her very often" was a refrain I heard often when speaking to people about Elaine. It's true, they don't. But they do, indeed, make them. Out there somewhere, hopefully, is another genius waiting to change our world and get into some trouble along the way.

The first rule of improv—a rule Elaine invented—is acceptance. If I say you're a duck, you're a duck. Fighting the idea doesn't make the scene any better, it just sinks it all. You don't have to like the setup, but you have to go with it. You can't control or change it. The only thing you can do is elevate it. In many ways, this book is just like that. It's an acceptance, grudging as it may be, and hopefully an elevation. There's still so much that is impossible to know, precisely because that's the way she wants it. Elaine has spent her entire life methodically laying an impenetrable wall between herself and the public, garnering the sympathy of friends and colleagues who fiercely protect her—perhaps in part because many of them don't even know her all that well themselves.

THERE'S A SCENE in *Ishtar* where Warren Beatty says to Dustin Hoffman: "You've got the guts to just say, *To hell with it.* You say that you'd rather have nothing than settle for less!" He means it as a sincere compliment, though its unintended cruelty gets the laugh. I keep coming back to that line when I think about Elaine, how prescient it was of her to write it for a film intended to be a comeback that was instead a death knell. This is the difficult part of loving Elaine May: knowing that she likely could have had a far more prolific career had she been more agreeable, had she compromised a little instead of always fighting for a white-knuckled grip of full control—and knowing how unfair it is to ask that of her. Why the fuck should Elaine have had to settle? Besides, if she had, she probably wouldn't have created a body of work—one that head-spinningly spans comedy, theater, and film; writing, acting, and directing—with such an intense and unique point of view, one that would come to define the latter half of the twentieth century. No one but Elaine could have told her stories the same way. Refusing to settle for less didn't entirely work out for her, but there would be others. The descendants of Elaine May are too numerous to count; her influence is everywhere.

What Elaine wanted most was to disappear. What she didn't count on was that some things, like the ashes of the cigars she chain-smoked or her defining voice, are impossible to get rid of that easily.

I Will Tell You Anything, but
I Warn You Now, It's a Lie

Imagine for a second that you're twelve years old and a recent transplant to Los Angeles, the new girl once again; you've lost count of what number school you're on now. Your beloved father, Jack, an actor in the Yiddish theater, has recently died, and your mother, Ida, is doing her best to hold things together. She's a good businessman, you tell people. It's the most generous description of her you can muster. The teacher asks you to tell the class a bit about yourself and you regale them with a tale of how you're from "all over," born in Philadelphia but a wandering nomad raised on the road as you toured the country performing in the vaudeville theater with your parents. While Ida handled practical concerns—printing tickets, running the box office, producing, that sort of thing—Jack had the dazzling multi-hyphenate role of being the director, the writer, *and* the star. So maybe his plays were a little more in the second-tier realm—he wasn't a Second Avenue* headliner—but he still managed to get a few good notices in the press and make enough friends in the business to have an audience he could turn to for support.[1] And you—well, you were more than just Jack's daughter. You were his costar. All right, so maybe you always had to play little boys named Benny, and maybe you had to stop when you started developing. ("And our people do not believe in breast binding,"[2] you would crack, beating everyone else to the punch line.) And sure, maybe you never seemed to stay in one place long enough to

---

* In the early twentieth century, the Yiddish Theater District was located primarily on Second Avenue in New York City.

learn the multiplication tables past five, let alone make real friends, before you were off to the next city. And okay, maybe the impoverished Chicago winters you endured were nothing like anything they could imagine, these suntanned children of Hollywood. But you didn't have to mention that. You could tell them instead how you were briefly a radio star yourself, making appearances on the Jack Benny show and playing Baby Noodnik in a Fanny Brice parody program. And how many of them could say the same?

It's a great origin story, dazzling even, one that could easily give a new girl an air of allure and mystery strong enough to, if not make fast friends and admirers, at least scare off would-be enemies until it was time to start all over again somewhere new. It's a story you'll stick to for the rest of your life, embellishing it at times for dramatic effect and always leaving people hanging on every word. Maybe it isn't the *exact* truth, but does that matter as long as it's good?

IF THERE'S ONE thing Elaine May knows how to do well, it's tell a good story. But where the truth—a detail she relentlessly fixated upon, at times to her own detriment—seems to be a sticking point in all her work, when it comes to her life, the facts are more malleable. As a writer, she knew which parts of her story were interesting and worth emphasizing, which parts were not just dull, but tragic and traumatic—things that needed to stay buried far from an audience's prying eyes. Elaine would not be the first twentieth-century artist to choose to mythologize her own life, and she certainly is not the last. In her earliest days with the Compass Players in Chicago, she entertained colleagues with tales of her birth "in a car trunk in Brazil or Argentina," her abduction by Yiddish comedy star Aaron Lebedeff, and life growing up in a suitcase.[3] As overnight fame with Mike Nichols brought an endless string of magazine profiles that would practically print anything they said verbatim, bending the truth became an entertaining way to break up the monotony, a game to see how much she could get away with before someone called her bluff. She spun herself into a woman who was fluent in Portuguese,[4] gave her measurements as "24–35–147½,"[5] claimed to be a distant cousin of Ed Sullivan.[6] The occasion doesn't even really matter. "You know that sometimes she changes stories just for fun?" Phil Rosenthal asks. "And she'll do it to me, her friend."[7] The story was hers to own and adjust however she saw fit, until the thread of the narrative slipped away from her and instead became a giant web of half-truths to untangle.

With Elaine's penchant for elusive privacy, the facts she personally presents as true must always be taken with a grain of salt. We are all, to varying degrees, unreliable narrators of our own lives, letting others know only what we *want* them to know. In life, this isn't so much malicious as it is incidental, a simple part of being a human who desires connection and acceptance above all else. "What truth can I tell that's as good as this lie they believe?" Elaine would reflect decades later. "The fact [is] that we kind of feel that we can choose the truth."[8] Well, sure. Elaine, though, wants you to know that you're being set up, wants you to question what is a fact and what is a good story. It's the mark of someone both acutely aware of the mind's ability to present alternate versions of reality— and of someone so distrustful of others that she expects the feeling to be mutual. "I will tell you anything," she once told an interviewer, "but I warn you now, it's a lie."[9]

The lies beg an important question: How much personal information about artists are their audience entitled to know, and how much does it even really matter? Artists come from somewhere, and their environments have an effect on the way they come to look at the world. But do we need to know all of it? Or is it enough to know that whatever the reality was, something about it was so unappealing that it could not be accepted without some sort of embellishment? We know that Elaine grew up in the Yiddish theater, a funhouse mirror of melodrama and vaudeville, where folklore from the old world met stories from the new world. Here the truth could be manipulated into something more entertaining, something that could offer escape from both the mundanities and the heartbreaks of everyday life. But audiences who attended these performances went home when they were over. Elaine didn't get that option. From birth, her home was among the people creating these alternate universes, with no line separating fiction from reality. As the screenwriter Jeremy Pikser would muse decades later, spending your earliest years enmeshed in that world "can't be good for your sense of reality."[10] Obviously it can't—which is perhaps why Elaine emerged from it with one of the most singular minds of the twentieth century, one whose view of the world and approach to her work she herself described as coming from "a tilted insight."[11]

HERE IS WHAT we know for sure: Elaine Berlin was born to Jack Berlin (a Russian immigrant from Pittsburgh) and his wife Ida (a tough woman from Chicago) on April 21, 1932, in Philadelphia, Pennsylvania. It was a birthplace that was more a matter of convenience to her parents' touring schedule than of any significance. They were constantly on the move: Just a few months before, Jack had been working in Los Angeles; less than six months later, the family was back on the road, living out of a hotel in Omaha. In America, the Great Depression waged on unrelentingly, while overseas, a refugee crisis was emerging as the Nazi Party made gains across Europe.[12] The only way to survive a world full of such sorrow and horror was to find something to entertain and distract yourself. Modern Yiddish theater, with its strains of both escapism and self-deprecating reflection, was good for that.

American Yiddish theater had always been for the masses—appealing to both rich and poor—but between the tight times of the Depression, the growing popularity of radio programs and movie houses, and Jewish immigration coming to a near standstill, vaudeville's audience waned.[13] Even in its prime, Jack was unable to climb out from under the shadow of his famous older sister, the actress Mollie Cohn, whom he often appeared alongside. Ida saw a star in Jack, though. She believed he could make a name for himself on his own and persuaded him to join the Hebrew Actors' Union to do so, a choice that outraged his family.[14]

"That family made the fourteen years I was married to Jack a nightmare," Ida wrote after his death. They found fault with everything she did, accused her of being a spendthrift—fresh, considering there was never any money to spend—and either shunned her from social events or invited her just to embarrass her. Once, in front of a group of actors, Jack's mother, Annie, loudly proclaimed that she would be "the happiest woman in the world" if Jack would divorce Ida.[15]

Estranged from his family in Pittsburgh, Jack hit the road, putting on productions all over the United States, Mexico, and South America, setting up shop in a city just long enough to build a troupe and produce a few shows about grim subjects like death and addiction until the money ran out and it was on to the next. He was, by all accounts, "a sweet guy,"[16] charming and charismatic, a doting father who would bring Elaine onstage with him to perform bit parts. He chased the work, not the money, relying on the kindness of others, often wiring his manager pleading for help when another show went under, a gig fell through, or he couldn't afford bus fare home.[17] It wasn't easy for Ida, working late into the night in production offices, a lone woman among men who didn't give a damn about her personal safety as long as they were paying her,[18] trying to support Jack's career, keep them afloat, and be an attentive mother at the same time. She lamented the fact that she never stayed in one place long enough to have a home of her own and was instead dragging herself around from one place to another with a child. But Jack was so good, she thought. No—Jack was the *best,* a rare talent whose genius was so deserving of her devotion and support that she was "satisfied to struggle just so we were together." Jack, though, was less satisfied by his failure to make it big, frustrated that he was playing to empty houses as the theater's popularity fell. Jack, Ida wrote, "didn't get much pleasure out of life. He struggled so hard to make a living and everything he tried to do came so hard for him. He ate bread with blood."[19]

In the winter of 1942, Jack left for a job he had taken in South America while Ida and Elaine stayed behind with Ida's family. He was sick, he told Ida, but no one would believe him. In dire need of money, he flew to Pittsburgh, where his mother and brother Harold agreed to help him, giving him a place to stay and advancing him enough to produce a show. It was a bitter winter; he would walk miles, coatless, to and from the theater to save carfare, telling Ida that she and Elaine would be better off staying in Chicago until he earned enough to return to them.[20]

Jack's performance was a modest success, earning $1,100 in one night, but Annie and Harold insisted they were entitled to half the profit for their investment, leaving Jack with $550 for two months of work. He couldn't find a way to argue with that, and anyway, things seemed to be looking up. Between the money from the performance and an offer in Chicago for a radio job, it seemed like maybe their troubles were over. It had been seven long months away from his wife and daughter, and Jack was anxious to get back to them. But Annie was less enthusiastic. Suspicious of a good thing and reluctant to give Ida anything, she agreed to give Jack only $50 of his cut—enough to travel home, but no money to spend once there. If the radio job worked out, she said, she would deliver the rest and then some to help him buy a home. All of Ida's jewelry was in the pawnshop. Elaine had no shoes. They were borrowing money to make rent. What else was he going to do? His only option was to return to Chicago and hope for the best.[21]

The radio show found an audience, but the pay was slower to come in. Every day for three weeks, Jack called his mother, begging her for the money he desperately needed that she had promised, always being met with promises of "next week, next week." Jack's share came, eventually, but he wasn't there to see it. One morning in March, on his way to meet a radio sponsor, Jack had a heart attack on the street. He wasn't a healthy man to begin with,[22] and all the stress had caught up to him. Even if he had time to call a doctor, he didn't have the money for it. All he had was a quarter in his pocket, which he offered to a woman in a drugstore with a plea for help. It was too late. He was forty-seven.

Bereft, Ida had more than her husband's sudden death to deal with; she faced the threat of imminent poverty. All she had to her name was 76 cents, nearly $600 worth of pawn tickets with interest due in less than two months, and a traumatized child to support. Jack's family promised to take care of Ida and Elaine, but not even that word was kept. They paid for Jack's casket with his own money, then left after the funeral without a goodbye. "I know I am a wreck," Ida wrote Jack's manager. "[His family] should be happy where I am concerned. I was left penniless and a wreck. Elaine is under the doctor's care for nervous disorder. That's what it did to her. She was so happy she had her daddy with her to stay and she was on the radio with him and all of a sudden this happened and she is bewildered and can't figure it out. Neither can I."

By the time she was ten years old, Elaine knew this to be true: People you love will leave. People you love will leave without warning, and the people you expect to take care of you in their place cannot be counted on, either. The world is a cruel, hostile, terribly unfair place, and betrayal is inevitable. Better not expect too much from anyone if you want to survive it. Best to keep your circle small and hold everyone at arm's length. Safer that way. *Safe,* a word Elaine eschewed in her work. "The only safe thing is to take a chance," she always said. But what if she just meant within the clearly defined confines of the page, screen, and stage, where everything has a meaning and an explanation? Real life is too messy to take risks and impossible to control. In real life, sometimes people just die, and there is no understanding or explaining it. So why not instead retreat inward, hide from it all inside fiction, first within others' writing and then within your own? "Physical reality," Mike Nichols once observed, "does not interest her."[23]

Elaine would submerge herself in her work, live inside worlds she could create herself, all the while fighting for as little credit as possible, fighting to disappear entirely. Professionally, there was no way she could ever be granted total anonymity. Her voice is too distinctive to go undetected, so strong that it spans generations, echoing and reverberating in the voices of others to follow. But personally, she's all but succeeded, always keeping her cards close, rarely giving any of her true self away. Why should she? Allowing your true self to be known, really seen—there couldn't be anything more terrifying than letting much more than a very select few into the soft and vulnerable parts of yourself. It's too dangerous. Performing a version of yourself is much easier, a way to control the uncontrollable, a way to not exist.

Elaine's preference for selective participation in the real world would have repercussions. By the twenty-first century, she would claim that much of her early biographical information wasn't entirely true but was simply the product of "her own idle inventions to the press over the years." She would claim to reporters so eager for the rare bit of information that they'd gladly accept her lies that she was born in Chicago, not Philadelphia, and that her Yiddish theater background had been exaggerated.[24] Blaming her idle inventions while continuing to drop idle inventions is the slick act of someone with a keen gift for self-mythologizing. The same can be said for her habit of disappearing for years at a time, allowing a narrative to form but never emerging to correct or confirm it. That's mythmaking in and of itself, allowing others to craft the narrative of your life in your absence instead.

LEFT TO FEND for herself, Ida moved with her sister—who had also been recently widowed and left with a daughter the same age as Elaine—into her brother Louis's home and went into business with him.[25] Uncle Louis was the kind of man who had a perpetual ulcer, an entrepreneur who involved himself in a multitude of disparate schemes to bring in a buck. His work ranged from buying surplus coffins from the army, to running a beauty parlor for straightening kinky hair (though he left the first customer bald), to owning two nightclubs under the name of Johnny Fogarty during Prohibition.[26] When he died, his estate was one big lawsuit.[27]

Life in Chicago didn't provide Elaine with any normalcy. It was just a new kind of dysfunction. "Whatever you're born into seems like the normal world," she said. "It was years before I realized that people didn't have a gun in the house and they didn't arrest you for booking every week. That seemed to me the way the world was."[28]

See, Uncle Louis was in with the Syndicate. Tangentially, that is—not *really* a part of it, but good friends with some of its prominent members. Rumor has it that one of his nightclubs was the infamous Al Capone haunt, the Green Mill Cocktail Lounge. If you believe the family folklore, it was Ida who nursed comedian Joe E. Lewis back to health after one of Capone's henchmen slashed him.[29] Uncle Louis's friends were like loyal family, but with a twisted and at times violent idea of what family and loyalty meant. Once, a friend of his blew up a cleaning store because the owners had been rude to Aunt Fanny.[30] Not even Elaine was immune to the pull of con work. By eleven, she had earned herself a reputation as a pitch partner for Chicago tinmen looking to sell aluminum siding. She had a knack for it; it wasn't just that she was young enough to endear herself to strangers. Youthful charm could only get people to answer the door. No, it was her ability to spin a story, to convince strangers that their home could be pictured in *Life* magazine, if only they added aluminum siding to it first. Sometimes she felt bad about it—all those beautiful historic homes being ruined by their lie—but a job was a job.[31] And what better job than telling a story?

By Elaine's account, Ida was "an absolutely respectable woman,"[32] but no one could deny that she was still a woman faced with the daunting and disparaged task of raising a child on her own. Ida, who hadn't attended school past the fifth grade,[33] was left to pursue whatever it took to survive, sometimes willfully or naively turning her cheek and working with Uncle Louis. As Elaine put it, "My mother once said of the Mafia: 'There's no such thing as the Mafia. Those Italians were our drivers.' . . . That was her world. That was the world she had been born into. It's sort of like cannibals. You think, 'How can they eat each other?' But that's what they do."[34]

Ida was undeniably hard on her daughter, a demanding presence. "Elaine can be a tough lady," Phillip Schopper, Elaine's former partner and frequent collaborator, says. "I understand that Ida could make Elaine seem like an angel." She was all Elaine had, yet she didn't exactly parent her with any sort of gentleness. Her outlook on life, especially on the losses endured throughout it, was decidedly unsympathetic. Life was tough, and that was just how it was. Elaine better get used to it.[35] She was funny and gregarious around others, Elaine remembers, but not around her. "I would hear her talk to other people so entertainingly, and when they left, I would say to her, 'Gee, I wish you were *my* mom,'" she said.[36] Theirs was a precarious relationship, one that would shape the rest of Elaine's life. In the eyes of her good friend Peter Feibleman, "Elaine was a postgraduate in the school of survival for people with difficult mothers."[37]

Elaine's later work is full of vulnerable women, victims, often made so by their mothers or by men. Her vision of the world was not pretty. One of her later students from the Compass Players, Annette Hankin, would assess: "I think she saw all things as trade-offs, and love in a cruel light. It was a terrible, awesome vision, that of a person who has survived an emotional holocaust."[38] Elaine learned early, from her own mother's example, that women would always have a harder time in the world, and even more so if they depended on a man to take care of them. Because one day he could simply leave you, and it didn't matter if he walked out the door or dropped dead of a premature heart attack. No matter which way his exit came about, an exit was inevitable, and you'd ultimately be left to your own devices.

UNCLE LOUIS FOUND a deal that took the whole family to Los Angeles, and Elaine, "by direct request of the authorities," was forced to enroll in school.[39] Formal education had been something viewed with disdain; she hadn't started until she was eight, and by the time she was ten, she had been enrolled in more than fifty schools, often for such brief stints that, she said, "I kept learning that Mesopotamia was the first city."[40]

Elaine, with her erratic upbringing and eccentric family, didn't fit in: "The despair of my youth was that I didn't wear braces and eyeglasses like the rest of the girls."[41] She abhorred Los Angeles, a smog-filled city grappling with its industrial boom in the wake of World War II. L.A. was dirty and ugly, a conservative town ravaged by red-baiting and bereft of any kind of core ideology or art. East Coast and European artists and intellectuals—Elaine's people— were not immune to the draw of Hollywood, but their work was not the standard-bearer; it was the exception. Their presence had had little impact on a community where lowbrow, superficial aesthetics dominated.[42] Hollywood was where culture came to die, and Elaine couldn't stand it: "I feel in opposition to almost everything anyway, but it comes to its height in Los Angeles."[43]

There, she bounced around from John Burroughs Junior High to Fairfax High to Hollywood High. She had an innate and infinite sense of curiosity but found school unbearably stifling. The only thing she could find any enthusiasm for was diagramming sentences. Forget about math—it was impenetrable—and forget especially about history. She couldn't even remember what year something happened to *her*, let alone when something happened to some dead man she didn't even know.[44] Finally, at fourteen, she quit. "Frankly," she said, "I was tired of it."[45] She could diagram sentences by herself. "The truancy people came around and threatened to take me to court," she said, but defiantly, she "called their bluff."[46]

Without classes to fill her time every day, Elaine read voraciously—"mostly fairy tales and mythology"—on her own, but that wasn't the only thing she found to occupy her time. She soon met Marvin May, a native Angeleno three years ahead of her at Fairfax High. Now a freshman at Los Angeles City College, Marvin was on his way to become a toy inventor and model maker.[47]

By December of 1948, the pair were married. Elaine was sixteen; he was nineteen. On their marriage license, Elaine lies, bumping her age up two years; she would say for years after that she wasn't entirely sure how old she was, assuming her mother cheated her age to make it easier for her to work young.[48] For whatever reason, so does he.[49] Teen marriage was not *as* taboo then as it is now; though marriage rates declined in the thirties, 17.1 percent of women between the ages of fifteen and nineteen were married by 1950. But that's not to say it was entirely acceptable, or common, with girls as young as Elaine.[50] The best thing—the only thing, really—a girl back then could hope to be was a wife and mother, but she would at least graduate from high school first, assume the role of house-wife second. Maybe there would be a brief detour at college, viewed more as a finishing school than as a place to learn a future occupa-tion. Either way, she'd be an adult by then; girls weren't supposed to get married until they were women, and at sixteen, a woman Elaine was not. But she wasn't like most girls, either.

Well, except for the fact that she wanted to fool around. "If I kiss, I fuck, and I don't want to fuck," she once said, turning down a would-be suitor.[51] Teenage Elaine didn't have the same self-awareness and self-control. Nights were spent going parking with Marvin, her cousin Jackie, and Jackie's boyfriend. The foursome would flip for the best rumble seat in the car; Elaine and Marvin were almost al-ways the victors.[52] A year after getting married and spending several nights in the rumble seat, Elaine became the seventeen-year-old mother of a baby girl she named Jeannie.

Did she marry Marvin to get away from Ida's rule? Possibly,

although it didn't take long for the marriage to go bust. Six months after Jeannie's birth, Elaine was separated and back under Ida's roof, on her own again, only this time with a child.[53] To eat, she picked up odd jobs: a spieler for a sidewalk photographer, a roofing salesman,[54] a secretary for a private detective who made passes at her. "At one point, he literally chased me around the desk," she said, "and I was thinking, 'I'm much stronger than this guy, and if he catches me, I don't know what he thinks is going to happen, but I'm really afraid I might hurt him.'"[55] Drifting and aimless, she one day found herself in the classroom of famed acting teacher Maria Ouspenskaya, figuring she had nothing to lose. Drama was, after all, in her blood. However, Elaine wasn't exactly a natural, at least not at the Method approach, right away. She struggled to play something she wasn't truly living, holding others back until she could grasp a concept enough to move forward. To her, exercises like the one in which the student portrays the lifespan of a tree—from seedling to budding skeleton to grown and full of leaves—weren't just illogical but untruthful. "I couldn't bud to save my life," she recounted years later. "I knew I wasn't a tree."[56]

It was around this time that Elaine had a revelation: "I thought I would go to college and become extremely educated."[57] Fulfilling that sudden desire wasn't going to be easy; few schools would accept her without a high school degree. But some of her theater friends were going to Chicago, and when she found out the University of Chicago would take her, she decided to join them.[58]

SO WHAT ABOUT Jeannie?

The year was 1952. Elaine was twenty years old, with her entire future ahead of her and a three-year-old child anchoring her to an infinite present. She made a decision: Jeannie would be raised by Ida, and Elaine would move forward. She'd return periodically, "and when she was home we were together," Jeannie said later. "She took me to the park and taught me how to make sandcastles. She wrote great fairy tales."[59] But they were visits. Jeannie wouldn't live with her mother full time again until she was nine.[60]

Men leave their families to pursue their art time and time again, a choice that often gets folded into the hackneyed narrative of the that there was nothing real to worry about."[7] Well, of course Elaine found it fun and worry-free; she never officially enrolled. Instead, she "majored in hanging out,"[8] dropping in on classes when she felt like it, holing up in her apartment and writing plays and script treatments when she didn't. When she did go, she had no qualms about sharing her own unconventional opinions, and chaos generally followed. Once she argued to a philosophy class—including the professor—that everyone in Plato's *Symposium* was drunk[9] ("that's the only way it makes sense," she insisted decades later),[10] walking out the moment she was sure she'd convinced them.[11] She was impossible to ignore; she claimed to have started a bar fight by saying *The Apology of Socrates* "was a political move."[12] It didn't take long for her to build an infamous reputation around campus. Everyone at the University of Chicago was smart—there was no arguing that—but Elaine was a world-wise woman among children, with a mind that seemed to run only at high speed, a cruel wit that could be weaponized at a moment's notice, and an intimidating raw and unbalanced intelligence that came from all those years of skipping school to devour books on her own instead. "She knew everything about the theatre and psychoanalysis," one of her suitors said. "She didn't know about anything else."[13]

Not that it mattered, because as if it wasn't enough to be brilliant, she was beautiful, too, with piercing gray eyes and a lithe body, the mere memory of which could reduce men to pubescent boys anytime they talked about her over the next fifty years. Her looks could be her power when she wanted them to be, but most of the time it seemed as if no person could be more oblivious to their own appearance. Clothes, makeup, even basic self-care—none of it interested Elaine in the slightest. She lived off huge numbers of apples—which she ate in their entirety, including the pits and cores—and wore her dark hair long and tangled. Her clothes were almost exclusively bought at Goodwill, and they rarely ever matched, let alone fit. She had a way of sitting that "could have been construed as flashing," though who's to tell whether she did it on purpose or simply didn't care.[14] A cigarette was always dangling from the side of her mouth. "She was like a gutter rat," one peer recalled.[15]

male genius. The same cannot be said for women, especially women in Elaine's time. The choice, in 1952, to not only raise her daughter as a young single mother but then to leave her, had to have been difficult at best, scandal-making at worst. It was the time of the nuclear family, when women not only weren't supposed to have any aspirations beyond being the ideal wife and mother, but were infamously advised by Dr. Benjamin Spock to "seek psychological counseling" if any arose. Saying Elaine left Jeannie with Ida and went on her way is too pert for the gravity of what that choice meant, the clear-eyed bargaining ability required to look at what you were going to lose with what you had the possibility of gaining.

Those closest to Elaine often seek to present a characterization of her as a woman who cares intensely about her work and nothing else. Or a woman who cares intensely about her work *at the expense* of everything else. The accolades or the money or the power—the by-products of the work—couldn't interest Elaine less. It's why she spends so much time in hiding, why she doesn't play the Hollywood game, refusing to promote her work or take credit or draw any kind of attention to herself. Like Elaine's nomadic childhood, this makes for a good narrative. It doesn't necessarily mean it's entirely true.

Elaine can disavow wanting fame or fortune or even the bare minimum of audience approval, but the one thing she cannot deny is her desire for an audience. If a joke lands in the woods and no one hears it and no one laughs, is it funny? If, truly, the work was the only thing Elaine has ever cared about, she would never have pursued theater or improv, leapfrogging from hole-in-the-wall Chicago stages to chic New York nightclubs and Broadway. She certainly wouldn't have continued to Hollywood, taking opportunities that came to her one after another, continuing to work doggedly behind the scenes—but still very much in the business—when her soured reputation had presented her with an out to go back to a life of anonymity.

But the difficult, alienating choice Elaine made in 1952 is the turning point, the hitch, the moment Elaine Berlin became *Elaine May*. Elaine May might truly care only about her work, but Elaine Berlin had to have had some kind of awareness of her own genius and some desire for that genius to be seen. Her father's daughter, she wanted the work and would chase it, no matter the human cost. And what other options did she have, really? She could stay in L.A., a place she loathed, and keep working odd jobs and taking acting classes, but where would that get her? Staring down the grim future that awaited so many girls in her situation: trapped in the cul-de-sac of domesticity, wings clipped. Going to Chicago was the only way she could make a real life for herself. The sacrifices were a small price to pay for freedom.[61]

CHAPTER 2

When in Doubt, Seduce

1952–1957

Elaine had seven dollars[1] in her pocket when she left home to hit hike her way to Chicago in 1952.[2] Chicago was everything Los An les wasn't, even if it was unfashionably deemed the Second City, art scene just a stop to pass through on the way to New York. At le it *had* an art scene. And then there was the University of Chica an island of beatnik culture, a hotbed of intellectualism, a place tl challenged its students to engage in thought for thought's sake the complete opposite of the rote learning propagated in the ri public school system Elaine had slogged through. It was the perf setting for her to become "extremely educated."[3] Its discussion-bas classes where attendance wasn't mandatory were full of bohemi students like herself—eccentric, analytical, and fiercely opinionate "We were all freaks," the editor Aaron Asher said. "We were w ahead of the country. There was sex. There was dope. There was subculture."[4] Paul Sills, who would go on to found the Playwrigh Theatre Club—which became the Compass Players, which then b came Second City, which opened doors to, well, everything else— put it simply: "You were where it was at."[5]

But admission to the land of where it was at wasn't as easy t score as one might suspect. You may not have needed a high schoc degree to enroll at the University of Chicago, but you did need to pass fourteen grueling entrance exams. And you weren't an easier off once you made it into its free-form classes, where punish ing final exams were the only tests given all year.[6] "Every weekenc someone would kill himself," Elaine said. "I mean, it was just the most neurotic place. So, really, it was sort of freeing. It was fun in

"I was both sexually attracted to Elaine and afraid of her," composer Allaudin Mathieu said. "She was over the top, but with great conviction. The only thing to say about everything she did was, *That's Elaine*."[16] Read through enough anecdotes from men who knew her at the time and you'll find this to be the common consensus. She was a flame for many moths drawn to the beautiful woman who was "about fifty percent more brilliant than she needed to be."[17] Perhaps they thought they'd be the chosen one, or maybe the victor, the one who could tame her or best her, in spite of all evidence pointing to their inevitable fate as the victim instead. She didn't do small talk and had no filter for politeness—let alone niceness—and with no interest in acquiring one, developed a reputation for being "dangerous to vicious, depending on the stimulus."[18] You were ill-advised to make any trouble with her; good luck and god bless if you got caught in her crosshairs.

See: An encounter on the streets of Chicago, when two men began to follow her down the street catcalling and making kissing sounds, allured by her good looks but unprepared for the pitchfork tongue that came with them. "What's the matter? Tired of each other?" she asked. "Fuck you!" one shouted, to which Elaine replied, with no hesitation or fear in her voice: "With what?"[19]

Severn Darden, who along with Elaine was one of the core members of the Compass, said it best: "You have a feeling that at any moment she might kill you."[20]

Paul Sills wasn't afraid of Elaine. Or if he was, he was too infatuated with her to let fear get in the way. He would be one of the many men who fell in love with Elaine, and one who would change her life. Or maybe she would change his. It seems fated that two people with similarly unconventional upbringings that spawned similarly unique brains happened to find each other in the same place at the same time. Sills, like Elaine, grew up in the theater, and knew little else other than a life melding reality and fantasy. Raised by Viola Spolin, the mother of theatrical improvisation, he had grown up watching her develop theater games intended to help players (Viola was averse to the word *actor*)[21] lose self-consciousness in rehearsal so they could fully embody their characters in performance. It was this sort of bohemian view of what theater was and what it could be that was in the back of the twenty-three-year-old Sills's mind when he got involved with the student theater group Tonight at 8:30. While his acting left much to be desired, he thrived as a director who took his actors seriously, no matter their skill level. He began running weekly workshops where he taught other green young actors Viola's games, using them "as a group formation device, as a way of working to make an acting company."[22]

MIKE NICHOLS AND Elaine May were never really a romantic couple, but they had a habit of romanticizing how they met just the same. Experts in narrative, they could turn the reality—which may have been more banal or more complicated—into a good story that was shared often over the years, perfectly constructed to hit all the right beats while almost always remaining lived in and worn, a script that grew more and more comfortable in its many retellings.

It started small:

Sills was a last-minute replacement director on a production of August Strindberg's *Miss Julie,* with Mike starring as Jean the Valet, though he arrived too late to save it from the "pathetic, awful" production it had become.[23] One night Mike observed from the stage "this evil, hostile girl in the front row staring at me throughout the performance." It was Elaine, not even trying to hide her withering disdain for the play her then boyfriend was directing. "I could fucking hear her *breathing* hostilely," Mike said.[24] He could feel her eyes on him the entire night, could tell that "she knew it was shit, and there was no way I could let her know that I knew it also."[25] Their mutual feelings were anything but amorous. "We loathed each other on sight," she said.[26] Days later, while reading an unexpected favorable review from the *Chicago Daily News,* Mike saw Sills walking with Elaine and, eager to share the good news, caught up with them. Mike, Sills told Elaine as he introduced them, was "the only other person on campus who is as hostile as you are."[27] "I couldn't believe Paul said that to me—and I was dating him at the time," Elaine said. More than fifty years later, "I've never forgotten it."[28]

So *this* was *the* Elaine May, the campus terror he had heard so much about. Well, perfect timing. He had a rave to impress her with.

He handed Sills the paper. As Sills read, Elaine scanned silently over his shoulder. Finally she let out a "ha!" and walked away.[29]

For two years, that would be their only encounter. Shortly after, Elaine took off on a hitchhiking odyssey across America with Sills and his friends. It was an "unsettling and wild" existence: running high on emotions and little else, they bounced around from Chicago to New York to Los Angeles, taking acting classes, planning for productions that never materialized, and writing furiously. It was, as anyone who has gone on a long road trip with friends in their early twenties knows, a combustible scenario. Sills, who wrote a Brechtian play with a character loosely based on her, was in love with Elaine. She liked him, maybe, but certainly not that much.[30] He returned to Chicago without her. It's here where the timeline skews, with Elaine traveling back and forth to Jeannie in California and elsewhere in between, the narrative of her life left to become folklore. Actress Mary Birdsong recalls hearing Elaine tell a story, decades later, about being young and broke in San Francisco and falling in with a group of derelicts (who may or may not have been into sex work) who, fascinated by her knowledge of literature, nicknamed her Shakespeare. "She would talk about it almost like a fairy-tale time, where she was lost and this land of misfit porn stars in hippie clothes rescued her and were her family," Birdsong says.[31] It was the kind of story, told as directing impetus, that left Birdsong thinking, "Well, even if it didn't happen, it could have."[32] Elaine herself demurs: "Well, if I was gonna be called anything, I'd like to be called Shakespeare."[33]

BUT THAT "HA!" isn't the end of the story of how Elaine May met Mike Nichols. No, the meet cute has a part two to it, one fit for the best of romantic comedies.

```
FADE IN:

EXT.—CHICAGO, 1954—NIGHT

The camera pushes in on the Randolph Street train
station. Commuters make their way out the waiting
room door and into the night. We slowly zoom in
on—
```

INT.—WAITING ROOM—CONTINUED

ELAINE MAY, our heroine, sits perched on a bench, hunched over a magazine. PULLING BACK, we see **MIKE NICHOLS,** the boy as hostile as she, staring at her from the other end of the room.

CLOSE ON Mike, thinking: what to do, how to proceed. Would Elaine remember him? Would she be uncomfortable if he said hello? Or worse, would she spare him no mercy and effortlessly eviscerate him again?

CUT TO Elaine, oblivious.

Mike strolls through the station and sits down next to her.

> MIKE
> *(slyly, with an accent)*
> May I seet down?

> ELAINE
> *(without looking up)*
> If you veesh.

> MIKE
> Do you haffa light?

> ELAINE
> Yes, zertainly.

> MIKE
> I het a lighter, but . . . I lost eet on Feefty-
> Seventh Street.

> ELAINE
> Oh, of course. You must be . . . Agent X-9?

FADE OUT.

The two of them got on the train together that night, carrying on their impersonations—their first *improvisations*—the entire way back to Elaine's place, a chaotically unkempt basement apartment on Chicago's South Side. The mundanities of domestic life did not interest Elaine; scribbled notes littered the floors, books lay everywhere. "She didn't know conventional dishes. She was utterly a rebel," Mike said. "That was part of the fun of it."[34] She made him one of her few cheap specialties: a hamburger with ketchup and cream cheese. It was love at second sight. In that moment, he "knew instantly that everything that happened to us was ours."[35]

About that love at second sight. People were always wondering . . . were they *actually* a couple? They certainly looked like a couple and talked like a couple and behaved like a couple. "Many think they are married," one profile acknowledged, before clarifying that they were both single. "'They understand and respect each other,' a friend says, 'and have a kind of love. But marry? It would be incest.'"[36]

Decades later, when asked if they were lovers or not, Elaine replied, "I will answer that. We were lovers or not."[37] In meaning to be characteristically evasive, quipping her way out of a question she didn't want to answer, Elaine inadvertently summed up their sexual past perfectly. They *were* lovers or not; the affair they had at twenty-two was so brief—at the Compass, it was known as "the three days that Mike lived with Elaine"[38]—that it almost feels wrong to call them lovers. Their love wasn't the lust kind of love; it was more intimate than that, that rare form of platonic love built on a foundation of *I* know *you*. It was the kind of love that could make a skeptic believe in destiny, in the idea that there are people out there who are connected to us in the most primal, ancestral way. Of course, that's probably too woo-woo for Mike and Elaine, too sentimental, especially for back then.[39] Let's just say they knew how to bond over their trauma.

Mike, like Elaine, didn't have much of a childhood. Born in 1931 to a Jewish family in Berlin, Michael Igor Peschkowsky immigrated to America at seven, fleeing Hitler with little more than two English phrases in his pocket ("I do not speak English" and "Do not kiss me.").[40] Well-off in Germany, Mike's family struggled in America, especially after the death of his father when he was eleven, which left him and his brother in the care of their mother, Brigitte, a sickly and easily wounded woman who loved few things more than playing the martyr.[41] Both he and Elaine "had extremely difficult Jewish mothers," he later said. The two could connect over the ways in which they found them funny—and eventually use them for material—but also all the ways in which they "had a pretty devastating, long-long-lasting effect on both of us."[42]

Growing up on the Upper West Side was lonely. The boy with the bad toupee (he had lost all his hair at the age of four after an allergic reaction to a whooping cough vaccine) living in bug-infested apartments didn't fit in at the elite private schools he attended on scholarship. "I never had a friend from the time I came to this country until I got to the University of Chicago," he said.[43] Elaine would be one of them.

"Everyone wanted Elaine, and the people who got her couldn't keep her," Mike said.[44] But there was something different about this, about who he was when he was with her, and vice versa, that told him she wouldn't leave him the way she had left so many others. Elaine, he soon discovered, wasn't as dangerous as she appeared. Like him, she had reasons to be hostile, and plenty more reasons to put up vicious defenses. But "her toughness was an illusion,"[45] armor she could suit up in to survive a world that she suspected would chew her up and spit her out without a moment's hesitation. No, this hostile boy and this hostile girl made good partners; who knew better than them how cruel life could be? They could bind themselves together with their "insanely judgmental" snobbery, create their own bubble where they "were safe from everyone else when we were with each other. And also safe from each other."[46] Sex—or, at least, sex long-term—would ruin it. They may have been only twenty-two, but they knew enough to realize that.

"We were not lost souls, but we were difficult people and we were difficult for others," Mike said, reflecting on their close bond years later. He conveniently leaves out that they were often difficult for each other as well—but more on that in due time. What he gets right in the romanticization of their tumultuous partnership is this: "We had not entirely successful relationships with a string of people, but kept returning to each other, as it were. We were the steady relationship and the others came and went."[47]

MEANWHILE, PAUL SILLS moved on from Tonight at 8:30. He could do only so much with nonprofessionals, and it was time for him to start his own repertory. In 1952, he found a partner in David Shepherd, a Harvard grad who had hitchhiked from New York to Chicago with a $10,000 inheritance from his stepmother ready to create his dream "people's theater."[48] Shepherd didn't know much about acting, but he knew he liked what he saw when he watched Sills's work. Sills wasn't entirely sold on the political theater aspect, but he couldn't pass up Shepherd's money, and the two came to an agreement that the company would be the best of both worlds. Every week, the players—mostly actors from Sills's class and recent U of C graduates like Ed Asner, Zohra Lambert, and Barbara Harris—would rehearse and perform works by Brecht and Cocteau alongside originals by its founders. They would call their new endeavor the Playwrights Theatre Club.

It couldn't have come at a better time. As the demographics of the neighborhood surrounding the campus shifted away from white and wealthy elites, the school became a mecca for the bohemian set. When they opened in June of 1953, they did so in an empty old storefront that had once been a Chinese restaurant. Actors weren't paid much. By day, they rehearsed productions of shows like *The Caucasian Chalk Circle* and *The Dybbuk*; by night, they slept rent-free in bedrooms converted from what had once been dining booths.

Sills was doing all right. But he needed Elaine. When she finally arrived at the Playwrights Theatre Club one freezing December night in 1954, she was wearing little more than a silk blouse and tennis shoes. She did not have socks, but she did have a baby buggy, in which she schlepped a draft of a play she had written on a collection of scrap paper.[49] "We were instilled with the fact that she was a person of consequence, worthy of note," Ed Asner recalls, "and we had to—we *should*—listen, because she was worthy to listen to."[50]

In the time that had passed since her days dropping in on classes, she had become even more "scarifying," a "mananizer," her lips never without a playfully savage come-on for one of many men she'd leave in her wake.[51] "I did not directly pursue her, but the young people in the theater did," Asner says. "They were all a-gaga. At the time, I suppose I considered that they were all eager to be castrated by Elaine May. And she did succeed in de-emphasizing a number of them."[52]

Sills looked to Elaine constantly for input on the theater's doings. He was now involved with Barbara Harris, but "what Elaine said was important to Paul. He had respect for her brain."[53] Their bond intimidated Harris. Only three years Elaine's junior, she felt even younger. "Elaine was very much into thought," Harris said, "and very sophisticated, and very smart. I was somehow more able to iron my clothes. Elaine was so . . . well . . . incompetent in terms of being able to get her clothes on."[54] She was awestruck by Elaine, who was as generous with other women as she was wicked with men. Elaine took Barbara under her wing like a wiser and cooler older sister, even as Barbara felt positively bourgeois when she compared her life to the bohemian existence Elaine had carved out for herself. Elaine was fiercely independent and answered to no one. She stole from supermarkets, wrote plays on the backs of cereal boxes, and accepted money from Sills to make rent. She'd rather beg than get an actual job, though even that was done theatrically and with unwavering confidence, as she taught Harris once. "She kept saying, 'We have to do it in Brechtian style,'" Harris recalled. "I said, 'What's Brechtian style?' And she said, 'I'll show you.'" Elaine approached a man on the street and told him matter-of-factly, "We're begging, and we want some money." Even begging she could make a man an embarrassed shell of himself. When he pulled out a quarter, she demanded, "And now one for my friend."[55]

"AT SOME POINT at Playwrights Theatre Club," company member Joy Carlin said, she and Mike Nichols "looked at each other and I said, 'I don't know how to act.' And he said, 'No, I don't either. What do we do?'"[56] Mike wasn't going to learn what he thought he needed to know if he truly wanted to be an actor from Sills. He couldn't stay in Chicago, not even for Elaine. He packed his bags and moved home to New York to study with Lee Strasberg, not sure if he'd ever come back.

Not that his absence distracted Elaine from flourishing at Playwrights, moving beyond acting in plays and teaching Sills's game workshops. In the summer of 1954, she began directing, starting with a production of Strindberg's *Miss Julie*. (This was one of Sills and Shepherd's fallbacks, consistently in rotation in Playwrights' limited repertoire.) "It probably was the worst opening we ever had in our lives," recalls Ed Asner, who had been cast, at Elaine's insistence, as Jean the Valet over an actor who had been brought in from New York specifically for the role.[57]

Elaine was "a very meticulous director," Joyce Piven said.[58] Details mattered to her. Details were what told the truth. Details never lied, never gave it away; even the smallest of them had to be attended to with great care. An hour of rehearsal time would be spent perfecting the removal of a glass from a tray; the recording of the show's ambient backing track was an all-night endeavor. Not naturally socially inclined, she never thought that her collaborators might have somewhere else to be or other things to do than spend hours accompanying her down her latest black hole of creative discovery. While Elaine stuck faithfully to Strindberg's script, she insisted that the truth of each moment be found organically, through improvisation, then refined from there—which meant her actors rehearsed long into the night. Often her cast would simply fall asleep onstage while she was somewhere in the wings, fixating on minute technical details. The night of the dress rehearsal, Asner remembers, they didn't start until midnight. When they were finished, "dawn was breaking through the skylights at the theater, just as it does in the play. It was not a good sign."[59]

The production was a disaster, but it didn't matter. Word on the street was beginning to spread about Playwrights, enough to keep them going for another year.[60] Elaine quickly became a force to be reckoned with professionally, someone you could count on to be brilliant at anything, whether it was playing Hippolyta in the Playwrights' Shakespeare Festival staging of *A Midsummer Night's Dream* or Åse in *Peer Gynt*, writing and producing a dark children's telling of *Rumpelstiltskin*, directing, or lending a hand with even the smallest of things, even if it meant sewing costumes.

But Playwrights wasn't meant to last. It was, in Shepherd's eyes, becoming less for the proletariat and more for the middle class. It was all Shakespeare and Brecht, too highfalutin and too safe, the same plays performed ad nauseam. There were external troubles, too; McCarthyist rumors swirled that the Playwrights Theatre Club was, if not scarlet, then at the very least pink. Two failed fire inspections (perhaps instigated by their unfavorable reputation) followed, and in February 1955, the theater shut down for good.

Playwrights may have been dead, but its cast and crew were already thinking about what was next. David Shepherd began to think: What if Viola Spolin's games weren't just theater tools? What if they could be the theater itself?[61] He needed a director, and who better than Sills?

THE COMPASS THEATER was a real hole-in-the-wall kind of place. Calling the narrow storefront space with plaster walls and plywood floors next to the bar of Hyde Park's Hi-Hat Lounge a theater was like one of the performers inside it pointing a finger at you and calling it a gun. It was a dump, but it was *their* dump: a place where this ragtag group of intellectuals could find themselves excited by the prospect of creating something new, something that could be both influential and irreverent, which they were young enough to have the blind confidence to go ahead and do. Things weren't as rinky-dink as Playwrights—they got a business manager, who negotiated for a portion of drink sales so they could make *some* money—but only just barely. For a while, most of them weren't even paid, and those who were—like Elaine, who got a cut because she was also directing—made only about $25 a week.[62] Rehearsals were chaotic, disorganized, and full of conflict. "What we would jokingly call rehearsals would usually end up in an argument with very little actual work being done," company member Bobbi Gordon said. With all the time they wasted yelling at each other—"a series of 'Absolutely not,' 'I will not do that,' 'No,' 'What do you mean? We certainly can't do *that!*'"—it was a miracle to all of them that they reconvened night after night at all, much less put on a good—sometimes even brilliant—show.[63]

With Sills directing, Elaine inherited the role of acting coach, teaching workshops with an approach that combined her Stanislavsky training with Viola Spolin's games. She rarely gave orders and allowed her players to improvise endlessly and take risks, even change the material if they were struggling, all in the service of discovering how to make the scene real for themselves.[64] There was no goal other than to find the truth and commit to it. She was Zen-like about it; truth was her religion. You might get to it a different way each time, but you could always count on it. The truth was the truth was the truth. "Everybody talked about the word 'organic,' but she did it," one of her students, Annette Hankin, said, "although I think her head always informed her heart."[65]

It's not just that Elaine was one of the few members of the company who could teach acting. While Playwrights had the classics to fall back on, the Compass needed new material. Lots of it. Elaine was one of the few who could write. She did so prolifically—manically, even. Writer's block never seemed to possess her. She would write late into the night, lying in bed with her typewriter propped up on her knees.[66] The ideas came faster than she could type, faster than she could piece them together: an idea for one play here, a scene for another there, stories that stretched for hundreds of pages, filled with minute details but no structure or end in sight. Everything was a possibility, nothing could be discarded. It would all be shaped and refined later. Friends—or more often, men who thought they had a shot with her, like Sheldon Patinkin—would try to help organize her, but it was no use. "Elaine would write notes on anything."[67]

And God knows the Compass Players needed those notes. They moved at a breakneck speed, performing five nights a week, with two shows on Friday nights and three on Saturday. Nothing was repeated. Each week was a brand-new show, with a set called Living Newspaper, in which the cast acted out excerpts from the day's newspaper as if it were a script, followed by a 45-minute "scenario play" they had rehearsed during the day. To keep the audience longer—more time meant more drinks, and more drinks meant more money—the finale was an improvised set built upon audience suggestions.[68] "All our work was inconsistent, attenuated, and belabored," Shepherd reflected.[69] But there was something interesting about the improv sets, something special about the way both the audience and the actors were trying to figure out what was happening onstage. People would hang around until early hours of the morning just to watch.

Chicago would eventually become a breeding ground for improv comedy, a wellspring of talent from which *Saturday Night Live* and sitcoms alike would poach actors. In the half century since, improv has grown from underground art form to mass-market genre. In major cities across the country, taking improv classes has almost become a rite of passage for every young wide-eyed transplant. In 2016, nearly 30,000 people were enrolled in classes at one of the Second City's three locations, not counting the number of company performers.[70] In 1955, you could count the Compass Players on two hands.

Not that any of them saw all of this coming. "We were in a game of blind exploration," Barbara Harris said. "It was an existential need almost. Once it began, there we were, and like little ants or beavers, we *did it.* Like ants or beavers, we just kept *building!* Even if what we did fell down. There was nothing else to do but work hard."[71]

They weren't even trying to be funny; it just happened, a byproduct of being a bunch of overeducated kids with no adults around to answer to. If mainstream pop culture was sterile and whitewashed—all *Father Knows Best* and *Ozzie and Harriet*—they were the underground antidote. And theirs was not the humor of Sid Caesar or Jackie Gleason or Abbott and Costello, with their outsize personas and lowbrow USO jokes. There was no straight man/funny man duo, no traditional "set up, build, punch line" joke structure, and certainly no cheap gags. Their humor came from calling bullshit on the status quo so many held dear, from digging into the psychology of the absurdities of human behavior and leaning into taboo topics others were afraid to touch.

It was all dark as hell. The players, like many young people before them and many to come, were not only unimpressed with the state of the world they were living in, but vehemently critical of it. "It was the University of Chicago—we talked about everything that was wrong. We did not speak about anything that worked," Elaine explained. "You don't have a scene if you do that. People don't have a comedy act if they do that. You are in some way, one way or another, criticizing."[72] Their plays reflected those cynical worldviews: authority figures, pretentious urbanites, middle-class parents, uninformed youth—they were all ripe for skewering. The world was not black-and-white; if you slid your razor across the surface, you'd find nothing but gray matter, full of greed and deceit and sexual hypocrisy meant to be exposed and examined. "These were people who were living out their liberation from their families," Shepherd said. "They were in analysis and they were using the stage of the Compass to liberate themselves from a whole lot of shit they had fallen into."[73]

But while the company was liberal in theory, in practice, the perspectives they presented were much more limited. If you were a white, well-read, young Jewish man on the lam from the middle-class American Dream life your parents were living, you could count on seeing your experience reflected back to you in their work. There was only one Black player in the group, and when it came to the core trust of writers, Elaine was the only woman, and her work was seldom appreciated. "I don't think anyone ever said it was good," said Compass member Mark Gordon. "Every time she came in with new material, it was 'Oh, my God, it's awful. It'll never work.' . . . Then we'd do it for people at night and the audience would be hysterical loving it. And then somebody maybe would say, 'Oh, I guess it's all right.' But there was never a recognition that Elaine's stuff was fantastic."[74]

Elaine's stuff was perhaps not recognized as fantastic, but it was certainly known that it was almost always unflinchingly honest. Brutal, even. The worlds she created on the page were merciless and unforgiving, the protagonists—often young women—aspiring for more only to be bulldozed over without sympathy. You couldn't help but wonder if there was an autobiographical element to them. "As Bill Shakespeare said, '[hold] the mirror up to nature.' Elaine held the mirror up to Elaine," Compass Player Walter Beakel once suggested.[75] Years later, as she and Mike promoted their Broadway show, she made her outlook clear:

Elaine: There are no darker sides of nature.

Interviewer: Are there really no darker sides of nature?

Elaine: Well, what would you call a darker side of nature?

Interviewer: Well, for instance, I think the pains of the poor, the griefs of the less fortunate people. All of those, I think—

Elaine: Well sure, if you're going to sulk about it.[76]

In many of Elaine's early plays, the material dealt almost exclusively with one darker side of nature: the abuse, assault, or mistreatment of women. There was *Georgina's First Date,* in which a handsome high school boy invites an overweight, unattractive girl to his senior prom as a joke, and assaults her afterward. Even though Georgina has some understanding that she's being used, everyone pushes her to accept because he's "a winner." When she returns home at the end of the night after being raped, she tearfully tells her mother "I had a wonderful time."[77] A "far-out" parody of *Ten Little Indians* ended with everyone dead onstage, and a satire of self-improvement classes called *The Real You* concludes when the characters' "improved" behavior turns off those they sought to impress. And then there was *Homecoming,* a scenario centered around a manipulative man who plants himself in another's conventional home during a college vacation, turns him into a rebel, and forces him to rape his girlfriend. The rest of the company balked at that one. It wasn't that her work made the male members of the group uncomfortable in its horrific vision of reality; they didn't even think it was plausible and amended it to match their views. "Elaine felt we had made a travesty of her idea. There was a display of anger. And we, being men, just ignored her. Nothing new about that," Roger Bowen said.[78]

During the early days of the Compass, Elaine spent much of her time distracted and distant, "annoyed at everything that was happening at the time"[79]—but perhaps, too, at always having to be on defense, at not being able to simply exist the way the men did. "She was one of those women who perceives herself as very vulnerable," Hankin said. "In fact, she was one of the toughest women I ever knew, a real tough cookie. It came from the perception that she had to defend herself in a world that would eat her alive."[80]

In life, she may have been vulnerable, but onstage she was something else entirely, daring and dangerous. One of only two women who performed regularly, she refused to conform to the psychological restrictions of traditional female roles like the wife or mother. Even if she "got all the parts that called for a girl who could wear a trench coat and a beret," she was no ingenue.[81] She fearlessly transformed into the spy, the psychiatrist, the mad queen. Watching her, you could forget entirely the beatnik slob she was in real life, could ignore the fact that she was often in disarray, skirts safety-pinned together and hair tangled. She was radiant, devastating, and gor-geous.[82] Elaine devoured improv like her apples. Onstage, all her wheels turned at once—writer, director, and actor—but she made it look effortless, never giving it away that she was once the girl who struggled to play a tree. The others knew they couldn't keep up. "She only had to touch her shoe, and the focus went to her," David Shepherd said.[83] Elaine may have been a standout, but she refused to be a selfish performer. She was generous, and always in service of the scene, whether that meant pulling scene partners through a rough patch or pushing them to rise to a difficult challenge. Every-one wanted to do scenes with Elaine; even if you were bad, you knew you were getting better.

Men in the audience couldn't get enough of her. Mike Nichols would recount one incident in which one challenged her to im-provise with him. The man would play the husband arriving home hours late and she would be his wife. She agreed and waited quietly as he staggered drunkenly around the stage, "acting," when:

BANG. Elaine went through the louver and was gone. Her lead-ing man began to follow her. "What are you . . ." BANG. Elaine was back with an armful of clothes, which she threw into the suitcase (we had prop bins backstage). She continued wordlessly to leave the stage and return with more clothes until the suitcase was filled. She snapped it shut and left the stage to an ovation.[84]

Another admirer showed up night after night, showering her with gifts and catcalls. Sometimes he would run onstage to profess his love. Unfazed, she worked it into the scene.[85]

But three months into the Compass, it was clear that the en-terprise was unsustainable. They were burning through scenarios, playing them for a week or two before moving on to the next, never looking back to revise and restage. And $25 a week wasn't enough to live on, not without inherited wealth (like Shepherd) or a willingness to live like an absolute bum (like Elaine). Even Sills took a Fulbright hiatus, and he and Barbara Harris were leaving for a year abroad. Shepherd wasn't equipped to direct the company the way Sills was, and with a limited company, improv amateur nights began to take precedence over new scenario plays. Improv was not an age-old art, and having people with no experience up on the stage with actors who weren't exactly experts themselves was a free-for-all. Chaos reigned at the Compass. Something had to be done if they wanted to save it.

YOU COULD CALL the life Mike Nichols was living in New York in the summer of 1955 sad. Go ahead. He would have agreed with you. He had been studying with Strasberg for two years, yet still had no career to speak of. He was broke, living in an unfurnished apartment and working odd jobs that barely paid rent. Some nights, his dinner was a soup made of hot water, free soda crackers, and ketchup packets.[86]

Shepherd and Sills needed outside talent. En route to England, Sills and Harris stopped first in New York to try to convince Mike to come back to Chicago. They knew he was good, knew he had something they were missing. And if they were going to start to pull in new talent to this unconventional enterprise, at least one of them should be someone they knew they could work with. Mike wasn't entirely convinced improv could work on its own, but it *was* $28 a week—and Elaine would be there. "I wanted to explore more Elaine and me. It was her and that train station and those hamburgers she made me in her apartment and what came with them," he said, "that I was thinking about when I decided to go back."[87] It sure beat ketchup soup.

His first day back, he found her. Though they hadn't kept in touch during the time they were apart, they had no trouble picking up where they left off. She was still the same hostile girl, except even more brilliant now, and he was still the same nervous, hostile boy. They sat together in the back room of the Hi-Hat "like a summit meeting," bartender Fred Wranovics observed. "It was a big deal. The two of them sat on those stools doing these routines, testing each other's ad-lib ability and spontaneity. Everyone was watching. It was like the Actors Studio versus the local fast gun. I'd come in every thirty minutes and they'd still be at it. I guess they hit it off."[88]

If he was going to have to go onstage with no safety net, he wanted to do it with her by his side. At first he was a disaster, always ready to burst into tears and sob his way through the scene the way he'd learned from Strasberg.[89] But he kept going, buoyed by Elaine's presence and encouragement. "She was the only one who had faith in me," he said.[90]

Improvising with Elaine was harder than it looked. They weren't playing spies on the Chicago train anymore; she had advanced in his absence, and he couldn't keep up. "The stuff never stopped coming out of her," he said. "She threw it away with both hands."[91] It was humiliating, difficult to watch without cringing. Though she respected her fellow actors onstage, she respected the truth of the moment more. If he went against the agreed-upon truth of a scene—by, say, pantomiming a gun without context—she refused to go along with it. "Why are you pointing your finger at me?" she asked.[92] Still, even as new players joined the company—actors more adept at comedy who could keep up with her—she mostly stayed with Mike. Mike was safe. Mike was known. Mike wanted to learn from her and work with her, not compete with her for laughs or attention. Elaine couldn't trust a lot of people, but she could trust him.

They were inseparable. She would cook dinner for him—steak and cheese sandwiches with no bread, since that was too bulky to steal—and they'd talk for hours about music and literature and their overbearing mothers.[93] She understood him, the hostile boy who had grown into a scared man whose cruel tongue came out only in private, and he understood her, the hostile girl who was really a delicate woman underneath her spiky veneer. When you're thinking on your feet, it's best to do it alongside someone who knows you well.

Onstage, they protected each other, even when they were fucking up, as in the first original scene they ever did. "You know how you're going to break up with someone and you call them and they don't answer the phone? They're not home and you think, 'Where could they be?'" Mike proposed. "And pretty soon you're calling them wildly, wondering if they've left you." It was a good observation, realistic, and funny—but it was impossible to dramatize, as they realized at the same moment, sitting on opposite ends of the stage in front of an audience. It was a humiliating experience, and she had no way to help him as he pretended to dial and mimicked the sound of the phone, *ring ring*ing into the void. He kept going, and she continued to sit silently. "I thought, 'I can't answer. Then the sketch will be over.'"[94] But she didn't have the heart to walk offstage and leave him there, either. If they were going to leap together, they had to fall together, too. After an agonizing amount of time, "the guy on lights just had to gradually fade us out. We just stood there. I never forgot it," she said. "It was the most painful thing I've ever done on stage. And it was the first thing we ever did together."[95]

Practice makes perfect, right? Yes, but the thing is, the goal with improv is never perfect; the goal is *real*. Still, practice enough, fumble through the discomfort of failing again and again, making a fool of yourself onstage in front of other people, and at some point, if you're lucky, you'll get a lightbulb moment where it works. And then that lightbulb moment becomes two, then three. Then you reach a point where your brain has become rewired to do it without even thinking about it, rewired in a way that even the bombing—and there will still be bombing—doesn't sting as much anymore, because the moments of transcendence outweigh it. "I don't mean to be mystical," Mike once said, "but such things did happen. Like doing twenty minutes of iambic pentameter that we had not thought of but just came pouring out. That was thrilling, and you'd be drained and amazed afterward, and you'd have a sense of your possibilities."[96]

Mike and Elaine found their possibilities in a shared interest in people's pretentious natures (including their own), a mutual fascination with betrayal, and above all else, an unending love for language, the draw of words and the crackling rhythms that could be sculpted from them. Their minds worked in tandem, with complementary perspectives. "We had the same kind of playfulness, we enjoyed the same kind of pretend, as kids do. If he had come and said, 'I'm a doctor. Are you sick?' I would've said, as if I was a kid, 'I don't feel good.' Because I wouldn't have said, 'What do you mean?' I would've known what he was doing," she explained.[97] They were, for better or worse, "in some weird way, each other's unconscious," Mike said.[98] For Elaine, an ability to improvise well with people came as naturally as conversation; there were some she got on with better than others. But for Mike, it wasn't as simple. Elaine was it for him. "I could always do it only with her. For me it depended on a certain connection with Elaine and a certain mad gleam in either her or my eyes when we knew something was starting and then the other one would jump in and go along."[99]

They began to deepen their craft, figuring out the edges of a still-boundless world and creating rules to guide themselves through it. Going for the obvious laugh was a no—it was a cheap move, "prideless and dangerous, and the audience loses respect."[100] Get the laugh the way anyone gets a laugh in real life: on the way to something else. After all, their biggest intent was to purely present observational sketches: "We started out, both of us, as Method actors, and just sort of turned out to be funny," Elaine said.[101] The Compass days of improv weren't *entirely* spontaneous; the concepts were preconceived, or, in the case of audience suggestion sets, brainstormed during intermission, with the players then building the scene and dialogue live on stage. But the phone call disaster alone had taught them that an idea wasn't enough; there had to be some hook with which to dramatize it.[102] If anyone thought improvising was simply getting onstage and winging it, they knew better.

No, improvising was just like writing, only done on your feet. They needed some of the same basic structure any good playwright would follow. Onstage, Elaine was the writer, Mike the editor shaping the scene and moving them through it. "She had an endless capacity for invention," he said. "She could go on and on in a character. I could not. I could make my few points, I had my two or three characteristics, then I had to move on to the next point because I was out. I couldn't do any more."[103] There had to be a core to the scene in order to pursue it at all, an answer to the imagined question of "Why are you telling me this?"[104] "Because it's funny" works, but got you only so far. "You're only going from laugh to laugh, and in between, there's this terrifying vacuum because there's no purpose," Mike explained.[105] That meant every scene needed a plot, and every plot needed character motivations. They floated a theory that there were only three types of scenes: a negotiation, a fight, or a seduction. When in doubt, Elaine said, seduce[106]—which is exactly how they finally nailed their first successful bit.

"Let's do two teenagers in the back seat of a car," Mike suggested.[107] To call postwar middle-class America *repressed* would be a massive understatement, but let's leave it at that anyway. Sex was at best a private act done behind tightly closed doors, and at worst, when done by anyone other than a married heterosexual couple, a harbinger of moral decline.[108] For people so afraid of sex, Americans sure were obsessed with policing it. In Hollywood, the Hays Code insisted that any major motion picture be "wholesome" and should never "lower the moral standards of those who see it."[109] On the radio, a song as chaste as "I Saw Mommy Kissing Santa Claus" sparked a national outcry.[110] Lucy and Ricky still slept in separate twin beds—and they were *married*. Forget about seeing any depiction of teenage necking anywhere.

But this wasn't America. This was the Compass, the one place where it didn't matter how out there the subject was, run by the kinds of young radicals who would usher in the coming sexual revolution from the underground up.[111] A year before Elvis would thrust his hips on television and send the nation into Puritan panic, Mike and Elaine were onstage at the Compass, playing two high school students clumsily navigating their burgeoning desires. As one of her ex-suitors said, Elaine "treated everything funny that men take seriously," and that included sex.[112] Elaine could find inspiration in a borrowed copy of the *Kama Sutra,* using it not for its intended use but instead for coming up with stage lines like "Let's do it like the Bending Lotus."[113] She ran with it.

The premise of the sketch is straightforward: Mike and Elaine are two teenagers parking. He clearly wants her and she wants him, but both crackle with palpable anxieties. He wants her to put out, she wants him to respect her. He fears rejection, she fears a tarnished reputation. Though they're both playing out anxiety, they wordlessly fall into its different manifestations: Mike is all verbal, clearing his throat and stammering, pubescent voice still cracking, while Elaine goes for the physical, playing with her shirt sleeves, picking at her wrists, squirming and stiffening and squirming again. She dithers on, playing dumb, hoping to drag out the inevitable, which eventually comes. Unable to take it anymore, he grabs her hard as she takes a drag from her cigarette and pulls her into a long, awkward, closed-mouth kiss. Midway through the unending embrace, she exhales a cloud of smoke out the side of her mouth.

It's no surprise the sketch was a hit they'd continue to build upon and refine over the years, eventually taking it to television and Broadway. People weren't used to seeing sex onstage at all—forget *teenage* sex—let alone sex displayed so frankly and truthfully for what it was: funny. All tangled limbs and nervousness, breaking voices and rambled musings about nothing, two people impossibly horny, simultaneously desperate and terrified to act on it and hoping the other can't tell. Maybe the skit appalled parents who didn't want to think about what their sons and daughters got up to when they borrowed their cars each weekend, but the young adults who had not too long ago been those sons and daughters were seeing their lives depicted realistically—and humorously—for the first time.

By the time the Compass moved into a larger venue at the Dock that fall, people were no longer coming to see David Shepherd's political commentary scenarios. They were coming to see Mike and Elaine create rich, relatable characters with beating hearts in the span of minutes, "being completely real, saying things for the first time."[114] The name-dropping Chicago disc jockey and his dumb starlet guest. The dentist and the patient who happen to be having an affair. The needling mother and her hapless son. They were coming to see Mike and Elaine play characters who were *real,* coming to see the two play people they knew—people they *were*—talk about the things people talked about in real life. Maybe Mike and Elaine were making fun of you, but they did so with such intelligence, such backhanded flattery that slithered up to and stroked the cheek of the narcissist in all of us. And anyway, what they were really doing was making fun of themselves. "We were very snotty, so when we made fun of ourselves, we were the ones who saw it and nobody else. It was a surprise to see that everyone was like that," Elaine explained. "That everyone had that mother. That everyone was that nervous on that date—man or woman or possibly creature—about having sex. As you learn it, that gives you a certain confidence, just that you think 'Oh, look how alike everybody is.'"[115] It wasn't just that you were seeing yourself reflected in Mike and Elaine; it was that you could feel a little special about it, like you were part of an exclusive club. David Shepherd's plays about current events were never going to have that kind of a pull.

WHAT HAPPENS NEXT is chaos.

The young cast would play games within their sketches and break onstage to both amuse themselves and purposely draw the ire of an increasingly prudish Shepherd. Shelley Berman quickly made enemies when he arrived with seemingly no knowledge of the Compass *or* improvisation and an affinity for turning every scene into a one-man show. "The next time you fuck me up onstage," Elaine warned him, "I will pull down your zipper and pull out your dick."[116]

Shepherd had moved the company, again, to a larger space, a chic nightclub on Chicago's North Side called the Argo Off-Beat Room, where the audience drank whiskey sours and the performers had to adhere to a suit-and-tie dress code. It was a far cry from the U of C undergrads drinking cheap draft beers in the back room of the Hi-Hat. When Paul Sills returned from Europe, he barely recognized it. Shepherd kept the theater alive in his absence, but it was growing increasingly commercial. The theater group that had prided itself on living on the razor's edge with an endless string of new material now retreated to safer grounds, freezing and repeating scenes that worked, taking so-so jokes from one night and polishing them for the next. The company grew drunk on the sound of laughter and were thirsty for more, much to Elaine's chagrin. This wasn't improv. At least it wasn't honest improv, and it was boring as hell, too. Forget fun. What good was it if it wasn't fresh, if tonight wasn't different from last night? Looking out at the audience that filled the Argo, you couldn't help but ask: Where did all the offbeat intellectuals go, and why were they suddenly playing instead for the people they had once ruthlessly mocked, "the rich kids from Evanston" who came into the city on weekends "to hear dirty words."[117]

By January of 1957, the Compass was over. Elaine didn't even bother showing up for closing night. For the next year, she and Mike took their act to a club on Chicago's North Side, briefly entertaining the idea of making their act a trio with Shelley Berman (the names Two Wigs and a Wag and Two Cocksuckers and Elaine were floated)[118] before Mike shut it down. They were a couple onstage and would stay one moving forward. She appeared in a production of *Lysistrata,* singled out as "very funny, but as Greek as bagels and lox" in what was otherwise considered the worst production of the play in two thousand years.[119] Mostly she wrote, filling her nights working on plays while Mike was off acting and cavorting with Pat Scot, who he would marry that spring. "Isn't it a beautiful first wedding," Elaine couldn't help but remark at the wedding.[120]

MEANWHILE, DAVID SHEPHERD went into business with Theodore J. Flicker. A friend of Severn Darden, Flicker had watched the Compass fall apart—but saw in the wreckage an opportunity. Improv *could* work. Maybe there are no second chances in the game, but there could be a second chance to create the game. They just needed to scrap everything and start over again. Shepherd agreed, and Flicker set out to open a new Compass in St. Louis with the hopes of then taking it to New York.

Flicker knew he needed Elaine, and though the thought of Missouri in the summer didn't exactly thrill her, Elaine accepted his offer for two of the most common reasons why any girl agrees to leave a great city for an abysmal one: she needed a job, and she needed to get away from a guy.[121] Mike was even less enthused, but he knew Elaine would be working closely with Del Close, a gifted young improviser she had met the year before when he auditioned for the Chicago Compass and had taken a quick liking to. "I really didn't know what to do up there," Close remembered, "but Elaine brought me through the scene and made me look good."[122] Mike reluctantly went along. If Elaine was going to make any partner look good, it was going to be him.

That summer, the pair moved into a boardinghouse with Flicker and Close and got to work. In that old brick house at 441 Westminster Place, they became a comedy think tank whose lives revolved entirely around improv. No longer curtailed as a means to meet Sills's and Shepherd's ideological ends, improvisational comedy was, in and of itself, the thing. And they needed to figure out not only how to make it true—particularly now that Close and Flicker had decided suggestion-based sets should *really* be created in the moment, and not after a brief backstage deliberation—but how to make it work. They did what any good scientist does: drafted hypotheses, tested, reviewed the results, and experimented again. Flicker was on the precipice of a breakthrough, and he knew that Elaine, "the most talented girl that I have ever known let alone worked with,"[123] was instrumental to it.

Today, the basic rules of improv have become something of a religion. Deified and glorified, they've long been commonly attributed to Del Close, by way of a book he coauthored, widely regarded as the improv bible, *Truth in Comedy: The Manual for Improvisation*. But what most people don't know is that they first came from Elaine.

Every morning that summer, Elaine and Flicker met in the Westminster Place kitchen for breakfast. There, they'd analyze the performances from the night before: What was working, what wasn't, and why. What made a scene flop? What made it soar? There had to be a logical method to the madness. Elaine was like a surgeon dissecting each scene in search of the heart, in search of what was necessary to make it beat. Improv—improv meant to entertain an audience, that is—needed rules. Elaine knew this, having set some for herself and Mike in their days in Chicago. But now the rules were being refined and would be practiced over and over to get them just right, then would be written down so they could be taught to others. Maybe then improv would have legs. Maybe then it wouldn't burn as hot and bright before spectacularly combusting the way it had in Chicago. In the span of a two-week burst of "white-hot creativity," Elaine and Flicker established what would become the guiding principles for decades to come:[124]

1. Don't deny. If Elaine says she has a drink in her hand, she has a drink in her hand.
2. Whenever possible, make a strong choice. The less obvious, the better.
3. You are you. What you think of as your "character" is really just a magnified piece of you. Therefore, onstage, be you.

When people cite Elaine as the godmother of improv comedy, it's not an exaggeration. Elaine was thriving, and in the collaborative setting used her skills to nurture and better the company the way she had back in the earliest days of the Compass in Chicago.[125]

Mike, though, was not happy. Here he was, a newlywed, and he couldn't help but be jealous of the new men in Elaine's life, the way Flicker got all her attention during the day and Close became her new scene partner at night.[126] Especially Close. Mike couldn't stand him, couldn't stand his "indulgent" capacity for endless improvisation,[127] couldn't stand the way Elaine was with him, teaching Del the way she had taught him. When the two of them improvised together, they were unstoppable; Del could keep up with Elaine. Del wouldn't rein her in the way Mike liked to, and they could explore worlds other than the neuroses of urban Jewish intellectuals. "Mike likes to dominate and control everyone around him," Ted Flicker said. "Elaine needs to dominate and control men. She trusts nobody." With these dueling psyches, the two "routinely manipulated the hell out of each other."[128]

And then, of course, there was the sex thing. Sex, that thing they knew would ruin their friendship if they engaged in it, still managed to instigate a rift. But Mike was married, and what was Elaine supposed to do? Sit around and knit? No, Elaine was straightforward about sex, liberated even, unashamed about wanting it casually and without any emotional attachment.

"Where does a girl get laid around here?" she asked Flicker one evening. He panicked—"I mean, she was a *very* strong, fascinating, brilliant woman, but I would just as soon stick my dick in a garbage disposal," he later recalled—and offered Del up in his place.[129] After the two spent the night together, Del was in love. And Mike was being a baby about it. The once-inseparable pair grew distant, then increasingly at odds. The company descended once again into the disorder of the old Compass, setting aside the trailblazing work of people far older than they in favor of acting out the emotional immaturity of who they really were—a bunch of kids who didn't know how to manage their incestuous relationships. The Compass was finally falling apart, maybe for good this time, with all the infighting and distrust and dramatics that would fill a very good reality show if it had happened today.

"Mike and Elaine crisis all day and all night," Shepherd wrote in his diary late that August.[130] It was clear that one of them would have to go—and it was going to have to be Mike, who "certainly can be a pain in the neck, an opportunist, a child who drags Elaine down to mediocrity and nonsense, all of that at his worst."[131] But the details of their spat—the story behind how they both ultimately ended up leaving the Compass—have varied over the years, swallowed up by the competing narratives of everyone involved, even by the ways in which their own telling of the story would shift over time.

Mike and Elaine said in their Broadway *Playbill*: "Because of an inability to raise the necessary capital [Flicker] was forced to give up this plan [to open the Compass in New York] . . . Mike and Elaine, who by this time had become friendly, were told to call a theatrical manager, named Jack Rollins . . ."

Ted Flicker said: "Elaine May called and said if I didn't fire Mike she was going to quit because Mike was trying to take the theater away from me."[132]

Mike said, decades later in an interview with *Playboy*: "I was basically fired for being such a pain in the ass."[133]

Elaine said: Well . . . Elaine, being Elaine, kept mum. She would let everyone else make up the story for her.

"It never occurred to us that we would go on doing this," Nichols said many years later. Performing was just something that was fun, a pit stop on the way from childhood to adulthood, when they'd eventually figure out what they were going to do and "have lives like normal people."[134]

Who were they kidding? Who was *Elaine* kidding, at least? Elaine had a normal grown-up life and an eight-year-old daughter waiting for her back in L.A., to which she was always free to return. She could teach or work odd jobs again to support her writing or settle for becoming a housewife again. She wasn't without options; it's that none of those conventional options were ones she even remotely wanted. Still, maybe Mike wasn't massaging the truth, skirting around their mutual ambitions to make the narrative seem more virtuous than it may have been in reality. Maybe they didn't think this streak would last forever. Maybe, ambitious as they may have been, they truly did think that the crushing reality would have to make itself known at some point and put an end to it. No, maybe they didn't know exactly what it was they did want, but Elaine sure as shit knew what she didn't. Elaine wasn't normal. Elaine would never be normal.

It took her about a week to realize she'd rather be miserable, with him, in New York than miserable, without him, in St. Louis. Mike had been calling her long distance for days. When he finally called with the possibility of a gig, she didn't hesitate. She would leave for New York that day.

CHAPTER 3

Nichols and May Take Manhattan

1957–1961

The way Mike Nichols liked to tell it, when Elaine joined him in New York in the fall of 1957, the two had about $40 between them and the phone number for Jack Rollins, a talent manager who was apparently looking for new off-beat clients. They figured they didn't have much more to lose. Why not spare a dime to make the call? The next day, over beef Stroganoff and borscht at the Russian Tea Room, they auditioned for Rollins cold, "wildly improvising a set of ad-libbed little skits we not only had never rehearsed, but had never even thought of until that desperate minute."[1] If they thought themselves woefully unprepared, Rollins didn't catch on. He was too mesmerized by their startlingly unique act: "I'd never seen this technique before. I thought, My god, these are two people writing hilarious comedy on their feet."[2] There was money to be made there, he was sure of it. "They were so un-show business they didn't know to be scared. They were remarkable immediately," he said. "They were complete. I knew they had something odd and wonderful, but I didn't know whether to laugh or cry."[3] They let out a breath they hadn't realized they'd been holding when Rollins picked up the check—and them.

At least, that's how it could have happened. But how about this:

Suspicious of Ted Flicker's ability to get a deal for the Compass Players in New York and convinced they could do a better job themselves, Mike and Elaine, along with Del Close and Nancy Ponder, decided to splinter off, venture to New York together, and try to create a new theater of their own in the summer of 1957. The group couldn't afford for all four to make the trip, so they pooled their money and sent Mike and Elaine as representatives. Things took a traitorous turn when Mike got fired shortly after their return—and the others were left stunned to find that the supposed four-some gig the pair had booked was actually meant just for the duo instead. This version, this betrayal, is the one Del Close spun and would stick to over the years, saying: "We were conned into betraying Ted [Flicker] and we were in turn betrayed."[4] He would remain admiring of Elaine for years to come, but his infatuated, idealized vision of her had taken a hit upon realizing that "the goddess was more evident in Elaine than in most people—in all her aspects—the beautiful one and the wrathful one."[5] It's a great story, a classic dramatic narrative with clear villains and victims. It's also not true.[6]

Okay, so what about this:

The group went to the city together to open the long-awaited New York Compass. But the fallout was more of a sad, sorry whimper than the kind of fireworks that tales of betrayal often promise: The money fell through, leaving them stranded. It's not as operatic as Close's, but it's just as messy. We never find out what happened to Close and Ponder, and the authors of the story's various versions never explain all the logistics of how—and given the timing of Mike's firing, when—Mike and Elaine ended up in front of Rollins. But it's a more forgiving version that Flicker went along with, and one Mike and Elaine shared most often in their early press[7] before abandoning it for a cleaner narrative. It's a funny form of revisionist history: A suggestion that they stumbled into fame circumstantially as indifferent bystanders to whom it happened, not two ambitious actors who actively engineered it. Charles Joffe, their first manager, alleges their actions fit the latter description more. Mike, he claimed, had pitched their act to multiple agencies to no avail before he and Rollins took them on.[8] But ambition isn't a virtue, and surely Mike and Elaine—those snide smart-asses whose work sneered at fame-hungry celebrities—knew enough to sidestep the possibility that they'd come across as a pair of hypocrites.

Whoever you choose to believe—and by now the absolute-facts version of the truth has been so twisted and long-buried, who's to say if any of the active participants even knew themselves, by the end, what the truth was so much as they knew the story they'd committed to memory—what happened next happened fast. Two days after their meeting, Rollins got Mike and Elaine a coveted audition with Max Gordon at the Blue Angel, a cabaret club on the Upper East Side. Gordon, a nightlife impresario, wasn't wild about them—he had an eye for spotting the next big things but had reservations about those who didn't emulate established and successful acts. Liking what he saw enough that he could trust Rollins, though, he took the risk.[9] They could open in two weeks when the current act ended. For a minute, their lucky break struck them more as an unfortunate disappointment. See, they were dead broke, they explained. They couldn't wait that long for work to come in. Shruggingly, Gordon gave them an opening slot at one of his clubs downtown, the Village Vanguard, to fill their time until then.[10]

You couldn't have picked a better time to walk into New York City nightlife. All around them, a new world was emerging. Stiff supper clubs and nightclubs with revue acts were still thriving uptown, but culture—*comedy*—was changing. The days of vaudeville acts full of shticks, comedians who dealt in formulaic punch lines and one-liners, were waning. Greenwich Village was where it was at if you were young and hip, its beatnik sensibility radiating outward. Comedy, after all, could be a lot like the jazz music so strongly associated with the neighborhood—free-form, boundary-pushing, and innovative. Mike and Elaine came in just at the pivotal point of transition, getting to experience a little bit of the old world and the new one, and finding they were a hit in both.

The Village Vanguard was perfect for them, cheap and casual and the charming kind of crappy, just like the bars they had played back in Chicago. Getting onstage and doing their act in front of relative peers—even if it was a full house of them—would be a comfortable wade into the New York scene. There they would open for Mort Sahl, a stand-up who presented himself as "candid and cool, the antithesis of the slick comic."[11] Though both acts practiced comedy by way of intellectualism, the delivery couldn't have been more different. Sahl was stand-up in the truest sense, his sets dealing in social commentary with blistering barbs aimed straight at the news of the day. Mike and Elaine, meanwhile, weren't getting onstage and telling jokes with short shelf lives. They were creating

Ibsen or Odets, Shakespeare or Chekhov? No sweat. "They would try to stump us, and the more they did that, the easier it got."[12]

They were a hit from the moment they stepped on the stage their first night: "The place was packed with people," Lorraine Gordon, Max Gordon's wife, recalled. "They were auditioning live. They had never been there. Max . . . said, 'Please don't laugh so loud. The agent is in the room and the price is going to go up.'"[13] They were openers upstaging the main act, the "hipsters' hipster," with routines that were "an interesting, if somewhat heady, change of pace."[14] Sahl couldn't bear it. By the time their second week rolled around, he started cutting them short. "No, no," he'd say. "Skip them. I'm ready."[15] The curtailing only made the buzz around their debut at the Blue Angel that much stronger.

Uptown was a different scene. The pot-smoking, turtleneck-wearing crowd of intellectuals were nowhere to be found at the Blue Angel. No, the Angel might as well have been the Argo Off-Beat Room turned up to eleven. It was downright swank, a plush venue with rosette-covered walls, filled with a chic clientele often distractingly talking over whoever was onstage. Everybody wanted something at the Blue Angel: wanted to impress a date, wanted to finalize a business deal, wanted to track down the waiter for another drink. It was not the kind of place where Elaine could wear her mismatched secondhand clothes. Because she was incapable of—or uninterested in—shopping for herself, Rollins's wife had to take her shopping for appropriate attire.[16] But there they were free to play their full set—"Teenagers," "Disc Jockey," "Pirandello," and "First/Last"—without Mort Sahl stealing their thunder. All the same Chicago stuff, of course. That is, until Mike got a call from his mother.

"Hello, Michael. This is your mother speaking. Do you remember me?" It was gold, a line so perfectly plump with guilt Mike knew he couldn't have written it better himself. "I said, 'Mom, can I call you right back?'"[17] He hung up and called Elaine to tell her he had an idea for a new piece. As he repeated the frostbitten line to her, she knew he didn't have to go any further. She knew it was funny, and she knew her way in. After all, her mother and Mike's mother could have been interchangeable.[18] Without saying anything else,

characters, their bodies hosting such a range of complex person
ities that it was impossible to really pigeonhole them as one *thi*
They were endearing but not saccharine. They were dark but n
bleak. Biting but not mean—or, well, maybe they *were* mean, b
mean in the sense that they were just brutally honest. Above all el:
they were creating entire worlds that encouraged audiences to retu
to them again and again. Returning, as an audience, to a stand-u
routine means dealing in diminishing returns; you can never r
capture the shock and surprise of the first time. You know th
setup, can hear it build to the expected punch line. Return to th
scenes of Mike and Elaine, though, and you count on somethin
fresh each night: the slightest change in body language might tak
a scene in an entirely new direction, a variation in a single lin
reading could render it funny in a way that it wasn't before. They
were building something new every night in the span of minutes
and doing it all on their feet.

Well, okay, not exactly *entirely* on their feet. Though the New York
crowd didn't know any better, Mike and Elaine's act was built mostly
on work they had developed and fine-tuned in Chicago. At the Vanguard, they performed a short set of two sketches—"Teenagers" was
a sure bet, followed by, depending on the night, the "Disc Jockey"
scene, a parody involving a name-dropping radio host and an eager
young starlet, or their tried-and-true "Telephone" bit, in which Mike
tries to make a phone call and Elaine plays a series of operators—
followed by something they had started experimenting with in St.
Louis. Asking for audience participation, they solicited a first line, a
last line, and a literary style in which to improvise the scene.

Today, First Line/Last Line is an improv mainstay. But to the
Vanguard audience in 1957, it was a brand-new art form, a trick act
audiences were in awe of, convinced they were being put on. No
one had seen something like this before. How did they do it? How
did they get from point A to point B like that? There had to be a
catch. The audience would return, trying to stump them or find the
invisible puppet strings controlling the entire endeavor. But they
couldn't. "The trick was, we had both read everything," Elaine explained. Only the easy ones were difficult; they weren't well-versed
in the popular paperbacks of the day. But throw out a Greek play,

the two took their spots that night and added a new sketch to their routine.

The nagging, overbearing Jewish mother joke of "Mother and Son" wasn't exactly original, but it didn't need to be. Although the core of the scene was an archetype—one that New Yorkers in particular could relate to—they would give it flair in the details. Across six minutes, they dug in not to the punch line, but to their characters: Mike as the rocket scientist son and Elaine as the manipulative mother raking him over the coals for the grand injustice of forgetting to call. If it struck viewers as all too real, too shockingly personal, as if the entire audience was being read, that's because it was. They both were acutely aware of the relationship between a busy adult child who shuts down when faced with a vicious mother who deploys one punishingly barbed line after another:

> "Someday, Arthur, you'll get married, and you'll have children of your own. And, honey, when you do, I only pray that they make you suffer the way you're making me suffer. That's all I pray, Arthur. That's a mother's prayer."
> "Okay, Mom, thanks for calling."

They both transformed the tired mother joke into a character piece, funny because both characters felt real, whole, flesh and blood—and they had only just been created. Elaine, especially, delighted in the scene, making a mockery of this woman while appealing to the audience's empathy at the same time. "We're called satirists, and I suppose in a mild sort of way that's what we are. Implicit in almost any comment is criticism," she noted when asked at the time about the origins of the sketch. "But I think that it's almost impossible to portray a character or do a scene unless you have sympathy with the character, unless you sort of admit beforehand that you could very easily do the exact same thing. If you don't do that, then you have something that's sort of smart-alecky."[19] If satire is revenge, then the best kind is that served from the empathetic place of knowing intimately that which you're mocking, so closely that you can bruise with a featherlight touch. "To attack something vicious viciously is nothing. Criticism requires compassion," she said.[20] There's a reason why you almost feel for the woman for a moment, almost take her side, if only she didn't make herself so ridiculous, all weak nerves and lethal tongue at the ready. "It's everybody's mother," Elaine would insist years later. But she wasn't playing it that way; she was playing it as if it were *her* mother, and was demonstrating how easily she could cut her daughter down. "We said, 'What is this scene about? It can't be that your mother calls you just to impose guilt,'" Elaine explained. "And we figured out that what it was is that it kept you a child; being guilty keeps you a child, no matter how old you are."[21]

"Our purest," Mike would remember it later. "It came out the way we improvised it and stayed there."[22]

In just two weeks, Rollins said, "they were the hottest thing in the city."[23] By the end of October, they were getting rave reviews from city papers. "The lines (they write their own sophisticated stuff) are the cleverest heard at any club in town," the *New York Journal-American* proclaimed. It didn't matter that they were playing the midnight slot; people were lining up outside the Blue Angel in hopes of getting in to see them (and often, not succeeding).[24] Their contract expanded to six months. Come December, they were in the pages of *The New Yorker:*

> Mr. Nichols, a fair youth with an alert and friendly mien, and Miss May, a brunette with lustrous eyes and an abject air that would fool nobody, carry on little dialogues, any of which would fit nicely into a revue, and do so with something of the same delightful interplay characteristic of that splendid vaudeville team the Lunts; the bantering tones, the repeated phrases, the artful covering of each other's lines—all these devices are present, and well mastered.[25]

But success in New York was different from success in Chicago. In Chicago, even if they were the biggest draw at the Compass and generating underground buzz, most audiences still acted unimpressed, too grounded in their own lives to really care about something even if it was trendy. They wouldn't humor you; they would laugh if you were funny, but if you weren't, you could expect a room of cold, uncaring dead air. If the reception during their first few weeks in New York was modest, their good press changed things. "When *The New Yorker* came out, *how* they laughed. We were horrified. We didn't know such things were possible," Mike said. Now the laughs weren't coming just from the stage when the two broke, but from the audience as well. People even laughed at the mere sight of the two walking onstage.[26] Even if Nichols and May were aspiring for success, becoming *fashionable* was something they had certainly never expected. Fashionable was a hop, skip, and a jump away from famous, and they were now firmly in the fast lane to it, on a journey neither of them quite anticipated. There would be no slowing down.

THINGS WOULD CHANGE even more when, in January 1958, Rollins booked the pair on a two-hour "Suburban Review" prime-time special of NBC's *Omnibus*. Just weeks before, they had bombed an audition for Jack Paar's *Tonight Show* and received a decidedly lukewarm response to their "Disc Jockey" bit on ABC's *The Steve Allen Show*. Their heady, sophisticated acts worked well in the dark, smoky rooms of New York City nightlife, where they were afforded the luxury of time to let their material build in front of an audience they correctly assumed was educated. But television was different. Television was short-attention-span theater, playing to millions of people at home you couldn't even see, in front of a live audience who didn't pay to see you. It's not that they weren't capable of having both "snob and mob" appeal; it's just that they needed to fool around with the proportions a little more before they were able to get the cocktail just right.

For *Omnibus*, Rollins negotiated a deal. They needed fifteen minutes, they needed no editing, and they absolutely needed a guarantee that no host would pull a Jack Paar, cutting them off short because the jokes weren't coming fast enough. Even though the *Omnibus* producers "wanted a sense of class,"[27] they landed on the material they knew could appeal to a broader audience. People at the Blue Angel would get the references that the jokes in "Disc Jockey" hinged upon, but there was no guarantee others would. (It's hard to laugh at one-two punch like *"Al is a lotta laughs [. . .] I haven't seen the old son of a gun for a while; I think he's in Africa. I told him, 'Al, baby, you're nuts. There's no money in Africa.'" / "I personally have never dated him, but the word gets back from those who have that he's, like, just the greatest"* if you don't know who Albert Schweitzer is.) But they could certainly relate to "Teenagers" and "Telephone." At least, the producers hoped they would.

The night didn't start particularly strong, though, and for a while, it was looking like this would shape up to be another appearance that would embarrassingly not work out in their favor. The special itself was a dud, with flop sketch after flop sketch. It'd be a tough crowd. As they went through their by-now-well-rehearsed "Teenagers" bit, the audience sat silent for an agonizing minute and forty-five seconds. Not even a line like "the entire lake is just *suicidally* beautiful tonight," which almost always hit, garnered a chuckle. But even though they look visibly nervous, no panic registers in their voices. If anything, the nervousness can be chalked up to being in character. Then it happens, like the onset of thunder, like a breath of relief: the laughs start to come. Slowly at first, timidly, then in loud cracks, Elaine winning the audience over with her perfectly executed exhale of a cloud of smoke mid-kiss. Any suspicion that they were stealing the show was confirmed during "Telephone," the audience roaring with laughter throughout. Elaine wowed them as she transformed from an impatient operator— seemingly unattractive, her voice gratingly nasal—to an early iteration of the archetypal "sexy professional" whose confidence Mike's character read as flirtation.[28] They went to bed that night knowing that no matter what, they had nailed it.

MIKE WOKE UP at four a.m. the next day and checked the papers. There it was in *The New York Times*: the show was dismissed for being "routine" and lacking in excitement, but nestled in the yawning criticism was a glowing recognition of their portions of it. "The only interludes of distinction," their sketches "had style and freshness." "Miss May in particular," they continued, "is a comedienne of very great promise."[29] Mike called Elaine immediately: "What do we do now?"[30]

* * *

SAY YOU'RE A relatively unknown comic. Maybe you have a few thousand followers on social media. You work steadily in a major city; a fair amount of people in the industry know your work; you've maybe gotten a good shout-out in high places here or there. But in the grand scheme of things, you're still very much in the minor leagues. You're not a regular on national television, and you're definitely not a household name. But then one night you post a joke video before you go to bed, and when you wake up the next day, you have five million views, a dozen missed calls from unknown numbers, and at least a hundred unread emails waiting for you. It's not that you're not used to attention—it's that you're not used to it on this overwhelming scale.

Elaine and Mike's *Omnibus* appearance was kind of like that. "Everyone had said to Rollins, 'Nobody will get them, they're too intellectual,'" Elaine recalled. "Well, everybody got us. We couldn't believe it."[31] They were twenty-five and twenty-six years old.

But it was more than that. People not only *got* Nichols and May—they *loved* them. The *Times* wasn't the only outlet to single out their appearance. The *New York Herald Tribune* raved that their "avant-garde humor" was "freshly observed and trenchant and marvelously funny comedy."[32] *Time* lauded their "fresh, inspired stuff"[33] and the AP called them "that extraordinarily funny young couple being talked about by so many people after only three guest appearances on television."[34] The country wanted to know: "Who are May and Nichols and where did they come from?"[35] and Rollins knew exactly how to engineer their longevity.

Omnibus was a game changer. "If that set of circumstances hadn't happened, it would have been a slow development for Nichols and May in the clubs," Rollins said.[36] Instead, their careers were on fast-forward. Less than six months after they arrived in New York, there was suddenly talk of touring, talk of recording LPs, talk of more television. They were no longer the late-night act at the Blue Angel; they were headlining. But even that was soon eclipsed. Ten weeks in, Rollins arranged for them to fulfill their remaining time later; there were bigger and better opportunities to cash in on first.[37] Everybody wanted a piece of Nichols and May—from higher-paying clubs in the city[38] to Perry Como and Jack Paar and the rest of the who's who of network television—and Rollins knew he could set his price high: $5,000 for each appearance. Elaine was used to living on $12 a week.[39]

ON THE RARE occasions she'd dine out in Chicago, Elaine would doctor the cheapest cuts of meat with a jar of Adolph's Tenderizer she kept in her handbag. Other times she'd ask the waiter, "How many shrimp are in your shrimp cocktail?"[40] Just a few short weeks before, new to New York in a way where popular was not yet synonymous with prosperous, she recalled that "we weren't exactly starving. We were just sort of involuntarily watching our weight."[41] Suddenly people wanted to wine and dine her and Mike on the finest steaks and champagne the city's hip restaurants had to offer. She didn't need her smuggled-in jar of tenderizer anymore, but who could blame her for being wary of letting go?

Here's the thing about fame: It's not natural, having attention and money thrust upon you, your life suddenly not quite your own. Elaine knew this and was suspicious of it. There were so many reasons to be distrustful: the fame had come too fast, it was too invasive, too disingenuous, too vapid. Too many prying eyes, strangers who thought they knew *her* when really, if anything, they knew only a *version* of her. Too many concessions to make—your art no longer just art, but a commodity. That was one thing that would take getting used to: The idea that her offbeat and sardonic observations could not just make her a living but could be viewed as a valuable product. Money was "an enormous kind of adventure," likely because it was something new to deconstruct and attempt to understand.[42] Unlike Mike, for whom wealth—as long out of shape as it may have been—was a muscle memory, Elaine had nothing to compare this entirely brand-new experience to. "How do you spend millions anyway?" she asked one interviewer. "Today I went out to spend some of my new money on clothes. And I can't find a dress that has a belt to it." As Mike observed: "Elaine has her protection built in. She just doesn't have an acquisitive instinct."[43] Department store saleswomen and famous hairdressers attempted to get her to turn in her worn tennis shoes and unset hair for heels and a chic bob, but she had a hard time changing her bohemian ways.[44] While Mike bought a Mercedes and a duplex on the Upper East Side, Elaine moved into a sprawling apartment on Riverside Drive, where for some time the only furniture to be found was a Ping-Pong table. "If I ever get organized," she told one reporter, "I know I'll enjoy every minute of this dream, too."[45]

Rich people were entertaining; she was both amused by and disdainful of the pleasurable lives of the privileged. "Did you know," she asked an interviewer, "that there are women who go shopping in the morning and then meet other women for lunch and then do more shopping and they do this six days a week all their lives?"[46] When one antiques dealer eager to furnish her apartment obsessed over a piece of furniture, she would goad him: "You mean it's secondhand?"[47]

No, even if she could understand it better, she would still find that money was a funny thing, something not to be taken too seriously at all. "Once you have it, you never have to use it—you just write checks or hand over your Diners Club card," she mused. If anything, she remarked, having more money made her only more democratic.[48] She had enough for her apartment, enough to bring Jeannie and Ida out to be with her, along with a housekeeper named Ruby to help care for Jeannie.[49] That should be enough. While Mike was gallivanting with the who's who of New York, befriending Stephen Sondheim and Jackie Kennedy and Richard Avedon, Elaine's idea of success was far simpler. All she wanted, she said, was to "make five million dollars, invest it all in AT&T, and have a sure forty dollars a week for the rest of my life."[50] Compared to twelve, forty seemed downright luxurious.

HERE'S THE OTHER thing about fame: Pretty quickly, the work it takes to maintain it replaces the work you did to earn it. The spring of 1958 was a blur of nonstop gigs. They traveled cross-country to embark on a bleak, laugh-less engagement at the Mocambo in Los Angeles, the West Coast's eminent hot spot that had the distinction of having an entire glass wall full of tropical birds. "Every night during our performance, one of the birds would die," Elaine recalled. "We would learn this because the next night the old wardrobe woman would come to me and say, 'Well, another bird died last night.'"[51] Then it was a hometown return to Chicago to head-line for a week at Mister Kelly's—at $2,500 a week, a hundred times more than they made the last time they were in the city.[52] Then it was back to the Blue Angel to finish their set. And there was still television to keep up with. TV, that thing that made them fa-mous, now exhausted them. The offers never stopped coming in, and Mike was always more willing to say yes.[53] Another thing about fame: Once you get it, people want more of the same.

This didn't sit well with Elaine. With no time—and no demand—to develop new material, the pair was stuck performing the same pieces they had been doing for years. "The bigger the nightclub we were in, the bigger the television show we were on, the more pres-sure there was to have the sketches we did be the best we had. And we found ourselves doing the same material over and over," Mike said.[54] An endless string of playing the two teenagers, the mother and son, the stranded motorist and the phone operator. For Mike, this was a nonissue. If anything, it was a welcome opportunity to refine each minute detail. They had based their work on a shared rule to never chase the laugh; now Mike was tinkering with the in-tent of garnering more. Laughs were a sign of adoration, a sign you had made a good impression. And he was good at polishing the veneer needed to do so. Mike, one friend had said, "believes that you can tell a book by its cover. Elaine is interested in the inside of the book and even more in the jelly stains and finger smudges on the pages."[55] Trying to operate in a stagnant world that valued per-fectly smudge-free pages was hell to someone like her. She resented the need "to start pleasing this tremendous unknown audience" where "you can only use safe material. But the only subject that's really safe is parking—and there's just so much you can say about parking."[56] She had success, but at what cost?

WE'RE ALL IN agreement here that the debate over whether women can be funny is, frankly, tired, right? Whether you want to go all the way back to William Congreve's 1695 letter "Concerning Hu-mour in Comedy" or Freud's 1905 book *Jokes and Their Relation to the Unconscious* or just a glance back at Christopher Hitchens's 2007 diatribe "Why Women Aren't Funny," we get it. Proclaiming that women are not only not funny, but will *never,* "scientifically speaking," be funny, is not only a long, time-tested parade of inane drivel, but a conversation that stretches far too close to comfort into our present lives.

Which is why it is objectively funny that at the tail end of the 1950s, Elaine May, a woman, was the toast of the town for . . . *being funny.* If we look back through all of the eager reporting on Nichols and May as they emerged, it feels as if there's been a mistake. Elaine gets nothing but praise—more often than not, she's singled out as the stronger player, acknowledged as the brains, the promising talent. There were no *"—for a woman"* qualifiers, no snide insinuations that her success was achieved only on the back of her male partner. Where were the profiles objectifying Elaine as a hot broad who, *huh, who woulda thought,* is funny, too? Where was the blowhard contrarian saying that he found her to be more grating than talented? How did Elaine seemingly sidestep the deeply entrenched misogyny of the era?

Just because the press was, for once, not grossly sexist doesn't mean Elaine existed in a world that was particularly welcoming to people who were not straight white men. Comedy was revolutionizing itself, that was for sure, but it wasn't bringing women along for the ride into the future. Though there was a female presence in vaudeville and cabaret, few who were prominent in those areas were brought along into this new era of comedy, one where you had to be fresh and boundary pushing, one where relying on tried and true theatrical archetypes wasn't enough to cut it anymore.

There had been plenty of female comedic actors in film since the days of silents and screwballs, and Lucille Ball was paving the way on television. But before the late 1950s, the chance of finding a woman performing comedy onstage was slim. Decades of hindsight make it easy to see their influence, but at the time, they were almost exclusively working in silos, performing to and for an audience that shared their identity. You could be a vaudeville performer like Sophie Tucker, but that meant basing your humor on bits and songs—and doing so, reluctantly, in blackface because producers told you that you were too unattractive to sell as you were. Moms Mabley may have been the highest-paid performer at the Apollo, but it wasn't until television appearances in the 1960s that she became more widely known. You had to either fit yourself into specific pigeonholes of female identity (like Jean Carroll, widely regarded as the first female stand-up, who told jokes about suburban life while dressed in her finest cocktail attire) or suffer the consequences if you rejected it entirely (like Belle Barth, who, after numerous lawsuits and an arrest on lewdness charges, was eventually banned from radio and TV).[57] If you were in a duo, you weren't equal with the man; you were Gracie Allen, playing the Dumb Dora to George Burns's straight man. Some of these women would make it past comedy's revolution away from these old formats, but not many. Comedy's revolution was one of a youthquake, and youth culture meant hip and happening, edgy and a little bit dangerous. There were two women who prominently crossed the bridge between vaudeville and stand-up, entered into the new world and shook things up: Elaine, and Phyllis Diller.

They could hardly have been more dissimilar: Elaine was beautiful, though slobbish and uncaring about her looks. So completely could she transform herself into a character that many weren't entirely sure what she looked like offstage.[58] Even though her looks could be a source of power, she had no interest in using them to fit into any conventional feminine stereotypes, even as she ascended in the public eye. Though plenty of people may have tried (and in small increments, succeeded) to get her to put a little more effort into her appearance,[59] she didn't need to be fully made up to exude an intimidating natural beauty. It wasn't something she hid, either—the way Diller did under her sack dresses—or made jokes about or centered her entire comedic sensibility upon.

Diller, though, made a name for herself with garish camp aesthetics and focused her act on lampooning the 1950s housewife. Elaine cared about character; Diller cared about jokes. Whereas Elaine could go on forever, meandering endlessly in someone else's skin, Phyllis was in and out. "A joke has *two* parts—setup, payoff. Forget this bullshit in the middle. The quicker you get to the payoff, the better," she said. "My idea is to edit. If one word can do the work of five, now you're talking."[60] Elaine liked words. She liked how she could lay them out in front of her like a path that would take her somewhere else, somewhere that wasn't here, deliver her to the truth. The longer the path, the more interesting it became. Editing was Mike's job, not hers.

They had one thing in common: They were both women fearlessly pushing back at a patriarchal system stacked against them. Although, of course, neither thought about it like that. This was the late 1950s; no one was talking about the patriarchy, much less about opposing it. Though Simone de Beauvoir's *The Second Sex* had been published in America in 1953, it would be another ten until Betty Friedan's *The Feminine Mystique* would set off the second-wave feminist movement.[61] Elaine and Diller were feminists in practice, but would never actually label themselves such.[62] (Even well into the twenty-first century, Elaine found feminism "really unnecessary," stating that she didn't get what the big deal was. Just do what you want, she'd reason.)[63] They were busy fighting for a seat at the table for themselves, with little thought of who else could pull up a chair behind them once they got there.

And even then, they may have gotten a *spot* at the table, but they still had to stand. They couldn't afford to sit down, couldn't afford to rest a moment, lest they give off the impression that they weren't strong enough to be there in the first place. So maybe people weren't debating whether they were funny, but there were still doubts that they could *sustain* their humor. Women, many thought, were too weak—physically and emotionally—to perform stand-up routines at a man's level. "The most taxing of all nightclub formulas, it is used by only two or three other women on the cabaret circuit; few have the tenacity to stick with it and develop into first-rate performers in demand across the country," *The New York Times* noted in an early profile of Diller. "Miss Diller explains the scarcity of her type of comedienne by pointing out that the work requires tremendous stamina, a thick skin, the courage to buck stiff competition in a predominantly male field and a speed that discourages hecklers and dispenses with the unladylike necessity of putting them down."[64] Elaine was too threatening to heckle in the first place, even by New Yorkers who had no idea of her venomous reputation. But even that didn't matter. They could have heckled her all they wanted. Her skin wasn't just thick; it was hidden behind a steely set of armor.

WHEN YOU REACH a certain level of success, you can start saying no. For most, this luxury comes years into a brilliant career; until then, no opportunity can be taken for granted. All press is good press; every offer for an appearance should be accepted or you'll disappear; every single paycheck matters. But Nichols and May weren't most people; they entered their era of choosiness less than a year after their meteoric rise.

The pace of their work wasn't sustainable, booking every gig in town and flying back and forth across the country to film television spots. That summer when they returned to the Blue Angel to finish out the last of their contract, they already had one terrible scripted television appearance (a CBS operetta called *The Red Mill*—it is, in their own words, not worth looking up) sway them enough to turn down a compelling offer from Lucille Ball and Desi Arnaz to develop and costar in a comedy series on CBS. Most actors would have been foolish to walk away from a potentially career-making deal, but all the exhausted Mike and Elaine could do was laugh. "Maybe we shouldn't," Elaine said. "I don't think I will," Mike replied.[65] They were content to keep television appearances to a steady minimum, just enough to maintain national exposure. They'd fill their schedules instead with radio appearances and interviews by day and appearances at the Blue Angel by night.

Elaine was getting listless. If she had to spend the night performing the same set over and over again, she had to find some excitement during the day. Interviews were the perfect opportunity for her to exercise her creative mind, keep it sharp, give it regular fresh air and feedings. By now the press was racking up—an endless string of interviews with somebodies and nobodies alike she constantly stressed over. What if, say, Dinah Shore playfully remarked to her on air, "Why, Elaine, you're wearing the same dress I am," and she—the woman unable to be anything but truthful, the woman who knew she wasn't a tree—sourly responded, "Certainly, didn't you see it at dress rehearsal?"[66] What a mortifying mood killer that would be.

Far worse than the ones who dealt in inane on-air banter were the ones who wanted to *know* her—at least, as well as any interviewer can know their subject in the span of an hour or two. They asked so many imposing questions about what was going on in her love life and how she shopped and just what she made of this whole fame thing. Elaine wasn't exactly shy, but she wasn't transparent, either. She wasn't capable of viewing an interview like a conversation with another person, one that, even if a bit transactional, was at the end of the day a human-to-human connection. An interview was at best a hostile interrogation and at worst treason. "If I don't like the interviewer," she explained, "I become not so much hostile as sullen and childish." Actually liking the interviewer was perhaps a worse position to be in; it gnawed at her insurmountable trust issues, at her intense fear that they, like everyone else, would inevitably hurt her. "If I *do* like the interviewer, I read the story and feel personally betrayed by what he's said."[67]

Once again, Elaine retreated into her fantasy world and pulled up the drawbridge. She could fulfill obligations to engage with the press and promote her work with Mike without getting hurt. She didn't have to be forthcoming. She just had to play someone who was, give them the Elaine May persona to avoid exposing any of her true self. So she began to bend the truth. The bending of truth turned into outrageous lies. They were gratuitous, piling up one after the other in print until you had to wonder what got cut. It was easy to do; half the time, she realized, the interviewer wasn't even listening to what she had said. "One radio man was interviewing us once," she said, "and he said to me, 'Are you and Mike married?' I said, 'No.' He wasn't paying much attention and he said to Mike, 'Fine, how long have you been married?' Mike said, 'But we're not.' The radio man, who was fooling with his tape recorder by this time, said, 'Wonderful! How many children have you got, Elaine?' I gave up and just said, 'Four!'"[68] The woman who valued truth above all else knew how often a good story could offer more currency.

MIKE AND ELAINE didn't take any time off after their run at the Blue Angel ended in the fall of 1958, heading straight to the studio to record their first album instead. Mike and Elaine were perfect for the medium. They weren't reliant on visuals to be funny; the jokes in their scenes were more verbal than physical. The album they released that year may have been called *Improvisations to Music*—eight vignettes set against a classical music background—but their patter was music in and of itself. The music was the rhythm of Elaine's nervous stammering as a secretary being seduced by her boss in "Cocktail Piano"; was their cartoonish accents when they returned to their favorite old spy routine from the Illinois Central Station in "Mysterioso"; was the coolly detached drawl of their voices as two bedded lovers in "Bach to Bach" getting off by indulging in incredibly pretentious intellectualizing and one-upping each other.

What set *Improvisations to Music* apart from other comedy albums of the time was that it, like much of their work, was all about sex. It's the running theme, with each track openly discussing the sexual relationships between liberated men and women. It was one thing for Mike and Elaine to perform these scenes in a club, where there was a guaranteed audience full of like-minded progressive urbanites. It was quite another to commit them to LP, to release these racy—yet simultaneously highbrow—boundary-pushing sketches to a nation who knew them primarily from their more family-friendly television appearances. "There was a kind of social vice that was existing around certain things," director Arthur Penn said. "You simply didn't talk about sexual behavior."[69] Incredibly, their risk paid off: That year, the album reached number 39 in Billboard's Top 200 and picked up a Grammy nomination in the Recording Academy's first ever Best Comedy Album category.[70]

They had secured their spot as the belles of the cultural ball, but all Elaine wanted to do was disappear. On the album jacket of *Improvisations to Music,* she and Mike wrote their own biographies: "Mike Nichols is not a member of the Actors Studio, which has produced such stars as Marlon Brando, Julie Harris, Ben Gazzara, Eva Marie Saint, Carroll Baker, and others too numerous to mention. He has never toured with *Mister Roberts* and has never appeared on such television programs as the *Goodyear Playhouse* and the *Kraft Theatre,*" Mike wrote. Elaine's said simply: "Miss May does not exist." It would be easier to take at face value as a joke, and not a desperate wish, if she hadn't been trying so hard to make it true.

Once Elaine said something, put something out there, it was there, for better or worse, committed to time and history. Her distrust of others grew. Elaine, who had previously never known when to bite her tongue, became increasingly quiet, letting Mike do most of the talking and make most of their business decisions as well—not at all unlike her father handing off most of the paperwork to Ida. If she couldn't quit, she'd make herself small instead.

THERE'S ONE PIECE that Mike and Elaine performed regularly during this period that they never recorded. At close to eighteen minutes long, "Pirandello" was the epic of improv comedy sketches, a fucked-up psychological funhouse of cards. They would start by playing kid siblings. Mike would challenge Elaine to a belching contest ("It would bring the house down," Elaine said) before they played the two children imitating their parents fighting.[71] The game would shift gears seamlessly from there, never fully giving away what was happening or when each wall would be blown down. They went from playing children acting like adults fighting to playing the adults themselves. Then that identity was smashed, and they became heightened versions of themselves, two actors having an increasingly uncomfortable argument in the burning hot spotlight. Elaine would suggest Mike was impotent; Mike would storm offstage. The audience would laugh—though only *sort of,* the lines blurred to the point where they weren't quite sure what was part of the sketch and what was reality, where the onstage action warranted amusement and where it warranted genuine concern. "The nice thing," Elaine said, "is to make an audience laugh and laugh and laugh, and shudder later."[72]

Each time they performed it, they would take it a step further, coming up with new awful cruelties to sling at each other, new ways to see how close to the edge they could get. They both knew each other's weaknesses and pain points, knew their own personal libraries full of devastating kill lines they had filed away out of self-restraint over the years. It would get physical: Mike would grab Elaine's arm and pull her toward him, ripping her blouse. She would sob. Were Mike and Elaine hurting each other in character, or were they honestly hurting each other? No one in the audience knew. As they began to react in shock, Mike and Elaine would break, proudly announcing with perverse delight at the *gotcha,* "This is 'Pirandello'!" before taking their bows. "Sometimes they still didn't believe we'd been acting," Elaine said.[73]

It was an act that was too physical to commit to one of their records and certainly one they never could have performed on television. It was too violent and too filled with psychosexual energy, for one thing, but for another, it was just too dangerous, the one sketch they couldn't set in near stone if they wanted it to turn out well. But in May of 1959, they brought "Pirandello" to the stage of New York's Town Hall, where they performed two back-to-back shows, selling out the 1,500-seat theater both nights. It was their biggest audience yet, and *The New York Times* singled out their performance of "Pirandello" in particular. It was "a scene that not only is extremely funny but that also involves a steady, subtle and, climactically, shocking shift of focus."[74]

But audiences who were hoping to see Nichols and May perform it again in a large setting would have to wait. For the first time in two years, they finally pulled back. That summer, they cut down the grueling club shows and instead focused on fulfilling lucrative deals to write and voice animated commercials for Jax Beer and record improvisations for NBC's radio program *Monitor.* It was a relatively comfortable gig, but one that Elaine enjoyed. For three hours every other week at the RCA Building, they could be the same kids they were in Chicago, endlessly improvising purely for their own enjoyment of it. No nervous television producers were signaling for them to wrap it up—the sound producer rarely inserted himself, and their sketches could stretch on longer than ten minutes—and no audience was waiting eagerly to be pleased. They weren't performing; they were working. And because they weren't live, they could start or restart however many times they needed until something clicked. In one improvisation, Mike began by playing a doctor and Elaine his patient, but it stalled, so they switched roles. Mike was now a patient in need of an "annual emergency ear checkup." It still wasn't right. "Elaine, we're not going anywhere. Let's figure out where we're going," Mike said. "No. That would ruin it," Elaine replied. "Let's keep going."[75]

Life, though, is not an improv, drifting along, waiting to see what happens and hoping for the best. Life needs some forethought, some planning if you want to actually go anywhere.

A NEWLY DIVORCED Mike spent that summer under the wing of Richard Avedon, vacationing and socializing with New York's rich and famous. Elaine, meanwhile, couldn't stay still very long. She spent the summer writing, working on a new play for producer Fred Coe, hoping to meet a deadline to stage it the following season.[76] When she wasn't writing, she was in psychoanalysis, spending five days a week in treatment with Dr. David Rubinfine, a rising star in the New York psychoanalytic community. Rubinfine was just as much a character as Elaine, not only a trained physician and talented therapist, but an amateur magician as well. He loved show business and creatives, almost, as some have said, "to distraction."[77]

Rubinfine was, by many accounts, eccentric, an overly romantic man who seemed to have missed his calling in the theater and somehow wound up in psychotherapy instead. Not only did his clientele skew toward those in the arts, so, too, did his social circle, as he befriended Stephen Sondheim and Hal Prince and spent evenings working behind the scenes at the HB Studio.[78] Elaine was his ideal patient: someone who not only loved comedy as much as he did (he kept a portrait of Buster Keaton above his desk) but loved analysis, too. There was order to it, theory behind it. Explanations for all the unexplainable phenomena of life. As her sessions progressed, she and Rubinfine grew increasingly closer.

IN THE SPRING of 1960, producer Alexander Cohen approached Mike and Elaine with an offer: Why not turn their act into a Broadway show? Having successfully staged a British duo's revue a year prior, Cohen had set his eyes on Nichols and May for his next big thing. It wasn't without some risk: They may have had sold out Town Hall, but this was Broadway. Town Hall was 1,500 seats for two nights. They were talking *6,000* for eight performances a week. It was a gamble, but an alluring one. What else were they going to do? The only thing safe was to take a chance, right? They said yes.[79]

But the size and grandeur of the show were the only real sources of risk. There would be no new material written for their Broadway show. Instead, they "found that the safest thing was to stick with the set pieces, which changed a little bit anyway, do the improvisation, and then get off with some set thing we had prepared."[80] Elaine, for reasons unknown, went along with this, letting Mike take over the practicalities.[81] That spring, they exported their act to San Francisco to test how their material played on bigger stages in front of new audiences. The ensuing reviews were mixed; though several critics loved it, calling Nichols and May "the funniest, freshest and most charming couple to have invaded the domain of comedy in at least a decade," "superb," and "the finest conversational humor in today's showbiz,"[82] some fairly called out what seemed like a cash grab to capitalize on their popularity.[83] (Ironic, given the amount of hustling they had to do to even stage a show in the first place. Vying for investors at $1,000 a pop,[84] Cohen often enlisted their talents, filling their schedules with luncheons with agents and meetings with investors and publicity photos with Avedon.)[85] If they wanted to make it on Broadway, they had to think beyond the cabaret mannerisms that worked in intimate nightclub settings but would never play on a large stage.[86]

Arthur Penn would be the man to pull it together. Already a well-respected television director, Penn was making a name for himself on Broadway, with two hit shows—*Two for the Seesaw* and *The Miracle Worker*—running simultaneously. A decade older than Mike and Elaine, he was the experienced elder, the guiding hand who also understood their particular brush with popularity. Mike and Elaine trusted his intelligence and his directing style, the way he was more like a valued friend making thoughtful suggestions than a director giving terse instructions.[87] Penn made mostly minor adjustments, like bringing in better furniture than their dinky stools and adding an intermission after "Pirandello," but it made a world of difference, elevating it from the nightclub to something more chic and far more structured for the staged setting. The fresh pair of eyes was exactly what they needed. "Suddenly it felt like a play," Elaine said.[88]

By the time their out-of-town tryouts started that August, the pressure had intensified. The investors were more than in ("I am listening to constant complaints from people who can no longer have a piece," Cohen wrote to Mike), but the material, though it was the same as they had done for the past few years, still wasn't clicking.[89] The review in the *Boston Daily Record* was unfavorable toward Mike, and Cohen had more notes for them, honing in particularly on what was still wrong with "Pirandello."

Oh, "Pirandello." Something was bound to go very wrong with the scene at some point. It was inevitable. You can skip back and forth across the third rail only so many times before you eventually trip. It was always a gamble; they both needed to go further into that performance than any of their other sketches, channel their Method training to fully blur the lines between fantasy and reality. If they didn't commit enough, the whole thing would fold in on itself; the audience would see the act at work rather than be sucked into it. But there was another way it could go wrong, a dangerous one. All the years they had spent chipping away at it—the one scene that they hadn't perfected, the one scene where there was always a nitpicky argument about its structure or its pacing—had taken their toll. While the audience couldn't differentiate between fantasy and reality, neither could Mike or Elaine. One night in Westport, Connecticut, "it went very far," Mike said. "I must have blanked out or something, 'cause I was hitting Elaine, back and forth on both sides of her face, and she had clawed open my chest, which was pouring blood, and we didn't know how we had got there."[90]

What had happened to them? How could it have come to this? Weren't they supposed to be the two people who would never hurt each other? "They brought the curtain down and we burst into tears and embraced and sort of controlled it after that," Mike said. "It was scary. It really got away from us."[91] But it didn't matter how shaken up they were; they didn't have time to stop and think too hard about *why* it happened, only that it couldn't happen again. The Broadway premiere was a month away; Cohen had built it up as an extravagant event of the year, from chauffeuring guests in a fleet of Rolls-Royces to dinner at Sardi's before the show to throwing a star-studded midnight block party after.[92] The month before, Mercury had agreed to publish an album recording of the show.[93] They couldn't fall apart. Not now, at least.

THEIR ANXIETIES WERE felt when *An Evening with Mike Nichols and Elaine May* opened on October 8, 1960, at Broadway's Golden Theatre. They were uncharacteristically restrained, cautious in a way that was perhaps unseen to those new to their work but glaring to anyone familiar with their fearlessness. "It was amazing," Elaine said. "Our opening night was the worst performance I think we ever gave because our friends were there. And they were terribly nervous for us. And it only seemed to show how nervous we were. We were absolutely certain that we had failed totally."[94] They did far better than failing totally, of course, although the reviews were sharply divided. In a sense, either you were young and cool and sophisticated, someone who got Mike and Elaine—and were open to expanding what Broadway theater could be—or you were tragically unhip, a stuffy, out-of-touch square who wanted to see the stage forever stuck in its set ways. *The New York Times,* for one, found it "amusing" but took issue with the improvised style showing its hand. "Sketches are becalmed for moments as if Miss May or Mr. Nichols seem to be reaching for the next move. Such hesitations are discomfiting: they rob a scene and its characters of definition; they give professional work an amateurish vagueness." "Pirandello," the show's most dangerous number for its performers, was "the flattest number in the show."[95]

Not that any criticism really mattered where the bottom line was concerned. The show was an immediate hit, regularly selling out. Mike and Elaine were making $3,000 a week, on top of the percentages of the gross revenue they stood to gain.[96] Sure, it was chump change compared to what they could pull in for TV appearances, but it was a steady gig that wasn't as dumbed down and rote as television, and audiences loved it. (Although for years after, they hung on to one lengthy complaint from an attendee who derided it for being "vulgar, disgusting, [and using] vile language.")[97] They were two of the most famous people in America, and Elaine was deeply unhappy.

Each show ended with their "First Line/Last Line" bit, and though the combinations could be as chaotic and as varied as "When the kissing had to stop" / "I went fishing and didn't catch any fish" in the style of Chaucer and "How can I smell my way to Dover, I have no nose?" / "Pine trees have long needles" from Dick Tracy's viewpoint, that was the extent to which they still improvised.[98] The rest of the show was set; not quite to the word, but it might as well have been. There wasn't room to be spontaneous on Broadway, not if the crew was going to be able to run the show smoothly. One night, in order to ease their work backstage, the stage manager transcribed each scene into an unofficial script. When Elaine got her hands on the transcription of their PTA act, she became stricken. "There isn't a joke in it," she said, dismayed. Dissatisfaction and self-consciousness colored her performance for the next several weeks; she couldn't shake the feeling that her words—the things she valued most—weren't getting across the way she had intended.[99] She would visit Mike's dressing room after another crowd-pleasing performance, terribly somber, apologizing for her perceived mistakes.[100] The ability to be in the moment was gone, replaced with rote repetition that she both detested and was paralyzed by. All the audience adoration onstage couldn't make a difference, and Elaine had no interest in the champagne-filled celebrity visits backstage. And there was always some celebrity waiting to greet them: Norman Mailer, Lillian Hellman, Richard Burton, Julie Andrews— the entire It Crowd of New York wanting to say hello. She could by now get through some polite socialization, but she'd just as soon sneak out before schmoozing was truly underway. Her dangerous wit and reputation hadn't faded, though. Just like in Chicago, men fell at her feet, simultaneously in love with her and terrified of her. It's just that now the men she was slaying without any effort weren't university boys; they were grown men, and accomplished ones at that. She claimed that on one occasion she found herself nose to nose with Richard Burton after she dropped something under a table at dinner and he followed her underneath it. "You're a damn fascinating woman," he told her.[101] If you don't believe Elaine, just look at what he wrote in his diary about her: "Elaine was too formidable . . . one of the most intelligent, beautiful, and witty women

I had ever met. I hoped I would never see her again."[102] Writer and critic Edmund Wilson, who became infatuated with Elaine after seeing *An Evening with Mike Nichols and Elaine May* four times, wrote in his journal that he "was sorry not to be young enough to fall in love with her and ruin my life."[103]

Her refusal to participate in the networking side of the business, to give people what they wanted and appear happy doing it, would hurt her in the long run. At a certain point, showing up to get-togethers, no matter how ostensibly casual, in old slacks and tennis shoes and with dirty hair would no longer seem charmingly eccentric.[104] A career is a game, one that can't be played by just betting on sheer luck, much as hers had been so far. At a certain point, it becomes shaped by your actions, by taking part in the usual rituals—business lunches and interviews, industry parties and fan interactions alike—an artist needs to both establish a reputation and continue to feed it. Mike knew this and tended carefully to his image both with his elite social circle and with the populace. "She was more interested in taking chances than in being a hit. I was more interested in making the audience happy," Mike said.[105] For Elaine, the work mattered most, not the rewards. The work was supposed to be the thing that begets more work, not fake friendships and ass-kissing.

Not only was the work no longer interesting or good—to Elaine's standards, at least—but there was no room for any relief, no time or energy to perform or develop something else simply to shake things up a little and keep her creative spark alive. "Their health is at stake," Cohen wrote to Jack Rollins, asking that he turn down all the numerous offers for additional appearances he had been receiving. "They are the only two performers in a long and arduous show. . . . Any such appearance will be a violation of their contract and place in jeopardy the length of the run of the show by needlessly taxing and exhausting them."[106]

Any love the pair had for each other was slowly bleeding out, replaced instead with the feelings of hostility they had harbored for each other the moment they met. Offstage communication froze. Soon even the backstage banter was gone, replaced with bitter exchanges where one reporter observed, "how-dare-you-treat-me-this-way is a recurrent theme."[107] They began showing up late, breaking during sketches. "Once during 'Teenagers'—I still remember it—during the kissing, we either hit teeth or something, and we began to break," she remembered. "And we stayed together in the kiss until we could pull ourselves together, and then we parted and something happened, and we broke up again, and we couldn't stop. At first the audience laughed with us, and then they began to get a little annoyed. I remember during intermission, Mike said we had to pull ourselves together—these people have paid an enormous amount of money to see us, and we have to be professional. So we went back onstage and just fucked the second act. We laughed, and we couldn't stop."[108] Mike would attempt to direct Elaine from the wings or within the scene, his own feelings of inadequacies—that she could endlessly invent in a way he just couldn't—rising. Elaine would ignore him, furious, taking advantage of the chance to improvise in the final "First/ Last" scene—the only part of the night she still enjoyed—and indulging her every whim until the show ran chronically late.

The situation wasn't just wearing on Mike and Elaine; they were beginning to test Cohen's patience as well. Earlier in the run, he had tried to guide Elaine into a more efficient mode of operation, but realized quickly it was a futile endeavor. "Elaine relates to things that are important, and she knows what's important," he said. "She may be late for half-hour call at the theatre or forget to comb her hair, but she never misses a dinner with Jeannie."[109] When he attempted to lecture or counsel her, she found a way to turn it back on him as a gag. One evening, he found a note from her on his desk which read:

Wake up (open eyes), get out of bed.

Get hair fixed.

Take bath (get towel, soap, washcloth; undress; fill tub).

Dry self.

Dress (put on underwear, dress and/or skirt & blouse, shoes).

Comb hair.

Do other things (as thou wouldst have them, etc.).

Correct Alex's souvenir program.

Look for hat.

Give insurance policies to Ronnie at 6:00.

BUY STAMPS.

Avoid answering phone in case it is Michael (or answer in disguise).

Avoid door in case it is neighbor (or answer in disguise).

BE AT ALEX'S AT 4:00![110]

But it wasn't funny anymore. There was an entire staff of people at work behind the scenes, and people in the audience paying hard-earned money to see them. It was time to grow up. By the winter of 1961, Cohen's correspondence became increasingly testy, like a stern father trying to corral his misbehaving children, not two grown adults who were supposed to be professionals. "WE ARE THE ONLY SHOW IN TOWN THAT GOES UP CONSISTENTLY LATE," he wrote in a memo to his stage manager. "Under no circumstances, at any time is this show to run into overtime and if you think it is going to come within one minute of running into overtime, cut the encores."[111]

"WHEN YOU DO a show for a year . . . you can't be best friends anymore," Mike said. "It's like you've lived with somebody and fucked each other's brains out and you're so sick of them, you just have to get out of the house."[112]

"I can't take it anymore," Elaine told Mike one day. "Take what?" Mike asked incredulously. "It's an hour and a half and all we do is talk."[113] See, that was the thing. That's all they had been doing. "She got so bored," Mike said. "All comedians want to change at a certain point. Your act becomes your enemy."[114]

"You can't go on for a year," Elaine said. Not even "First Line/ Last Line" was enough to keep her from going crazy every night. Repeats were inevitable. "By the fourth time you've gotten Shakespeare, it's very hard to do new things because you've done it four times."[115] And besides, she was suspecting that their act had a social expiration date. Kennedy's election had changed the mood of the nation. The egghead, self-serious days of the Eisenhower era were coming to a close. Camelot was glamorous and sexy. The president *laughed* at himself. No, the only thing worse than being stale would be an audience knowing you were stale.[116] "I told Mike there was no way we could top ourselves," Elaine said.[117]

She had a clause in her contract: As long as she gave four weeks' notice, she could get out. It was time to use it. "I have enjoyed my association with you, but I do not wish to continue in the Play as it is too great a strain upon my strength and time," she wrote in a terse, formal resignation to Cohen on June 1, 1961.[118] A month later, after more than 300 performances, the show officially closed. It had grossed more than $35,000 (equivalent to roughly $358,000 today)[119]—a bigger commercial success than anyone involved could have anticipated—and Elaine just walked away, with no plans for what to do next.

CHAPTER 4

What the Hell Happened to Elaine May?

1961–1967

INT.—LOS ANGELES, WINTER 1967—DAWN

Elaine is in the car again, half asleep on her way from her hotel room—the one with a cheap view of the Sunset Strip where strangers slip desperate love letters meant for someone else under her door each night—to Columbia Studios. Hollywood is suspicious of Elaine. Or, rather, Hollywood doesn't know what to make of Elaine, a "smart New York lady," with no publicist and no desire to get one, annoyed with all the attention she has to endure every day. She's black deli coffee served to those who drink only champagne.

She's not Mike: charming and genial, ambitious and eager to prove himself. No, she couldn't be like Mike: someone who had outgrown his scorn for the Hollywood ecosystem and was now conscious of his status within it. Even when he behaved at his worst, his most personally arrogant or insufferable or professionally indulgent, it didn't really matter. There were certain things he could get away with that she couldn't. Not anymore, not without him by her side to be the nice one, the one to soften the blow, garner the forgiveness of those she had pissed off. That winter, she had watched as Mike received his first Academy Award nomination for Best Director for his debut, *Who's Afraid of Virginia Woolf?* Nominated for thirteen awards, the film won five.

It's 1967, and Mike is an Oscar-nominated director, while Elaine doesn't even know how much she's being paid for the two forgettable films she's shooting back-to-back. It's 1967, and Mike is the talk of the town, while Elaine is showing her credentials at the gates of

Columbia Studios. She's worked there twice in the past six months. Security still doesn't know her name.[1]

What had gone wrong? How could they have drifted so far apart? How was it that Mike was *there* and she—arguably the better half—was, well, *here*, drifting, stumbling from project to project with no thread connecting them together in a way that might resemble a career? Less than ten years ago, people couldn't get enough of her. Now the question was not *Who is Elaine May?* Now the question was: *What the hell happened to Elaine May?*

WHEN MIKE AND Elaine called it quits in 1961, it was an amicable split. They were sad about it, even. No one was the enemy here. "He felt guilty that he had been mean to me," Elaine said, "and I felt guilty that I had left the show."[2] The story they told themselves and everyone around them was that they were long overdue for a rest, for a break from work that they both agreed had become "so dehumanized and so unreal."[3] It was time for them to pursue their other interests. They had spent far too much time together in such an intense way. This was their chance to safely part, to detangle the messy knot their limbs had made. Better to do it now, before it got so bad that all they could do would be violently cut themselves free.

Of course, no one could ever believe that they were really calling it quits while they were still on top. The end of the show couldn't be the end of Nichols and May; the door would remain open to work together in the future. In six months, they would reconvene for an obligatory weeklong run of *An Evening With* in Toronto, but other than that, there would be no new sets, no return to TV or nightclubs. While Mike drifted through the rest of 1961, socializing, dating, and making the most of his newfound spare time, Elaine spent the year writing feverishly and developing new plays, one of which would bring them back together.

MAKING HER NEW York playwriting debut in 1962, Elaine returned to what she knew best: damaged women—victims dealt a bad hand by life—and the hapless men who surrounded them. A short one-act,

Not Enough Rope, found Elaine dealing in the most pitch-black of gallows humor: A lonely young woman living in a boardinghouse decides to hang herself, but she doesn't have any rope. When she asks her new neighbor if he has anything she can borrow, all he has to offer is twine. But once she's finally strung herself up, she has a sudden change of thought—and finds that she's unable to free herself. As the girl balances precariously in her room, she calls out to him—the only tenant home—for help cutting her down. In a tragicomic twist of events, she finds that he's even more psychologically disturbed than she is.

At a scant twenty-five minutes, though, it doesn't seem like a fully fleshed out play, even as a one-act.[4] And to audiences who knew nothing of her playwriting, it could easily have seemed like an ill-formed Nichols and May castoff. The reviews were withering. *Not Enough Rope* had but "scattered reminders" of the brilliant humor associated with Nichols and May; she was "as tearful as the somber prophets of a man's failure to communicate."[5] Derided as a "jolly little piece just this side of necrophilia," the play was little more than "a blown-up version of a sick joke."[6]

Elaine had earned a built-in audience for whatever plays she would write on her own, but it was an audience earned from material that, despite its prickliness, was ultimately welcoming. You listened to a Nichols and May sketch and felt like you knew these people; they were you, or they were your snappy friends trading barbs at cocktail hour. But to watch an Elaine May original was a different experience entirely, uncomfortable and perhaps a little frightening, an unrelenting display of life's cruelties.

Alone with her work, delighted by the own twist of her joke, she meandered, losing the shape and point of *Not Enough Rope* entirely. She was supposed to be better than this. All it showed was a writer in need of an editor. An Elaine in need of a Mike.

STILL FIGURING OUT how to be an Elaine without a Mike professionally, she sought partnership in her personal life. That April, Elaine suddenly married lyricist Sheldon Harnick. Though they had been seeing each other for about a year, their marriage caught everyone off guard, most of all Mike. Elaine wasn't the marrying kind; for as long as he had known her, she treated men as if they were disposable, never hanging in long enough to get serious. To marry Harnick, of all people, whose work—which would soon include songs for musicals *She Loves Me* and *Fiddler on the Roof*—was wry and witty, but almost always laced with earnest optimism, just didn't make any sense.

Sure enough, it didn't last long. By June, with Harnick in London overseeing the West End opening of *Fiorello!*, they separated, agreeing to divorce when he returned. "It's not a question of any other person being involved with him or myself," she said. "It just didn't work out."[7] The marriage was so brief, she joked that she got custody of the cake,[8] while more than fifty years later, Harnick had to be reminded that the short-lived union had ever transpired.[9]

The same week that she and Harnick called it quits, Elaine's latest play, *A Matter of Position*, starring Mike, closed during its Philadelphia tryout without ever making it to Broadway.[10]

A MATTER OF POSITION was doomed from the start. Okay, so maybe she shouldn't have written a play where the protagonist—a man who desperately longs to be liked goes to bed for a year in a fit of depression and refuses to get up—was based on Mike. Or maybe she could have, but she shouldn't have let Mike play it. Or she could have, but she shouldn't have *told* Mike it was about him. There had to be a more tactful way to do this, right?

Or maybe Mike should have known better. When had Elaine ever written a sympathetic character? And had she ever been shy about critiquing those closest to her? Although she insisted that she couldn't really explain where the character had come from, that the ideas would come to her in the middle of the night, divine inspiration, and she was just the messenger, he could sense what was real. Her perception of him was less than friendly, contemptuous even. To her, he was "a moral monster whom the audience couldn't like."[11]

Things had seemed good between them. Hadn't things seemed good between them? At any rate, they were doing a good job of putting on a show for the public. Remember John F. Kennedy's birthday party at Madison Square Garden in 1962? You know, the one where Marilyn Monroe serenaded the president with "Happy Birthday" while wearing a sheer sequined dress she had to be sewn into? Mike and Elaine performed that night, too, had stood behind Marilyn as she sang and had seen, clear as day under the glow of the stage lights, that she wasn't wearing any underwear.[12] They seemed fine then: funny as they read their silly little fake telegrams of congratulations, perfectly cordial as they retired to a smaller private party at the home of film executive Arthur Krim later that evening. Had Elaine been hiding her resentment that entire time, letting it simmer long enough so that it would make useful material?

That was May. By September, things were falling apart. As *A Matter of Position* headed toward Philadelphia, Elaine dropped out of the play as his costar and was replaced with Rose Arrick. She reasoned that she could better observe how it was hanging together if she had distance to focus on the script and everyone else's performance of it, rather than fixating on her own. The script was what mattered to her above all else. Even if the general assessment by everyone else was that, despite a "brilliant" second act, the rest needed a significant amount of work, nothing would twist it in a direction she didn't intend.[13] Not Mike's performance—which she was unhappy with—and certainly not Arthur Penn's direction. Disagreeing with his request for cuts, she quickly replaced him with Fred Coe, who would direct on top of his producing duties, despite his own shortcomings.[14] Now none of it was working. "There was this pall of fiasco that hung over the entire production," said John Lahr.[15] The first reading set off panic in Elaine. Coe didn't understand the characters, she felt, or what they were supposed to do. Rehearsals were worse; each performance failed to meet her expectations.[16] Even if Elaine claimed she didn't care what audiences thought, that didn't mean she didn't want people to understand it. And she couldn't argue with the fact that you had to win over *some* people if you wanted to continue to work. *Not Enough Rope* was a fumbled first impression; to avoid a repeat, she needed full control over her intended Broadway debut. She would be vicious about it if necessary:

Q: Have you had any quibbles with the director or the cast on their
   approach to your play?
A: No.

Q: Has this led to bloodshed?
A: Occasionally.[17]

Without Elaine beside him, Mike was lost and self-conscious, back in an eerily familiar position from all those years ago: staring down at the hostile girl sitting in the audience judging him, chain-smoking anxiously in the dark. "It was disastrous," he said. "It didn't work for me, it didn't work for the play, it didn't work for her."[18]

The chasm only grew when the producers began insisting upon what Arthur Penn had called for from the start: Elaine had to cut forty minutes from the play, particularly the third act, which had reached an absurdly excessive length. "You can't have people streaming out of the theater at one in the morning," Coe pleaded.[19] But that just wouldn't work for her. (Can't you just hear her replying, "Why not?") There had to be another solution. "I usually believe that anything can be fixed—even terminal cancer, if they try," Elaine said. "But somewhere in Philadelphia, I realized I had absolutely nothing to say about the making of my play. They didn't even want me in the theater."[20] She had already made changes to the script earlier in rehearsals.[21] If she made these additional, far more significant cuts, she argued, she would no longer have a truthful story about real human behavior. She wouldn't even have a play. She would have "a formula made up of words and jokes and scenes."[22] Rather than let them "emasculate"[23] her work, she offered to trim the length by working with the actors more directly, in effect sidestepping Coe and taking over direction herself. But after a few days, it was clear that wouldn't cut it, either.[24] Turning to Mike with the expectation of support, what she got instead was betrayal.

The abrupt change in the power dynamics had shaken something loose, both within and between them. Now that it was no longer them "together against everyone else," it became each person for themselves, each fearing humiliation for their own separate reasons.[25] Mike, panicked about his own inadequacies as an actor who no longer had Elaine as an onstage crutch, sided with Coe. "Get her to cut the play or I'm leaving," he threatened the producers.[26] Elaine, knowing Mike had to singularly represent her vision onstage—and wasn't up to it, especially given the stakes—balked. The problem wasn't her script; it was him. Get another actor, she argued. Mike would be judged as an actor, but by then he didn't even really *want* to be an actor, so what did it really matter? A subpar performance wasn't going to affect the rest of his career, especially when the text itself could be blamed for it. But being a writer was *it* for Elaine, what she had considered herself before improvising with Mike took off, and what she had given up their act to return to. For Elaine, this wasn't just business. It was personal.

They both betrayed each other, but Mike's was a greater betrayal, crueler and more devastating. "It was not a pleasant experience," he said. "I behaved very badly toward Elaine."[27] She had gone for his ego, but it was a weak swipe, nothing that would derail his entire career. Because there never was a power imbalance—not really. Mike may have felt the sudden shock of realizing he was no longer in the wings of the Golden Theatre giving direction to Elaine, and that it was the other way around. He may have felt emasculated by this, even, but at the end of the day, he inherently would always have more power in the world than she. He'd always have the ability to protect his dear friend, as he had so many times before. This time he simply chose not to.

It was three against one; Coe and coproducer Arthur Cantor seized control of the show, making the cuts they wanted, to Elaine's dismay. But it didn't matter what they did. "There was something about the play itself that nobody liked," she said. "It went so badly that at intermission I went out in the lobby and heard someone say, 'Who can I write to about this?' It was tough."[28]

With critics and audiences both against it, the play folded in October, after seventeen performances and $125,000. Mike and Elaine folded, too. "They simply were not destined to work together forever," Jack Rollins conceded. "They could drive each other up the wall."[29] But they had gone too far this time. They may have thought they were the two people who could never hurt each other, but it isn't possible for anyone to move through life without inflicting pain on someone else. Not even they could escape that.

"Once we'd gone through that experience of trying to screw the other one, out of panic and discomfort on our own parts," Mike said, "it was sort of over."[30] They were able to hide their split from the public for nearly a year, but to anyone who knew them, it was like living with separated parents who continued to share the same house for the sake of the kids. "We stayed in each other's lives. But it wasn't the same. We had seen each other every day, we knew each other's lives, we made fun of each other's dates," Elaine said.[31] At benefit and television appearances they had committed to and couldn't back out of, they spoke only onstage; they eschewed doing any publicity for their third album, *Mike Nichols and Elaine May Examine Doctors,* a compilation of sketches from the radio program *Monitor.* They had become just like the people they made a mockery of, putting on the pretense of having it all together, trying to fool everybody else into thinking that was the truth. After that, "we had some years where, it's not that we didn't speak, but there was no contact," Mike recalled.[32]

"In my memory," Elaine said nearly fifty years later, "I thought our estrangement was longer than it was. But we were estranged in that forever we felt guilty."[33]

Neither could be fully blamed for the uncoupling of Nichols and May, but when it came to the dissolution of *A Matter of Position,* the producers had no trouble pinning it on Elaine: "Elaine is a very talented girl," Fred Coe said. "Elaine is a very difficult girl. I have found the two are synonymous."[34]

Difficult. The word hangs in the air, damning, demeaning, dismissive. *Difficult* is a death sentence if you're a woman. Attempting to wrangle that much control over your work is a no-win situation. If you're successful, you're a narcissist, someone who seeks to undermine and take credit for the collaborative work of others. If you're not, well . . . the only thing worse than not being a team player is being the team scapegoat, the one all fingers will point to when failure strikes. Mike would be fine. He would go through a bit of an identity crisis, unsure of who he was when he wasn't with *her,* but his career wouldn't suffer. Elaine, though, was *difficult.* A difficult *girl,* despite being a fully grown thirty-year-old woman. She took her play back and began to rewrite.

IN THE SPRING of 1962, before *A Matter of Position* went into production, Elaine was commissioned to adapt Evelyn Waugh's *The Loved One.* A short comedic novella about the funeral business in Los Angeles, it clocks in at 176 pages. Elaine turned in a screenplay that pushed 200.[35] Despite star buzz—"Richard and I think it's the best script we ever saw,"[36] Elizabeth Taylor told Mike—executives were less than enthused. The studio assessed her draft: "There's too much death in it."[37] Elaine dropped out. The 1965 picture, filmed with an entirely new script, was a disaster.

There were other projects, too: a half-hour sitcom for CBS about two elderly women running a boardinghouse for recently released convicts, a pilot of which the network's then vice-president of programming said, "would be made only if Miss May is satisfied with her script."[38] It was never produced. Another sitcom that was forty-five minutes long, much to the bewilderment of network execs, who informed her that it couldn't be done. "That's irrational," she argued. "The BBC isn't a half hour or an hour. It should be what it should be." They passed on it, but she was persuasive enough that, as producer John Calley recalled, "all these major network guys from the network . . . ended the meeting apologizing for network policies."[39] Plans to write a one-act about a family of thieves, to be paired with a one-act adaptation of *Nights of Cabiria* as a star vehicle for Gwen Verdon, fell through when the producers decided to drop her part and make a full musical adaptation of the Fellini film instead. (It became *Sweet Charity.*)[40] Talks of a role in a new Gower Champion play dissolved when he left the project.[41]

She returned to teaching, working closely with her friend William Hickey—who had starred in *Not Enough Rope*—at the HB Studio in New York on a new play entitled *Name of a Soup.* The workshop was billed as a "Hickey/May" production,[42] but "she was sort of half directing," Judd Hirsch, who, as one of Hickey's students, served as the stage manager, remembers. "We all sort of got trained by her, in her odd way of teaching."[43] Just like *Not Enough Rope* and most of her plays, it was centered around an outcast, unattractive woman and the ways in which she's taken advantage of by society. After finally meeting a nice man on a date, she starts a relationship with him in spite of others' warnings that it's too good to be true. She eventually learns that they're right: the man isn't even human.

"While it was going on, some producers came and said, 'Why don't you shorten the play?'" Hirsch says. "Because this play was like three hours and it needed an ending that *she* liked a lot. So she took about four seconds out of the play and said, 'There. How do you like that?' And of course, they never did it. Unproduced. It was all difficult, because she had to have her way, which is really what a true writer wants. And if a producer gives it to them, they have to suffer, but that's okay. She's a very particular person. Very particular about how her plays should be done."[44] But Elaine had run out of capital to leverage. Until something hit, she didn't have the room to be particular.

IT WAS OFFICIAL: Elaine was in what we can now call her "flop era."

Even though we use terms like "flop era" with some mocking affection these days, it wasn't always the case, particularly not in the early 1960s. Just because Elaine avoided blatantly sexist criticism in her height of fame with Mike doesn't mean that it didn't exist. It was just waiting to get her on her own, to hold her—like every other woman—to a different standard from her male counterparts. Men can write plays that bomb, can have deals that fall through and pitches that never sell, can produce mediocre art and withstand the criticism of the world. Their flop eras aren't even really regarded as flop eras because they work steadily throughout them anyway, getting second chance after second chance. A woman rarely receives the same opportunities and cannot afford to produce anything that doesn't excel, lest her success be written off as a fluke. And no matter how brilliant men thought Elaine was, she was still, at the end of the day, a woman.

The problem with the flop era is how low the bar is set for a woman to enter into one, and just how much power it can hold to derail her career altogether. How many women were pushed out of Hollywood entirely after one project that was anything less than a sweeping success? How many women were told that it was just like this for everyone, that it was just hard, that it was a constant fucking struggle no matter who you were, even when all facts pointed to the contrary? Elaine, whether treated like it or not, was an anomaly wherever she went; Broadway was no more welcoming to women than comedy. In the two decades that led up to the feminist movement's reaching the theater in the 1970s, female playwrights were largely considered a rarity; you could count the number of successful ones on a single hand.[45] It was no accident that *A Matter of Position,* had it made it to Broadway that year, would have been one of only four productions opening in 1962—out of a total of fifty-one—written by a woman.[46] Screenwriting was no better; although women had enjoyed moderate success early within the studio system, they, too, were being shut out. By 1960, only 5 percent of American films were written by women, down from a high of 20 percent in 1920.[47]

But context didn't matter then. By 1963, Elaine was struggling to get her footing while Mike was directing a hit Broadway show. Maybe she was better with Mike, after all, people wondered. Maybe she was wasting her talents, or maybe those talents were so innumerable that those who wanted to give her work didn't quite know how to make use of them. Maybe she was just directionless. Who knew. Elaine would climb out of this flop era eventually, lagging behind the male peers she had once been miles ahead of, but still doggedly in the game. She would have more flop eras to come, ones that would last longer, ones that would be far graver, having fallen from even greater heights. But they would be ones she knew she could weather by keeping in mind the memory of this period, the knowledge that she had already stared failure in the face when it seemed to matter most and somehow made it through to the other side.

In the meantime, though, she got married.

DID ELAINE AND David Rubinfine start their romantic affair while she was still his patient? We'll probably never know. In a normal situation,[48] David would have been a catch: a blue-eyed, soft-spoken man who wasn't in show business himself—no competition there—but interested enough in it to understand and care about her career. And his job was great, too, respectable and prestigious, in a field that she found just as interesting as entertainment, maybe even more so. If only his job hadn't been treating *her*. During their time together, Elaine's interest in psychology deepened. She'd taken to reading enormous amounts about it, imbuing her writing with a deeper understanding of human behavior.[49] But it's not like they were a dry and stuffy intellectual Upper West Side couple. Together, they were a madcap pair, Elaine the insomniac and David the magician, who was "capable of being very wild and crazy, just like Elaine."[50] Once when David's friend, psychiatrist Ralph Greenson, was hospitalized, "David and Elaine came storming into the hospital at eleven o'clock at night with a bag of green apples. They said, 'We heard you like apples.' So that was when they came for a visit."[51] What a couple they were, indeed.

And the infatuation wasn't one-sided. Just as Elaine could find much to like about David, there was plenty for him to be drawn to. Or excused by. "I can certainly understand why David was attracted to Elaine," psychoanalyst Milton Wexler said. "She is so witty and so sharp. But I don't think it's the best idea to find your wives on the couch."[52] Marshall Brickman mused, "She went in there obviously and twirled him around. She was fascinating, brilliant, attractive. Who's going to be able to withstand that? Well, he didn't."[53]

There was another catch to their relationship. If David being Elaine's psychoanalyst weren't enough of an ethical burden to overcome, he was Elaine's *married* psychoanalyst. Shortly after Elaine filed for divorce from Sheldon Harnick in June 1962, David left his wife of twenty years, Rosa, with whom he had three young daughters, for Elaine. The following April, Rosa, distraught, died by suicide after overdosing on sedatives. Six weeks later, on June 8, 1963, Elaine and David were married.[54]

"David Rubinfine thought of himself as an orthodox analyst," his former supervisor, Dr. Margaret Brenman-Gibson, said. "And to become sexually involved with a patient was a sin for an orthodox analyst . . . He had to feel very guilty about that whole thing. If you then add to that Rosa's suicide, which of course was her way of saying how *she* liked the whole idea of his leaving her, he has to have had a very unhappy life thereafter."[55] Their marriage didn't just rock the analytic community—David was ostracized from the New York establishment and stripped of his right to train at the New York Psychoanalytic Society & Institute—but it made waves in entertainment as well.[56] Suddenly it wasn't Elaine's plays that were being talked about at cocktail parties; it was her unconventional relationship, and the husband that often showed up on the set or backstage. "It was a beaut of a scandal exacerbated by Elaine's prominence," Arthur Penn said.[57] Interviews instantly became more personal; the more people wanted to know about her home life, the less she gave. "Why don't you just say I'm married to a doctor?" she asked skittishly.[58]

Elaine was now the instant mother of four girls: a teenage Jeannie, whose life as an only child was upended, and three stepdaughters, ranging in age from six to eleven, who had just lost their mother. All that maternal domesticity she had fled nearly a decade ago was suddenly thrust upon her. Days were spent fulfilling the duties of a typical housewife: running a six-story brownstone on Riverside Drive that burst at the seams with squabbling sisters and two dogs, a mutt one of them brought in off the street named Bernice and another named Susie who was suspected to be part wolf.[59] How was she supposed to work when she was busy dealing with the mundane inconveniences of Con Edison[60] and hemming and hawing over different shades of white paint?[61]

She had outrun it as long as she could, but it had finally caught up to her. It would always catch up, the curse of the female artist. Hadn't Elaine had it all, even if briefly, decades before Helen Gurley Brown introduced the concept to workingwomen everywhere? Well, maybe the illusion of it, but not really, because there is no having it all. Not when you're a woman, and certainly not when you're a woman in America in 1963. A successful career, a successful marriage, and a happy, well-adjusted family? Not possible. Something would have to give, and it would usually fall to the woman—the mother—to give it. By the 1960s, more women were entering the workforce, but plenty more were staying home. How terribly ordinary, how disappointing but unsurprising it was that Elaine would be one of them.

Really, though, what was she going to do? Three traumatized girls needed a mother, and although she had help from her own mother and housekeeper, it was up to Elaine to fill that role. She hadn't planned for things to end up this way, but she did her best to rise to the challenge of uniting the blended family. She'd take the girls to the zoo or style their hair, hold family game nights or play readings in the evenings after dinner, give the young girls advanced books to read at school.[62] David, though looked down on by the psychiatric community, was no pariah; the man who had married Elaine May had become a psychoanalyst to the stars,[63] counting Tuesday Weld, Anthony Perkins,[64] and Alger Hiss[65] among his clients. And couldn't the argument be made that he was *saving* them, *healing* them, *helping* them with their problems? What were Elaine's plays doing for the greater good? It didn't matter how in awe of her talent David was. At the end of the day, hers was work that could take a back seat, done at home in between giving the children reading lessons or taking them to various appointments. David may have been a psychoanalyst with patients depending on him, but did that mean that his work was more important than Elaine's?

PLAYING THE ROLE of a homemaker was stifling, but Elaine welcomed its limitations. Elaine, who sat on a trove of unfinished work—plays, screenplays, and sketches—and wrote prolifically but rarely productively, saw avoiding writing as an integral part of the process. Her inability to let go and move on extended from the stage to the page. She didn't have to write anything new if she could keep rewriting her drafts, over and over again, "attacking them with a fierce black pencil until no one but she could possibly decipher them."[66] To write was to struggle, to wrestle with the string of words forming a choke hold around your neck that wouldn't loosen until you had arranged them just right. Even then, they wouldn't let you rest. Motherhood meant Elaine could no longer stay up writing manically all night, with a typewriter propped in her lap. Instead, she took to her basement office, only when she felt things were calm enough in the house for her to do so. But even then, she found ways to avoid the intimidation of a blank page:

I would usually take two weeks to make sure that all the pencils were sharpened, that the pens had the right kind of points, that I had the perfect amount of three-hole notebook paper, good erasers, plenty of hot water, apples and coffee. Then, rather than sitting down to write, I would rearrange furniture for days. Then I would make long lists of instructions like "Don't bother mother under the penalty of death for anything." Then when I couldn't find anything else to do, I would start to write and immediately I would hear the kids yelling and I would run upstairs—spared.[67]

"She was very shadowy," recalls Deborah Hautzig, a childhood friend of the family who spent most afternoons at the Rubinfine house. "I saw her, but she spent most of her time behind the door, and I was not invited in, nor [were the children]. She just sort of slithered around her life, but she was a good mom to my friend, so that says a lot. It wasn't even her kid."[68]

The work she did manage to stage during this period reflected her new position. *Rumpelstiltskin,* a children's theater production,[69] was a wacky contemporary adaptation of the Grimm classic that she had started back in Chicago and updated for Jeannie.[70] "My mother promised she would write a play for me based on Rumpelstiltskin when I was a little girl," Jeannie said.[71] Now a teenager longing to perform—but looking more to emulate her idol Barbra Streisand than her mother—she received the finished play as a Christmas gift in 1963. The following year, the play held three performances each weekend over the course of winter break, followed by a summer tour in Connecticut, New Jersey, and the suburbs of New York. What little press attention the play received was focused on Jeannie, whom *The New York Times* featured in a profile of three ambitious teenage girls. Elaine's name was barely mentioned; in its brief appearance, Jeannie "flinch[es] at the inevitable pairing of her name with her mother's."[72] It was almost as if the press was ready to move on from Elaine and focus on her more charismatic and forthcoming daughter.

But it wasn't just a professional sense of perfectionism that was holding Elaine back, nor was it motherhood. Without Mike, and publicly casting about for her own identity, Elaine found herself paralyzed in another way: by her own boundless potential. Friends she knew later in life would marvel that she seemed to have emerged fully formed, skipping over all the self-doubting years of early adulthood.[73] She had spent the past decade blazing down a singular path, whether intentionally or not. But now that she had willingly walked away in favor of something new and unknown, what she found was that she was not so much standing at a fork in the road as she was at a roundabout. "She could sell out—write gag plays like Jean Kerr and make a fortune and be on magazine covers like Mike Nichols," a friend assessed at the time. "She could take pratfalls and be funnier than Lucille Ball. She could hole up somewhere and write tragedies blacker than Lillian Hellman's. Hell, she could teach philosophy at Radcliffe. She has so many things going for her that, in a curious sort of way, I don't think she'll ever be happy."[74]

EVENTUALLY ELAINE HAD to get back to work. Playing the part of mother wouldn't be new or interesting forever. The only problem was that in moving forward, she grasped desperately at the past.

Remember Ted Flicker? The guy running the St. Louis version of the Compass who said he'd rather get his dick stuck in a garbage disposal than sleep with Elaine? The man who helped invent the rules of improv with Elaine just a few short years ago at the kitchen table had moved on. In 1959, he found himself in New York after taking *The Nervous Set,* an avant-garde musical about the beat generation he had written with Del Close, to Broadway. By the following year, he launched an ambitious improvisational theater in the Village. With a group of players who would share in a percentage of the theater's profit, the Premise was Flicker's way of "putting into practice both my ideas on group dynamics and the techniques Elaine and I had come up with."[75] But it's hard to maintain a socialist-minded repertory and turn enough profit to keep the lights on. In 1964, he sold the theater to Michael Brandman, who, in keeping with the theater's off-kilter ethos, brought in Elaine to stage an improvisational revue of her own called the Third Ear.

Elaine stayed firmly behind the scenes, directing with the same intensity she had made a name for herself with in Chicago. She had no tolerance for mediocrity, eschewed easy laughs, and showed no patience for anyone looking to showboat in lieu of serving the scene. "She'd audition actors," Mark Gordon remembered, "and she'd say, 'Okay, you try to pick me up at this bar.' A cat would come in and order a drink and he'd say to her, 'You want a drink?' She'd say, 'Yes.' And he'd say, 'What do you want?' She'd say, 'Go to your place?' And he'd say, 'You're really very pretty. You have beautiful eyes.' And she'd say, 'Go to your place?' Well, an actor who didn't hear couldn't be in the company. What Elaine was saying was, 'No verbal shtick. This scene should be over in ten seconds. If your task is to pick me up and I say yes right then, you've reached your objective, so go out!'"[76]

But if you happened to be an actor who listened, an actor who was open to work for others, you might make the cut. And those chosen by Elaine got to see a different side of her, one that was not exactly soft, but supportive. If Elaine saw your potential, she would help you reach it, though maybe more by shoving you in its direction than by holding your hand and walking you there. The four up-and-coming actors who joined Gordon to make up the Third Ear—Reni Santoni, Peter Boyle, Louise Lasser, and Renée Taylor—each benefited from her ability to see their specific strengths, sometimes before they could see themselves. "She would direct you and bring out your best qualities," Taylor says. "'This is your quality as an actress: You're very brave. And I want you to go all the way in doing this sketch about a mother giving advice to a bride on her wedding day.' She was very encouraging to me as an actress, and me as a writer. I didn't even know I was a writer, but she said that's what improvising was—writing on your feet."[77]

Unlike Nichols and May material, the Third Ear leaned more topical than evergreen. There would still be scenes skewering human foibles (like a scene about distractingly dramatic funeral mourners or one about a man whose obsession with his television ruins his marriage), but the real focus was on current events. Commentary on LBJ and the War on Poverty, the ongoing conflict in Vietnam, and the assassination of President Kennedy—still searingly fresh in the eyes of a stunned nation less than six months later—were all fair game. "When Kennedy got shot, I followed the papers, and the papers said that he was shot from the mall, that he wasn't shot from the mall, shot him from here, then was shot from there, and I invented a game with my cast, which was if you could put two clues together, you won," she said.[78] The way Elaine saw it, saying the quiet part out loud wasn't cheap shock, even though others may have interpreted it as such. "You have only to mention the assassination to cause enormous silence," she said. "But I don't think we should ignore it. I don't think we can ignore anything that is so much in people's minds all the time."[79] As a showrunner, she relentlessly held a mirror up to society, no matter the personal cost. (Even if that meant suffering through years of—allegedly—having her phone tapped after giving JFK assassination conspiracy theorist Mark Lane a chance to speak on her stage.)[80] And as a director, Elaine felt her job was to "say it's marvelous if [the actors] do a very good scene. And if it doesn't work out, I'm there to try and figure out why."[81]

But it was never really that simple. In a position of power with no one to challenge her, she fell back into the painstakingly meticulous habits she had developed all those years ago at Playwrights Theatre Club. Once again, the truth of a scenario was of the utmost importance, often at the expense of the laughs. What Elaine would not acknowledge was that, in theory, good comedy must always be rooted in truth, but it cannot always stay there; more often than not, the simple truth of a situation lacks the kind of heightened dramatic conflict needed to make a scenario move. Workshopping a scene about the recent stall-in by rogue civil rights activists at the 1964 World's Fair, Elaine rejected the easy jokes about inconvenienced straphangers. "That's not what would happen," she insisted. "What would happen if you were really on a train and it stopped?"[82] The actors then proceeded to improvise the listless, actionless act of simply waiting. Realistic, sure. An audience member could get a good knowing guffaw out of it. But Elaine insisted on extending it to the height of realism; the bit dragged on for forty-five minutes until Elaine was satisfied it should go into the show. "Everyone said, 'You can't do that,'" Gordon said. "She said, 'Well, they waited all this time and they're rebelling. Maybe we ought to experience a little what the waiting is like.'"[83] Still, she trusted that the audience was smart enough to get the jokes, that "if you do something honestly they will respond to it."[84] It was a wild change of tune from someone who had once been more comfortable with an audience *not* liking her work. It was also entirely wrong.

When the show opened that May, it fell flat on its face. The reviews were brutal. The performance, a mix of set pieces and spot improvisations, was "either mild or shoddy"[85] and "more glib than perceptive."[86] Critics suspected that any laughter from the audience was more because they feared being seen as squares than because they thought it was actually funny.[87] The few sketches that "reach[ed] marvelously funny heights" were often undone by droning on long after the curtain should have closed.[88] How was it that Elaine May, who had the foresight to know that Nichols and May would soon become passé in the changing culture, could not see that this show was a "tired gimmick"[89] full of "unlucky little bores"?[90] How could she have produced such an "unusually mediocre evening"[91] full of improvisations where "nearly everyone fell on their faces and stayed there"?[92] The kindest thing to be said about it was that the portions that worked were not so much satire as they were basic "good entertainment, occasionally excellent entertainment,"[93] with "the distinct feeling of that Spring-like May touch."[94]

It couldn't have helped that earlier that week, Mike had both won a Tony Award for his Broadway directorial debut, *Barefoot in the Park,* and had a triumphant, raved-about opening night Off-Broadway with *The Knack*—a fact that Elaine's critics couldn't help but point out, their reviews laced with pity for the partner left unexpectedly in the dust.[95] "You've got to say one thing about the old-timers," said one reviewer. "They knew when to get off."[96]

THEY COULDN'T STAY mad at each other forever.

There was a party on Riverside Drive. She hated parties, hated all that cheap small talk and social fakery. Hated how she could never remember names or faces, hated the hot flush of embarrassment that came when she inevitably said "nice to meet you" to someone she'd had an intimate conversation with just weeks before.[97] And yet here she was with David, making the best of it but probably looking for the nearest exit. And then there he was, the one face in the crowd she could never forget: Mike.

Mike and Elaine's reunion wasn't the kind of grand and romantic moment you see in movies—they were too honest for that. It was small—quiet, even—a brief exchange of pleasantries. He introduced her to his latest girlfriend; they traded a few quips. Perfectly polite, perfectly nice.[98] And then, as they parted ways, he heard it: "See," Elaine said to David, "I told you Michael was wonderful."[99]

Freeing themselves of any lingering personal animosity allowed them to reunite professionally. Over the next several years, they would perform their greatest hits when an occasion called for it. There was the occasional money grab, like a series of appearances on Jack Paar, but more often than not, they could bring themselves together for a good cause or fundraiser.[100]

Having grown increasingly politically active on her own,[101] Elaine convinced Mike to join her for a celebrity performance for the civil rights protesters marching from Selma to Montgomery, Alabama, in 1965. "Elaine said, 'I'm going. Do you want to go?'" Mike said. In preproduction for *Who's Afraid of Virginia Woolf?*, he hesitated. The producer had told him no, he said. "And she said, 'It's up to you.'"[102]

Arriving in Montgomery, they were met by federal agents, "who gave us each a dime to call the FBI in case anything went wrong," Nichols remembered, and a crowd of 20,000 people lined up in the heat. "Everybody got a little nervous," he said. The stage that night was a makeshift one, built out of coffins since "it was all they had."[103] As the night wore on, the stage grew crowded with members of the audience who had fainted and now sat at their feet, their bodies passed overhead to the only space left to breathe more freely.[104] Following an introduction from Martin Luther King Jr. and performers like Harry Belafonte and Peter, Paul, and Mary, the pair performed their telephone operator sketch, updating it as if Governor George Wallace were trying to get in touch with President Johnson. It was a hit.[105]

ALTHOUGH REUNITING WITH Mike from time to time kept her in the public eye, it wasn't enough. There had to be some way to establish her own identity. Maybe not as a director or even as a writer. Maybe it would be as an actor, what she had been from the very start. Yes, maybe returning to the stage in that capacity would be a better fit. At any rate, it was another idea to throw at the wall, another risk to take for the sake of trying. If things went wrong again, at least they couldn't put all the blame on her. When the opportunity came in 1966 to work with "longtime fan"[106] Jerome Robbins on a new play for Broadway, she said yes.

The Office, a "neither conventional nor realistic"[107] contemporary comedy about the interpersonal relationships at a struggling shipping company, looks promising on paper. It was the first full-length play by María Irene Fornés, who had just won an Obie Award for two Off-Broadway one-acts the previous season, helmed by the visionary Robbins—coming off Tony wins for his direction and choreography of *Fiddler on the Roof*—and starring Elaine and Jack Weston. But there was one big problem: The show wasn't there, and no amount of star power could fix what costar Tony Lo Bianco calls "a *crazy* play."[108]

The problem, lighting designer Jules Fisher explains, was that the show was "not fantasy in any way, but it was internal and intellectual in the sense that the jokes were not broad. You'd have to see into Elaine's mind, or that character's mind, to understand why that was funny."[109] Making things more confusing, the show itself wasn't even sure if it *was* a comedy. Elaine playing an incompetent new secretary lent itself to some comedic moments, but the rest of the show flitted between unexpectedly serious and inexplicably bizarre. "Elaine elevated it because of how good she was,"[110] Fisher says, but she could do only so much. Surely Robbins could save this, though, right?

"It was a total disaster," Lo Bianco says. It was in the middle of the first act of the first preview when Elaine, alone onstage, heard the boos start. The audience was booing—*booing!*—a sound she had never heard before in her professional life. There was nothing to compare it to, not even that excruciating failed sketch with Mike all those years ago at the Compass, and this time she was all alone. And it didn't stop. Stretching throughout the rest of the play, by the end, the boos were so loud "the asbestos curtain came back at us as we were getting ready to take our bows," says Lo Bianco.[111] It was too much humiliation for Elaine to take, and it wasn't even her play. All that toughness and apathy about audience acceptance was smoke and mirrors concealing a far more sensitive soul. When it came time for the cast to come out and take their final curtain call, she wouldn't budge.[112]

Robbins jumped ship, quitting the production "either before the first preview or after the second," Fisher says. "Early enough that he left the place stranded. Here's the play now without a director. And it was scheduled to open quite soon. Nobody would replace him, because if you were another director, you'd say, 'Well, if Jerry can't make it work, how am I going to do it?'"[113] Unable to find someone to replace him, the play closed after ten previews. Critics never even got the chance to see it.

FOR A MINUTE there, it didn't look like Elaine's career was going to survive the 1960s. Maybe it was inevitable. Maybe you could call it fate, could blame it on the universe. Maybe you could argue that in her professional life she'd had it too good for too long, had practically coasted her way to success without any real criticism or troubles. It couldn't last. Everything costs something in the end. Maybe it was just circumstantial that she found herself paying the price now.

Or maybe it was just that the work she was turning out was shot after shot in the dark, spotty at best and disappointing at worst, and never all that brilliant. And it's not like she was the easiest person to work with or someone willing to make the changes needed to take something from fine to fantastic. Compromise—the element so essential to any creative who hopes to maintain a career in any mainstream corporate setting—was not a word in Elaine's vocabulary.

But maybe it was the sexism that she had evaded for so long creeping in, only more insidious and far less obvious. Sexism in show business doesn't always manifest itself as a room full of men dictating the way you should look or getting your ass slapped by a club owner. Sexism in Hollywood is about the work, about the haves and the have-nots, the people for whom there are always hearty meals and the people who have to scratch and claw and fight for scraps. It's about those an industry puts its faith in not to fuck up its chief concern (profit), and about who is afforded an unlimited number of second chances when they inevitably do. It is about the way subpar work from men is accepted—praised, even, as Elaine had once presciently mocked[114]—while women have to prove their worth by being brilliant at every single turn. It is about who just gets "their way" and who is told they're "difficult" over and over again, enough times that they start to believe it, fold in on themselves, and go home.

It didn't matter *why* Elaine's career wasn't working out, though. It just mattered that it wasn't working out. By 1967, even the press was beginning to comment on her career stasis. Talk about kicking her while she was down: *Life* went so far as to publish a premature postmortem in the form of a profile titled, bluntly, "Whatever Happened to Elaine May?" In retrospect, it makes sense that it was the last time she'd give an in-depth interview.

THERE WAS AN upside to the profile, though, a reason for it being written. That year, she'd star in two feature films—her first screen roles—back-to-back: Carl Reiner's *Enter Laughing* and Clive Donner's *Luv,* alongside Peter Falk and Jack Lemmon. Both film adaptations of hit stage shows, they seemed like foolproof choices—*smart* choices, *calculated* choices, even—destined for success.

Elaine had been offered film roles before,[115] but none of them lived up to her standards. As she put it, "they were all female Tony Randall parts."[116] Not that her role in *Enter Laughing* as Angela Marlowe, the boy-crazy actress in a second-rate acting company in the late 1930s, is much better. Even Reiner admitted the character felt flat on the page. "We needed an actress who was bigger than life," he said, "who could make something out of it. I just thought of Elaine right away."[117] She accepted Reiner's attempted rescue from career stasis (in part, she claimed, because "my typing finger needed a rest").[118] She was tough, but only so tough. If she wanted to survive, she couldn't do it on her own. She needed help. And so, like many before her and many to come, Elaine traveled west to the land of opportunity. Los Angeles was still the same city it was when she had left it as a teenager, but the sound stages of Hollywood were a wild new frontier. "Elaine didn't know a damn thing about making movies at first," Reiner said. But Elaine had the gift of observation on her side, and a genuine desire to learn whatever she could. She stood on set and "soaked up everything."[119] She didn't know nothing for long.

Already, Columbia was courting her for their adaptation of *Luv*. Casting about for a leading lady to star opposite Lemmon, producer Martin Manulis floated Elaine's name. "My god, she's perfect," Lemmon replied, but not without knowing the catch: "Can we get her?"[120] To their surprise, she had been having such a good time on *Enter Laughing* that she agreed. Filming wasn't that bad, actually. Unlike television, you had time, and unlike the stage, it wasn't live. You didn't have to play it so safe or put pressure on yourself to get it right on the first try with no do-overs. Your performance might be frozen in one form to live on forever—the drawback that set it aside from the unpredictable thrill of theater—but at least there were takes, and the opportunity to do something new each time, until you were satisfied that the one going to print was your best.

But Elaine could do only so much with the one-note Angela. Originated onstage by Vivian Blaine, the character is just a sketch with little to do and even less backstory. Was the thin characterization of an airhead actress who still calls her father "Daddy" meant to be a grown woman stuck in a state of arrested development, or were the actresses selected to breathe some semblance of life into her just woefully miscast? Elaine plays her like the starlet in the old "Disc Jockey" scenario, adopting the same high, breathless voice and wide-eyed demeanor. It's not a great screen performance, but it's not bad for her first time. Finding a kindred spirit in Reiner, who encouraged her to improvise and gave her the power and freedom to suggest changes, was a lucky boon. Elaine's enjoyment of the filmmaking experience was largely due to the fact that Reiner all but brought filmmaking to *her,* playing to her strengths in a way that made the foreign experience more familiar. But not every film set operates the same way, and *Luv* was about to prove that the collaborative atmosphere of *Enter Laughing* was more an exception than the norm.

Which brings us back to the six a.m. car ride.

Making one film is exhausting. The day starts early and the hours are long. If you're a New York theater actor, you're spending months away from home, all alone on the other side of the country in a vapid city you likely loathe. There are lines to memorize and rehearsals to be had and take after take after take—*do it this way; now do it that way; now again for a close-up; with the same intensity, but for your costar's close-up*—each requiring your all. If you're Elaine, you're doing all this by day, then retiring to your hotel room to spend what sliver of night you have to sleep staying up writing before the studio car comes to fetch you at dawn to start all over again. Now imagine making *two* films, back-to-back, with no rest in between.

But there's something else about making movies, or at least acting in them, that would prove detrimental to Elaine's enjoyment of them. When the news of her film debut broke, Mike called it: "Elaine is going to suffer in Hollywood," he said. "She must have complete control of a given situation. Out there she will be at the mercy of many people."[121] There it was. On *Enter Laughing*, Elaine had the benefit not only of a smaller role in a character ensemble (she's only on-screen for about thirty-five minutes, most of which is spent in the background), but of a writer and director who, as a performer himself, understood how to collaborate with actors in a way that made them feel secure with their own performances. But Clive Donner, the young British director coming off *What's New, Pussycat?*, didn't work that way.

It didn't take long for *Luv* to come to a grinding halt, an entire crew waiting as production staff flitted between Elaine's trailer and the director's bay and back again in desperate attempts to talk her down from the ledge. The problem: She wasn't happy with her performance in a scene and insisted that it needed to be reshot. Elaine's acting style was, as Lemmon marveled, "touched with genius, like Judy Holliday. She approaches a scene like a director and a writer, not like an actor, and she can go so deep so fast on a scene."[122] But whether that's a good thing depends on the situation. The back half of Lemmon's compliment gets at, even if unintentionally, how easily genius can become less a buoy that pulls everyone else up and more a ball and chain that drags everyone down: "Her mind works at such a great speed that it's difficult for her to communicate with other actors."[123] Now it was playing out in front of them, Elaine's brain clicking into director mode to insist that she and Peter Falk were unacceptable in a scene they had just printed, and that the whole thing needed to be filmed again. Out of the question, Donner and the film's producer replied. It was good enough, they assured her. This wasn't high art; this was a studio comedy with a fast-paced schedule, and they had to keep moving. But Elaine couldn't be appeased. When the guilt-tripping ("We all go down the drain together") and snide remarks ("This is a great way to get a comedy—fill everyone with an enormous sense of rage") didn't work, she resorted to desperate generosity, offering to pay for the retake herself.[124] On and on the crisis went, resentment building among the crew. Finally the producers gave in. The scene would be reshot, though who's to say if it was to appease her and keep things running or if it was because they had realized she was actually right. Regardless, the rest of filming went well enough that the difficult situation left no hint of ill feelings with either of her costars—Falk became a lifelong friend, while Lemmon called her "the finest actress I've ever worked with"—or her director. But Donner would say what everyone else was thinking: Elaine was good. Maybe *too* good. "The devastating thing about Elaine," he said, "is that she's better at everything—writing, acting, directing—than almost anyone else I know."[125]

Much like Angela Marlowe, Ellen Manville isn't exactly a feast of a character for Elaine, but she at least gives her a bit more to work with as a lead. Sexually frustrated and pissed off, an emotionally damaged but brilliant woman (men resent her for it, she'll explain later, in a moment of art painfully imitating life), she has the great misfortune of being sandwiched in the suburbs between two loser men. Milt (Falk), her used-tchotchke-selling husband, sets her up with his old college friend Harry (Lemmon), who is not only strange but also suicidal, as part of his plan to leave her for a perky young blonde in the city. Eventually Milt realizes he loves Ellen, and Ellen realizes she loves Milt, and the two scheme to undo the mess they've made for themselves.

The film is a relatively forgettable sex farce—the single-setting play isn't robust enough to translate into a multilocation feature, and any edgy humor it attempts seems to be more of the "because we could" motivation than because it serves the story. Elaine, though, stands out—far more than she does in *Enter Laughing*. She's a natural on-screen, grounding an otherwise relatively flat character in truth, giving weight to her backstory, and, knowing her medium, rooting much of her performance in the smallest moments: a wicked glare or resigned downward glance, a deadpan drawl or a high, flirtatious giggle. Watching her relaxed performance, it's easy to see why Reiner suspected she "could be a major movie star. But not in drama. She thinks only in curves."[126] She had not only the talent but also the charisma and—particularly when done up—the looks for it.

Critics were split on that, though. The response to both films—often reviewed together, as if the fact that they were both adaptations of Broadway productions, starred Elaine May, and came out within the same week meant they were inextricably linked—was mostly negative. *The New York Times* warned, of *Luv*, "if you're in a mood for heady humor or satire of a sharply lined-out sort, you might do well to be wary of this frivolity,"[127] while *The Village Voice*, in a joint review, said "*Luv* fails ambitiously whereas *Enter Laughing* fails coyly without even the courage of its own vulgarity."[128]

Still, Elaine managed to survive. Her reviews, when good, were glowing. In its review of *Enter Laughing, The New York Times* called her out as one of the film's three strong points, squeezing out "the laughs in their material like washwomen wringing out clothes" and turning the film into a "sheer low comedy farce."[129] And *The Village Voice* regarded her performance as "a very esoteric imitation of Barbara Stanwyck, . . . an intellectual with a heart of gold, a walking tribute to the satiric potentialities of old movies."[130] In reviews of *Luv*, she was often singled out as the best in the film. "Elaine May glitters," one reviewer wrote. "She makes every syllable count, often dipping them in acid first, then devouring them in a dour, cynical expression that one critic has likened to a camel."[131] "Elaine May comes on like Rosalind Russell with a Ph.D.," wrote another. "Fortunately, she has the best lines and delivers them complete with her critique of them. . . . She should be immune to criticism from us lesser mortals."[132]

In retrospect, what Reiner said was true. Elaine *could* have been a true star, with the charm of Judy Holliday, the versatility of Barbara Stanwyck, and the fast-talking wit of Rosalind Russell all in one package. The timing was right; New Hollywood's wave of offbeat comedic heroines was just beginning. Leading ladies were still often Waspy blond hothouse flowers, but room was being made for new stars, for character actresses like Barbra Streisand or Shirley MacLaine to find that they could be leading ladies, too. Why not Elaine?

Well, because being a movie star didn't suit Elaine any more than being a Broadway star did. For one thing, she'd have to move back to Los Angeles, and that wasn't going to happen. Then there was the lack of control over the final product. If she was to act full time, she'd have to build up clout to finally have the power to be more discerning about her parts, and how was she going to do that when she had only so much time? Elaine could have been a movie star, all right—if she had been about ten years younger. At thirty-five, she knew the end of her prime on-camera years was already quickly approaching. She knew she was a good actress, but she also knew that no matter how much Hollywood was changing, they still didn't give a shit if a woman could act as long as she was young and beautiful and fuckable. Being a movie star wasn't about being an actor; it was about being a celebrity, someone who let a team of people tease and touch and primp and paint her, someone who put on a smile and participated in the kind of insipid press cycle she so often mocked. Why submit herself to that, to a career where she'd have a limited amount of power, a place where she'd be put out to pasture to fade into obscurity within a few short years, when she could "achieve immortality" as a writer?[133]

Faced with the need to promote two new films back-to-back, Elaine found that she was "a full-time celebrity" again.[134] She had been down this road once before already, had seen the expectation that she share who she was off-screen with strangers, and hadn't enjoyed it the first time. This time, without Mike to hide behind or act as her spokesperson, would be even more difficult. "I've no time for gossip, chitchat or conversational inanities," she explained to one reporter at the time.[135] For the very few interviews she conceded to, she prohibited any questions about her childhood, first marriage, Jeannie, her second marriage, and her "reasonably happy life."[136] What else was left? The most she would offer about her move to film was that "it was very nice to get my nose in the Hollywood feedbag."[137] Not even *The New York Times* could convince her to do a sit-down; instead, she offered to write her profile herself. Penned under the byline Kevin M. Johnson and reportedly cut down from seven thousand words,[138] the resulting piece is partly satire, a knowing jab at the formulaic Hollywood profile with questions both frivolous ("What do you sleep in?") and banal ("What approach did you use?") But more tellingly, it's partly self-mocking performance art, with Elaine creating an exaggerated version of herself, playing the character of Elaine May to avoid exposing the real one. She plays up her reluctance to "go Hollywood," leans into her manic reputation with an extended aside about wanting to adapt Sartre's *No Exit* as a Technicolor romp about apartment hunting in Chicago, and turns the dial of her paranoia and distrust up to the highest possible level and keeps it there:

> "I suppose you'll rewrite all that when you get home," she said cynically. "Oh well. Go ahead. I knew this might happen. Write what you want. I don't care."
>
> I asked her if she was always this nervous about being interviewed and she protested loudly that she was not nervous, that she loved being interviewed, and that if I wrote she was nervous she would send a public denial to the New York Times.[139]

But buried within the dry humor is an explanation. A human moment, a glimpse behind the curtain. For someone so unconcerned with others' opinions, she seems to want readers to know why it is she's like this, why she'd rather take on the work of writing an entirely fictional interview than submit herself to spend even a single hour with a reporter:

> "Have you had bad experiences with interviews before? I mean are you generally misquoted?"
>
> She stared glumly at the coffee pot. "No. But I'm always sorry for what I've said afterwards . . . and a couple of times I've been misquoted . . . and I've had friends who were misquoted . . . and

you know how it is. It's like that terrible feeling you get after you drop the letter in the mailbox. It's too late."[140]

Then she did damage control, cleaning up after herself before she'd shun publicity all but entirely. "I have no earthly idea how [*Luv*] will turn out. It's up to them now," she told *Life,* not without a hint of wary distrust, as if the vague "them" was the enemy.[141] It was the last in-depth print interview she ever gave.

It was an interesting blip while it lasted, this Hollywood thing. But it would never last. It was time to go back to New York. Back to writing. Back to reality. Elaine May would not be a movie star, after all. But it wasn't for nothing; the experience would just get the wheels turning in a different way. Elaine wasn't a movie star—but she was a director. She just didn't know it yet.

ELAINE RETURNED TO what she knew best, but it was clear that what she knew best was chaos. That spring, while waiting for both films to be released, Elaine booked a guest appearance on an episode of *The Smothers Brothers Comedy Hour.* A once rather vanilla duo, the brothers' network variety show was becoming increasingly engaged with current events in an attempt to meaningfully connect with younger audiences. Insisting on pushing the envelope would eventually lead CBS to fire them, but the first great offense came from . . . who else? Elaine.

Elaine wasn't any old guest star showing up and reading the lines crafted for her by a team of writers she had never met. Instead, she contributed her own writing, most notably with a three-part sketch with Tom Smothers[142] in which the two play a pair of censors who object to the word *breast* in a film they're reviewing. The scene grows increasingly goofy, one gag after another, until it's revealed that they're having an affair. By today's standards, it's tame, but back then—pre–*Laugh-In*, pre–*Saturday Night Live*—its critical cultural commentary was daring. No one on network television was speaking to youth culture, and certainly no one on the air was willing to mock the stiffs in charge who put them there. In an act that was comedic in and of itself, CBS executives censored the sketch. All that language about breasts that drove the fictional censors crazy drove their real-life counterparts up the wall, too. And then there was the even bigger problem—the fact that Elaine's sketch was tearing away a curtain of artifice, exposing the inane, and at times ugly, creatively stifling policing that went on behind the scenes. Let audiences *know* that censors even existed, let alone let them be characterized like this? Absolutely not. It didn't matter that Elaine insisted her original version of the sketch was far dirtier. It had to go.[143] "I thought I was toning it down," she said. "Now the myth will probably be that it didn't work."[144]

But the story doesn't end there, not with CBS retaining the upper hand. The script was leaked to the press—though no one knows who exactly did it. It could have been Smothers, exerting creative control, though he insists it wasn't him. It very well could have been Elaine, in search of cheap revenge. Either way, *The New York Times* printed the first section verbatim in its Sunday Arts section. Below Elaine's byline, the subhead says simply that the following sketch "was ruled out for 'bad taste.'"[145] It was her first brush with brazenly defying and publicly shaming a studio for their interference with her work. It wouldn't be her last.

In the decades to follow, Elaine would build a reputation for herself as a trusted collaborator, someone who could make your project better, often at the eleventh hour. She would become known as something akin to a savior, not a script doctor so much as a script *surgeon,* precisely diagnosing a story's problems and methodically correcting them under pressure. But in 1967, she was still figuring out to do so with tact.

That November, she took a job writing and directing a new revue for Mort Sahl, tasked primarily with figuring how scripted portions of the show would run alongside Sahl's stand-up act. By the time *An Evening with Mort Sahl* reached its final week of rehearsals, there was no script; Elaine had rejected all but one of the sketches Sahl had presented to her for consideration. "Probably 35 sketches and 58 hours of material," he fumed.[146] He didn't even show up for the technical or dress rehearsal.[147] The show was canceled a day before it was set to open.

*   *   *

WITH THE END of the 1960s fast approaching, Elaine found that she was barely any further ahead than she was when the decade started. How the hell was she going to get out of this one?

The answer: Elaine would write herself out. She would always find a way to write herself out, but her next giant step would be more like an accidental stumble.

CHAPTER 5

You Make the Crew Nervous

Adaptation/Next and *A New Leaf*

1968–1971

Hollywood was hemorrhaging.

Always the slowest moving and most expensive medium, by the mid-1960s, the film industry was barely hanging on by a thread. Did anyone really expect an archaic monolith run almost entirely by a group of men who had assumed their positions thirty years ago to relate at all to the current youth culture? The kids of the sixties, the baby boomers with buying power, had had enough of film's formulaic bullshit. Movies weren't interesting and exciting anymore, at least not ones made in America. Bloated musicals and pert Doris Day rom-coms and Dean Martin schlock could all eat it. And they did. Losing money left and right, studio takeovers and mergers were unavoidable. Universal went to MCA while Trans-America scooped up United Artists, MGM got bought by a billionaire, and an industrial conglomerate acquired Paramount.

By 1967, Hollywood was hovering at a crucial crossroads, with a chance to turn it all around. The unexpectedly wild success of *Bonnie and Clyde* and *The Graduate*—one film made reluctantly by a studio and the other made independently after every studio turned it down—signified that all bets were off. There was a new way to make a picture, and if Hollywood wanted to hang on any longer, they better get hip to it.

At Paramount, where the two new heads of production—Robert Evans and Peter Bart—were under the age of forty, this meant adjusting the focus. In January of 1968, they announced to the press their ambitious new plan to get Paramount back on top. "Movie-making is like building a house," Evans said. "You have to start with a foundation. We believe that foundation is the story."[1] Writers were the stars now, and Paramount would do anything to fill their house with those of the highest wattage possible. Executives formed relationships with literary agents, film rights were optioned for books still in galley form, and the studio formed contracts with forty-one screenwriters, many of whom would also produce or direct.[2] No one knew an in to a hot deal like Hillard Elkins, an agent, super-manager, and producer who had managed artists like Mel Brooks and Steve McQueen. By March of 1968, he found a spot for his new client Elaine May on Paramount's payroll.[3]

The job: to write an adaptation of *One Hundred Dollar Misunderstanding*, Robert Gover's salacious 1962 bestseller, followed by an original screenplay, which she'd direct, too. "To tell you the truth," she said of the reversal of fortune, "I don't know what I'm doing. Mr. Elkins became my personal manager a few hours ago."[4] It was the kind of deal you couldn't turn down, a good deal that wasn't just good, but historic, even: the first studio film to be helmed by a woman since Ida Lupino's *The Trouble with Angels* in 1966; the first at Paramount since Dorothy Arzner's *Merrily We Go to Hell* in 1932. The studio was already bragging to the press "with self-congratulatory glee at its good fortune that a woman has assumed such a triple-threat role"[5] for the first time in film history.[6] Except . . . Elaine didn't want it.

Or rather, she didn't *not* want it, but she certainly wasn't expecting it. Elaine's desires were much simpler: "I wrote this movie script that I wanted to sell for a lot of money so that I could be richer," she said.[7] She thought she had a golden ticket in a short story she had optioned from *Alfred Hitchcock's Mystery Magazine* called "The Green Heart." The story of a lazy, spendthrift bachelor who reaches the bottom of his trust fund and finds himself, broke and miserable, looking to solve his financial woes by marrying, and subsequently killing, a rich woman intrigued Elaine. "I liked it because I realized the guy, the hero, was going to kill this woman. And he actually kills somebody else. And I thought, 'He's going to kill her and he's not going to realize that he likes her,'" she said.[8] It checked all her boxes: a vulnerable and victimized woman, an insufferable and duplicitous man, and a pitch-black comedic bend that would make the audience shudder for ages before they got around to laughing. In Elaine's twisted mind, that all added up to hit potential. "I was certain it was absolutely commercial. It had two murders in it, so it could be a mystery, and if it wasn't a mystery, it could be funny, and if nobody laughed, it could be a love story. I didn't see how it could fail."[9]

She had written the part with a Cary Grant–like figure in mind, and was surprised to get a call from Cary Grant himself to say he was interested in starring—on one condition.[10] "I couldn't do that ending as it's written because my public wouldn't accept that I was trying to kill her. You would have to change that a bit," he told her. Elaine, shocked that she was turning down Cary Grant, replied, "Oh, Mr. Grant, I've worked so hard on this screenplay, and I couldn't possibly change it at this point. So I'm going to have to say no."[11] With Walter Matthau attached in his place, nearly every major studio passed on it before Arthur Penn set her up with Elkins, who took her to Paramount. "It wasn't received with overwhelming enthusiasm. I pitched very hard on the fact that having a woman director would be of consequence. The pitch seemed to work with [Charles] Bluhdorn," Elkins said.[12]

But wait a minute. Directing? All Elaine had asked for was director approval. "It's very frightening to give your stuff to a director, because you would not believe that a scene that seems as clear as day to you can turn out the way it does," she explained. That ask would turn into a backward opportunity. "They were offering me an enormous amount of money, $200,000, I think. And [Hilly] came back to me—he'd been my manager for two days—and said, 'I've set a wonderful deal. I produce. You write and direct. And you get $50,000.' And I asked, 'What happened to the other $150,000?' And he said, 'You can't expect to get that much the first time you direct.' And I said, 'I don't want to direct.' And I think he said something like, 'They can't afford it if you don't.'"[13]

So that was the hitch. Follow the money, and it became clear that it wasn't so much a decision born out of a genuine desire to be inclusive as it was a way to cheaply solve a problem. "[Bluhdorn] told me, 'Do you know who Ida Lupino is?'" Elaine remembered.

"I said, 'I've heard of her.' He said, 'I can make you another Ida Lupino.' And I thought, 'Can I not accept this offer?' But I had no choice."[14]

It was a win-win for Paramount. They could bolster their image—hire a woman to appease growing pressure from the women's movement—and be cost-effective at the same time. By pushing all three duties onto Elaine, they could hide their maintenance of the status quo—paying a woman less for more, exploiting both her gender and her inexperience—under the guise of progress. No decision in Hollywood is ever made without checking first how it will affect the bottom line, least of all progressive decisions, and Paramount made sure they could pad their pockets well with this one. Out was the $200,000 check for just a script; in was $50,000 for Elaine to write and direct—*and* star in it, too. "They wanted to have Carol Channing play the woman," she explained, "and I said, 'No, it has to be someone who really disappears. It's the guy's movie.' I said, 'Can I pick the person?' And they said, "No, but you can play it. And all for the same money.'"[15] Meanwhile, Matthau would take $375,000 plus profit participation bonuses, and producers Elkins and Koch would each get $50,000. After Matthau received his share of grosses, Elaine would split 35 percent of the film's earnings with the three men.[16]

Of course, she had to write it first. But even that would have to wait. It was 1968, and Elaine was on the up, balancing more opportunities than could have seemed possible just a few years earlier.

THE BERKSHIRE THEATRE Festival had invited Elaine, along with playwrights William Gibson, Jack Gelber, and Terrence McNally, for a summer residency in Stockbridge, Massachusetts. The opportunity was seemingly simple, but an artistic dream: the chance to develop and test plays "free from the blight of success."[17] Straight plays, the festival's founders surmised, were a dying art form crippled by the rising costs of staging them—not to mention testing them on the road—the increasingly shrinking window of what was considered commercially viable, and the added pressure of celebrity. "When there is big money at stake, there is always the atmosphere of panic," Elaine assessed.[18] Berkshire, free of any of that, was the perfect environment for her to experiment again, staging two of her own plays and directing a third.

First up was *A Matter of Position,* still churning in her mind all these years later. She knew it could work, if only she could figure out how to get it there. "I made some major changes and rewrote the third act several times," she said. "Usually the changes were because you could see that the direction or the acting wasn't working. You keep asking, 'Why can't they act it right?' but then you realize that the problem has to be in the writing." She spent that spring rewriting it, pulling it apart and putting it back together again, approaching it with a more clear-eyed vision than she had the first go-round: "There's no point in preserving that beautiful idea if nobody gets it but you," she acknowledged. "I spent a lot of time just cutting and shaping—and I sobbed a lot."[19] Fixing the play was more for her own personal satisfaction than it was for any kind of professional atonement. Even she knew that the ability to look at something from every angle—the writer, the actor, and the director—could be advantageous, but just as often created gridlock. She kept her expectations low: Just get past that. Just make it work. The rewrites were one way to solve the problems. Leaning on Arthur Penn to direct so she could act in it was another. Already, she had fixed the biggest mistakes she had made the first time. As the show approached its four weeks of rehearsal, she showed no concern about it being a wild success or attracting enough attention to finally bring it to Broadway. "I just want to see it—like doing it in your living room," she said. "And see if people throw things this time."[20]

Luckily for her, they didn't throw things. Not even close. What a relief it must have been—if Elaine had been the kind of person to even read the reviews—to see a rave from the *Boston Globe,* praising it as a "first-rate piece of work," a play that moves "with a kind of logical insanity that carries her comedy right to the borders of farce without letting it wander into alien territory."[21] What a moment of righteous satisfaction she must have had, reading another proclaim: "May's comedy is a comedy rather than a series of comic sketches, and it is a very good and very funny comedy—on the order of, say, 'A Thousand Clowns' but funnier and with more substance."[22] And what a smug, knowing laugh she could have had seeing how much the sole dissenting pan centered on the critic's issue with the way Elaine "never gives her emasculated hero the benefit of a few scraps of human dignity" or her heroine "the dignity of womanhood."[23] You can almost hear her response: "Are you new here?" *A Matter of Position* was no longer the out-of-town flop; it was a hit, setting a box office record for the Berkshire Theatre Festival and taking in more than $25,000 in its three-week run.[24] Elaine, unfazed, went back to work.

Next on her agenda was *Adaptation,* a psychologically charged, episodic one-act where she transposed the cycle of life into a game show, with the protagonist earning points and moving forward and backward across a board as he makes his way through life. An infant coddled by his mother becomes an adolescent who can't connect with his father, then a young man who blunders through school and learns about sex. Soon he's an adult trapped in a loveless marriage. Then finally he's an old man of little importance staring at his own death. It's not a particularly robust idea, but what it lacks in dramatic potential, it more than makes up for in wit. *Adaptation* is less a play than a chance to poke holes in American society and all its fixations on superficial values, and no one gets off easy—not average-bordering-on-mediocre men, not Jewish mothers or distant fathers, and definitely not cloying girlfriends or nagging wives. The result is a dagger in the side of the American Dream, plunged there by characters whose creator clearly spent a lot of time deconstructing the ego in psychoanalysis.

Adaptation would share a bill that August with a last-minute addition from Terrence McNally, *Next,* about a middle-aged misfit drafted into the army by mistake, with Elaine directing both. Even though the point of the festival was to relieve the pressure they would have experienced elsewhere, both had personally high stakes in the show. Elaine had found redemption as a playwright with *A Matter of Position,* but *Adaptation/Next* would be the first plays she directed professionally. And for McNally, it was a chance to prove himself as a playwright, only his second work staged after "a famous disaster"[25] of a first play. Their relationship was symbiotic: Elaine, the industry veteran, found herself being taken seriously as a director, while McNally, still green, found himself soaking up the wisdom she would generously impart. "She is my real teacher in the theater," he said. "Just about everything I learned, significant, in the theater, I learned from Elaine."[26]

"Every day at rehearsal, all she'd ever talk about was what the characters were doing," McNally said. "She would just say, 'What are they doing? What are they doing?' and I'd say, 'But they're *saying*—' and she'd say, 'Theater is not what they're saying, it's what they're doing.'"[27] Though Elaine's capacity for self-editing was limited, when it came to others, she was a scalpel, killing darlings with precise logical reasoning. Plays operated with the same rules she and Mike had established for their sketches. Never go for the easy laugh, she taught McNally: "When characters deal in gags and jokes, you pay a terrible price for them. You're left without characters, and you're left without a play," she explained. And never preach: "Write people instead of symbols. Audiences come out to the theater to find out about the people on the stage, not to be lectured by Terrence McNally on the social and political state of America."[28]

Elaine thrived in the bubble-like environment of the festival. Berkshire wasn't the real world, hampering the creative process with daily distractions of children to care for and houses to keep or doubt-inducing producers constantly eyeing the bottom line. Though critics would attend performances, they were mostly local; even if you got a pan, it wouldn't show up in *The New York Times*. Free of stress and surrounded by people focused on the same creative goal, Elaine could indulge in her inclination to focus on the details. She would work around the clock, chain-smoking and guzzling coffee and diet soda, so rarely stopping for food that the cast joked that they had to hand-feed her. Often she'd arrive at rehearsals with an entire act she had rewritten the night before.[29] "We improvised until we knew every nuance of the situation," said James Coco, who, after a supporting role in *A Matter of Position,* stayed on to play the lead in *Next.* "And of course Elaine doesn't know the meaning of the word 'stop.' We'd rehearse nine, ten, eleven hours and then we'd plead to go out to dinner and she'd say, 'Fine. We'll stop and talk about the play.' For another five hours."[30]

To her actors, she could be tough, even frustratingly illogical in her vague instructions to get to the truth of the scene—but only seemingly so. Elaine's mind was always three steps ahead of everyone else. Instead of giving actors step-by-step instructions to meet her, she'd simply point them in the right direction and watch, trusting and empowering them to figure it out for themselves. In one of *Next*'s biggest comedic moments, Coco strips for a physical examination. For weeks in rehearsals, Coco—balding, overweight, and self-conscious—played the moment from behind a privacy screen. Then one day, he walked in, and it was gone. "You don't expect me to strip in full view of the audience, do you? Where's the screen?" he asked Elaine, panic-stricken. "Whoever heard of a screen at an army induction center? No screen," she replied. They argued for hours until Coco finally realized that he could cover himself with the American flag prop. "And then I stopped and practically fell to my knees in relief," he said of his revelation. "I ran over and draped myself in it. Elaine gave a loud sigh. 'I wondered how long it would take you to think of that,' she said. Well, *she* had thought of it. She thinks of everything, but she makes you discover it for yourself."[31] She was always looking to push the game to its furthest possible end point, always asking, "What is this like in real life?" But she was not without limits; she wouldn't ask her actors to do something she didn't feel she could do herself. At one point in Coco's flag debacle, she insisted he be fully nude—it was the only way to keep his moves realistic and genuine. Coco refused and told her to play it for herself and see. Undaunted, she stepped behind the flag, stripped, and wrapped herself in a sheet. But before she could get too smug about being right, Coco told her to drop it. She hesitated. "Absolutely not," she said. "Because this is make-believe, and I'm naked underneath, and I don't have to." He had made his point. She didn't ask him to be nude again.[32]

Both plays were a gamble that paid off, opening to favorable reviews. "Some of the satire is familiar, if not secondhand, but the best of it is fiercely funny," the *Boston Globe* ruled.[33] Another critic singled out Elaine's writing: "There is no doubt that she is a human machete in cutting through the clichés of a certain segment of our society. She is sharp, observant, has an ear for dialogue and can be extremely funny while engaged in desperation."[34] To the uninitiated, though, her view of the world could be polarizing. Age hadn't altered her perspective much from the bleak view she had while writing plays at the Compass. Her characters were still ones whose "hearts are used only for coronary occlusions, nothing else."[35] She was, for better or worse, the same woman who had written *Georgina's First Date*: "The only time a man tells a woman he loves her is when he wants to score," one critic observed.[36]

Nevertheless, in February, *Adaptation/Next* opened Off-Broadway. Deemed "one of the best this season,"[37] it quickly became one of the hottest tickets in town. Finally, after all this time, Elaine had struck gold. "There is malice aplenty in Miss May, but it is uniformly distributed and so never dishonest. And there is no can't in her, no can't at all, which is what makes her, finally, a serious playwright."[38]

By the time the double bill ended its run more than 700 performances later in October 1970, Elaine had won two Outer Critics Circle Awards and a Drama Desk Award for her directing and playwriting. She had proven herself on the New York stage, but she didn't have time to stay there. Instead she turned to another Sisyphean task: proving herself in Hollywood—behind the camera this time.

IT DIDN'T TAKE long for the suits at Paramount to start sweating.

One Hundred Dollar Misunderstanding wasn't working. Not even Elaine could turn a sexually explicit satire of America's deep racism into a film that could actually be shown in any proper cinema. "I think in the whole book there are only three pages where there is no sexual activity," she said.[39] But that didn't matter; their concerns were now on the other film Elaine was still contracted to make. By the time they received the completed script for *A New Leaf* in the winter of 1969, their nervousness was pronounced. Stretching to 147 pages, it was filled with jokes about Hitler and pedophilia and suicide,[40] bizarre fantasy sequences, and at least one murder backed by a soundtrack of "The Star-Spangled Banner." It was by no means a nice romp. "I've gone out of my way to avoid compassion," Elaine declared.[41] In an internal memo to Evans, Bart expressed his concerns about the script, which ran into the same kind of trouble as her plays: It was long-winded, with scenes frequently meandering gratuitously without ever really getting anywhere.

More concerning was its disjointed nature. "What we have here are two movies, not one," Bart wrote. "The first is comedy-satire. The second is bald farce. The first has characterizations. The second has only schtick. I like the first. I dislike the second."[42]

And then there was the dark comedy. Maybe it was *too* much. They needed to reframe the story as a quirky romantic comedy and shift it away from whatever homicidal tale Elaine was concocting,[43] and they needed to do it fast. Elaine's script revisions were already delaying the start of production; the budget had ballooned from $1,875,000 to $2,200,000 before a single frame had been shot, with production advocating for another $300,000 buffer and fifteen to twenty more days on the schedule in case Elaine, a first-time director, ran into trouble.[44] Time was money. They would sit back and watch, biting their nails, and hope for the best.

When *A New Leaf* went into production that June, "I began sort of on one foot and just continued that way," Elaine said.[45] She wasn't completely inexperienced, going into it with at least some strengths as a screenwriter—she knew how a scene should be constructed and how she wanted it to look—as well as an actor and stage director— she understood what she wanted from a performance and how she could get it. But that wasn't enough. As a film director, she would need more technical knowledge than she possessed, more than she could have possibly learned in her brief time on the sets of *Enter Laughing* and *Luv*. The tone was set the first day, when she found herself stumped by the crew's question about camera placement; she thought the camera was one of the lights. When it was finally pointed out to her, she said simply, "I don't know." "There was a hush," she remembered. "There was a seventy-man crew which had been babbling incessantly. And everybody stopped in a row. It was like that movie scene when all the heads turn. And there was a long silence. And then somebody took me aside and said, 'You make the crew nervous.'"[46]

Of course she made them nervous; she was already at a disadvantage as a woman in charge of a nearly all-male crew and an unnatural leader. "You're supposed to be crisp," she said. "You're supposed to say 'Cut, print, beautiful, next setup.' You're supposed to say it for the morale of the crew, like a captain on a ship. I couldn't say

'Cut, print, beautiful, next setup.' I couldn't even say 'Action.'"[47] Showing up transformed as Henrietta—soft-spoken, girlish, and fragile—paradoxically helped win the crew's favor, but only in a way that made them view her as a delicate creature in need of their protection,[48] not as their boss. Every day, Matthau would come to set ready to undermine her with a filthy joke he told the crew in front of her. "And the first day when he did it, the crew just looked horrified, and I realized that it was up to me to tell a filthy joke back, or else I would have an embarrassed crew for the rest of the movie. I could never match him, but something so that the crew would not feel that I was horrified."[49]

She could have made up for what she lacked in leadership ability with the kind of decisiveness that comes from experience, but she didn't even have that—though it's worth asking how much she, or anyone who had never made a movie in a time before film schools were ubiquitous, was supposed to. "There's no way to know unless someone teaches you or you screw up," she said. "And when you start a movie by someone saying, 'You can't pick a director, but you can direct it,' you really start knowing nothing."[50] Mike had gone into *Who's Afraid of Virginia Woolf?* with the mentorship of Billy Wilder, the veteran director advising him on everything from what to wear on the set to how to effectively craft a narrative.[51] With no similar figure to guide her, Elaine went into survival mode. "Every day became about trying to remember just what [the story] was about and not screwing up too badly," she said.[52]

But not screwing up too badly didn't mean not screwing up at all. Production fell behind schedule almost immediately; by the fifteenth day of shooting, they were twelve days behind.[53] There was a disconnect between Elaine May, a director of actors, and Elaine May, a director of film. She filled the supporting cast with old friends and close collaborators, from James Coco and Rose Arrick to her own mother and stepdaughter in bit parts. Renée Taylor, who had a small role as one of Henry's eligible dates, remembers, "She said, 'I'm writing a part for you. Can you water-ski?' And I said no. She said, 'Well, don't tell them that when they call you. We'll figure out how to get you to do it.'"[54] She was open and giving with her actors,[55] constantly encouraging them to play a scene differently and improvise from take to take, much to the camera operators' dismay. "The cameraman would say to me, 'You can't move over here. You have to just stay within this six-foot framework.' And she'd say, 'Don't listen to him. You go wherever you want to go, you do whatever you want to do. And the camera will find you,'" says Taylor.[56]

Scenes weren't rehearsed until they became rote. They were games. In one, where Henry's attorney breaks the news to him that he's broke, knowing the actor actually knew tax code, she declined to give him a script and instead had Matthau ask him one absurd question after another. "The guy who was playing the lawyer really looked like he would have a breakdown," she remembered.[57] In another, Elaine, as Henrietta on her honeymoon, asks Henry to help her fix the Grecian style nightgown she's wearing incorrectly. Its two minutes of pure slapstick screen time are the result of Elaine sewing herself into the dress without telling Matthau. "He genuinely couldn't get me out of the nightgown. We had to do a second take, so by the time he did the second take, he knew, and he was a good sport, but for ten minutes, he couldn't get me out."[58]

It's to the credit of her knowledge that the best performance is often the one least planned that these risks paid off in the final film. But it certainly wasn't the most efficient way to direct. She burned through film, shooting take after take after take, much to the producers' chagrin. "The first day, we did the scene five times," Koch remembered. "We thought, 'Tomorrow, we'll start again,' but it went on and on and on. 'Do this again.' She kept complaining she wanted it to be better."[59] No performer got off easy, least of all herself. With no one to trust for honest feedback but a closed-circuit TV set in which she could watch her own performance, it was the *Luv* debacle all over again. Even if she finally landed a take she liked enough to print, it didn't help that for the entire first week, she shot only the master, not knowing that she had to shoot close-ups, too. "I was way ahead of schedule," she claimed. "In the first week I had jumped four weeks ahead of schedule with no coverage, and I was very proud. And then they wanted to go in and cut it. And I said, 'Well, this is too long. Let's take some time out.' And they said, 'Well, we can't.'"[60] Fixing it with reshoots, on top of an already overstuffed script that no number of day-to-day revisions could bring down, delayed production even further. "We will have a very, very long movie," Bart wrote in a memo from the set in June.[61] By July, when the film "finished shooting its thirty-second day on a thirty-three-day schedule, and they were forty percent into the movie," Koch was pulled and replaced with Stanley Jaffe in a desperate attempt to instill some sort of control on set.[62]

But trying to control Elaine was a hopeless endeavor. "She's a fucking maniac! Jesus, Howard, what am I going to do with her?" Jaffe reportedly said to Koch, just weeks after insisting she was a breeze to work with.[63] "She's a tough little lady, that one," Matthau said. "You suggest one thing, O.K. Then a minute later, if you deviate by one single comma, you find out who's in supreme authority."[64] But her toughness was an illusion, the same shield she deployed every other time she had felt threatened. She was as paranoid as she was indecisive, desperately in need of help with the technical side of things, but afraid to accept any. Studio heads tried to boost her morale, to no avail. "They kept saying this movie would be funnier than *The Odd Couple* and I didn't need to work so hard," she said. "I told Charles Bluhdorn, the head of Paramount, 'I'm not as good a writer as Neil Simon. It's not as good a script, so I have to work harder.' 'You *are* as good a writer!' he said. 'No I'm not,' I said. 'I'm not as funny.' 'Don't say that!' he said. 'You're *funnier!*'"[65]

And anyway, maybe it was all just lip service. Maybe they were just pretending to encourage her, pretending to let her think that she could pull this off just so they could watch her fail. She knew they didn't really want her there but were staring at a $200,000 penalty if they fired her.[66] Wouldn't it be easier, she thought, for them to just let her march herself off the side of a cliff instead?[67] Not even her costar liked her all that much. Despite liking the script enough to sign on, Matthau said, "I had doubts about Elaine directing and acting, too, and from her own script, and I told her so."[68] His first day on set, he asked her, "You're not going to direct me, are you?"[69] To him, Elaine was as gratingly naive as the character she was playing. "I was sitting next to Walter in our first scene and they did this clapper where they say 'sound' and I said, 'Action!' And he said, 'Don't look in my face and say action! I've done thirty movies! I know when action is!' And I never said 'action' again," she said.[70] Any hard-won fondness the two eventually built up between them—he was only difficult, by Elaine's estimates, for "the first four-fifths of it"[71]—was gone by the end of production. See for yourself what Matthau had to say about her as soon as the cameras wrapped:

"Elaine is one of those brilliant, brilliant, brilliant people who's a terrific pain in the neck because she's crazy. She's a full-fledged nut."[72]

"She's an impossible broad."[73]

"I mean, who would give *Elaine May* a job as a director?"[74]

With few she felt she could trust, she instead clung tightly to whatever she could control. If she could do as much as possible herself, if everything could just be done her way, then maybe she could beat them at their game. Maybe she could make it out of this alive. She knew she had a strong story, and that was all that mattered— protect the story, keep it unchanged from the page, she thought, and she'd be okay. After all, wasn't that why she was directing it in the first place?

She worked sixteen-hour days,[75] smoking constantly, wearing the same clothes day after day. "Most of the crew says she's brilliant but spooky," one report said.[76] She haggled with her makeup man to let her go barefaced, convinced her hairdresser to let her sloppily fix her hair herself to make Henrietta appropriately unappealing. "Everyone said that to me, 'You're too attractive for the part,' but I managed to downplay my looks by simply no makeup, bad hair, and everyone treated me as though I weren't that good-looking," she said.[77] She scouted locations long after dark, and her arms were often carrying a mess of papers, scenes she had rewritten overnight. "Elaine May makes Hitler look like a little librarian," Matthau said. "She can literally do anything she wants. Give her five minutes, and she'll master it. She doesn't need or want anybody's help. She may look frightened and insecure, but I don't believe it. She's going through an I-must-do-everything-myself stage now. She can, I guess, but she'll be dead first. She's using up the energy that six truck horses and six geniuses use in any given day. How can you pour out that kind of steam and not pay for it?"[78] Was it not needing or wanting anyone's help, or was it that no one was really offering it—at least not in a way that wasn't condescending? So her terminology may have been lacking—"I want them to be full-figure but not tiny," she'd tell the director of photography when framing a scene—but did that warrant others telling her, "You don't have to know about lenses, little girl"?[79]

Maybe she had brought it on herself, trying to play both sides of the coin—the passive, fragile lady director and the competent supreme authority on set. Acting like a girl meant she was treated like a girl, which she resented when it wasn't in her favor. "There is always some idiot who will come up to you and say, 'You're just great for a girl. You think exactly like a man,'" she griped on set one day. "For Crissake, I always thought intelligence was neuter."[80] Being a woman behind the camera, the first in years, meant navigating a catch at every turn: Behave in too feminine a manner, and you're perpetuating the stereotype that to be feminine is to be weak, confirming the notion that women couldn't direct, after all. But behave like a man, and you're a traitor to your gender, perpetuating the patriarchal belief that masculinity reigns supreme, that you can't be womanly and qualified at the same time.

Just as there was no one to teach her how to direct, there was no one to teach her how to strike the right balance. If the girlish act had started from a place of fear, eager to please those in charge and convince them she wasn't "one of those women who are not nice women," it had mutated into something that undermined her. Maybe it would have been easier for her to play nice, shut up, and let herself be a hollow studio puppet, but when had she ever been easy or agreeable? It was a facade she could keep up for only so long until her true self was exposed, and the time eventually came for her to take off Henrietta's mask and make Elaine's demands. "People would leave me saying, 'She's a nice girl. What is this big thing about? She's a nice girl,'" she said. "And the thing is, of course, I wasn't a nice girl. And when they found this out, they hated me all the more. In the end, when it comes down to it, you're just as rotten as any guy. You'll fight just as hard to get your way."[81]

ELAINE MAY WOULD like it very much if you never saw the version of *A New Leaf* that exists today.

Once filming wrapped in early October,[82] Paramount could tell they had trouble on their hands.[83] They had barely finished the pickup shots in Jamaica before Elaine started reconsidering the editor assigned to cut the film. "The fact that she has reservations about him probably does not reflect on his inexperience, but on the fact that this is the only area left for her to bitch about," Jaffe wrote to executives.[84] It didn't matter who the editor was; the writing was on the wall that the process would be like pulling teeth. "Elaine May, being one of the more indecisive people, will probably require more editing time than is presently estimated," Jaffe warned. "Overall, I would say that the picture in its first cut will be extremely long. . . . I believe the picture will be cut well but, of course, we will only know this when the actual cutting begins."[85] By the time Elaine spoke with *The New York Times* in January 1970, despondence was setting in as she cut and recut:

> "Do you feel you broke any new ground in this film?"
>
> "No, none. But I tripped over a lot of old ground."
>
> "How would you describe this film?"
>
> "It's adequate."
>
> "Do you have any hopes of winning an Academy Award for your work?"
>
> "Certainly not. It's not good enough for one. I'm just hoping that people will stay awake."[86]

Even if it was a self-effacing gag, if people were going to stay awake for it, they at least had to have something to *see*. Editing wasn't going any faster than shooting had. It just gave her even more options to mull indecisively over. On and on it went, stretching far past her contracted sixteen weeks of edit time[87] for nearly ten months, until finally she turned in a sprawling, three-and-a-half-hour-long, murder-filled film.

Early in production, studio executive Bernard Donnenfeld acknowledged the one thing they were all fearful of happening, a decision that they might have to make: "We certainly have the right to step in and take over the completion of the picture; but as we all know, this is a highly volatile procedure and does not work."[88]

But now the choice was inevitable. They couldn't put a three-and-a-half-hour-long movie in theaters. And they couldn't expect her to chop it down in a timely manner. If they wanted to have any picture ready to show, they were going to have to recut the film themselves. Well, that wasn't going to work for Elaine. In September 1970, she sent Paramount a list of seven demands, ranging from wanting another sixteen weeks of cutting time—with Paramount providing "ample" postproduction facilities and a $500 per week nonaccountable allowance—to insisting on using her choice of music (Paramount would have to secure the rights) and doing whatever dubbing she felt was necessary. Demands, Paramount retorted, that were "totally unacceptable," and would get her removed from the picture.[89] They were done playing her games. "Elaine May and Elaine May Inc are and have been in breach of their agreements with Paramount Pictures Corporation . . . and by her actions, Elaine May has caused Paramount to suffer substantial damages," Paramount's vice-president wrote in a cable to her lawyers. "Elaine May and Elaine May Inc shall be held fully responsible and accountable for any action that they or either of them may take against Paramount, The New Leaf Company, or the picture itself."[90]

Denying Elaine her contractually promised preview screenings of her cut,[91] Evans, Jaffe, and Koch stepped in to oversee an entirely new edit. They had always had the right to the final cut of the film, and now they had to enact it.[92] They immediately slashed the two murders Henry commits while preparing to kill Henrietta,[93] effectively throwing out Elaine's idea that this was a film about a man who gets away with murder. "Right to the throat," she said. "I mean, they do not cut out the peripheral stuff. They cut out exactly what you wrote the thing for. They know, somehow."[94] The fantasy sequences were chopped—though a few shots linger in the at-times-disjointed final cut—and the ending softened to something more sweet than sickening, a man who is redeemed by love, rather than one who reluctantly accepts it. She was so offended that she refused to cooperate with redubbing the final scenes. (If you watch carefully in the last four minutes of the film, you'll spot her lips moving with no sound, then speaking in an obviously different voice.)[95] "It wasn't *just* a love story," she protested later. "I never meant it to be. It was a love story, but what was interesting was that he murdered a guy."[96] Though the resulting film was still far more cruelly funny than the "cliché-ridden, banal . . . total disaster"[97] she feared it would be, it was undeniably watered down. She couldn't let them release it without a fight. In January 1971, as Paramount eyed an Easter release, she sued for an injunction. This wasn't *her* movie anymore, it was Robert Evans's and Paramount's after they had effectively rewritten and redirected it in the edit. She demanded $150,000 in damages[98] if they didn't take her name off the picture—use of her name, she argued, would be "willful misrepresentation and damaging to her reputation"[99]—and insisted that the studio be prevented from "doing any further editing, cutting, looping on the film" or publicity for it.[100]

They went to court, where the judge—Irving H. Saypol,[101] the chief prosecutor on the Julius and Ethel Rosenberg espionage case—asked to see a screening of it himself. She didn't stand a chance. "The lights went down, and the judge sat there and he screamed and laughed and screamed and laughed, and the lights go up and he says, 'It's the funniest picture in years. You guys win,'" Koch said.[102]

IN RARE INTERVIEWS in the years to follow, Elaine recounts her experience making her first film with hesitancy, a little pride mixing with more parts pain. She calls it "a hair-raising experience," a "very tough movie" that she "struggled through."[103] The nicest thing she can remember about it is how fun Matthau was, though "paradoxically, because I had so much struggle with him."[104] She concedes her responsibility in all of it—"with every movie I have done, I may just be a pain in the ass"[105]—but just the same, who hasn't, at some point in time, been a pain in the ass when working through a shitty situation?

Matthau may have thought she was tough, but not asking for help and insisting on doing it all yourself aren't the actions of someone tough. They're the actions of someone scared. And how could she not have been scared? Making a movie was supposed to be the biggest moment of Elaine's career, but she hadn't asked for this opportunity; she was thrown into it blind, and those in charge had little confidence in her. She knew she wasn't their first choice for the job, so why should she have trusted any help they may have offered? What a miserable way to make your first film, expected to show up and behave as your best self day after day while learning as fast as you can. It's understandable why she would put up defenses and hope they would somehow protect her from the worst.

Not that Elaine would ever call any of this traumatic. No, she wouldn't allow herself to be victimized like that. It wasn't about her, and it certainly wasn't about her gender. It was just how it was. "The studios are always stupid," she insisted. "They're going to be stupid for everybody."[106] The most she would do was talk about it sideways, use the injustices of sitting on hold with a major corporation as a sort of allegory to say how she really felt: "We all know that there's something about the tiny things in life happening to you that devalues you, that lessens you, that makes you numb. You have to become more and more numb not to get offended. And pretty soon you get pretty sick. But it seems to me, at some point what you really want to say is 'I won't deal with a company that doesn't have a real [telephone] operator. For one day, I'll make them lose that much money.' . . . For one day, you'll take the trouble to make trouble for someone else, because it's the only thing that keeps you from getting sick, from sort of retreating."[107]

IN SPITE OF it all, the film was a success. *A New Leaf* would be the last time Elaine would play a lead role on film—and the only time she would direct herself—and it's her best on-screen performance by far. A feat of physical comedy, a grand exaggeration of her own real-life graceless idiosyncrasies, all dropped teacups and spilled glasses of cheap wine, walking around with price tags hanging off her clothes and softly exclaiming "Heavens!" Henrietta doesn't disappear, as she had initially wanted her to. Rather, Elaine disappears into her. For two hours, it's easy to forget that she had ever been perceived as hostile or dangerous or formidable.

Critics for the most part loved the film—and loved her, both as an actor and a director.[108] In a warm review for the *Chicago Tribune*, Gene Siskel wrote, "Miss May writes and directs with uncommon grace," and compared *A New Leaf* to *It Happened One Night* and *Bringing Up Baby*. "Miss May may be right," Vincent Canby wrote for *The*

New York Times. "Her version may be better than Paramount's, and, theoretically anyway (not having seen the other version), I'm on her side. Still, the movie . . . is so nutty and so funny, so happily reminiscent of the screwball comedies people aren't supposed to be able to make any more, I'm quite satisfied to let things stand."[109]

By 1972, *A New Leaf* had grossed $5 million[110] and was nominated for two Golden Globes (for Best Picture and Best Actress) and a Writers Guild of America Award. Had the lawsuit not taken up most of the press coverage and had Elaine actually participated in its promotion, it might have done even better. Not that it mattered. She had delivered great reviews and made Paramount money, and that was enough. Elaine didn't just survive by the skin of her teeth; she found herself suddenly established and respected, a member of the Directors Guild of America—only the third woman—and already at work on her next film, a second chance she had predicted she would somehow get:

> "Will you do anything different in your next movie?"
> She thought for some time. "Yes," she said.
> "What?"
> "Everything."[111]

CHAPTER 6

Laugh and Laugh and Laugh and Shudder Later

The Heartbreak Kid (1972)

The way Charles Grodin tells it, "If I hadn't run into Elaine May, I don't know if I would have been in the movies."[1] The actor had been having a rough go of it come 1971. "Careerwise," he said, "I was kind of treading water at best."[2] Then he got a call from Elaine May.

That fall, she was hired to direct a new film, *The Heartbreak Kid,* about a man who leaves his bride on their honeymoon for another woman, by independent ABC subsidiary Palomar Pictures. She would lighten her workload for her second outing in the director's seat. This time, she would stay firmly planted behind the camera— "in fact, I feel terrific about not acting," she insisted—and would leave the writing to Neil Simon, whose screenplay based on a short story by Bruce Jay Friedman she swore she wouldn't even so much as tinker with.[3] "Why should I?" she asked. "I think 'Doc' can do his stuff without my help."[4] Simon would have a clause in his contract preventing her from doing so, just in case, but that wouldn't stop her from stamping her perspective all over it anyway.[5] If they wanted her to direct, they were going to have to accept her tilted insight on Neil Simon's very un-tilted world. From the start, Elaine made it clear to her producer Edgar Scherick that she was no hired gun: "He said, 'I am going to give you a really tough producer, because he's got to keep an eye on you.' And I said, 'No one can control me but you, Ed. You have to produce it.' He said, 'Well, I'm running this little studio.' I said, 'It's a small studio. Don't you want this movie to come through on time? Don't you want to keep me from doing something crazy? Don't you want to keep control of me?' He said, 'Maybe you're right.'"[6] She'd twist her logic to get what she wanted every step of the way.

It all started with the very foundation of the film: finding the right ensemble. With Simon coming off two back-to-back hits— one, a film adaptation of his Broadway hit *Plaza Suite,* and another, an original script, *The Out-of-Towners*—and Elaine making a name for herself as the surprise underdog director of the year, *The Heartbreak Kid* was a hot casting. "I found out much later that every young movie star in Hollywood who knew of the project wanted to do it," Grodin remembered.[7] But Elaine already knew the person she wanted for the lead. Lenny Cantrow—the schmuck who finds himself infatuated with a bored shiksa coed as his feelings for his new bride deteriorate just days after their wedding—needed to be an unknown. And that unknown had to be Charles Grodin, the tall, awkward actor who had stumbled over a joking pass at her at a party a few years before.[8] Since then, she had followed his career closely, telling anyone she could that he was *it.* "In fairness to other actors," Grodin said, "I don't think Elaine was getting out and around that much, since she was spending a lot of time alone writing, and Elaine has never been one to stay on top of the latest show-business news (or, for that matter, anywhere near it)."[9] But never mind that. She knew that others would see in him what she did once he got a part that would show it off. Now she had the power to give it to him. After a screen test for her, Simon, and Scherick, he was in. But Elaine didn't stop at Grodin. There was another power flex to make: She cast Jeannie in the role of Lila, the jilted bride.

Growing up, Jeannie and Elaine would have private acting lessons together. "She used to take me into the study and lock up the doors, and it would be the two of us for a couple of hours," Jeannie said.[10] As a teacher, Elaine could be tough, never offering praise if something wasn't truly worthy of it, but enormously patient and encouraging if it was clear you were trying your best, giving advice on how to pull the emotion out of an action. "I was around eleven. I remember singing this song to her—'I'm Gonna Leave Old Texas Now, Ain't Got No Use for the Long-Horned Cow'—I was singing this song, because I wanted to be a singer, and I had just left all my friends in California, so my mother said to me, 'Sing the song again, and when you come to the word Texas, think of California, and all your friends, and everything you left behind.' Well, I sang the song again, and I started to cry while I sang. But I kept on singing, because I saw what she was getting at. Just that little idea of substituting added so much color to the song."[11]

After a brief disappointing stint at New York University's acting school,[12] Jeannie moved back to Los Angeles. Unlike Elaine, she loved it there, although she found that while it was full of places where you could "park in front of where you're going" without paying,[13] it had an abysmal number of acting schools that actually cared about anything beyond the superficial. "No one can see beyond your height, weight, and clothes. I was usually hostile because I knew I was being looked over," she lamented.[14] Rather than shoehorn herself into the type of class meant "for character actors who say they want to play different parts but keep on playing the same character they've been playing for twenty years," she started a school herself, which she ran while writing a screenplay about her grandmother's life on the side.[15] As an actor, Jeannie found herself typecast in small roles in youth movement films like *Alice's Restaurant* and *Getting Straight*—"a revolutionary in dungarees," she called them.[16] *The Heartbreak Kid* would be the perfect opportunity to show what she could really do.

Was nepotism responsible for Jeannie winning the part? "I would hope to think that my mother was a little prejudiced," Jeannie joked,[17] but she insisted that handing over a role wasn't in Elaine's nature, that she had to read and screen-test and wait through rounds of auditions like everyone else.[18] Which, sure, but it was likely just a formality. Erik Lee Preminger, an associate producer on the film, remembers: "There really was never a question that [it would] be Jeannie, and for good reason. Although Elaine would never say, I think because she had this picture in her mind, it made agreeing to do the film easier."[19] It certainly added a curiosity factor to the film, audiences eager to see if Elaine was capable of pushing her own daughter to give it her all. "Will the artist or the mama prevail in Miss May's direction?" one report questioned at the time of casting news.[20] But even if Elaine had a hand in winning Jeannie the part, she would have to fight for her to keep it.

See, Simon wasn't happy about two unknowns fronting his film. It didn't take much to convince him not to fire Grodin—"You already saw him perform it," Elaine reminded him[21]—but Jeannie would be a harder sell. Jeannie, he thought, wasn't attractive enough. "I wanted Diane Keaton to play the first wife, and Diane is a very attractive girl," Simon said.[22] But everyone else thought Keaton was too much like the gentile princess to be the abandoned Jewish wife. "He kept telling Elaine to get someone better-looking," Grodin remembered, "and Elaine said, 'Okay, if you can bring me someone who looks more attractive who can act the part, I'll do it.'"[23] The whole time he had no idea that the girl he was calling unattractive—the girl who looked, talked, and moved jarringly just like Elaine—was her daughter. It didn't even matter that it was Jeannie. What mattered was the principle of it all, the violation of truthfulness Simon was insisting she enact, all of which stemmed from a fundamental disagreement on the source material itself. "I never wanted it to be the story of a guy who meets a homely girl, then meets the most gorgeous girl in America and wants to leave one for the other. That's too simple," Simon argued.[24] In Elaine's interpretation of the original story, Lila is "atrociously ugly." She agreed with Simon, but with a twist: Just as there's no drama in a man leaving a repulsive girl, there's no truth or nuance in his leaving a pretty one. With that logic, Elaine said, "I want somebody reasonable. Like Jeannie, who's just average."[25] Simon was later able to acknowledge that "those were very special circumstances. The girl, Jeannie Berlin, was Elaine's daughter; and she obviously gave a very good performance." Still, he said, "it was *not* the picture that I had in my mind. I was very upset about that."[26]

Rounding out the trio was another contentious casting, with Cybill Shepherd—in her second on-screen role—as Kelly, the blonde on the beach. The role had initially gone to the girlfriend of agent Freddie Fields, but there was one problem: She was a brunette. "I kept saying, 'But, Elaine, this role is about being blond,'" said costume designer Anthea Sylbert, "and she kept saying, 'But you'll fix it.' By the time we had the first reading, her hair was the color of a bright orange carrot. Neil Simon wasn't pleased."[27] And it only got worse from there; her bleached hair falling out in clumps, "she was paid off and sent back to L.A. with a scarf over her head," Preminger says.[28] Shepherd became the last-minute save, despite the fact that Elaine, she said, "had seen me chattering mindlessly on Dick Cavett's show and decided I couldn't play this or any part."[29] Just days before they were due to begin production in Miami Beach, she read for Simon and Elaine in a tiny Manhattan office. "I told you she was perfect for it," Shepherd remembers Simon saying.[30]

THE BATTLES DIDN'T stop there. There was also the issue of the script to be dealt with. Simon was well aware of Elaine's reputation, for better and worse. He respected her talent enough to hire her to direct the independently financed film, but he also knew enough to be cautiously protective of his work. With more clout and power than most screenwriters, he inserted a clause in his contract: Elaine couldn't change a word. Not without his prior approval, that is.[31]

But that didn't mean that Elaine wouldn't make her own tweaks to the story elsewhere. Preminger recalls spending weeks with her before rehearsals going through the script line by line. "She would look at a scene, and she'd ask me, 'Now, why does the character do that?' And I'd have to make up a backstory to give a rational explanation for why the character behaved in such and such a way."[32] In rehearsals, she would push the actors to explore the subtext of the dialogue, all the different interpretations they could bring to each line, all the ways they could fill up the space where nothing was written. She had Jeannie and Grodin improvise what songs they would sing together in the car as two happy newlyweds blissfully en route to their honeymoon. "Where does it say they sing?" Simon asked. They reached an agreement: Elaine had to print one take where the scene was played exactly as written, then she was free to improvise as much as she wanted. The final film would be hers to put together as she saw fit. "I assume he found the whole situation extremely trying and, after the first couple of days of rehearsal, he was never again seen around the movie set," Grodin remembered.[33]

"I could have really screamed about it," Simon said, "but some of the changes I liked. Some of them I *didn't* like, but it was not worth it to go through what she herself did, taking her name off *A New Leaf* when they were going to open it because Paramount had reedited the picture . . . I was for the most part very happy with *Heartbreak Kid,* so I said OK. So I lost a few battles here and there."[34] The biggest of which happened to be the chilly ending Elaine used, one that deviated from the original script. "I thought the ending of the picture that I wrote was infinitely better than what Elaine had. It was the one thing that I really regretted," he said. "They shot it. They filmed it and never showed it to anybody. I begged the producer to at least screen it in front of twenty people. He said, 'No, I won't even do that.' I was really furious at that. I'm *still* furious at him for doing that. I'm not furious at Elaine for wanting to try it, because she did it both ways; but it was the obligation of the producer—and it just makes sense—to screen it and see how others feel about it."[35] Nearly a decade later, Simon would concede that there was a "very complicated interplay between Elaine May and myself," but if he had to do it again, he would still ask her to direct the film "because I think I could reason with her more now."[36]

In Elaine's version of the story, the two got along well until their casting dustup, after which Simon spoke to her only through Scherick. They never reconciled after their working relationship turned sour, save for one conversation: "He said, 'I like that movie best. It's very Chekhovian. It won't get a laugh.' Because he wanted to write like Chekhov. And he said, 'I think you did the movie to give Jeannie a part.' And you know what, he was probably right."[37]

PRODUCTION ON *The Heartbreak Kid* was a breeze compared to *A New Leaf*. Elaine worked well with firm guardrails in place, be it the objective distance from the script or the pressure of a strict shooting schedule. *The Heartbreak Kid* being independently financed meant there was little room for screwing around. There was no Paramount to go back to asking for more, more, more; they just had what they had, and the knowledge that running through it would be done at the risk of making artistic compromises.

No longer a novice, she knew what she wanted and, obsessed

with finding the kernel of authenticity, was relentless about getting it. An inability to change the lines didn't keep her from seizing any opportunity to improvise physically to get her desired effect instead. In one scene, in which Grodin has to take a running leap from a dock onto a moving yacht, she would increase the distance between him and the boat incrementally each take "until she got the desperation in the jump that she wanted."[38] Similarly, in another sequence, she instructed Eddie Albert, as Kelly's father, to never look at Grodin when he was speaking to him, just to continue eating his dinner. "The direction was simple," Grodin said. "The result was devastating."[39] She would don a wet suit and wade into the ocean herself for a scene that could have been shot from the shore, directing Grodin and Shepherd from feet away as she was thrown around in the surf.[40] Her idea of authentic wasn't always tactful, though. When filming moved to the University of Minnesota, "she wanted to make a contrast between Miami and Jewishness, and Minnesota and white, upper-Midwest," recalls production assistant David Streit. She put out a call for all-white extras. "All white, all blond. As many blond-looking people as possible to make the contrast. And it was, at that time, offensive, as it is today, to say only the white, blond people can be extras." Filming stopped when Native Americans protested, and started up again once they were paid to join, although "they were kind of put into the background of the extras, so that they could be a part of it and Elaine could have her contrast."[41]

She would shoot an unscripted version of the film's ending, instructing everyone on the set to improvise as if they were at a real wedding reception themselves, often hanging back and letting them go without interruption. In one take, Grodin improvised a conversation with Albert and one of the wedding guests before walking away to the far end of the room. Elaine called out to Albert to react. It was no use. "Elaine," a cameraman said, "we already cut." Incredulous, she tore off her headphones: "Don't cut 'til I *say* cut!" she said.[42]

"We had extras, we were a film crew on location, and we were going into overtime and the scene had been covered. Believe me, she was very, very meticulous," says Streit. "And Edgar said, 'You gotta stop. We're going home.' And, she said, 'No, we're not. I've gotta get this shot, this shot, that shot . . .' And he said, 'No, we're going home.'" Filming halted as they left the set to work it out. "They went into the next room, and there was shouting and there was furniture being thrown around. I could only imagine. But we did shoot. We did stay and finish the shots."[43]

But this all sounds just as chaotic as *A New Leaf*. All that improvising? All those cameras running, running, running? That same stubborn insistence on doing things over and over again, even after getting a take that was good enough? How did she avoid repeating the same disaster? The reality is that it was controlled chaos, improvisations and demands kept in check by a team that neither undermined nor coddled her. Just as having guardrails in place helped her work more efficiently, so, too, did her crew. She could still easily become very controlling: "She insisted on having one of those filters that the director of photography uses to sort of gauge the lighting, because she didn't trust the director of photography to get the lighting right. And that was because *once,* he didn't," Preminger says.[44] But more often than not, she worked in lockstep with a support system of producers she could trust, people who cared about and respected her, even when she could be maddening. They understood best the ways she needed to be supported in order to work well, the ways in which she could become so consumed by her work that she ignored all outside reality. Rather than let her struggle by herself, they stepped in.

"You really had to take care of Elaine," associate producer Michael Hausman says.[45] On the set, she fueled herself on cigarettes and Schimmelpenninck cigars—sometimes smoking both at the same time, one in each hand[46]—and fistfuls of NoDoz.[47] So hyperfocused and engrossed in a scene could she become that, on one occasion in Minnesota, she hadn't even realized her feet were frostbitten until Shepherd noticed she was limping.[48]

When not on set, she had no sense of time or place. You were wise to not let her wander off on her own. That lesson was learned early on when, after seeing David off at the airport at the end of a weekend visit, she got into a cab to return to her hotel and requested simply, "I'd like to go to the Holiday Inn." "There are seventeen

Holiday Inns in Miami," the driver said. "Which one is it?" Elaine couldn't remember. "I don't know," she said. "Let's go find it."[49] The day of the move from Florida to Minneapolis, cars running and full of crew members ready to go to the airport, Elaine still hadn't packed. Hausman had to go up to her room, "literally throw everything she owns in suitcases, pack them up, put them in the car, and bring her," Preminger says. "She needed that sort of handling to move on."[50]

BUT IT WAS worth it, they reasoned, because no matter how monomaniacal she could get on set, she had a special touch with every actor. "Elaine wasn't the kind of director who slaps you on the back or anything, so you could never be 100 percent positive what she or anyone else felt," Grodin said, remembering a bout of paranoia in which he thought Dustin Hoffman would replace him. ("Are you crazy?!" Elaine replied when he finally took her aside to confirm his fear.)[51] But she was intuitive, always knowing the right questions to ask, the best way to communicate and direct them to the outcome she thought was right. "I had never attended an acting school," Shepherd says. "I don't have a degree in anything, except I did go to the Peter Bogdanovich School of Film and I worked with Elaine May on my second film. That's like working with another genius after Peter Bogdanovich."[52] When Shepherd felt pressured by the male producers to approve a shot of the body double they had scouted from the Playboy Club to take her place in a nude scene, she refused, arguing that the nudity, as a whole, wasn't necessary to service the scene. "I held my ground," she said, "and Elaine agreed with me."[53]

"She loved her actors," Preminger says. "And she let her actors interpret and work the way they felt they should and was very gentle in the way she guided them. I never saw her lose her temper with actors. The gentleness of Elaine's treatment was a joy."[54] She didn't play favorites, least of all with Jeannie. On set, Jeannie called Elaine "Miss Mother"[55] and insisted that working with her was strictly "a director-actress relationship. That's *all* it was. There was nothing about mother-daughter relationship. She directed me the way she directed everybody else, which was allowing you to 'go'—to do what your impulses told you to do." And not even Jeannie was immune to the perplexing feeling of following the twists and turns of Elaine's mind. "She's so many steps ahead of you! I mean, she'll start talking about something that seems from left field. You have no idea why she's talking to you about a particular subject. Then, suddenly, you do the scene, and it comes out right."[56]

IN SPRING OF 1972, after *The Heartbreak Kid* had wrapped, Mike and Elaine danced around the idea of reuniting professionally for the first time in twelve years. They had turned down so many opportunities, big and small, since their split.[57] But while Mike had all but sworn off performing, maybe Elaine was starting to miss it. There was a rush from performing live—that pit in your stomach just before you step in front of an audience, the uncertainty about whether you'll fall flat on your face, that rush when you kill—she could never get from writing and directing.

Feeling ambitious, they booked and quickly sold out ten nights at Chicago's Playboy Club in anticipation of a reunion special on NBC they'd tape later that summer.[58] But less than a week before the run, Elaine pulled out, and they canceled it.[59] Perhaps having learned a lesson about dragging out an edit for too long on *A New Leaf*, Elaine cited pressure of finishing *The Heartbreak Kid* on time.[60]

But they did trot their act out that June for a benefit concert Warren Beatty had organized for George McGovern at Madison Square Garden. It was a night full of star-studded reunions, with Nichols and May joining Simon & Garfunkel; Peter, Paul, and Mary; and more. "This is a lot of fun," Mike said. "I don't know why we've waited so long."[61] Onstage, they made cracks about Vietnam ("I've always wanted to get out of Vietnam—even before we got in," Elaine joked) and Hubert Humphrey's proposal to give everyone $1,000 a year before performing a variation of their operator sketch, lightly amended with jokes about phone tapping.[62]

That night, they set the blueprint they would follow every time they'd reunite over the next few decades: Play the hits. The material could deviate a bit to keep up with the times—and for the sake of Elaine's sanity—but never again would they do something new. For most other acts, an endless greatest hits parade could have seemed tired or sad, especially as the seventies progressed and Nichols and May—sitting on the cusp between the old guard and the new—could so easily have been deemed irrelevant. They still talked about doing the television special, but even that didn't materialize. Nichols and May would never do that special, not even the new version, which by then was just to be a type of best-of revue.[63]

They knew how to read the room. "The rhythm and the tone of the world have changed," Mike acknowledged. "There's a lot to be said for letting the past be the past. What I love most is that when we stopped, we stopped."[64] They saw what happened to those who tried to forever revisit their former glories, the pitiful ways it often ended, the ways they could so easily disappoint. No, they would leave the discovery of new things for their individual lives, and together thrive on scarcity, appearing just often enough to indulge an audience's craving for nostalgia, but never staying long enough to bore them. Until the early 1990s, when the time came for tributes and galas thrown in their honor, the McGovern concert and Jimmy Carter's 1977 inauguration—where they performed a version of their "Mother and Son" sketch from the perspective of Carter and his mother—were the only times they appeared onstage together. The more time they spent apart, the more they were missed—and the easier it became to get away with continuing to do the same sketches over and over again, joking, "we said for our 65th anniversary we'd dodder out and do 'Teenagers' for the 50,000th time."[65]

IT OPENS, NOT insignificantly, with the title credits: "Neil Simon's The Heartbreak Kid." A beat passes, and Simon's name fades away. Below the title: "An Elaine May Film."

Here is what we expect from a Neil Simon story:

- Something comedic.
- A lot of zingers.
- Two-dimensional characters.
- If it's a movie, camerawork that is flat and uninteresting, your standard shot/reverse shot kind of deal, no better than taping a play.

Here is what we expect from an Elaine May film:

- Something comedic, but often darkly so.
- A lot of zingers, but few that get immediate loud laughs so much as a cerebral nod. "That's funny," you say to yourself. So many zingers that you may not get half of them until later on, finding yourself simultaneously amused and horrified.
- Characters that appear one-note at first glance, only to reveal their complexities upon closer inspection.
- Long takes, strange angles, and scenes within scenes . . . [66]
- . . . Which draw out that horrific nature of how many jokes are just casually thrown out, without any acknowledgment that they're jokes to begin with.

And here is what we get from *The Heartbreak Kid*, a Neil Simon story directed by Elaine May:

A comedy of the most discomforting variety. How she lingers in the silences, refusing to snap through lines at a rapid-fire setup/punch line pace. How she forces the audience to squirm, dealing in voyeuristic long take after long take, camera close, refusing to let you look away. How she makes you internally cringe, watching Lila hopelessly infatuated after losing her virginity on her honeymoon as the reality—he married her because she wouldn't give it up before marriage—sets in all over Lenny's face. How much secondhand embarrassment you feel as Lenny tries to win over the parents of his college coed crush, how you want to scream, "Do you even *hear* what you're saying?" Don't you wish she would cut away, for god's sake, as she draws out, to agonizing lengths, the climactic scene where Lenny finally dumps Lila over a lobster dinner? There's no farce here, just excruciating unease. You don't want to see Lila's pain. It's snotty and sad and desperate. Don't you feel like you're right there, one of the diners in the restaurant that night who had the great misfortune of watching a private moment play out in public? Can't you feel your cheeks growing hot?

Rather than playing Simon's script as broad comedy, going for easy laughs without interrogation, what Elaine does instead is lean hard into reality. She doesn't just want you to laugh at these characters; she wants to analyze—and pass judgment on—why they are behaving the way they are. Like *A New Leaf* is Henry Graham's film, *Heartbreak Kid* is Lenny's through and through, and we are meant to watch and judge his desire for assimilation, how he expresses disgust for everyone around him to mirror his own self-hatred, only to be on the receiving end of that same disgust later when he thinks he's found a way out. Yet every character is played with a kind of empathy that causes your allegiance to constantly shift. Yes, Lenny is right to want better than Lila. No, Lila isn't as off-putting as she seems—we're seeing her through Lenny's eyes, and how, in his panic, he has exaggerated every slight annoyance to an unbearable level. No, it's not okay for Lenny to destroy the lives of others when what he's really trying to do is destroy himself. Yes, Kelly is manipulating him for sport, and we shouldn't feel sorry for her. No, that doesn't make it okay for him to follow her to Minnesota without her consent. Yes, we should empathize with more than scorn this man who now feels guilt for blowing up not only his own life but the lives of others. No, we should be satisfied that in the end, he's right back where he started: still empty inside, still an outsider. Back and forth and back and forth until you realize: there's no one to root for here.

At the end of the day, it's just as much a tragedy as it is a comedy. Underneath the humor of it all—which helps us digest how awful it all is—it's just sad. And isn't that just like real life? Elaine seemed to think so. "Humor sort of happens, sometimes against your will. It's more a way of looking at things," she said. "You look at something one way and it's a disaster, you look at it another way and it's humorous. It depends on how you tilt your head."[67] Elaine's *Heartbreak Kid* gets right to the heart of being a person: We are all, men and women alike, flawed, capable of being awful, cruel, petty, and disgusting. Inside all of us is a monster, and sometimes it doesn't take much for it to come out. Whether or not that's funny depends on how you choose to look at it.

IF *A NEW LEAF* was an uncertain first step, *The Heartbreak Kid* was a confident stride, one critics met with praise, particularly for her ability to interpret Simon's work in a new way. Vincent Canby called it "an unequivocal hit" and a "first-class American comedy," made so by someone who brought Simon's script to life beyond the easy laughs and gave it "for a change, a real understanding of character."[68] Roger Ebert agreed: "The movie doesn't constantly bow to Neil Simon's script (as most movie versions of his work do). Elaine May is willing to improvise, to indulge (and exploit) quirks in acting style, and to examine social hypocrisy with a kind of compulsive ferocity."[69]

Even Pauline Kael, who wasn't sold on *A New Leaf* and claimed to despise film adaptations of Simon's plays, worried she might "risk damaging the pleasures of *The Heartbreak Kid* by overpraise," writing: "Elaine May has the rarest kind of comic gift: the ability to create a world seen comically. Her satirist's malice isn't cutting; something in the befuddled atmosphere she creates keeps it mild— yet mild in a thoroughly demented way, mild as if impervious to sanity."[70]

The praise carried into awards season, where it received two Academy Award nominations (Best Supporting Actress for Jeannie and Best Supporting Actor for Eddie Albert) and three Golden Globe nominations. Grodin earned his own accolades, but the true breakout star was Jeannie. All the concern about whether Elaine could direct her own daughter to go deep into the role was unfounded; it was Jeannie who was singled out time and again, going on to win a New York Film Critics Circle Award and National Society of Film Critics Award for her performance.

But the near-unanimous critical adoration didn't keep it from stirring up controversy. Hollywood may have been founded by Jewish immigrants, but their version of expressing the American Dream entailed actively working to erase their identities.[71] Studio heads changed their names and self-censored their Jewishness in life and on-screen, rarely, if ever, telling Jewish stories, hiding behind the puritanical Production Code to defend against anti-Semitism as Nazis rose to power in Europe. And for decades, even after World War II, many of Hollywood's biggest stars—actors like Lauren Bacall, Cary Grant, Hedy Lamarr—followed suit, changing their names, assimilating and dissociating from their identities in the face of the Hollywood blacklist, which often suggested Jews were the link between Communists and the movie industry.[72]

By the late 1960s, as the Production Code was abandoned and the culture became less repressive, New Hollywood emerged full of young Jewish filmmakers and stars who would more implicitly and explicitly assert their identity.[73] "In the movies, actors like Zero Mostel, Elliott Gould, and Barbra Streisand began to establish themselves as international celebrities, not by suppressing their Jewishness, but by exploiting it. Why not? Suddenly it was 'in' to be Jewish," *The New York Times* observed at the time.[74] But Jewish representation still rarely meant telling traditional Jewish stories; instead, it became packaged in a way that was deemed more palatable for American society at large, delivered in a New York—read: Jewish—comedic sensibility (part of which Nichols and May had a hand in developing). Neuroticism, anxiety, and self-hatred, nebbishness and emasculation—they all became synonymous with Jewishness, even if they weren't actually. Author Henry Bial refers to this as double coding, an ability for a text to "communicate one message to Jewish audiences while simultaneously communicating another, often contradictory message to gentile audiences," which often "functions to negotiate between the desire to assert the specificity of the Jewish experience and the apparently competing desire to speak to the universal human condition."[75] And whether overtly Jewish or just Jewish-coded, these films were almost always about men. Save for the exception of Barbra Streisand, Jewish women were all but entirely shut out of leading lady roles, told they were "too Jewish" or "too exotic," only slipped into supporting roles in other people's stories, there to play the wisecracking best friend or the nagging wife. The rare occasions a female lead was written as Jewish, she'd likely be played by a non-Jewish actress instead, a particular form of dilution of representation that runs rampant today.[76] *The Heartbreak Kid* very easily could have followed that route if Neil Simon had had his way and Diane Keaton (a Methodist) had played Lila. But Elaine knew enough to keep it true, refusing to play the Hollywood game of whitewashing a character who is in large part shaped by their Jewish identity. What she didn't anticipate was that this decision would cause such a sharp backlash.

The Heartbreak Kid is a satire of Jewish stereotypes, playing with the archetypes of the kvetchy, insipid yenta and the nebbishy, shiksa-goddess-chasing Jewish man. But more important, in Elaine's hands, it's a film about self-hatred, a disdainful read on a subset of Jewish men who have an intense desire to assimilate into gentile society. Critics, though, argued that the film was more realism than satire, which made its portrayal of Jewish identity wildly offensive. Lila was a particular cause for concern, with some suggesting that the film insinuated: "Why be married to a cloying, unsophisticated, slightly overweight Jewish girl who speaks with a discernible singsong Jewish intonation when you can perhaps conquer a very Waspy-looking, knockout blonde shiksa type?"[77] And so much for representation. For once, actual Jewish actors had been cast in explicitly Jewish roles, but the parts were "cramped little molds, which the actors are unable to enlarge."[78] In the end, with all the infractions piled up, "Simon and May bypass the issue of Jewish appeal in favor of standardized Hollywood comedy."[79]

They have a point; the film walks a fine line between satirizing stereotypical Jewish depictions and presenting those stereotypes as reality. "It's satire" is so often used as a lazy defense against criticism of poor writing; it would be easy to apply the same criticism here. Simon's wink and nod "just the jokes, folks!" narrative variety brings the film up to the edge of a problematic cliff; the only thing that holds it back is Elaine's insistence on bringing psychological depth to it. If Elaine hadn't given each character more of a backstory on her own, taken the time to flesh out the film beyond its surface level, laugh-on-every-line dialogue—which, on the page, reads flat and toxic—it's possible that it could have been viewed even more harshly. "If they don't feel bad for her," she explained, "we've really fucked it up."[80] Jeannie, too, developed Lila beyond the wisp of personhood she is granted on the page. "I didn't want to make that girl stupid," she said. "It would have been so easy to do Lila stupid. I don't think Lila was stupid. I think every single thing she did was justified to her. I mean, she thought she was being nice. And she was really terrifically in love."[81] What's more, she had modeled Lila partly on an old summer camp friend, a Christian girl from a tiny suburban Pennsylvania town. "She was so naive she'd make you look intelligent," she said. "I'm the kind of person who will take a chance in conversation and get very sarcastic. I'll say anything. But she would come back with an interpretation that would make you feel like a louse."[82]

Elaine's intent wasn't to make something anti-Semitic; she wanted to take audiences into the psychology of broken men—a choice that is both upsetting to audiences and one that is difficult to catch if you're simply watching the movie as entertainment and not analyzing it. If anything, she thought, casting Grodin—"who is a Jew, but doesn't look it"[83]—instead of Dustin Hoffman, who was Simon's pick, was a deliberate choice to avoid anti-Semitism. "For this beautiful woman to walk down the Miami Beach and see this short, sleeping Jew, is going to make this an antisemitic movie, because everybody's gorgeous on the beach but Dustin. I can't do it," she argued. "I don't want the whole movie to seem like they're making fun of a Jew, because it's not what it's about."[84]

She couldn't quite understand what the issue was; were her critics watching the movie she'd made? In an interview a few years after the film's release, Elaine addressed the criticism with dismay: "*The Heartbreak Kid* didn't seem to be anti-Semitic to me at all. I was really surprised when it seemed that way to other people. It never entered my mind. It was written by Bruce Jay Friedman, who's a Jew. And it was scripted by Neil Simon, who's a Jew. And what would they write about? The Welsh? I think that when Jews write movies, they are very concerned with being a Jew, because it's still a specific thing, just as being a southerner is. There are very few Americans who still have real cultures."[85] For her, the issue seemed to stem from the intersection of identity and drama; these characters were found offensive because they weren't heroes, but making a character a hero is rarely interesting, let alone funny. What she didn't acknowledge was that it was more than the fact that Lenny wasn't a Jewish hero; it was that, in a highly reactive time, she presented him as a Jewish antagonist. It was just a coincidence, she claimed: "I really don't think Hollywood would dare—even if they wanted to—to portray a Jew unfavorably. I don't believe they would portray anyone unfavorably."[86] Though who's to say whether she meant it or whether the comment—suspiciously ignorant of the possibility for internal subconscious bias for someone with such an vast breadth of knowledge about psychology—was just a feigned naive defense, Elaine playing dumb when it benefited her.

Feminist critics, already suspicious of Elaine after *A New Leaf,* were also up in arms. How much of an advancement could it possibly be if the only woman directing studio films—and one of the most prominent women directors, period—was perpetuating such harsh portrayals of women?[87] *The Heartbreak Kid* had taken things too far, they argued. Lila was too much of a stereotype, too needy and insecure, slobbish to the point of grotesque, and too stupid to see through her husband's farfetched lies. She was, as Barbara Quart argued, "one of the most negative images of a Jewish woman on film—created by a Jewish woman, with her own daughter in the role of the offensive woman." (Forget the fact that the Christian girl was just as awful in her own right, as was the Jewish man, and never mind the fact that they were all written by Simon, not Elaine.) This was work that "reflects the wounds of an earlier and lonely generation of women directors. Some may murmur about May (as has actually been written about [Lina] Wertmüller) that such women directors got so far just because of their ferocity to women, which made their cinematic visions acceptable while those of others with equal gifts are not."[88] Casting Jeannie in the part was "punishing,"[89] they claimed, a "conception born of considerable hatred—of women, Jews, and, at some level, her own daughter."[90] Critic Marjorie Rosen went so far as to accuse Elaine of being "an Uncle Tom whose feminine sensibilities are demonstrably nil." She expected more from Elaine, suspecting she must have resented watching Mike's career blossom while hers flatlined. *"She's been there,* as they say. She knows what's at stake."[91]

But Elaine was never that simple. Her films adopting the point of view of misogynistic protagonists didn't mean she was misogynistic herself. Forcing an audience to look at something is not the same as endorsing it. Rather, it's her goal to "make an audience laugh and laugh and laugh and shudder later" taken to its furthest possible end point. They're sociological interrogations, the work of someone who wants to know: How badly can these characters behave before an audience will turn on them?

What's more, nothing in an Elaine May film is what it appears to be on the surface, including her female characters. They may not be robust, but they're not the flat caricatures her critics would like to believe. Henrietta contains multitudes: She may want to marry a man who clearly views her with contempt, but she doesn't have to—she has her own money—and she may lack confidence, but she's good at her job and loves it, and despite her timid nature, can at least whisper that she wants recognition for it. Elaine's performance infuses her—and the rest of *A New Leaf*—with an undercurrent of sad sweetness, a thread that Jeannie picks up, under her direction, in *The Heartbreak Kid.* Lila is grating and obnoxious, but there's undeniable warmth granted to her, a sense of humanity that this is a real person, and not some shtick. "Are you going to be grouchy for the next fifty years?" she asks early on, quietly, a little hurt that this is what she got on her wedding night. It becomes a constant refrain: "I married a grouch," she mutters, less a sitcom catchphrase than a quiet realization of her own very real and valid disappointment. She's no idiot. She knows what's going on. All she wanted was to live a quiet, ordinary—dull, even—but happy life, and the man she trusted to give it to her has no intentions of sticking around to do so.

Quart wasn't entirely wrong in speculating that Elaine's cinematic vision was shaped by her past wounds. After all, Elaine had been working for fifteen years, so her perspective—and the fact that it would never change—should have been clear. It's not that Elaine hates women, it's just the fact that she's an equal opportunist when it comes to ridicule, thoroughly unconcerned with the likability of *any* of her characters, regardless of gender. Still, there's a generosity afforded to her women that isn't applied to her men. There's always an acknowledgment that they're "good girls," that their treatment by the men in their lives is undoubtedly cruel, although it's never empathized with so much as presented as a simple recognizable fact. In Elaine's eyes, she's not passing judgment; she's merely reflecting her vision of reality. And anyway, maybe it's a good thing they remain so unexplored, that their pressure points aren't pushed repeatedly. If Henrietta and Lila were considered offensive, what would they make of a fully realized female character in Elaine's world, one who was just as awful as any of her men?

In retrospect, there's a hollowness to the feminist critiques of the time, the way rhetoric is warped and weaponized. Statements like "She's been there, as they say. She knows what's at stake" reverberate in the empty language of girl power feminism of today, the derisive "as a fellow woman" critique that to be less than praiseful and supportive of other women, regardless of their individual behavior, makes someone antifeminist. It is fair to be personally disappointed that an artist's work does not reflect your personal values, but it is also unfair to expect them to in the first place. How fair—or feminist, really—was it to demand Elaine make films that were about women, or depict women in a way that met one group's unexpressed standards, simply because she was a woman? Isn't that just another form of sexism in and of itself? And besides, were they familiar with any of her past work? What exactly did they expect from her? Elaine had no interest in making an identity film simply for the sake of asserting her own identity. No, there had to be something more compelling than just gender to interest her. When asked, in 1975, if she would ever make a film about a woman, she said, "If it was an interesting film I'd be interested. I wouldn't be interested in directing because it was about a woman. I don't think anybody would unless it was to exploit some star or some market."[92]

True representation means allowing women the freedom to create anything, not just art that is kind to or about her own gender. So maybe Elaine's feminine sensibilities *were* nonexistent. But is that such a bad thing? Their absence allowed her to hold true to her singular vision, refusing to be siloed into what was expected of her as a woman, and in doing so, proving to male gatekeepers that women were indeed capable of making films about *any* subject—including men.

But if second-wave feminist critics hated her now, they could just wait. There would be more to blame Elaine for before the decade was over.

CHAPTER 7

Two Stolen Reels and a Clown Car

Mikey and Nicky (1976)

Barry Diller is not a particularly large man, but on a summer afternoon in 1975, sitting under a sloped ceiling in the back seat of a tiny Ford Pinto, effectively held hostage by Elaine at the wheel, the then CEO of Paramount seemed mammoth.

Diller was in the hot seat, but he wasn't the only one on edge. *The Heartbreak Kid*'s success served as proof that Elaine was now "a major American director,"[1] that the mishaps on *A New Leaf* were just the flubs of someone extremely green. A second film with as few on- or off-set shenanigans as *The Heartbreak Kid* indicated that she had figured it out somewhere along the way, how to make a good movie without losing control in the process, right? Or maybe it was just wishful thinking.

Paramount and Elaine approached their second chance at a working relationship with more caution than optimism; when signing the thirty-three-page contract to produce *Mikey and Nicky* in 1973, both added special clauses to protect their own interests. The studio, wary about embarking on another unending production, issued strict stipulations about the time and money Elaine would be granted. A delivery deadline was set for June 1, 1974; any costs that exceeded the approved $1.8 million budget would come out of Elaine's fee; once she ran 15 percent over, they could take over the film.[2] Elaine, in return, would get the highly coveted final cut and would have to deal only with Paramount president Frank Yablans—who was so in her corner that he agreed to play a hit man in the film before he was subsequently pulled—and wouldn't have to set foot on the Paramount lot. But by late 1974, Yablans was out (the foray into acting with one of the studio's most unmanageable auteurs didn't sit well with Paramount's Wall Street investors), Diller was in, and *Mikey and Nicky*'s budget was pushing $4.3 million. Now a year late on her delivery deadline, Elaine looked at her negotiation options. She rented a Ford Pinto.[3]

But let's go back to how we got here.

The center could not hold for long. With *A New Leaf* a modest enough financial success, and *The Heartbreak Kid* an even greater one, Elaine realized she had acquired a bit of power in an industry whose top priority was not creativity, but the bottom line: "If it made good money Paramount would invest in it. If Hitler were alive today, as somebody said, I guarantee you, twenty million at the box office," she cracked.[4] The box office returns from her past two films not only buoyed her own confidence in her directing abilities but earned trust from the studios as well. "The first movie, they thought I was insane," she said. "The second movie, after the first movie made money, they thought I had my way."[5] Having proved her "special way," she set her sights on her past for her next project, all the way back to work that had followed her ever since her days in Chicago.

Chronicling one endless night between two estranged best friends, low-ranking mob men who double-cross each other, *Mikey and Nicky* was not only one of Elaine's earliest pieces, but her most personal one. That draft on scrap paper stowed away in the baby buggy she brought with her when she showed back up at Playwrights in 1954? That was *Mikey and Nicky*.[6]

It was a story born out of personal history and practical need. At the Compass, improvisations would often simply run out, leaving actors to their own devices to fill time with one-acts instead. Elaine leapt at the opportunity to have her work seen, even if it was an opportunity driven more by desperation than by an invitation. "I thought, 'What can I do with two guys and no scenery?' . . . I had no ambition to write about gangsters; there were just people in the company who could do that," she explained.[7] Whether or not she intended to write about gangsters, the subject material was certainly something she knew about firsthand.

Peter Falk recalled Elaine telling the story to him in one long night on the set of *Luv* back in 1967. "It was based on real people in a real neighborhood, people that were close to her, whom she had known since she was a child," he said. "She remembered it very vividly and it caused in her a need to write it. I thought it was a helluva story."[8]

"The Syndicate was very big in Chicago, and [my family was] sort of part of it. My uncle was very good friends with an Italian guy who once blew up a cleaning store because they were rude to my aunt Fanny," Elaine explained. These small-time gangsters, the ones just trying to make enough money to get by and maybe open their own booking joint one day, only ever took out hits on those in their innermost circles. They were paranoid men; because only their most trusted confidants were close enough to have access, it was almost a given that your best friend could eventually be your killer.

Once again, Elaine returned to her fascination with the complexities of interpersonal relationships, the tenuous ways we build trust with one another while betrayal remains plainly inevitable. "You know, we're kind of primitive and then we learn sort of not to be," she reasoned. "Civilization teaches us something and really rouses us, or else we would just kill each other. But these guys don't have that overlay. Nobody teaches them that other way. They have a code. God knows what it is, 'cause it's constantly broken, but they live by it—and they break it. They have a perverted sense of what honor is, but they *do* have a sense of what honor is."[9] In her titular characters, who feel an equal pull of an obligation to kill to protect their leader and to kill to protect themselves—and the constant need to police that delicate balance—Elaine felt a kindred spirit: "I recognize that in me," she said, "but I'm fortunately too weak to carry it out."[10]

Whereas other characters Elaine used to explore the nuances of imperfect relationships in her films were purely fictional, whether derived from outside source material like the short stories *A New Leaf* and *The Heartbreak Kid* were based on or from her own mind, like the to-come *Ishtar, Mikey and Nicky* stands apart. These men were real: "I don't know if they're interesting as characters, but they were interesting to me as people. I can't tell you why they behave that way, but I really can tell you—I've hardly ever said this firmly about something that I've done—that that's truly what they're like."[11]

IF *MIKEY AND NICKY* is based on people Elaine knew, then it's worth bringing up the one whom it was not, at least not explicitly, about: Mike Nichols. If you made this assumption, you wouldn't be the only one. It's so obvious that the very nature of its *too* obviousness makes it seem all the more plausible. Why would Elaine, direct as she is, bother to beat around the bush? Bestowing the name of her former best friend on her protagonists, then forcing the characters in the film to reckon with their complicated—often treacherous— relationship, seems, on the surface at least, like a thinly veiled attempt at a two-hour-long dig at her own ex-partner.

Mikey and Nicky confronts the nature of childhood friendships, the people we keep in our lives long after we've outgrown them simply because they know things about us that no one else can ever really understand. These people were there for our transformational events, big and small, the ones we can now only recount memories of for spouses and new acquaintances. They know all shades of who we are and who we once were, not just the polished version we present to the world. Maybe we hate them, maybe they're not good for us, but how much—if at all—does our shared history outweigh all that?

Mike and Elaine were not friends since childhood, but pretty close, especially given the fact that neither had a real childhood of their own. Embarking on the climb to fame together as young people on the cusp of adulthood, putting each other before spouses and children as they traveled from club to club, show to show, night after night, then arriving suddenly at a surreal moment of unexpected stardom—this was an experience unique to them, and them alone. No one else can understand what it was like, not really. They can just hear the stories. If Elaine and Mike were paired rocket ships, at a certain point, their paths had to diverge or they'd run the risk of collision. Much like Mikey and Nicky, one ascended higher and faster, leaving the other—who, depending on who you ask, had more sheer talent but not enough dealmaking charisma—behind. As Nichols climbed through Hollywood's ranks, the distance between the two inevitably grew. Things could never and would never be quite the same.

The parallels binding fiction and reality together are undoubtedly strong, but not strong enough to form the entire foundation of a film. Early in *Mikey and Nicky*'s history, murmurs floated around that it was loosely based on Nichols's and May's own relationship; they continue to occasionally resurface today, even after being dismissed. It's easy to see how Nichols and May were set up to be read in reference to each other (even shipped, if you will),[12] with people creating narratives where there sometimes aren't any. They were attractive; they had off-the-charts "will they or won't they? did they or didn't they?" sexual tension (a reminder: they did); and their lives were forever entangled even decades after their professional split. To even the casual fan, theirs is a relationship brimming with intrigue; more than half a century after they burst into the public consciousness, there are still gaps in the story, more questions than we have answers for. Of course, part of the reason they continue to be talked about is because their story has never been told the whole way through. It's a story told mostly from one side—Nichols's—and, even then, it's not complete. We are always trying to figure them all the way out, even though we can't.

It's natural for the mind to wander when trying to fill in the holes with a little creative nonfiction, especially when the subjects give you so little to work with in the first place that they almost, in a way, make it easy. But at the same time, come on. These people—and this production—are dramatic enough on their own. They don't need us to grasp for or create revenge theories to amplify the chaos even more. What's more, to distill Elaine's original script down to a flattened "it's really about her ex" doesn't give her enough credit as a writer or a filmmaker capable of crafting a nuanced portrayal of unfamiliar experiences without relating them back to a romantic entanglement of her own.

The truth is that *Mikey and Nicky* isn't the thinly veiled revenge narrative many believe it to be. Certain emotions and dynamics may have been loosely pulled from their relationship, but the similarities stop there. The real story isn't as sexy as many hoped it would be. In fact, it's downright pedestrian. By the time *Mikey and*

Nicky began filming, the two were on terms as good as they had ever been.

Elaine only ever seemed to damage professional relationships, not personal ones. Even today, most who found themselves on the receiving end of her sharp judgments or at the mercy of her deficient leadership on set hold no hard feelings. If anything, they speak of her with great fondness and amusement. Elaine, it appears, would behave badly to get what she wanted when it came to work, but it's no coincidence that her personal relationships escaped relatively unscathed. Loyalty and trust mattered deeply to Elaine. Her characters may betray others, but she would never do this. Most of all, not when it came to Mike.

MIKEY AND NICKY opens with Nicky (John Cassavetes) holed up in a fleabag Philadelphia hotel, on the brink of a nervous breakdown, dirty and drenched in sweat, looking like he hasn't slept in days and wincing in ulcer-ridden pain. Thank god you can only see him and not smell him, though Elaine's portrait is so unflinchingly visceral you can almost feel the walls of his stale, piss-stained room closing in around you. Convinced there's a hit out on him after he stole from his mob boss, he contacts the one person he thinks can help him: longtime—but estranged—best friend Mikey (Falk). Mikey, with all his level-headed charm, manages to talk Nicky out of his room and tries to plan his escape from town, but Nicky—in a fit of mania or, so certain these are his last hours alive, an attempt at a last hurrah—changes plans constantly, leading Mikey to one maddening destination after the other. All the while, a hit man is hot on their trail—and Mikey might be the one leaving the bread crumbs. Their endless night together reveals, in slow, brutal layers, the ugly truths, betrayals, and regrets that plague their friendship as they inch their way toward whatever daylight brings.

To anyone who has ever had to greenlight a project, particularly in Hollywood, the concept sounds promising on paper. The setup seems to be a buddy comedy: two Mafia men played by Falk and Cassavetes—the *Columbo* star and the prolific independent screenwriter, actor, and director—stuck together for one long night, trying to avoid getting killed or killing each other in an original Elaine

May film. *The Godfather*, but funny. Early publicity for the picture would define it as "the story of a life-long friendship, compressed into a half-dropped Halloween mask of a comedy."[13] Elaine herself alluded to a comedic tone when asked, by *The New York Times* in 1971, if the film would be similar to her first two features: "I certainly hope so. It's the story of a very loose Italian and a very uptight Jewish guy who grow up together and work their way into the numbers racket. When one of them discovers he's going to be 'hit' by the organization for embezzling, he begs his old friend to get him out of town, and then things really start popping."[14]

Of course, Elaine's tilted perspective would put a refreshingly dangerous twist on the buddy concept, opening it up to the same sort of examination of broken men and the trails of collateral damage that follow in their wake that she used to revive the romantic comedy with her two previous features. Sure, the first one ended up being about murder, and okay, the second revolved around infidelity, but as bleak as both got, they still, at the end of the day, could be plainly categorized as comedies, films that made people laugh, no matter how much they cringed while doing so. And maybe this production would run more like *The Heartbreak Kid* and less like *A New Leaf*. How complicated—and costly—could it possibly be to shoot a film with such a small cast and so few locations? Paramount was in for a shock: Not only was it distinctly *not* a comedy, it was far from easy to make.

The fact that *Mikey and Nicky* wasn't a comedy and was instead something much darker was just the film's first problem. "It's not *The Godfather*," Julian Schlossberg said. "Elaine wanted to show what it really was like, not how it's glamorized."[15] The film Elaine eventually turned in was much more complex than anyone could have expected, genre-hopping from neo-noir film to buddy comedy to crime drama throughout its two-hour runtime. Audiences and studio heads alike expected Elaine to make them laugh—and to be fair, in *Mikey and Nicky*, she does, but the laughs don't come easy. They are often buried in heart-wrenching moments or follow harrowing scenes, lodging themselves in the back of your throat, just as difficult to swallow as the rest of the film. Throughout filming, Elaine fretted over the possibility that the film was *too* funny, that her inability to resist writing a laugh line or finding the underlying humor in a situation was working against the dramatic tone she wanted. She worried that it would become predictable, just like what everyone expected from her.[16] Good marketing could get around all that, but to market a picture, you need a picture. Wrenching that from Elaine, though, would prove to be nearly impossible. Her perfectionism clouded the set; now coupled with Cassavetes's own demanding vision, and with no one to rein them in, it spelled trouble.

Early on, Michael Hausman, who moved up from his associate rank on *The Heartbreak Kid* to serve as one of *Mikey and Nicky*'s producers, got the sense that the production would be radically different from that of *The Heartbreak Kid*. The previous film's schedule chugged along in large part because Simon's strict contract forced her to shoot a scene and move on to the next without much delay—there were only so many ways to improvise without changing the lines. *Mikey and Nicky* had no such guardrails. It wasn't so much a premonition that it was going to go *badly,* but that "it was going to go the way Elaine, Peter, and John wanted it to go."[17]

In the decades since its making, it has been difficult to speak about *Mikey and Nicky* without talking about the myth of *Mikey and Nicky* and its notorious sprawling production that resulted in some 1.4 million feet of film. To put such an incomprehensibly large number into perspective: 1.4 million feet of film is 259 *hours* of raw footage—nearly three times the amount used to film *Gone with the Wind* (which had a final runtime nearly double that of *Mikey and Nicky*'s). It's 265 *miles* of film; the drive from New York City to Washington, D.C., is 30 miles shorter. But why so much? And how, when the shooting script ran the average industry length? Many have blamed improvisation, saying Cassavetes and Falk changed their lines from take to take and rarely followed the script, a claim Elaine has since disputed as false. "It's not possible to improvise this because, although it seems not to be, it's really plot-driven," Elaine argued. "You can only fit these small incidents that tell the relationship, and they have to be narrow and they have to really say exactly what they are going to say. You can't ad-lib around them."[18]

She's not pulling our legs, not telling a slightly altered version of the truth with that one. *Mikey and Nicky*'s shooting script is pains-takingly detailed to the point that it often reads more like a novel. The building blocks of how each scene logically progresses before reaching the climactic moment are laid out with methodical pre-cision. Not even the dialogue on-screen deviates too much from her written word; early in filming, Elaine had a note slipped under Cassavetes's hotel room door: "Elaine says learn the lines."[19] Some improvisation did occur, though not in what her characters say, but in the ways in which they say them, and, most particularly, where they are in frame when they say them.

Believing that any formal blocking would lead to unnatural re-sults, Elaine ran three cameras simultaneously and left the move-ment entirely up to her actors. If trust was one of Elaine's biggest creative drivers—something granted to her actors, who she believed were capable of drawing on their real-life friendship and level of craft to realistically portray these men on film—logic was the sec-ond. In one of *Mikey and Nicky*'s pivotal scenes, the two men get into a knock-down, drag-out brawl in the middle of a dark Philadel-phia street. On most films, the sequence would be choreographed to the nth degree, not only to protect the actors but to determine how to best capture the action on film. Elaine, though, eschewed the use of a fight coordinator; every fight scene she'd ever seen in movies never seemed real to her—rather, derived from artificial de-pictions of violence in old Westerns. The real-world logic mattered to her: "I just let them go. They knew they knew they weren't going to punch. I've never seen a fight—and I've seen them—where a guy punched a guy. They push, they wrestle."[20]

For her actors, her specific, unpredictable direction was a boon. In his memoir, Falk details a moment of difficulty he had while film-ing one pivotal emotional scene, a continuation of an intense scene shot nearly two weeks earlier. Falk was having trouble recapturing that specific set of emotions. The first take was weak, as were the following two or three. Just before a new take began, Elaine pulled him aside. "I want to remind you of something," she whispered. Falk leaned in closer to hear her, put his arm around her waist, his cheek to her cheek. He didn't hear her say anything. Instead, after a split second of confusion, he felt the sensation of teeth—Elaine's teeth!—on his lip. "My first thought was this is a gag," he wrote, "but then it started to hurt and I was about to push her when she suddenly, savagely, sank her teeth as deep as they could go into my lip. I was in the middle of my scream when I heard Elaine in her small voice say to the cameraman, 'Action.'"[21] The following take was not only a winner; it left Falk stunned with awe, admiration, and appreciation.

As for Cassavetes, the two had become friends before the production began, having met when, according to Elaine, the filmmaker tried to give her a $10,000 grant from Screen Gems, and ever suspicious of a good thing, she turned him down.[22] When Falk asked Cassavetes if he'd be interested in the script, Cassavetes had only three questions: "Are you gonna be in it? Did she write it? Is she gonna direct it?"[23] When filming began, the two were in constant consultation, discussing not only Cassavetes's performance but his opinions on the script and the shot list for the day.

While "letting them go" was an artistic choice that benefited the actors, behind the scenes, it was a logistical nightmare. God help any unhoused drunk who stumbled across the set; if Elaine caught sight of them, they became material. "The old man Elaine sees. 'I like him. Let's use him.' Drunk. Doesn't know what's going on. Really frightened when John Cassavetes points a gun at him. Kicks him in the rear. Twice. They do the scene twice. Gave him $10 and a pack of beer. Old man says, 'I feel sorry for you.' Elaine says, 'He's only projecting our pity for him,'" unit publicist Tom Miller recalled. Even interior shots were filmed at night because, Method to their core, they believed they'd act more convincingly then. The entire set would have to be lit—because Elaine would never give them clear marks, and no two scenes were performed the same way—for the cameraman to truly capture the action.[24] It wasn't unusual for her to fully commit to playing others' parts off camera when directing the supporting actors' sides. On one instance, filming a scene with the man playing the hotel clerk, "Elaine would dash into the elevator, close the doors, and then Sy would run over, deliver a screaming, reprimanding speech and pound on the elevator doors. A pause. Then this voice sounding far, far away—Elaine, unseen in the elevator, still directing, would yell 'Cut.'"[25] Then there was the ill-fated occasion someone dared yell "cut" in place of the director. Cassavetes and Falk, having finished a scene, walked away from the camera until they were out of frame: "After about seventy-five yards, Peter and John take a left. There's no one on-screen, so the cameraman yells cut," Hausman says. "Elaine comes up to him and says, 'Why did you yell cut!?' He says, 'There's no one in the street.' The film is still rolling. She says, 'Don't ever cut. They may come back.'"[26]

"There's a big technical side to the visual stuff, which she could never master," Paul Sylbert, the film's production designer, explained. "She can't light a cigarette without burning her hand. She works on impulses, intuitions. It's easy to do on a typewriter, but impossible to do when you have other people standing around."[27] Elaine herself would go along with that. "I'm not a pro as a director," she claimed at the time. "I'm a pro at thinking about movies. I'm a pro at talking about them. You ask me anything about a movie and I can answer you in movie language: budget, schedule, gross, net, distribution. I'm a pro at that."[28]

But it was not her own technical ineptitude or intuitive way of working that Elaine blamed for the excessive amount of material or the seemingly unending shoot. If the studio was so upset about the extravagance of it all, she tried to claim that the call was coming from inside the house: "They kept canceling the movie, 'cause they kept looking at the dailies and seeing that it wasn't a comedy. And then we would be off. We would go off, we would start."[29] Was the studio really responsible for the erratic stop-start nature of the shoot? "Forget about it! Paramount didn't shut it down," Hausman says, shooting down her thin excuse.[30] Instead, he counters, it was Elaine's own erratic behavior that served as the conductor of the runaway train *Mikey and Nicky*'s production was quickly becoming.

Elaine was running herself into the ground, sometimes editing until late in the morning after filming all night. She was exhausted, living off yogurt and protein drinks, and impossible to get through to or keep on any sort of schedule.[31] Everyone was held to her exacting standards, whether it was her assistant or,[32] often finding herself dissatisfied with what she saw in the dailies, the cameramen she repeatedly fired.[33] By the time it was finished, *Mikey and Nicky* had five credited directors of photography, with a few more working without credit, including Hausman, a group of teenagers Cassavetes found who "looked like delinquents from the street,"[34] and Cassavetes himself, who had his own ideas about what the film should look like and how it should be shot. On one night shoot, Cassavetes turned off all the lighting, much to the gaffer's exasperated objection, swearing it would turn out brilliantly when the print was finished. The next day, Hausman recalls, the crew gathered to look at the footage. "The comments were like: 'Oh, there he is. Oh, no, no—that's not him. Oh, I think I see him. No, that's the door. It was all black. You couldn't see anything."[35]

The paranoid energy of the film permeated the set. Unit publicist Tom Miller was instructed to stay out of Elaine's sight for the entirety of his time on the production for fear she'd think Paramount was spying on her.[36] He left it never having met her. "Me, the unit publicist. Sort of shows you what she thinks about publicity during the making of a film, right?" he wrote.[37] But not even he could stop curious reporters from prying. Dan Rottenberg, then a reporter for the *Chicago Tribune,* snuck onto the Philadelphia set and observed some of its chaos firsthand: Elaine, standing in the middle of the street, chain-smoking and arguing with Hausman about the scene that's scheduled to shoot in a few hours:

> All May wants to do is move the scene from South Street to Front Street, around the corner. . . . The crew had spent several days on South Street putting up false storefronts and arranging the lights. . . . This change will require the crew to move the lights and create a few more phony stores . . . and to repave a stretch of Front Street. Oh, and if it isn't too much trouble, May would like all this done tonight, so a few takes of the scene can be shot before the sun comes up.[38]

When compromise did come, it wasn't easy. At the start of shooting, Elaine intended to film one long scene in a sprawling Philadelphia graveyard. On a summer night, this proved to be a problem. Soundman Chris Newman informed Elaine and Hausman that there were too many crickets; they'd make getting good sound nearly impossible. Reluctantly, they moved the next night to the nearby Woodland Cemetery. At this site, situated near a major interstate, they had an even bigger problem to deal with. The sound of overnight trucking traffic could be heard from the set. Hausman and a production assistant set up shop with walkie-talkies on the side of the highway, using free coffee to win over the truckers, who stopped long enough for Elaine to run a few takes.[39] They pulled it off somehow, but she didn't make it easy for them.

Elaine didn't deal in quick takes. Hers stretched on impossibly long, long enough that a thousand-foot load of film—which lasted roughly ten minutes—would nearly run out by the time each was done. Director of photography Victor Kemper remembers a situation like this happening that night in the cemetery. During one take, he warned Elaine that the film was running low, but she emphatically warned him not to cut. Not wanting to upset her while she was entranced with the scene in front of her, he decided it best not to say anything when, sure enough, the camera ran out. Somewhere around the fourteen-minute point of the scene, Cassavetes must have realized that time had stretched on too long and broke character. He asked Elaine if they were still rolling. What Kemper says next is the key to Elaine's on-set style: she didn't care. She loved the work he and Falk were doing so much that she wanted them to finish even if they weren't being filmed. The work they were doing, the emotions they were exploring in character, were more important than the end result. Later, deep into the editing process, Elaine asked Kemper what happened to the footage of that one perfect take. She hadn't remembered that none of it was actually caught on film.[40]

Of course Elaine had her own distinct vision of what the film should look like and how her actors should perform; it had been brewing in her mind for the past twenty-odd years. But she and Cassavetes—"we became friends because he felt that I was more insane than he was"—fed off each other's energy, with no one else on set strong enough to rein either of them in. According to Elaine, Cassavetes's only demand on the film was "that he be good." He could deal with breakdowns on set, late shoots, changed plans, even having to helm the camera for a bit himself. "But if he thought he wasn't good in a take, he would walk."[41] Elaine found this demand reasonable—after all, she had had the same exacting standards for herself as an actress when filming *A New Leaf*—but meeting both of their demands proved to be impossible to do on an industry average shoot. By the time filming had completed in both Philadelphia and Los Angeles, the production had ballooned from $1.8 million to nearly $4.3 million spread across 120 days. And the difficulty wasn't about to stop there.

ELAINE SET UP shop in West Hollywood's Sunset Marquis, where she and her team turned half of the hotel's grand floor into their own editing lab, with two rooms and a full-time librarian dedicated to storing and cataloging the insurmountable bulk of film alone. It quickly became clear that cutting this behemoth would be an all-hands-on-deck situation. Her crew grew to nearly a dozen people who worked in double shifts six days a week, often editing into the early hours of morning.[42]

"There was always something going on at the Sunset Marquis," says critic Todd McCarthy, who began his career in Hollywood as Elaine's assistant on *Mikey and Nicky*.[43] While Elaine and her team edited in one set of suites, Miloš Forman was doing preproduction for *One Flew Over the Cuckoo's Nest* out of another. Russ Meyer and Roger Ebert set up workspaces and residencies there, and it wasn't unusual to see David Bowie hanging around. The windows in *Mikey and Nicky*'s swath of rooms were sealed shut with black vinyl and tape to keep out the light,[44] but the door to the suite was always open; you never knew who would walk into the endless night, welcome or not. On one occasion, deep into the early morning hours (for those who were keeping track), an unknown and uninvited guest sat down to watch the editors in action. When the stranger ignored Elaine's requests to leave—"I'm enjoying what I'm watching. Just keep going"—Elaine finally turned around and said, "Well, then. Take off your pants." He didn't stay much longer.[45]

The process, to Paramount's horror, stretched on for more than a year. Editing suited Elaine. She was good at it; with a writer's eye for structure, she actually enjoyed the granular process of taking the story apart and putting it back together in as many varying combinations as possible, sometimes wanting to see ten or twelve different cuts of the same scene. With a typewriter, this process is easy. With film, though, it takes time.

"Working with her was like an advanced course in editing," says editor Sheldon Kahn. Together they would work long nights side by side. Most directors would give edit orders with clear objectives for what each scene should convey. Elaine, though, viewed editing more as another tool for discovery than as a means to a predetermined end. "You were able to go through and try the scene this way, try the scene that way, try the scene another way, and all that kind of stuff before deciding on which way is probably the best way to put the scene together for an audience."[46] Twelve cuts would be done of a single scene in the span of a week; she'd decide on the third version—remembering every frame of it. Initially hired for a four-week stint to sync dialogue with night shoots, Kahn, Elaine discovered, was a natural fit who worked well with her. He ended up staying on the film for nearly eighteen months. Once, when his children came to visit, upon meeting Elaine for the first time, his daughter asked, "'Miss May, why don't you ever let my daddy come home?' I got to tell you, it's the first time in my life that Elaine had no answer."[47]

Her work was as erratic as it was obsessive. "Her ideas moved so fast through her mind that she would not complete one thought before going on to the next thought," Kahn says. "She would be explaining to me how the scene should be put together, but not completing the thought, and therefore I didn't know what to do. But I would sit there and listen to her and listen to her, because she'd come back to the first idea, back to finishing the thought on everything."[48] It didn't take long for him to learn to speak her language. She would often disappear for hours at a time at night to shoot B-roll footage of downtown L.A. with Cassavetes. Returning to the hotel after the editors had gone home, the two would undo everything that had been accomplished that day.[49] Rarely did she socialize with anyone other than Cassavetes, Falk, and Jeannie, who had a suite of her own at the hotel. David came to visit, although the pair had become less than together. She rarely would break to have dinner with him when he was around; sometimes she sent Kahn in her place instead. "He came into town to be with her," Kahn says, "but when she was working, she was working."[50]

Preoccupied, she subsisted on health food McCarthy delivered periodically.[51] She was too suspicious to let hotel maids near her suite—strewn with books and clothes, old food, and film cans full of cigarette ash—so it had to be aired out for two days when she left.[52] Her mood was determined by what she was smoking, McCarthy recalls. She chain-smoked cigarettes when things were running *smoothly*. You'd know things were getting dicey once she pulled out her skinny Schimmelpenninck cigars. And if the shit had really, truly, hit the fan, she would puff away on oversize cigars that were fit for Orson Welles but looked downright comedic hanging from Elaine's mouth.[53] According to one account, Paramount executives began to joke that the only way they'd be able to get to Elaine was through the county health department.[54]

The oft-repeated portrait of Elaine as the obsessive recluse *is* entertaining, but it's shaded with damning judgment that makes it difficult to consume with the same kind of giddy delight as most gossip. Elaine is certainly not the first artist—not even the first director—to devote herself so fully to a project that it supersedes her own desire or ability to take care of herself. After all, is that not the kind of behavior we often hold up as being that of geniuses? But if such behavior is considered a trait of geniuses, then it takes us to the question of who is allowed in that club, and if granted access, who gets slotted into a special category of "mad" genius. More often than not, women are sectioned off as such, allowed to be geniuses only if their brilliance drives them crazy. And their madness—perceived or otherwise—will cost them something sooner or later. Genius can explain away the problems of men time and time again; it's rarely that simple for women.

"We think she didn't want to finish it," an anonymous source speculated in 1976, "because she had worked on it so long it had become her whole life. She loved editing it. They would come down to the cutting room and she'd say, 'Today we're going to do the last scene.' But she'd never do it."[55]

Perhaps by dragging out the edit stage of the film, Elaine was trying to achieve a kind of unattainable perfection, getting the film to match the exact way it had played in her head for so many years. Or maybe there was safety in forever being at work on something that was known, something that was concrete, staving off the depression that follows the completion of any major project. If she never finished it, she never had to face the dreaded question of what's next. Elaine's paralyzing indecisiveness never resulted from the question of what she should do. Instead, she had too many gifts and options in front of her, so her indecisiveness stemmed from a tougher question: What *shouldn't* she do? It was an endless calculation of just how much rope she could use before reaching the end.

Elaine was well aware of the possibility that being a maverick attempting to just say "fuck it" in an environment that regarded artistic work "like a credit rating" would not always work in her favor. "You experiment and you fall on your ass," she said in a rare appearance at the New School in 1975. Chain-smoking her way through the evening, hopped up on Benadryl and red wine, she was in an uncharacteristically truth-telling mood: "The world does not offer it to you, no. This country does not offer it to you. It's a bad setup for people who are in the arts. It's really hard to work here."[56] If endlessly editing was a way to delay the possibility of failure, then it backfired, dooming *Mikey and Nicky* before it even had a chance to succeed.

Or maybe it was just a matter more technical and less dramatic than that: "Do you really want to know why *Mikey and Nicky* has taken six and a half years to complete?" she asked the New School audience. By this time, the film was still nearly a year away from its eventual release. "The sound! Somehow, something went wrong with the sound. And that's the truth. I wish I could say I was probing for artistic truths. Actually, I'm just trying to get it so you can hear it." It was one of many excuses she gave Diller during the prolonged process of his "repeated attempts to be able to see the film."[57] The audience clapped when she revealed she thought she had finally gotten it down; Elaine cut them short with an ominous warning: "Don't applaud. Wait'll you see it."[58]

The sound *was* a hopeless, staggering mess. And it wasn't because of on-location incidents like that time in the cemetery, but because Elaine had been persuaded that it would be beneficial to record the sound on two tracks, one for each of the principal actors. With over two hundred hours of separate tracks that wouldn't mesh together or match with what was happening on-screen, post-production fell even further behind.

Finally, Paramount put their foot down. Hausman had succeeded in keeping the production afloat for some time, but enough was enough: "Finally I said, 'Well, we've got to see the results of wherever you are, however you can get it together,'" Diller says.[59] Still only about a fourth of the way through the sound mix, Hausman and Elaine scrambled to pull together something presentable by the next day. The viewing started off fine enough, but when the third reel went up: silence. Elaine improvised. Reel after reel, she verbally performed the soundtrack of the film, mimicking the voices of Falk and Cassavetes, slamming doors, and honking cars. It was entertaining, but in no way was it enough to make up for the fact that she was now a year past her delivery date, the film was still far from finished, and Diller's patience was quickly running out.[60]

Which brings us back to the Ford Pinto.

Elaine decided to negotiate. "She disappeared for two days, and then came out and said, 'Todd, rent me a Ford Pinto,'" says McCarthy. "Elaine spent two days trying to figure out, 'How can I get the upper hand here with Barry Diller and get myself more time?'"[61] Knowing she didn't have to set foot on the Paramount lot, she acquiesced to lunch with Diller—but she'd pick him up. "I think, of her waking hours, the majority of her time was spent concocting avoidance strategies to do what someone else was expecting her to do," McCarthy says. She and Hausman forced Diller into the back seat of the Pinto, whereupon they drove with him to one of downtown L.A.'s greasy spoons—"one of their favorite divey places where winos and drug addicts were hanging out"—in hopes of causing enough discomfort in him to eke out a desperate, exasperated extension from him.[62] No one remembers what words were spoken that day. If you ask Diller, he doesn't even recall the event happening in the first place,[63] though he admits that Elaine and company "tried everything they could, simply because she wasn't really ready—or didn't want—to screen the film."[64] Who knows *what* Elaine could have possibly said to talk her way out of the mess she had gotten herself into, but somehow, both parties came to a tentative agreement. The film would be completed and delivered by September 15, 1975.[65]

But on September 26, Elaine was not only *not* done; she was now in New York, where she had spent the rest of the summer editing,[66] and she was asking for another $180,000 to finish.[67] "Once she was on something, it was very, very, very difficult for her to give it up and let it go through the systems that you have to do. You finish your editing, and then you hand it off to the postproduction people and then the distribution people," says McCarthy.[68] But everything about handing over the movie "made her worried and paranoid. She felt that other people had it in for her, or that they were going to somehow rubbish her work or something."[69] To her, $180,000 was nothing compared to what Paramount had sunk into the project already, and it would enable her to get *her* version done. To Paramount—and Diller—it was her final strike. The games were "a distraction" for him, he says. "I was running a fairly large movie and television operation and somewhat as a side job was trying to rescue this footage, so to speak, so it took time away from my real job."[70] Things couldn't keep going on like this forever, which was what it looked like would happen if Elaine got her way. The studio ordered that she bring the film to them, where, under her supervision, staff editors would finish what she started—but in less time and for far less money. As if Elaine—who hadn't for a moment forgotten what they had done to *A New Leaf*—would ever let that happen. The ensuing fuckery is the stuff of legend, what critics focused the bulk of their initial review upon and what outlived, until recently, the film itself.

"Why should I be loyal to a big mountain with some stars around it?" she is claimed to have said.[71] No one—not even Paramount—was going to take Elaine's film away from her without her consent. So she sold it. The price: $90,000. The buyer: an unknown production company called Alyce Films. For a minute, it seemed like she had cleverly kept the upper hand. Then the lawsuits started.

Furious at her disloyalty, Paramount sued Elaine for breach of contract (*of course* they sued her for breach of contract); Elaine countersued, arguing that the studio was willing to, indeed wanted to, sabotage all the work she had done simply because it had been started under the direction of Yablans. It was quickly discovered that Alyce Films was little more than a front for Peter Falk and a number of Elaine's friends and associates.[72] According to Diller, Elaine's lawyer, Bert Fields, "rigged a scheme where it passed from person to person so no one could be held responsible."[73] Likely hoping they'd luck out with a settlement, they were no match for Paramount's legal department. Elaine lost (*of course* she lost; she couldn't possibly have thought she'd get away with that thin argument, could she have?) and was forced by a New York judge to hand over the film.[74] Which she did. Sort of.

New York sheriffs were sent, guns drawn, to the editing studio to collect the film, protocol Elaine found hilarious in its excessiveness: "I'm sorry to laugh," she said years later when telling the story, "but it's *a movie*."[75] The problem was, two reels were missing, without which the film couldn't be completed. The scandal quickly escalated Paramount's lawsuit in New York's Supreme Court, as the studio charged Elaine and David Rubinfine with criminal contempt. According to court documents, less than an hour after Paramount ordered the removal of the film, Elaine—who had been instructed by Fields to give her editing staff the day off and leave town[76]—went to Rubinfine's apartment to consult him. That night, he went to the postproduction suite and "removed between eight and twelve cartons" that he hid in his car trunk. The next day he drove them to the home of a psychiatrist friend in Connecticut;[77] jurisdiction wouldn't allow New York sheriffs to cross state lines. But it was a messy heist. After leaving Connecticut, Rubinfine called Peter Falk, who told Rubinfine to tell his friend that someone would come pick up the reels. Falk, brought into the lawsuit under allegations of aiding and abetting, wouldn't admit or deny his marching orders. "I might have said it," he acknowledged.[78] Somehow, things would get only more complicated: Once the reels were picked up, they disappeared entirely, with *everyone* involved swearing they weren't in on this part. Elaine's best defense was to play dumb and pray a technicality would get her off: She couldn't possibly be guilty, because she had no idea about the court order. She and David hadn't been personally served; it was her attorney who had received the papers.[79] In recent years, this act of unwavering fuck-you bravado has won Elaine almost unanimous admiration. If only she'd accept it.

SEE, ELAINE REMEMBERS things differently. Her retelling remains vague, avoiding nearly all association with the theft and letting herself off the hook with relatively clean hands, despite what facts were committed to court record. According to Elaine, "someone" stole the reels; she doesn't know who it was or where they kept them, just that, when she put out word for their return, they came back in one piece.[80] Things were solved by Fields, who was just as secretive. "He was what you always thought Perry Mason was," Elaine said. "He did everything, and he did it without pay because I had no money. I paid him, finally, a year later, but he didn't know I would."[81] In her version of the story, she presents herself as a hapless bystander. It's a role she'd often assume when finding herself backed into a corner, presenting herself as "kooky and fragile, a delicate flower, someone unequipped to deal with the real world."[82] But as a filmmaker who is intensely controlling of her work, down to the very last detail, and highly attuned to any attempts to mess with it, she can't always carry off this role convincingly.

It makes sense that she'd feign ignorance in her active years as a director as an attempt to not dig the hole she found herself in any deeper and alienate any remaining chances for work. But in recent decades, why has she remained tight-lipped, never once taking credit for an act that famous fans like Natasha Lyonne and Patton Oswalt have lauded not as self-destructive or disruptive, but as "legendary" and "punk-fucking-rock"? There's no chance for punishment anymore; the critical disdain is gone, replaced instead with acclaim for having the guts to stand her ground. What's the point in not owning up to it now?

"Elaine is very secretive. I think she's paranoid," Michael Hausman suggests.[83] But paranoid of what? If there is scant criticism to fear now, then maybe it's the praise. It's an aversion that dates back to her time at the Compass, when she refused to be moved in the slightest by it. "Elaine didn't give a shit if the audience didn't like her work," Compass alum Mark Gordon remembered. "When you talk about elitism, that's her snobbery. She worried when the audience liked it too much."[84]

Elaine could take criticism, rise above it, sure that she was just smarter and better than her harshest critics; their misunderstanding her work was *their* problem, not hers. In fact, she was almost certain they wouldn't like what she had done, convinced that people were out to get her, in spite of a mountain of loyal friends and colleagues always standing behind her. ("I don't know who her real enemies were other than in her own mind," McCarthy says.)[85] Praise was a trickier beast altogether, far more complicated and unfamiliar. It might be nice if people liked what she did, but it might also mean that maybe she wasn't as intelligent as she thought. Unlike Mike, she had no desire to be a crowd-pleaser. Instead, "Elaine thought of what the audience *should* want. She didn't give a damn."[86] The more praise Elaine receives for actions previously written off as bad behavior, the harder it is for her to not only change her stance on acknowledging them but also continue to hide in anonymity. Attempting to glaze over the incident is perhaps not as much an unwillingness to take ownership of a perceived negative narrative as an attempt to just make all the attention go away so she can continue to live her life unbothered, just the way she likes it.

AS THE LAWSUITS dragged on, friends of Elaine continued their attempts to fix things on her behalf. Cassavetes advised her to flex her influence and "give a party and invite all the important people you know, including the head of the studio"[87] (She found it ridiculous and declined, though not without some palpable regret that she didn't at least try.) Warren Beatty called Barry Diller up and tried to talk him into letting it go; what was the harm in throwing a wad of—in the grand scheme of things, insignificant—cash at the situation to just get it over with? Diller refused; there was only one way Elaine was keeping her film *her* film, and that was if she did as told, returned the missing reels and worked on the Paramount lot. "She is a brilliant woman and a wonderful woman," he said, "but she can go to jail or the madhouse for ten years before I submit to blackmail!"[88]

Paramount's lawyers issued a subpoena, only to subsequently attempt to take it back after Diller realized it would be "crazy" to be "the only studio that jails a director for going over budget."[89] The New York judge was not amused by the drama playing out between Elaine and Paramount and threatened to use the court to force them to deal with this in a civil manner. Finally, Diller budged, pledging his word over the phone—though refusing to put in writing—that "things will go right for you" if she would just hand over the reels. "Will you be in your office for fifteen minutes?" Elaine asked. "Someone will come with the film."[90]

Sure enough, within moments, a box of film appeared outside Diller's office. After all her stubborn refusal to work under Paramount's watchful eye, Elaine spent the fall of 1976 on the lot supervising *Mikey and Nicky*'s final cut for a December 10 release. Decades later, Elaine remains hazy on the particulars of the lawsuit; the entire ordeal, she conceded, was traumatic and exhausting, even for her: "Shel Silverstein once said to me, 'If there was an earthquake and all the film was destroyed and all the editors were destroyed, would you be happy or would you be distraught?' And I said, 'I'd be so happy.'"[91]

Years later, after she and Diller reconciled, Elaine finally asked him why he felt the need to act so harshly toward her during his time at Paramount. "He said 'I don't know.' He said I was so miserable." The only explanation she can come up with is that if she wasn't collateral damage in an ongoing feud between Yablans and Diller, then it was all one big misunderstanding. The assumption that this was a comedy had set her up for failure. Even if the studio thought they could reshape it into something lighter than it actually was, like they did on *A New Leaf,* they were outmatched. "It was a very odd movie. It was a gangster movie. It was funny only for a limited amount of time—they just didn't expect it. They didn't like it. They weren't prepared for it," she said. "I keep looking for reasons, but I never did understand it exactly. And it went on for a very long time because they couldn't recut it because they didn't have the negative. But I want to tell you that no matter how you cut this, it wasn't going to be a comedy."[92]

BY MID-DECEMBER, HAVING settled the lawsuit, Paramount knew the film needed to be released, and Julian Schlossberg, Paramount's then vice-president of worldwide acquisitions, realized that giving it a proper rollout wasn't on anyone's agenda. "It wasn't spoken about at all. What was spoken about was *King Kong* [the 1976 remake], *Marathon Man*, *Black Sunday . . . those* movies were the excitement.[93] Excited about it or not, they were obligated to put it out, though Elaine still wasn't convinced it was ready. At an industry screening in Hollywood, she went "running up the aisle to the projector's booth in her attempt to halt the screening. It didn't work, but she was given assurances that she would be able to do additional work on the film before it was released."[94] Such was not the case. A week later, a studio-approved version of *Mikey and Nicky*, rife with continuity errors, and as Elaine confirms, absolutely not a comedy, was dumped unceremoniously in theaters for a few days in December to fulfill contractual obligations. With Christmas right around the corner, they offered little more publicity than an ominous tagline: "Don't expect to like 'em." The onus of promotion fell to Schlossberg and Elaine, who, in taking up a grassroots strategy, putting up posters together all over New York City, cemented an extremely close friendship together.[95]

Mikey and Nicky played barely long enough for audiences to see it, but few critics who had a chance did so with unfavorable results. Although *The New Republic*'s Stanley Kauffmann ranked it as one of the ten best American movies of the seventies, at the time of its release the bulk of the reviews were not kind. *New York* magazine's John Simon derided her "unhealthy ability to be finished with something, to let go" and called the film "a celluloid death wish."[96] Perhaps most scathing of all was that from *New York Times* critic Vincent Canby: With the film "told in such intensely claustrophobic detail," he said, "to watch it is to risk an artificially induced anxiety attack."[97] It would not be until 1978, when she and Schlossberg bought back the rights, that Elaine would be able to release her own cut.

"Miss May is a witty, gifted, very intelligent director," Canby allowed in his review. "It took guts for her to attempt a film like this, but she failed."[98]

CANBY WAS CORRECT in that assessment; it did take guts. Films written and directed by men in which women were central characters were only just beginning to find critical and commercial success. The next logical step would have been to have women direct those types of films; only after that could women attempt to make a film about men. Elaine refused to be constrained by that slow build; she jumped straight ahead, rational timeline be damned. But *Mikey and Nicky* wasn't made in a bubble; its production directly crossed paths with the rise of women struggling to gain a stronger foothold in Hollywood.

In 1979, the Directors Guild of America enacted a task force to address the underemployment of the union's few—less than 2 percent—female members.[99] Their findings were troubling: Between 1949 and 1979, Hollywood's major distribution companies released 7,332 films, of which seven women directed fourteen, or 0.19 percent. Elaine, with her three releases—second only to Ida Lupino's seven—was responsible for 20 percent of the entirety of female-directed films in that time frame.[100] And no one seemed to care. To many producers, writers, and casting directors, profit mattered more than progress; hiring a woman over an established man wasn't a risk they were willing to take.

"The worst thing that could happen to a woman director, even at this point, is that she should have trouble on the set, go over budget, over schedule, that kind of nonsense," Verna Fields, a Universal vice-president for production, told *The New York Times* in 1978. "I think it would be very easy for a lot of people to blame it on the fact she had no control—that she didn't shoot well that day because she had her period."[101] Where Fields was sly enough to reference Elaine without a direct mention, one of Hollywood's top agents at the time, Harry Ufland, was more direct and unflinching in his take: "It's easy to blame male chauvinism, but it's quite simply that no woman except Elaine May has ever made a good movie, and her last one, *Mikey and Nicky,* never got finished. Everyone knows how brilliant she is, but no one will trust her with a film. The rest of the women's stuff I've seen is just awful."[102]

As if one round of critical backlash against *Mikey and Nicky* wasn't enough, Elaine was now facing a second wave, even larger and more insidious. The stakes were high; when one woman failed, all women suffered. And here she was, the most prominent one employed at the time, offering support to all the excuses male studio heads used to justify their unwillingness to employ women directors: They were too weak to keep up with the grueling pace of a shoot, too emotional and uncontrollable, and most of all, too stubborn and inflexible. "People who could not want to work with the women could use this as an excuse. 'Well, I've heard all about Elaine May,'" McCarthy says.[103] The progress of an entire gender was resting on Elaine's shoulders, but Elaine was not built to carry the weight. She was a small woman, iron willed but bird boned.

No one will trust her with a film. The phrase rings with a double standard, despite Ufland's protests. It's true that Elaine's behavior on *Mikey and Nicky* was erratic, even a little selfish in some ways. But she was no worse than many of her male peers, who worked without the added weight of an entire gender's progress on their minds. Francis Ford Coppola's *Apocalypse Now* premiered at Cannes as an unfinished "disaster" after more than doubling Paramount's initial $12 million budget. The principal photography alone on *The Shining* took more than a year, with Stanley Kubrick shooting upward of sixty takes of each scene, much to his actors' detriment. Martin Scorsese began big budget *New York, New York* with a plan to improvise in lieu of a finished script while deep into a cocaine addiction that would wreak havoc on the production schedule.[104] Peter Bogdanovich's *At Long Last Love*, with a complicated production that hinged on filming all musical numbers live and with a cast of primarily non-singers, was such a failure the director took out newspaper ads apologizing for the film. If any of these directors' missteps drew bad press or had landed them in director jail, their sentences didn't last very long. Meanwhile, Elaine was settling in for her first lengthy stretch behind bars, for crimes far less egregious.

If Elaine was being discriminated against for her gender, she supposed later that it was only because, well, she had acted too much like her gender. It wasn't that she was a woman, it was that she *acted* like a woman, playing nice and docile, then getting into trouble when she flipped the switch, said fuck it, and stood her ground. As a woman, you're damned if you're too nice, damned if you're not nice enough. Elaine, years later, thought it better to stick to the not-nice route from the start. "I think the real trick is, for women, start out tough," she said. "They don't start out tough. They start by saying, 'Don't be afraid of me. I'm only a woman.' And they're not *only* women, they're just as tough as guys. In that way, I think I did have trouble. But only because I seemed so pleasant."[105]

Was it Elaine, or was it just the state of the even bigger movement Hollywood was dealing with when you zoom out even further? By the late seventies, feminism was a household word, but it was no longer the hot-button issue it had been earlier in the decade. The women's lib momentum that had been building when Elaine inked her historic deal to direct *A New Leaf* had reached its crest and was now beginning to drop. Support for the Equal Rights Amendment, which had boomed throughout 1972 and 1973, slowed to a trickle, holding steady at thirty-four states ratified by 1975 after a roadblock arrived in the form of Phyllis Schlafly and conservative opposition. By 1977, not even the National Women's Conference could breathe new life into the movement; instead, then radical issues like abortion and gay rights drove away the on-the-fence women the movement needed to incorporate in order to grow. To many who had been skeptical from the start, it was beginning to appear that the women's movement was just a flash in the pan. If Washington wasn't going to prioritize gender equality, why should Hollywood?

Throughout the eighties, more female directors followed a one-and-done pattern in the studio system. Executives no longer felt obligated to commit to even an air of equity; if a woman's debut was not an enormous commercial success, it was rare she would be given the opportunity to make a second. Moderately successful men could enjoy long careers in the studio system; moderately successful women did not have the same luck. Instead, they made their way forward in independently financed features and, in growing numbers, in television and documentary work, where budgets were much smaller and easier for them to acquire.

For now, though, Elaine was done. Even if she hadn't been blacklisted, she was burned out. During that night of red-wine-induced honesty at the New School, she thought aloud about how strange it was to get paid to play make-believe, to avoid real life. "I guess it's sort of like you feel: Will they find out? I don't think it's that you enjoy it so much, as that it's something that's in your mind that you are going to impose or inflict on an enormous amount of people and get paid on top of it. And every once in a while you think, 'Well, gee, I'm getting away with it.' But not because you enjoy it, but because it's better, god knows, than a lot of other things. It's not wild fun. But what is? What is?" she asked. She couldn't deny that directing could be a physically taxing and at times tedious way to make a living, but still, it was "not as bad" as working at a shoe store.[106]

But there had to be some other option, something that fell between the brutal tedium of moviemaking and working retail, because she couldn't keep putting herself through this. Building experience hadn't taught her anything except that she'd had it better when she started, naive and unassuming of all the challenges she would face. "I was much smarter twenty years ago," Elaine said that night. "I was much smarter in my first movie than in my second. I was much smarter in my first play than in my second. The only thing I think experience teaches you is what you can't do. When you start, you think you can do anything. And then you start to get a little tired."[107]

It would be eleven years before she directed again.

CHAPTER 8

Nothing Was a Straight Line

Heaven Can Wait, Reds, and Tootsie

1976–1985

Well, wait a minute. Elaine had taken quite the hit, but she didn't stay down very long. By now she was used to the taste of blood in her mouth that accompanied the inevitable poor response to a swing and a miss. But it was personal this time. *Mikey and Nicky* wasn't just the first film she had crafted in its entirety; it was about her family. She couldn't help but be hurt that her perceived labor of love blew up in her face. Still, as upsetting as it was to have her work rejected, it would be even more upsetting *not* to work. To be a writer was to go several rounds with rejection. Win some, lose most. Wasn't that the saying? She got back up, shook herself off, and figured out what was next for her in Hollywood.

The better part of the next decade would become something of a missing period for Elaine. Her career would skew in one direction, then in another, an assemblage of jobs, but not necessarily cohesive—a flashback to her disjointed period of professional stasis just twenty years prior. She acted—as the straight woman opposite Walter Matthau in Neil Simon's *California Suite*, where she gets lost in one of the ensemble's more forgettable storylines, and later, in a return to the stage opposite Mike in *Who's Afraid of Virginia Woolf?*—and worked on developing comeback features that never materialized. She even, with Mike, took up a six-figure deal to record car commercials.[1] (Better get cash wherever she could.) Mostly, though, Elaine laid low. The wallop she had taken after *Mikey and Nicky* only granted the press-averse Elaine the ability to retreat inward even more. Here she had been handed a chance to disappear—wasn't that what she really wanted?—but she didn't take it. Not entirely, that is. Though much of the work she would do in this time was largely uncredited and behind the scenes—a form of erasure in itself—she still found herself shoulder to shoulder with some of Hollywood's most powerful players.

It all came back to the work. It all came back to redeeming herself, to reminding anyone who underestimated her that she was always the smartest one in the room. Maybe you didn't see it at first—maybe you'd see only the crazy—but she'd make sure that eventually you would. Quitting wasn't an option. Quitting meant only that *they* won, and Elaine would sooner have them kick all her teeth in, one by one, before she'd allow that to happen. No, they could laugh with her, they could laugh at the jokes she cracked—the ones she was in control of—but she refused to let them laugh *at* her. There was always work somewhere. Maybe it wouldn't be directing. Not for now, at least. For now, she'd have to keep a low profile, work with friends she could trust, and let them fight battles with the studios for her. Writing, the one thing she knew she could always rely upon, remained untouched, still there to bail her out when she needed it most. Not only was it a good fallback; it was the perfect setup for what she both wanted and needed most: anonymity. A writer, unlike an actor or even a director, could be anyone, anything, flying under the radar, nameless and faceless, taking as much or as little credit as they desired. It was the perfect solution: Even if her name wasn't on a picture, if it was good, people would know she was involved. And if it was bad? Well, for once it wouldn't be her problem. For once, she'd be able to pass the blame on to someone else.

EVER SINCE THE end of Nichols and May, Elaine's name had floated around the film industry as someone to turn to when your script needed punching up—though few actually succeeded in booking her for the job. Elaine was as picky to the point of evasive about professional commitments as she was about doing press interviews. "It seemed like every time we were having an issue with a script, [Otto Preminger] would say, 'Try and get Elaine May to doctor the script,'" Erik Lee Preminger remembers.[2] It wasn't until the

Premingers' third picture together, 1971's *Such Good Friends,* that they had any luck. In production limbo for years, the adaptation of Lois Gould's novel had already gone through multiple drafts, including passes from David Slavitt and David Shaber, as well as Joan Micklin Silver and Joan Didion and John Gregory Dunne.[3] But it was Elaine who would crack it with her offbeat vision, more interested in nailing the finer, more truthful details than exploring the script's feminist undertones. One of the first critiques she lobbed at Preminger was that "this is a medical story, and there are medical flaws in this." Not that he really cared about the level of research she had done; he just wanted her to go and write him something he could finally put on-screen. She gave him her few requirements—$175,000 and absolutely no credit for her work— which he agreed to on a handshake deal.[4]

Otto Preminger worked closely with his writers, meeting with them regularly to review their work in progress and, in most cases, to tear it apart and tell them how to do it better. He was dismayed to realize Elaine didn't operate like that. "He made an appointment with her for the following Monday. He gave her a whole weekend to work on the first scenes," says Erik Lee Preminger. "Monday: No Elaine. No sign of Elaine, no answering the phone with Elaine. Elaine was not there. No Elaine for a week. No Elaine for two weeks. No Elaine for *three* weeks. And then she picks up the phone like nothing had ever happened."[5] She had finished a third of the script, sent it to an impressed Preminger, then repeated the cycle of disappearance and non-communication until she reemerged with a finished script in just ten weeks.[6]

But not giving her credit and not associating her name with the finished film were two very different things in Preminger's mind. When *Such Good Friends* was released in late 1971—just months after Elaine had made headlines for trying to take her name off *A New Leaf*—she was shocked to see that seemingly everyone knew that the writer listed in the credits as Esther Dale (which happened to also be the name of a veteran character actress) was really Elaine May.[7] More shocking was that the leak had come from Otto Preminger himself, who had maybe not exactly gone back on his word, but had found a loophole around it, and made no secret of her involvement in hopes that it would help promote the picture. "She was very unhappy about this," Erik Lee Preminger says. "She really felt that Otto had betrayed her."[8]

Couldn't have that happen again. Hollywood was crawling with people who simply could not be trusted, out for their own way and willing to do whatever it took to get it. Anyone who was capable of hiring her for a project and being a pleasant colleague was equally capable of turning and walking right over her if it meant getting what they wanted. Everyone respected Elaine when they needed a favor from her, but the respect just about stopped there. She should have known well enough by now how expendable she really was. Elaine was unable to ruthlessly separate business matters from personal ones, not when her work itself was so personal. Better to instead surround herself with the few she allowed into her circle, the people she trusted not to fuck with her and who could be reminded that she knew where they lived if they did. From then on, she'd all but exclusively collaborate with friends, filling the rest of the 1970s—when she wasn't directing a film or in battle over one—helping Marlo Thomas or Herb Gardner with their work, consulting with Charles Grodin, and giving every script of Mike's a once-over before it went into production. It would be this kind of reliance upon friendship—real friendship, not the networking Hollywood kind—that would pull her out of the mess she had made for herself with *Mikey and Nicky*. Once again, Elaine's rescue from career suicide came in the form of one of the industry's most powerful men. Enter Warren Beatty.

Beatty had an idea: "It's a remake, and I'm not going to be in it. I'm putting this together as a starring vehicle for Muhammad Ali. It's about a boxer who, he dies and he goes to heaven, but it's a mistake, so they bring him back, but his body had been cremated, so they put him in the body of a CEO whose wife has just murdered him. And then CEO comes back, and when the CEO comes back, everybody in the movie sees the CEO as the CEO, but the audience sees the CEO as Muhammad Ali. And then Muhammad Ali meets a girl and then a boxer dies and he goes into his body. It's a love story."[9] And he wanted her to help him make it.

The crazed way Elaine tells the story of her first collaboration with Warren Beatty is funny, but she's not totally exaggerating. Beatty was known for ideas that were, if not exactly farfetched, certainly ambitious. His planned directorial debut, a remake of the 1941 film *Here Comes Mr. Jordan,* with its chaotic-on-paper plotline, was no exception. Elaine, though often just as crazed, could ground him in reality.

The two had first crossed paths more than a decade before, in 1964, when he sought her out to polish *What's New, Pussycat?* (She declined, and eventually Beatty left the project.) In the years since, Beatty had grown from golden boy to aspiring auteur, producing his own material long before it became the Hollywood norm and successfully bringing French New Wave aesthetics stateside with 1967's *Bonnie and Clyde.* Beatty had spent the better part of the decade that followed as a multi-hyphenate filling his plate with prestige acting jobs (*McCabe & Mrs. Miller*), screenwriting (*Shampoo*), and political organizing (producing a series of star-studded benefits for McGovern), not to mention keeping a very active, tabloid-worthy social life. By the mid-seventies, Beatty realized that the idea he kept coming back to was one "of a romantic fantasy, because that's what *I* wanted to see."[10] He was in a slump: tired, a little depressed, working relentlessly on developing far heavier material, and grieving the deaths of friends. A film like *Here Comes Mr. Jordan* felt like it was just what he needed, lighter fare that didn't sacrifice thought. "Something about the size of the theme didn't seem small," he said. "It was dealing with death and reincarnation. That made me want to see it particularly."[11] But wrestling those themes into a well-structured and entertaining farce would be a tightrope act. Lean too far into the farce, and it's stupid; play up the original's sentimentality too much and you run the risk of alienating an audience full of 1970s cynics—even the ones looking for a feel-good flick. "That was one of the reasons I brought in Elaine," he explained. "I wanted to be on guard about the sentimentality and I thought she would take care of my reservations."[12]

In October 1976, still tied up in desperate last-minute attempts to get her final cut on *Mikey and Nicky* before the film would be unceremoniously released against her wishes, Elaine found the time to crank out a first draft of a screenplay for Beatty.[13] She wouldn't be the first writer on the project—Francis Ford Coppola took a crack at a draft back in 1968[14]—and wouldn't be the last. The thing about Warren Beatty was that he was never satisfied, not even with the work of someone he regarded as highly as Elaine. Though much of her original script created the framework that would eventually be seen on-screen—so much so that the Writers Guild's tentative credits initially gave her sole writing credit[15]—they eventually reached "some differences of opinion," Beatty said. "I thought, 'I want to be collaborating, I want to argue, I want to go back and forth.'"[16] Beatty's philosophy was that a script was never truly finished, and it never had just one author. It was a never-ending group project, something that could be tinkered with and reworked all the way from early drafts through shooting and up until the very last second of the eleventh hour in the editing room. And even then, it wasn't *finished* as much as conceded to. *Heaven Can Wait* was no different, and a number of voices would have input over the course of its production. Peter Feibleman, one of Elaine's close friends at the time, would be brought in to contribute. Beatty would throw in his own ideas. And then there was co-director Buck Henry, who would go on to write new dialogue—mostly for himself and for Julie Christie, whose casting meant her character had to be rewritten as British—as shooting was happening, though even that wasn't up to Beatty's standards. "I think he had more confidence in Elaine than he did in me," Henry said. "Perhaps rightly so, because Elaine's stuff was brilliant, off-the-wall brilliant. Warren was always yelling at me, 'Will you finish the fucking scene and stop writing jokes!' Then we'd tear it up. I would write a scene, and then Warren would say, 'This is just a joke, isn't it?' 'Yes. It will make the audience laugh.'"[17]

By the end of shooting, Elaine's original script—not only far colder, but also front-loaded with scenes that practically make it a medical farce—would be mostly kept intact. Her presence, though muddied, is undeniably felt. At its best, *Heaven Can Wait* does exactly what she was brought in to make it do: It rejects sentimentality, veering away from Beatty's idealized romantic fantasy with a preachy message about mortality and instead toward a slapstick comedy of errors, primarily through the film's two standout performances from Dyan Cannon as Beatty's high-strung murderous wife and Charles Grodin as his secretary and Cannon's co-conspirator/lover. "The film sort of wilts when Miss Cannon and Mr. Grodin aren't on the screen," Vincent Canby noted in his review at the time, "but when they are on the screen, it acquires a very funny lunatic life."[18] Together, the two crackle with classic Elaine energy. While there are multiple occasions in which the group endeavor hangs together so seamlessly you can't quite credit a single line or action to any of the myriad authors unless you were to go straight to the script, Cannon and Grodin's scenes remain almost entirely as Elaine originally scripted them.[19] Their banter is pitch-black wit, duplicitous and treacherous, full of paranoia that occasionally hinges upon absurd hysteria but never lingering there long enough to feel untrue. It's their Macbeth cosplay—Elaine's creation—that steals the film, a pair of performances that might not have happened without her input.

For Cannon, the part of Julia Farnsworth initially seemed too crazy. "I don't understand her," she told Beatty. "I don't get who she is. And usually I can get into character and characterization right away, but this woman is nuts and I don't understand why."[20] But Beatty, refusing to accept any of Cannon's three rejections, had her meet with him and Elaine in the hopes they could talk her into accepting the role. The woman who had breathed life into the off-the-wall character, Cannon recalls, "was quiet. She wasn't effusive, but whenever she said something, it was gold."[21] Beatty had taken Cannon's noes for maybes, thinking she was playing hard to get without considering her valid concerns about the role. It occurred to her that Elaine was there to do something he couldn't: give her the female point of view. Having unlocked something that she could be comfortable playing, Cannon was in. Now they just had to find her counterpart, the smarmy and neurotic Tony Abbott. Elaine knew there was only one man for the job: Charles Grodin.[22] The character had practically been written with him in mind, but Beatty was, according to Grodin, "reluctant." "I heard you were crazy," he told Grodin. "Maybe it's because you're an actor, a writer, a director, and a producer, and anyone who does all that would have to be a little crazy." "*You* do all that," Grodin said. Beatty replied: "That's how I know."[23]

On *Heaven Can Wait,* Beatty's directing style was just as slow and, at times, as painfully meticulous as Elaine's. He ran actors through twenty takes of the same scene; agonized over every decision, no matter how big or small; wanted to shoot more, more, *more,* no matter how impractical it was. Only no one tried to stop him or corral him the way they did Elaine. "He never did anything that would hurt the movie," Paul Sylbert said in Beatty's defense.[24]

At least Elaine didn't have to hang around to see Beatty rewarded for the same behavior for which she'd been punished. By then she was already at work on *California Suite,* taking a bit part that would reunite her on-screen with Walter Matthau. There's no rhyme or reason to the choice. It's not a great role or even a great script. Simon's *Suite* anthology seems stale and dated, even by 1978's standards. The entire cast is a who's who of in-demand actors, but one can only assume most took the part for an easy paycheck and the chance to work with a script by one of Broadway's biggest playwrights. The most that could be said for Elaine was that she figured why not when presented with the opportunity to play opposite Matthau again—as if she had forgotten all those times he called her Mrs. Hitler.

Both films came out within a year of each other. Though *California Suite* would be a relatively forgettable endeavor (despite making the most of a tired plotline, Elaine is rarely mentioned in the film's so-so reviews), *Heaven Can Wait* would win Elaine her biggest industry accolades yet. That spring, Elaine would be nominated (along with Beatty, who now took on a cowriter credit)[25] for her first Academy Award and go on to win a Writers Guild of America Award for her screenplay.

By the following year, Beatty needed her help more than ever. He had developed a fascination with John Reed—an American journalist and leftist activist who documented the birth of the Soviet Union—and had spent the better part of a decade, in fits and spurts, trying to turn the story of his life into a film. This ambitious passion project would be an uphill battle every step of the way. *Reds,* on the most basic level, is a movie about history, a docudrama about Reed, his time documenting the Russian Revolution, and America's burgeoning radical movement in the early twentieth century. But it isn't simply about history—which is to say, a film about a bunch of dead people with a plot we already know the outcome of—as it is a film about the way history is remembered, the ways in which memory, in all its failures, shapes the chronicling of time. Oh, and it's also a love story; intertwined is Reed's affair with Louise Bryant (played by Beatty's then girlfriend Diane Keaton, which would complicate things even more), a bohemian artist and aspiring writer who eventually becomes his colleague and on-again, off-again wife. Elaine couldn't help, years later, but crack an exasperated joke about its impossibly complex plot, calling it "about this communist who was born in the late 1880s, saw the Second Comintern, and he marries another communist and he goes back to . . . and he's the only American communist who's buried . . . and, well, whatever."[26]

New Hollywood may have been in full swing, but investing money in a sprawling historical epic that was soft on communism, big on messaging, and weak on cleanly discernible plot wasn't exactly a gamble any studio wanted to take. The success of *Heaven Can Wait*, though, changed things. After that, Paramount production head Robert Evans said, "Warren could dictate what he wanted to make. *Reds* was his come shot."[27] But first he'd have to get his script in order, and the draft he had at the moment was in sorry shape. Written by Trevor Griffiths, a successful London playwright and intellectual, it was, to put it plainly, a total drag. Beatty thought it was "too British,"[28] which was a polite way of calling it a stuffy, bone-dry history lesson. There was no spark between Jack and Louise, no conflict, no humor *or* drama—and it was quickly becoming clear that Griffiths would not be the person to pull off the difficult and delicate dance of making the internal squabbles of early twentieth-century leftists informative for clueless audiences *and* sexy enough to entertain them. Elaine, though, would. She may not have known as much about the rote facts of history, but her capacity for understanding human behavior would make up for that. Even as Beatty sought the input of several writers during the long, tedious process of making *Reds*—Robert Towne, Peter Feibleman, and Lillian Hellman, among others—Elaine's input would be the most significant.

WARREN BEATTY LIKED to work out of hotels, and Elaine would meet him wherever he was staying in the world. In Los Angeles, you could find him at the Beverly Wilshire; in New York, it was the Mark or the Carlyle. Sometimes it was Paris, at the Athénée, and he would fly her in on the Concorde just to work on scenes over the weekend.[29] Jeremy Pikser, who started on *Reds* as an apprentice of Griffiths, then, after his departure, became the film's research consultant, recalls that no matter what city they were in, the work always started the same way: "We would meet and talk and argue."[30]

Everything was an argument. To write a script was to write a battle ledger, stubborn will and wit grinding against stubborn will and wit. Chairs and typewriters were thrown, screaming matches would ensue. On one tense occasion, Elaine—sidelined with an ankle injury, walking with a cane, and at the end of her patience—tried to call it a night, only for Beatty to grab her cane to keep her from leaving as she screamed.[31] It wasn't so much about ego (well, maybe some of it was about ego) as it was about serving the story best, a convoluted idea of creativity, each person fiercely protective of how to make something work, convinced that *this* was absolutely right and *that* was absolutely wrong. "Elaine's a fighter, and Warren's a fighter," Pikser says. "That's how they'd relate."[32] If you weren't willing to fight to the bone to defend a line of dialogue—or, later, take 3 over take 27, cutting a scene here or twelve seconds earlier—then maybe your opinion wasn't good enough.

When she wasn't writing or arguing about writing, Elaine presented herself as someone who needed to be taken care of, seemingly playing a version of herself that was almost too inept and cautious to function. A request for a ride to the airport could escalate into an anxious plea to "come with me just as far as New York?"[33] When Feibleman wasn't by her side to support her, Pikser was indispensable. She insisted upon keeping him close as her personal historian while she worked her way through the script, protesting almost *too* much that she knew absolutely nothing about the material at hand. "Explain it to me," she would say to him, inviting a history lesson on early twentieth-century politics. No one really believed she was as clueless as she acted. It was just that playing dumb was far easier than letting on how much she did know, which always came with the risk of being proved wrong. "So, this labor thing," she once said to Pikser, "it was, like, a whole movement?"[34]

Holed up in her hotel room, rewriting scene after scene, she would transform the script as only she could: with intelligence and ferocious observations of character that didn't sacrifice attitude or biting wit. She knew that this couldn't be a stale, stakes-less history lesson, a bunch of people sitting in rooms and talking without any clear motivations or needs. Aware of the fact that it had to serve Beatty as a leading man and that the love story part of the equation had to feel current for an audience to really care, she focused on building out the Reed-Bryant relationship and the third wheel of Jack Nicholson's Eugene O'Neill that comes between them. Along the way, Pikser became not only someone she mined for research, but someone whose nascent writing skills she picked up on and encouraged. "She would say, 'Okay, we need a scene here where John Reed and Emma Goldman fight. What year is this?'" Pikser says. "I would say, 'It's 1919.' She said, 'I don't know what they would fight about in 1919. Write me a fight.'" She would hand him a yellow pad and take it back when he was finished, swiftly and surgically rearrange it line by line, then give it back to him. "It's good," she'd say. "Write it again."[35] Her only method of editing was to do it over. As always, maids were barred from entering her room. Probably for the best. They'd have been horrified at the sight of Elaine's workspace: the floor, which she used in lieu of the desk, covered with notepads that tracked multiple variations on the same scene, stacks of dirty room-service dishes, and a film of cigar ash covering it all.[36]

Rewrites went on throughout the film's grueling nine-month-long shoot,[37] and by the time postproduction moved from London to New York in the summer of 1980, Elaine was still there. Cutting *Reds* would be an ordeal not unlike *Mikey and Nicky*, with an alleged 2.5 million feet of film—"an entire room of footage"[38]—for editors Craig McKay and Dede Allen to assemble. Beatty worked late nights and weekends, tinkering obsessively, thinking of ideas for reshoots, keeping other apprentices and editors[39] on call or on the clock at all hours—including holidays—just to keep up with the sheer scale of it all.[40] In Elaine, Beatty found someone cut from the same obsessive cloth, someone whose creative counsel could be called upon at any time. Any number of Beatty's frequent trusted collaborators would stop by the postproduction suite to share their thoughts, but Elaine "was his ultimate trusted person that he wanted to come in," says first assistant editor Cindy Kaplan Rooney. "He supremely trusted her, more than anybody."[41] For one, she never got involved with him as anything more than a friend. "Elaine was too savvy to be one of those girls on Warren's list," Feibleman said. "The minute sex got into it, she would have been dead in the water. She became the person he talked to. She was like a guy when the three of us were together."[42] For another, she had the benefit of being one of the smartest—and most opinionated—people he knew, and she had no real skin in the game. Elaine was pulled into the project as a writer and trusted friend to kick ideas around with, and her name would not, under any circumstances, appear in the final credits. She didn't have the kind of fierce ownership as did others on the team toiling away at making something perfect—a sound mix, an edit of the scene—and so the opinions she shared were free of any agenda. "She gave it her all. It wasn't really her film, [but] she basically lived there and put input into it," says Rooney.[43] She wasn't fighting for validation of her work. She was fighting for the story, at just enough of a remove that she could catch minute details that those who had been so submerged in it would never see. "Elaine has this unbelievable ability to, every time she sits down to look or work at the film, it's almost as though she has never seen it," Phillip Schopper explains. A film editor who started on the project doing photo treatments, Schopper hung around long enough to become another voice in the collaborative mix. On *Reds,* he made a lasting impression on Elaine; she would enlist his help on nearly every project she worked on for the next decade. "She has this ability to just kind of wipe it out, and she can go a long way—many, many months into the project toward the end."[44]

So good was her eye that once, after Beatty screened a new cut of a scene that he hoped to have tightened up, she remarked as soon as the lights went up, "What *is* it with this reel? It feels like every shot is four frames short!" Warren brought Dede Allen into the screening room: "Would you tell Elaine what I asked you to do for this scene?" he asked. "Well, you asked me to take four frames off every shot," Allen replied.[45]

As postproduction settled into the following summer, Elaine

became a staple in the editing room at Trans Audio on West 54th Street, both a blessing and a curse to everyone else there. "Nothing was a straight line," Rooney says of her work habits. "Everything was all over the place. So even though I'm sure she was giving a lot of good trusted advice, the spinout from it sometimes caused chaos. Everyone was kind of already at the end of their rope, and then she came in and it created a new whirlwind."[46] Elaine and Beatty were good collaborators, two perfectionists who valued hustle and the company of intelligent partners to work and argue with in equal measure. (It's no fun to fight with a lesser opponent, you see.) The catch, of course, was that in order to fight with Beatty or Elaine, you first had to win their trust, and that didn't come easy. That was another thing they shared, a deep-seated belief that "a man who is not paranoid is a man who is not in full possession of the facts."[47] It wasn't the Mafia, but it might as well have been, with all their outsize sense of the importance of loyalty, trust, and respect. But theirs was a mutually beneficial—if not, as some have suggested, a bit manipulative—relationship.[48] In Beatty, Elaine had a powerful protector again, someone who would respect the unconventional ways in which she worked, someone who wouldn't apologize for her when she said the wrong thing, but would probably join in telling authority figures to fuck off when it was warranted. And Beatty knew that Elaine was quite possibly the best thing that could ever happen to your picture. She was an unending well of ideas you could take from, so long as you gave her the kind of support she needed to keep going and kept at least one foot steadily on the ground.

Elaine's influence on Beatty throughout the huge undertaking of postproduction was undeniably strong. "Warren, as ballsy as he was and brilliant as he was, he was insecure about it. So here comes this brilliant Elaine May, and then her word kind of took precedence for a while," says Rooney.[49] Elaine, the outsider, came in with critical opinions that often spun the work into a completely different direction—even though, most of the time, she was right, often because the distance was her greatest asset. A sound editor could spend weeks meticulously crafting a sound mix for a crucial scene only for Elaine to make the simple observation that something had changed—"and not for the better." They would stick with the scrappy temp mix—the sound that was just intended to be a placeholder—and find it was more honest and compelling than anything they spent all that time and money trying to painstakingly re-create.[50] On and on the restless doing and undoing went, Beatty and Elaine feeding off each other's energy right up until the last possible minute, with the pair writing new lines of dialogue the night before the negative had to be en route to Rome for its Technicolor printing.[51]

But the obsessive labor would pay off. *Reds* may have been only a modest commercial hit when it finally opened in December 1981—due, in part, to its long runtime preventing multiple showings, and Beatty's reluctance to do press around it—but what it lacked in box office returns, it more than made up for in critical acclaim. By the time the Academy Awards rolled around in the spring of 1982, the picture was up for twelve nominations—the most any single film had received since *Who's Afraid of Virginia Woolf?* scooped thirteen in 1966. *Reds* was nominated for Best Original Screenplay, an accolade it had already won from the Writers Guild of America—though credited to Beatty and Griffiths only. "In a really fair world," Pikser says, "that should have been 'Script by Elaine May.'"[52] To him, Elaine spun a story to justify her anonymity, explaining that she wouldn't take credit for her work because she *couldn't* take credit—and *especially* couldn't take any money—because she was in trouble with the IRS. "I personally don't believe that story," he adds, "but that was the story she told me. She liked to say that she was a criminal and that she came from a family of crime. I think she liked the idea that she was in trouble with the law, to put that out so she couldn't take any money and she couldn't get any credit."[53] But even without a good story to provide an excuse, she knew that relationships were transactional, that no friendship was immune from keeping a score.

So even though her name wasn't on the print when all was said and done, Beatty still found a way to make sure she got her due for all her contributions, floating the idea that he'd work with her on one of her projects down the line as a sort of payback.[54] In the meantime, in his speech accepting the award for Best Director at the Academy Awards, he thanked Keaton and Nicholson, then re-marked, "I know I do one thing well. I get good people." A good person he couldn't let stay anonymous, much as she may have wanted to: Elaine. Hers was the next name he mentioned, the first in a string of contributors and collaborators who "happily saved him."[55]

She was back in business. Or at least everyone in Hollywood who had hiring and firing power knew she was. To Hollywood, she had a new calling card: script doctor extraordinaire. Elaine would be the one to come in and save your ass, and by refusing credit, make you look good doing it. To much of the general public, though, Elaine had sunk into the carpeting of the room where things happened, holding the room together while remaining all but invisible to any-one who wasn't paying close enough attention. It was "Whatever Happened to Elaine May?" all over again, except this time, no one was asking. No one was writing a prying profile. No one really cared. And Elaine liked it that way.

SHE COULDN'T SIDESTEP the public eye forever, though. In the spring of 1980, while *Reds* was shooting in Europe, Elaine and Mike would reunite onstage for their first production together in more than a decade.

Their canceled run of shows in 1972 had planted the idea of officially reuniting, just in a different capacity. "There's something sort of sad about a crone and a geezer doddering out to give us their well-loved routines for the millionth time," Nichols said.[56] (Never mind the fact that they were middle-age, not old.) By 1975, the idea of teaming up to play George and Martha in a production of *Who's Afraid of Virginia Woolf?* was floated in earnestness.[57] Fi-nally, after five years of attempts to rearrange too-full schedules, both were in deep need of something new—Elaine looking at her options outside of directing, Mike coming off another divorce and a string of projects that would never see the light of day—and real-ized it was now or never.

Six weeks in New Haven, a tight quartet with James Naughton as Nick and Swoosie Kurtz as Honey, and absolutely no press cover-age: That was the promise Mike made to finally convince Elaine to join him in playing one of the most disturbing couples of modern theater. It could work. It could be good, even. They had grown, hadn't they? So what if they were stepping into such an emotionally explosive play—they were better equipped to keep their work and their personal lives from melding inextricably into each other this time, weren't they? And anyway, it would be good for both of them to remember what it was like to be just an actor again, to challenge themselves with material they couldn't sleepwalk through, to relinquish a little bit of control and give themselves over to another director and the collaborative nature of the stage.[58] "It was a play I had never liked that much," Elaine claimed decades later. "But he really wanted to do it."[59]

Yet she jumped in with full force. From the first read-through, "it was clear that they were going to be able to bring something so unique to it," said Arvin Brown, the show's director.[60] Elaine was a true player, full of infinite curiosity, all what-ifs and how-abouts, game and ready to follow a creative impulse down whatever unknown path it would lead her. "I thought from the first moment of rehearsal that she was fucking brilliant," says Swoosie Kurtz.[61] Her choices were fresh, explorative, and completely unexpected. In Elaine's hands, Martha was, for the first time, not the braying earth mother type played again and again but, rather, "very slender and seductive and sort of used her body in a kind of legato way," Kurtz says. "And so subtle. She would just throw lines away. I just remember being knocked out by that, having this memory of Uta Hagen, who was unbelievably amazing. But I don't think any of us had seen Martha that way. It wasn't embarrassing when she started coming on to Nick. I mean, it was emotionally, age-wise and everything, but it wasn't that kind of *Oh, here's that older, sort of beyond her prime, kind of slightly overweight woman coming on to this handsome young man.*"[62]

Quickly, though, the weak points presented themselves. Elaine was able to come up against difficult material she hadn't yet entirely figured out how to play and give the CliffsNotes version instead to get through it. Mike, though, proceeded with far more careful attention. He was slow and methodical in his approach to the play, needing to understand all the hows and whys of each beat before moving on to the next, a product of both his nature—ever the editor to her writer—and the concern that he didn't have the same natural ability as she to immediately put a long dormant muscle to full use. It had been decades since either of them had been onstage performing anything but their well-worn bits, and *Virginia Woolf* is hardly an easy evening jog to get the juices flowing again. At that point in their lives, neither had anything to lose or prove—and they certainly didn't need the meager pay that Long Wharf offered—yet here they were agreeing to run a marathon night after night in a tiny Connecticut theater in front of all their friends and the New York celebrity crowd who had come up from the city to see it. There was a palpable nervousness among the entire cast, but for the two of them, the thrill of the challenge overwhelmed the stark terror any day.[63]

Except, that is, when it came to the elephant in the room: the play's third act—aptly nicknamed "The Exorcism"—in which George and Martha grow bored with terrorizing Nick and Honey and instead turn inward to destroy each other. Mike and Elaine began showing up to rehearsals like kids who were hoping to distract the teacher from checking their homework until the bell rang, telling anecdotes at any chance the opportunity presented itself, insisting on working on material that was already well covered. They knew what unspeakable cruelty they had to tap into, and just how dangerous it could become. What if they weren't as older and wiser as they thought they were? What if they were still at heart two kids who were mean and Method, with little control over the collateral damage that could come from it? After they reunited, Elaine said, "we were careful of each other's feelings as we had never been before. There was a formality between us that only happens when you hurt someone."[64] The chance that it would be "Pirandello" all over again—that in meaning to hurt each other in character, they would go for the real-life jugular instead, and ruin what they had built back—was almost too much to bear. "It was like the two of them were sort of circling a bomb that was about to detonate," Kurtz says. "And we didn't know when, so [we did] whatever we could do to not just keep circling and hope that we can be far enough away and it wouldn't go off."[65] As the short three-week rehearsal period stretched on, the production fell more and more behind. Suddenly, the first previews were imminent, and they still had yet to run the third act in its entirety.

The third act stood to threaten the new, grown-up relationship they had cultivated, the warmth and gentle kindness with which they treated each other offstage. Together, they were a shared brain. "There was Mike and his big personality," Naughton says, "and Elaine and her big personality. But when you were with the two of them, you were in the presence of a third personality. Whoever they were together was somebody else."[66] Their young costars marveled in their company, watching their history unfold as they finished each other's sentences at post-show drinks or shared laughs in one of Long Wharf's two adjoining dressing rooms. Maybe it was maturity, lessons learned from all their ups and downs and the great love that remained. Maybe it was a bond of mutual fear, a desire to overcorrect in real life the atrocities they'd commit against each other every night onstage. Mike's shaping of scenes became softer; gone were the days of coldly directing Elaine from the wings. Instead, whenever he had a suggestion, he would pop his head casually into the women's dressing room, jokingly calling out: "Irene? Arlene? Eileen? I have a little note for you—in an otherwise flawless performance. You know that line in act three?" he would say as lightly as possible. "You're coming in a bit late with it and it's ruining my laugh on the next line."[67] And Elaine, rather than take issue with being told what to do, was serene and accommodating, even when his process proved difficult for the rest of the cast. "If she was frustrated with Mike, she wasn't gonna let anybody else know that, because they were a team," Naughton says. "They were loyal to each other. That's the way it was."[68]

They had come to realize that often their criticisms weren't really about the other person; they were projections of themselves, their own fears and insecurities. "I had the feeling that she knew he needed help, too," Kurtz says. "He wasn't just judging something she was doing. It was kind of like, 'I need you to do this so that I can get this laugh.' I felt like maybe he thought, 'I'm not doing it right, so maybe you could help me by coming in quicker with that line.'"[69] And if there was one thing Elaine was going to do, after all the protection she had gotten from Mike over the years, it was that she was going to protect him back, both offstage and on. In one performance, as George antagonized Nick from across the stage, Naughton found himself so provoked that instead of responding with another barb of his own, he lunged across the stage to physically attack Mike. Elaine, positioned between the two, "was off the couch like a shot. 'No, no, no, no, honey.' She got up in my face, just grabbed me by the shirt, and was not gonna let me get there."[70]

Sure enough, after a few previews, they were on it, moving through the play with their own fierce tilt. Elaine in particular was fearless, varying her performance night after night, spontaneously trying new things in the moment in a way that not only made Martha more intriguing, but kept her costars on their toes as well. "Whatever happened, she reacted in the moment, not in the way she had practiced reacting," says Kurtz. "She was a very, very great listener onstage and really picks up on what the other actors are doing and follows that, whatever happens in the next moment. She definitely has her own blueprint of where she's going, but wow, she has a split-second reaction to this and the next moment and the next one."[71] There was no telling what she would do in the moment. On one occasion, at the top of act 3, when Nick and Martha return to the living room after supposedly being together during the act break at the end of act 2, Elaine curled up next to Naughton and, wearing little more than an oversize men's shirt, moved to refill his drink as she carried on with her four-page monologue. On and on she talked—and poured—until the bourbon spilled out over the edge of his glass and into his lap. "I'll never forget how much fun it was to watch that bourbon come up, up, up, up to the top of my glass, wondering, 'Is she gonna stop pouring?' And she didn't, until it kind of dripped over the edge," Naughton says. "So then I poured a little off into her lap. Then she kept talking, but she looked at me and sort of smiled. She had this bottle of bourbon, I had a glass full of bourbon, and she also had her glass of vodka still in her other hand. I thought, 'If I go any further with this, she's going to take that whole bottle of bourbon and just pour it out my down my shirt.'"[72] To work with Elaine, he had realized, was to dance with one of the best, someone with whom you could be free to make choices, knowing they'd follow your step wherever you led them.

Mike might have promised Elaine there would be no reviews, but he couldn't keep all of the New York media from making the short train ride up to Connecticut to see their rare reteaming. That included *The New York Times*'s drama critic Frank Rich, who circumvented the press blackout by simply buying a ticket for himself. "It is the happiest possible reunion," he wrote. "Here, after far too many years of waiting, are Mike Nichols and Elaine May—finally together again, alive and well, on the very same stage." Forgoing a predictable, easy comedic play like *Plaza Suite* or *Same Time, Next Year* and instead heading straight for one of the American theater's most demanding and recognizable dramas was a challenge not for the actor out for an ego boost. "Is it still possible for any actors to make *Virginia Woolf* seem fresh?" he asked. The answer, he found, was that, in bringing their own lived-in lacerating humor to George and Martha, Mike and Elaine transformed the couple's knock-down, drag-out fights into spiky battles of wit, and in doing so, shifted the meaning of the play away from the dramatic. In Mike and Elaine's game, the premise became: "What if George and Martha are in fact a happily married couple who play grotesque games merely to while away the night?" While Rich rightly noted that the show's "grueling momentum" fell short in the third act, it overall exceeded expectations. "We arrive expecting to watch two rusty stand-up comics do a novelty act. We leave having seen four thinking actors shed startling new light on one of the great dark plays of our time."[73]

But the glory of the acclaim was short-lived; by the time Rich's review appeared in the papers, it was apparent that the run was over. While speculation swirled about something far more dramatic—that the play's cruel Olympics had taken their toll on the pair, that one of them developed stage fright after their cover was blown by Rich—the reason was far simpler, a fizzle and not a bang. Mike got pneumonia, and after a few days of uncertainty, the producers finally called it. There would be no resuming the last few dates, and certainly no bringing it to Broadway, as some suspected would be the case after such overwhelming out-of-town success. They had run the marathon together, and it was a good experience while it lasted. They didn't much care to do it all over again. Besides, it was for the best that *Virginia Woolf* ended when it did. Had it continued any longer, Elaine might not have been free to make her "most spectacular save"[74] yet.

DUSTIN HOFFMAN HAD spent the better part of three years—a century in an actor's life—developing *Tootsie*. He liked the original screenplay—a self-described "$4½ million extended sitcom"[75]— enough to sign on, but his demand for full creative control landed the film in years of development purgatory as it became a revolving door of attached script revisionists and directors. By 1981, the film was still stuck on a revised draft by a fourth screenwriter that, though it had evolved into a much more intelligent and nuanced comedy about chauvinist out-of-work actor Michael Dorsey, who learns to become a better man by pretending to be a woman, still wasn't up to director Sydney Pollack's standards. What Hoffman and Pollack wanted was another new set of eyes. What they needed was for those eyes to belong to a woman. It was Hoffman's lawyer Bert Fields, who also happened to represent Elaine, who suggested to him that she was the perfect woman for the job.[76]

They're called script doctors for a reason, even if many of them aren't particularly fond of the title. "That implies the subject is sick, and that's not always the case," Feibleman once explained. "Often, it's just a matter of people working on material for so long that it just needs the input of those with a fresh perspective."[77] Still, Elaine's ability to come in fresh enough to both diagnose the ailments—big or small—in a screenplay and quickly present a solution with exacting precision was unparalleled. Any person with a strong opinion can make a critique or point out something's weaknesses. Few are able to solve such problems, and often only after someone else has done the identifying. Rare are people like Elaine, who can take one look at the material and, within the same breath, do both. There was something almost comedic about the contrast between Elaine the filmmaker and Elaine the consultant, the way a woman who so rarely wrote tight scripts herself was able to trim the fat from the scripts of others, or present one decisive, strategic answer instead of throwing twenty ideas at the wall. Meeting with

Hoffman and Pollack, she gave them a rundown of everything she thought needed work. "God knows what I've written here," she wrote on the first of her 145-page revision, chock-full of killer added jokes, sharp character observations, and a number of slashed scenes marked up, ironically, with "Do you really need this?" "Some of these changes may be useful, some may not," she said of her notes and additions. "At this point I only care if they're legible."[78]

Michael needed a roommate ("Someone he can tell his feelings to. For the audience"),[79] and the flat female leads needed some life breathed into them. "I'm telling you right now, you have to have a girl already in your life and I'm going to write her with Teri Garr in mind," she told Hoffman.[80] She crafted Garr's Sandy in her own image, endearing, but with a bevy of neuroses just grating enough to keep her from being too sympathetic. (The constant challenge, Pollack acknowledged, was "getting it right up on the edge of cruelty" without actually crushing hearts.)[81] And to get Lange on board, who nearly turned down the part of Michael's soap costar—and love interest—Julie, Elaine expanded her beyond a character who on paper was "a symbol more than anything"[82] and into a full-dimensional modern woman. A single working mother with an asshole boyfriend[83]—Ron, the soap runner—and a hopeless romantic father, she ends up resembling the archetypal Elaine May heroine: vulnerable, not entirely unaware of the ways in which men are taking advantage of her but too self-loathing to really do anything about it. "Elaine wrote a terrific scene for [Lange] in bed—which was a scene where you had to make Dustin fall in love with her—where she's quite lyrical about the flowers on the wall in her bedroom. But the rest of it," Pollack explained, "she's a kind of a victim. A beautiful victim, and somebody that was just universally understood as the girl you would be desperately in love with."[84] The soap opera within the film needed an overhaul—which she would spend a great deal of time working on with Pollack to make as close to truthful as possible, crafting authentically frothy soap dialogue and building out a backstory of the show's plot—and a spectacular house-of-cards collapse at the end. An early party scene, which no one had been able to crack, she informed Pollack, simply could not be scripted. "I can't write a party because there's no way to write a party," she told him, urging him instead to just improvise the whole thing. "They're never real in movies, anyway," she said. "You gotta find a life for the party."[85]

Most of all, she understood the movie Hoffman and Pollack were trying to make. This wasn't a sophomoric cross-dressing farce full of wisecracks about getting to see naked women. It was a real, truthful drama about how one character grows as a person, about how a man experiencing life as a woman can become a better person for it. Her changes weren't major, she insisted, just "a tilt."[86] But she could sniff out even the slightest artifice in a scene and push it closer to the truth. A single line like "but he treats you badly" in a conversation between Dorothy and Julie warranted a complex critique: "I'm not sure what you want here," she scrawled in the margin, "but there's something so gross and intrusive about Dorothy's saying this. It's based on his seeing Ron with April. It's his first time at her house. He's there under false pretenses, being a man. Old friends are careful about saying this."[87] She continued the note, her thoughts extending down half the page.

"Elaine is the one who made the movie work," Dustin Hoffman said.[88] She would complete her revisions in three weeks and walk away with a $325,000 paycheck—plus an extra $15,000 just for taking an initial meeting with Pollack.[89] Most important, as her contract stipulated in a separate clause, her work was to remain confidential, not only waiving Writers Guild credit but insisting that Pollack could not use her name in association with the film in any way.[90] Despite refusing credit, Pollack would send Elaine a congratulatory telegram when *Tootsie* won Best Screenplay at the New York Film Critics Circle Awards. "You really earned it," he wrote. "I'm deeply grateful and very happy for you."[91] The film would go on to be nominated for nine Academy Awards, including Best Original Screenplay. Jessica Lange, who was also nominated in the Best Actress category for a harrowing portrayal of Frances Farmer, walked away instead with the Best Supporting trophy for *Tootsie,* in large part thanks to Elaine, and that sweetly sad whispered monologue about floral wallpaper.

TOOTSIE WOULD MARK a turning point in Elaine's career, firmly cementing her in a new era of largely invisible work. If we're to believe her side of the story, by the mid-eighties, she had gone from someone who was practically unhireable to someone who was not only constantly booked and busy, but able to turn down work left and right, agreeing only to scripts she found truly interesting or exciting, no matter how high the paycheck. "I've had major producers call me," Julian Schlossberg claims, "and say, 'Can't you talk to her? I've offered her a million dollars for three weeks and she won't do it!' I said, 'It's not about the money, it's about the project. She doesn't like the project.'"[92] "Elaine is the exact opposite of everyone else in Hollywood," Charles Grodin said. "She's always fighting to get as little credit as possible, to keep her name off movies, to *not* be invited to the parties. She's happier without any of that."[93]

And maybe that's true; maybe she could afford to live a life of artistic purity. It's not like she wasn't making money elsewhere. There were those car commercials, not to mention, now that she was living in a co-op in the famous San Remo building on Central Park West, a side hustle playing the lucrative New York real estate game by renting out apartments in her Riverside Drive property.[94] And it wasn't as if she didn't surround herself with famous, wealthy friends who could take care of her if she needed. She could live for months with Marlo Thomas when she went to L.A.,[95] fly as a guest on David Geffen's private plane,[96] celebrate Thanksgiving at Herb Gardner's apartment[97] and Christmas Day with Lillian Hellman,[98] check out the hottest theater openings with Beatty.[100] It's easy to continue to play the role of the starving artist you were when you were young when you have a safety net to provide you the comfort and luxuries that you've grown accustomed to in middle age.

So what were some of the projects she *did* like over the years? Bill Murray, who professed that "she saved my life on numerous occasions, professionally," came to her for help with *What About Bob?*,[101] while Jim Henson had her do a quick polish on *Labyrinth*.[102] Warner Bros. tried to get her to do a rewrite on Jonathan Demme's *Swing Shift*, but she turned them down. ("What a wonderful movie, it's fabulous!" she told Demme, before asking the executives, "Are you guys out of your mind?")[103] There was *Ghostbusters II*, in which it was more her questions than her suggestions that helped Dan Aykroyd and Harold Ramis better structure their story.[104] She of course came to the rescue on any film best friend Marlo Thomas made and was called upon to help Herb Gardner make edits to *I'm Not Rappaport* while it was still in tryouts.[105] And she always had a say in any play or film Mike directed. "She came and saved my ass," he'd often say, though she would pass it off as hyperbole: "If you say to Mike, 'Gee, the credits could be shorter,' he says, 'You've done it! You have saved this movie!'"[106] The save could be as little as a line here or there, like in *Heartburn,* when Elaine "came in and, just by talking to Nora, got her to come up with the best line in the movie, where her character says, of men, 'You want fidelity, marry a swan.'"[107] And, though never confirmed, it's long been speculated that Elaine was behind some of *Working Girl*'s most memorable cracks.[108] Sometimes it was bigger, identifying the spine that separated *a story* from a collection of jokes: "Mike, this is about how we can't help who we are. We will always default. No matter how much we try and reinvent ourselves, we will always default to who we've always been," she told him during *Social Security*'s out-of-town previews. "The minute she said it," Caroline Aaron says, "Mike restructured everything. He went, 'Oh, okay.' He so trusted her and her perception."[109]

Who really knows how many brilliant films and plays were made better by Elaine's input? Elaine wouldn't talk about them then, and she won't talk about them now, either. If *Tootsie* was the moment she truly earned a reputation as one of Hollywood's most valuable script doctors, it also marked the moment she made shirking credit no longer an odd preference, but an absolute rule. It was different before, when she'd seek anonymity on films like *Such Good Friends* more because she would be one of many taking a pass at what everyone knew would be a relatively unsavable script. And it was different when she helped out those in her inner circle, people like Nichols or Beatty, Grodin or Thomas. Theirs was an incestuous hotbed of creativity that saw no lines between work and friendship. Putting in unpaid, uncredited work—even if it was just a fresh set of eyes and ideas—knowing someone would do the same for you down the line when you needed it was maybe a transactional type of friendship, but they only saw it for what it was: friendship.

This time, though, and every time to come, Elaine felt a sense of loyalty to her fellow writers. She had benefited from the protection of others, and now, having scratched back a little bit of power, it was her chance to pay it forward. By 1980, she, along with Feibleman, Joan Didion, and John Gregory Dunne, formed a collective called the DBA (short for Doing Business As) Company. Hoping to "only do production rewrites on films already shooting or on pictures with a budget, start date, and pay-or-play cast" and working as a collective—producers wouldn't know which writer (or combination of writers) was responsible for the work— and taking no credit, they hoped to fight shady studio dealings. Too often had they seen one writer wrongfully fired with another brought on to overly rewrite a perfectly fine movie; they couldn't count how many times they'd been asked to take meetings or read scripts for free. As the DBA, not only would they be fairly paid, but they'd be protecting their colleagues.[110] "We'll represent no threat," Feibleman said. "We're out there to protect the writer—not ace him out."[111] On *Tootsie,* she had been assured that Larry Gelbart—the last writer to work on the script and the one who would receive final credit—knew she had been recruited to offer her thoughts on his work and was fine with it. When it came to light that Gelbart, a friend of hers, had actually been left in the lurch, both parties were upset. "I really felt that's really like fingering someone," she said.[112] She vowed that it would never happen again. And it didn't. After *Tootsie,* she would insist that the last writer on any project she had been hired for personally call her and give their blessing, or she would not take the job.[113]

It's worth pointing out, though, that there was a self-serving angle to her sanctimonious act of looking out for the underdog. Not taking credit wasn't just about helping others; it was about helping herself, too. When in conversation with Mike for a 2013 *Vanity Fair* profile, Elaine was asked, point-blank, "Don't you like credit?" She answered: "Well, I didn't have any control." A gloriously easy cop-out, an explanation that lives in the half-truth, almost daring someone to push back with a skeptical "*Elaine . . .*" She continued: "You can make a deal if you're going to do the original writing. But if you're going to do the original rewriting, you can't. You're a hired gun. No matter how much you write, what you write, you're still a hired gun, and you have no control." She would insist that the only time she'd take credit was when working with Mike, simply because she knew he wouldn't screw her—or the script—over. The beauty of not taking credit and ceding all control, she explained, was that you actually "have great control because you can say your name isn't on this. I'm getting nothing out of this."[114]

She would play up the martyr role years later, insisting again that her work on *Tootsie* was free: "I must say that after, [Gelbart] made an enormous amount of money, and he never gave me a dime."[115] But it's not entirely true. She wasn't getting *nothing* out of it. She was getting a great paycheck, for starters, not to mention the biggest boon of all: Not asking for any public-facing credit in saving a film meant she got more opportunities to do exactly that. Just as she didn't want to make another writer look bad, she didn't want to make a film look bad, either. Although some may have thought having her name attached would be a big enough draw that they should leak it, her position was otherwise: If someone else was brought in to work on a film, then the public would reason that the film was a real mess that wasn't worth seeing, and that helps no one. She could let the work speak for itself, let word travel throughout the business that she did it well and was unassuming about it. You got more work by playing nice and keeping your mouth shut.[116]

A MONTH BEFORE *Tootsie* opened, David Rubinfine died suddenly of a heart attack. His heavy smoking habit had rivaled Elaine's, and despite having a heart condition, he refused to quit. The two had—publicly, at least—kept separate apartments since at least 1975, when, during the *Mikey and Nicky* lawsuit, Paramount charged that Elaine went to David's apartment an hour after receiving the order to not move her film.[117] By 1982, he and Elaine had been living all but separate lives. He was alone in his Santa Monica apartment for hours until Peter Falk broke down the door and found his body.[118]

When they met, Elaine played the fragile role, the one in need of a partner to take care of her, someone to quite literally hold her hand on the set of *Enter Laughing* and stay up late at night with her when she worked. And David was good at that. But as time wore on, the dynamic became strained.[119] "David and Elaine couldn't stay married," Arthur Penn said, "but they loved each other."[120]

David was something of a playboy;[121] his behavior with clients was unconventional and, at times, of questionable ethical standing. Consider his relationship with one patient, the poet Bernadette Mayer, who began seeing him—free of charge—once a week in 1971 and escalated her sessions to every day. "I can't remember for how long it was," she said, "but it was way longer than I would ever want to remember."[122] It was a remarkably intense doctor-patient relationship, especially since the doctor was married. He penned an effusive introduction for the 1975 edition of her book *Memory,* writing, "Her writing is so original that it seems very much like her own invention. But I had better stop here since I realize suddenly that I am so envious that I am struggling with strongly competitive urges."[123] Letters from him to her in 1975, in which he both answers her psychological questions and provides recaps of his personal Saint-Tropez vacation, are signed "Love, David."[124]

David and Elaine separated, with David moving to California and Elaine splitting her time between the two coasts. One of David's patients recalls him saying, "We have a terrific arrangement. I love Elaine. She loves me. We live separately."[125] They never divorced and remained good friends, and he was "absolutely crazy about Elaine right to the day of his death."[126]

"David was a very important person in her life, right to the end of his life," Schlossberg says. "Certainly, it was upsetting and it came as a shock."[127] Their separation caused her relationship with her stepdaughters to dissolve, her attention waning in David's absence.[128] But while she drifted further and further from being the only mother the three Rubinfine girls had, she found reconciliation with Jeannie. After *The Heartbreak Kid,* Jeannie decamped back to L.A.—and away from Elaine. "There came a time where they just couldn't get along and didn't speak to each other," Schopper says. "There were a lot of years where they were sort of apart."[129] In L.A., Jeannie could climb out from under Elaine's shadow. With her own acting school taking her focus, and reports of on-set difficulty rife with gossip that she was "taking orders from her mother,"[130] she practically dropped out of film entirely. But with Elaine spending more time on the West Coast, and now alone, the two became close again, forming an indomitable, inseparable pair.

While the obvious tragic parallel between the loss of David and the death of her father exactly forty years prior was impossible to ignore, it went unacknowledged. Not even a person with as dark a mind as Elaine could have scripted a narrative like that. Instead of dwelling on it, she would get back to her work, bury herself in it if she had to. Six months later, she would act in a Chicago staging of a new play she had written, a one-act about a bitter New York woman phoning a counselor at a suicide prevention hotline, demanding to know what about this cruel life was worth sticking around for.[131] "Elaine is a writer," Schlossberg says. "She loves to write, and she would, and I'm sure did, find a way to continue to work. Nothing's going to stop Elaine. Nothing."[132]

BY 1985, THE decade was shaping up to be some sort of a sick joke, all too reminiscent of the floundering she had done twenty years before. A period of profound success had been followed by personal and professional instability. The David saga had come full circle; he had entered her life as an agent of chaos and left it as one, too. And what had started as a pivot to pay the price for *Mikey and Nicky* was turning out to be less than temporary.

It would be easy to say that this was what Elaine had wanted all along: creative power without any personal responsibility or accountability, the chance to have her cake and eat it, too. A chance to vanish into thin air, become a ghostlike presence scattering her cigar ashes all over the entertainment industry with no one being the wiser that it was her. But the truth was that Elaine was now tending to a small graveyard of personal projects. There was a romantic comedy called *Million Dollar Baby* she was writing for Marlo Thomas in 1977[133] that they were still talking about in 1983.[134] A science fiction work that was deemed "the hottest screenplay in California . . . worth $1.5 million—at least" in 1979 never materialized,[135] nor did her rumored rewrites on the doomed Robert Towne/Warren Beatty project *Mermaid,* since *Splash* beat them to the punch.[136] Gossip about a reunion with Mike was a constant, whether it was about the possibility of remaking *Grand Hotel* together in 1979[137] or directing (her) and producing (him) a play by Renée Taylor and Joseph Bologna[138] in 1980 or writing an adaptation of film industry tell-all *Indecent Exposure* in 1984.[139] She worked on an early version of a screenplay that would become *State and Main* with David Mamet,[140] but it wouldn't be produced for another fifteen years— maybe because their process could only be best described by Mamet as "we sit around; we smoke cigars; say funny things; write some down"[141]—and an adaptation of *The False Inspector Dew* that didn't go anywhere.[142] It's normal in Hollywood to have some unrealized projects under your belt. Deals fall through, actors drop out; passion projects fizzle and are abandoned or rejected all the time. But Elaine's string of unproduced work was not just bordering excessive; it was gutting. All this talent, going straight into the wastebasket. And forget about directing. "It was difficult for me to get directing jobs because I seemed sort of crazy. They accused me of taking the [*Mikey and Nicky*] negative," she said a decade later.[143] How much time had to pass since *Mikey and Nicky* for a studio to trust her with a film again? Elaine had spent the better part of nearly a decade making other people's films better, never making any of her own. Her luck would change soon, though. Warren Beatty and Dustin Hoffman both had debts to her to repay—but not even that would end up working out the way she'd hoped it would.

CHAPTER 9

Dangerous Business

Ishtar (1987)

Elaine was in the middle of the Moroccan desert, covered head to toe in so much fabric that you could barely even see her underneath it all:[1] long sleeves and pants; a robe for good measure; a scarf across her face held up, improbably, by her oversize sunglasses; a straw hat that wouldn't be enough to keep her hair from eventually frying in the beating sun,[2] but was better than nothing for now. This was not New York. This wasn't even Los Angeles; at least that great desert sprawl operated in a way she could make sense of.

Elaine didn't know how to operate here. She had gone with a companion who posed as her husband so she could buy a rug "which could not be sold to me, because I was a woman," she said. "I met the man and he gave me a price for the rug and I said okay and he looked really hurt. They said, 'You have to negotiate.' So I gave them a price back that was low, and he said to me, 'I will take your price, but if I do, we can never be friends again.' Now, I'd met this man five minutes ago, but I found myself saying, 'Rather than never be your friend again, I will raise my price.' And then I finally got the rug. But it was such a different way of doing things. It was such another culture, and such another language and code."[3]

Buying a rug in Morocco would be easy. Making a film there would not.

EVEN IF WARREN Beatty didn't owe her for *Reds,* she liked working with him enough that she wanted to team up again. Beatty wasn't just an ideal collaborator and source of support, someone who could make her better; he was, like all her best partners, a symbiotic complement, someone she could make better, too, unearthing parts of his personality and talent he hadn't fully mined before. She knew Beatty wasn't the self-serious playboy he could appear to be. "I wanted to think of what to [write] for him, because he's funny and he's a southern boy, really," she said.[4] Wasn't he great in *Heaven Can Wait*? Shouldn't he follow up *Reds* with something more like that—lighter and funnier? Something sort of goofy and feel-good—or, well, the closest to feel-good as she was ever going to get. Elaine had been watching old *Road To . . .* movies—those Bob Hope/Bing Crosby buddy flicks—and it clicked. How fun would it be to write one of those, she thought, and how perfect was the timing? She had always had a kind of prescient knowingness, an ability to capture the zeitgeist before nearly everyone else even realized what the zeitgeist was. Look at all there was to lampoon: It was the mid-eighties, and if you were paying the slightest bit of attention, it wasn't hard to see all the conflict stirring up in the Middle East, and America's messy involvement in it all, whether it was backing both Iraq and Iran in a war of attrition or selling weapons to Afghan resistance groups to fight the Soviet Union. And it was all overseen by a movie star in the White House whose only knowledge of the Middle East, you would think, was derived entirely from those Hope and Crosby movies. "At that time, Reagan was president, and I met him. And he's an amazingly naive, innocent, charming guy who really, really cared about show business! So he was the president. And nobody really knew what was going on, actually," Elaine said. "I thought, 'Really, there's something very endearing, if terrifying, about this kind of innocence, this kind of naiveté.'"[5] Not only was something in the *Road To . . .* vein an appropriate send-up for the current climate; it was also right in her wheelhouse. "As you know," she added, "I write for two men all the time."[6] This, she thought, would be her next movie.

Over dinner with Beatty and Bert Fields, she began tossing around the idea, making up scenes about two hopeless dolts and riffing on the premise.[7] They could be performers of some sort, perhaps songwriters—characters for whom you could "write bad songs that you might conceivably, if you were really talentless, think were okay"—whose innocent cluelessness would symbolize how foolish she found our involvement in the Middle East.[8] For Beatty, it was as if she had punched up an idea he had been thinking about himself: He had long been mulling over an idea about a director making a movie about a revolution in Central America who gets caught up in an *actual* revolution that breaks out during the shoot.[9] It was one that the pair, along with Peter Feibleman, had briefly entertained, going so far as booking a trip to Central America for research before it fizzled out. But Beatty knew that if it wasn't Elaine's own idea, it wasn't going to go anywhere with her at the helm.[10] More important, he knew that if Elaine thought that the better story was in the Middle East, not Central America, who were you to question her? Elaine wasn't always right, but she was never wrong.

The plot was established. Aspiring New York singer-songwriters, Lyle Rogers and Chuck Clarke, two hapless middle-age men with an indefatigable well of drive and passion, but an astonishing lack of any discernible talent, take a gig in Morocco, foolishly thinking it will be their big break. Instead, they find themselves ensnared in a proxy conflict between the country's right-wing ruling government, its left-wing rebellion, and the CIA. Sure, there'd be commentary, but she wouldn't serve it to you straight; on the surface, the film would be an easygoing farce full of music, romance, and adventure. Elaine would wrap her cutting indictment—of fame, of men who fail up, of American politics—in pure silliness. On paper, it would appear to be her most commercial and accessible comedy yet, tailor-made to the box office trends of the time. Hollywood had changed since Elaine last made a film; its new era had crested and was fading fast. Out were psychological character studies, in were big budget comedies and action-adventure films like *Ghostbusters, Beverly Hills Cop, Romancing the Stone,* and *Back to the Future.* So many of her peers were graduating from small seventies comedies to match the tone being set by filmmakers like Steven Spielberg and Robert Zemeckis; why shouldn't Elaine try her hand at it, too? In the game that was Hollywood, this was a level up. How could she resist making a run at it?

While Beatty was a lock, there was still the balancing other end of the schmuck equation to figure out. Fields knew right away: Dustin Hoffman was their guy. Not only did he also owe Elaine a

"The goddess was more evident in Elaine than in most people—in all her aspects—the beautiful and the wrathful one," Del Close would say of his former flame, Elaine May, here in an early publicity photo from 1960.

Elaine May, the gutter rat, 1961.

May and Mike Nichols at a private after-party celebrating President John F. Kennedy's forty-fifth birthday party, May 1962. By the end of the year, the pair would no longer be speaking.

May with Shelley Berman and her brief second husband, Sheldon Harnick, on the opening night for the stage production of *A Family Affair*, 1962.

A reconciled Nichols and May perform for the civil rights protesters marching from Selma to Montgomery, Alabama, in 1965.

On set with director Jerome Robbins rehearsing *The Office*, 1965. The disastrous stage production would be one of May's post–Nichols and May flops.

"You make the crew nervous." Elaine May, director, on the set of *A New Leaf*, 1970.

May and costar Walter Matthau sharing a laugh behind the scenes of *A New Leaf*. The two had a contentious relationship on the film; his first day on set, he asked her, "You're not going to direct me, are you?"

Directing Charles Grodin and daughter Jeannie Berlin in *The Heartbreak Kid*, 1972.

Behind the scenes on *Mikey and Nicky* with John Cassavetes and Peter Falk, early in the film's runaway-train production.

Nichols and May bring their long history to the parts of George and Martha in the Long Wharf Theatre's 1980 production of *Who's Afraid of Virginia Woolf?* "We arrive expecting to watch two rusty stand-up comics do a novelty act," Frank Rich raved. "We leave having seen four thinking actors shed startling new light on one of the great dark plays of our time."

Elaine May, at eighty-seven, accepting the Tony Award for Best Actress in a Play for her performance in *The Waverly Gallery*, her first stage performance in twenty years.

favor, but imagine the deranged gleam of madness that might have appeared in her eye as she thought about another comedic under-current his casting would bring to the movie. What if she deliber-ately wrote both of their characters against type, making Dustin the heartthrob and Warren the dopey outsider? Though the two men had only ever met in passing, she knew they "were compatible in a comic way," Hoffman said.[11] It was just too good to pass up.

Elaine drafted the script—which would initially be called *Blind Camel*—in three months while Beatty got to work selling the idea to his friend Guy McElwaine at Columbia Pictures[12] and to his potential costar. Convincing McElwaine wasn't hard. "Everyone thinks it was a tough decision to do *Ishtar*," McElwaine said. "It was not a tough decision. . . . My trust was in Warren—and his ability to merge artistic propensities with populist taste. His track record is almost unmatched." What's more, McElwaine had "spent a lot of time with Elaine, talking about this project. And she assured me she was not going to misbehave."[13] It was no secret that Elaine's relationship with studios was still chilly. She could make all the promises they wanted, but it was Beatty's involvement as a pro-ducer that would get them on board. The only difference between investing in Elaine and investing in Beatty was the return; as long as Beatty's wild gambles kept turning out to be big moneymakers, they could accept that his overlong productions and rule-skirting behavior were just part of the deal.[14]

Hoffman, though, would be a tougher convert, with several res-ervations about coming on board. There was the whole Morocco plot point, for starters—Hoffman and his frequent collaborator Murray Schisgal felt that, rather than an action film, this was really a much smaller movie about two delusional Simon & Garfunkel wannabes trying to make it big in New York. He didn't find playing against type necessary, nor was he exactly comfortable with it. And then there was the more concerning problem: Elaine's prickly, pro-prietary demeanor. Meeting with her, "I couldn't get any movement on the things that I didn't think worked," he said. "Murray said to me, 'They're not going to change anything.' I replied, 'That's my feeling. They as much as said it.'"[15] Forget about all of that, Beatty urged him. The problem was not Elaine; the problem was the lack of supportive producers and execs on Elaine's side. If she appeared to be immovable and resistant to change, it was only because so many had so radically changed her work without her consent in the past. But he had the power to fix all of that: "You saw those movies that Elaine did," Beatty told Hoffman. "You know she's never had a good producer? You know that they never surrounded her with the right people? . . . I'm going to be there, and I'm going to make sure she has the room to do her best work." He insisted it would work. "Don't worry about the script, go with her talent, go with us."[16] Hoffman hadn't made a film since 1982's *Tootsie*. The clock was ticking. He was getting old, and the times were changing; there was a new star every month. Relevance was currency in Hollywood; the longer you didn't work, no matter the reason, the more you lost. He wasn't like Beatty, someone whose long absences from the screen could be explained away as time spent developing his own projects to write and direct. He could no longer count on being as selective as he was and still stay a guaranteed bankable star. "I'm probably going to take it," he told Schisgal. "Partly as a favor to Elaine, and also because Warren is so persuasive." He could brush aside his reservations and let them keep their vision of the story as is, trust Beatty that going with her talent would work out for the best.[17]

The rest of the cast and crew would be filled out with an A-team of trusted collaborators. Elaine got Charles Grodin to play the inept CIA operative, and friends like Jack Weston, Carol Kane, Rose Arrick, and Herb Gardner to fill small supporting roles. She and Phillip Schopper had just begun a romantic relationship that would last the next thirteen years; on *Ishtar,* he would serve as her "artistic consultant"-cum-right hand man. Beatty, meanwhile, tapped *Reds* cinematographer Vittorio Storaro, brought on his cousin David MacLeod as an associate producer, and put his latest girlfriend, Isabelle Adjani, in the role of the revolutionary love interest. Paul Sylbert, who had worked with both May and Beatty on *Mikey and Nicky* and *Heaven Can Wait,* would sign on as production designer—though, later, he would serve as one of *Ishtar*'s primary inside sources as the criticism and negative press mounted.

To write the so-bad-they're-almost-kind-of-good songs, Beatty flew Paul Williams, who had done the music for *A Star Is Born* and

The Muppet Movie, to meet with him, Elaine, and Dustin in England. From the start, indecision and evasiveness reigned supreme. "There were two tasks at hand that were interesting," he recalls. "One is to get the job, to get Warren to actually say, 'Okay, I want you to write this.' And then to have Elaine tell me what she is looking for. I got into the characters—to me, it was like an acting job. I started writing the songs based on what I felt. She would nod and say, 'That's wrong, I don't know . . .' But she wouldn't give me any directions on what she wanted from me."[18] Write a song and demo it for Elaine. Wait for her feedback, which there was never very much of. Write another song. Demo it for Elaine. Wait for her to say something, anything, again. That was Williams's process, over and over, until one day, he walked in to share his latest, a track he called "That a Lawn Mower Can Do All That." "I had the lines about 'I can see her standing in the backyard of my mind / She cracks her knuckles, and the scab that's on her knee won't go away / I can see the woman waiting in her eyes, and I can see the love, and I can see the Brooklyn Dodgers in L.A.,'" he says. "And she nodded. She said, 'That's exactly it.'"[19]

Williams would find himself working on *Ishtar* for a year and a half of the film's production, staying all-expenses at the Waldorf Astoria when working in New York. When the production moved to Morocco, Williams, who typically only ever spent a few days on the sets of films he scored, went with them. What if Elaine needed a new song in the moment of shooting? She had only written so many snippets of lyrics into the script and forget about prerecording any of the tracks to lip-synch to when they shot the scene later. That would be too artificial, would suck all the spontaneous energy of a true live performance out of the air. And besides, better not to plan things too much. Because suppose somewhere around the twelfth take of a scene she realized that what the scene actually needed was a brand-new song entirely. Who would write that? It didn't matter that she would actually use only one or two of those lines. She needed an entire new song—because who knew *which* two lines she'd end up wanting to choose later in the edit room. By the time shooting wrapped, Williams estimates he wrote more than fifty songs for the picture.[20] Of the twenty-three original songs credited in the final film—three of which were on-set ad-libs and ten of which Elaine had written into the script—only five of Williams's full original compositions made the cut.[21]

MOROCCO WASN'T EXACTLY the kind of place where anyone in Hollywood would ever want to make a movie—it's easier and cheaper to film desert scenes outside of L.A., with English-speaking extras and all the props and location resources you could need nearby—much less in the fall of 1985. Within the span of a week, Israeli forces had bombed the Palestine Liberation Organization near Tunis and Palestinian terrorists hijacked the *Achille Lauro* cruise ship—all while the Moroccan government was dealing with its own guerrilla situation. Even without all the terrorism, the Moroccan shoot was off to an ominous start: Just before filming commenced, reports leaked that a "youngster" was killed by the film caravan after running out into the street. Even though the driver was exonerated, and Elaine was in another car, it seemed a bad omen for how the rest of the ten-week shoot would shake out.[22]

You'd have to be crazy to be an American—especially a Jewish American—and still go forth with making a movie there. Crazy, or have some sort of financial incentive to do so. In the decades that have passed since *Ishtar*'s release, it's been suggested that filming in Morocco—often singled out at the time as another extravagant line item in a sky-high budget full of extravagant line items—wasn't actually an extravagant choice, after all. Columbia wasn't the only one fronting the movie; part of HBO's 1985 deal with the studio for exclusive TV rights to their films required paying a license fee equivalent to "a substantial percentage" of the films' production costs.[23] Not to mention that it was a convenient way for Coca-Cola, Columbia's parent company, to spend some of the millions in frozen assets they had in the country. It's a good explanation for an otherwise illogical choice, one that even plausibly checks out. Coke had, after all, been asserting an aggressive campaign with private and government groups in the Middle East to get themselves off an Arab boycott list that had kept them from selling their soft drinks across most of the region since 1967.[24] (Which also makes a seemingly throwaway line, in which Grodin's character is offered a Pepsi—which gossip columnists were quick to hound as an ungrateful author's chomp at the hand that fed her[25]—less a clever barb and more just, well, truth.) Maybe Coca-Cola really did think *Ishtar* could put to use some of its nearly $1 billion in corporate assets earmarked for Europe and Africa.[26] Or maybe it's just another good story, one of many good but plausibly deniable anecdotes that surround the film.

By now, the myriad apocryphal stories about its production—which range from scandalous and damning and too strange to possibly be fiction to redemptive and vindictive—have become legend. It's nearly impossible to know how many of them are really true or to what degree. In all likelihood, there is truth in the wildest of them and revisionist lies in the most mundane. "From any small thing you can make a million truths," Elaine once said.[27] She wasn't talking specifically about *Ishtar,* but she might as well have been. No matter whose point of view you take—Sylbert's, Schopper's, Elaine's, or anyone else's—they all have an agenda. Some have an ax to grind with the subject of many of these stories, some were her close friends (and in one case, her romantic partner), and one is the subject herself. Had the film done better, maybe things would be different. Maybe then there would be a singular clear version, with no one jockeying to tell their side the loudest and with the most authority. Instead, the story of one of Hollywood's biggest disasters has become a multiplayer blame game.

IF ONLY THEY hadn't been suspicious of something coming easily from the start, hadn't taken it for granted. Maybe then things would have gotten off on the right foot. It's hard to tell, but in the case of acquiring the then-titular blind camel, they almost had it made. In lieu of a near-impossible-to-find actually blind camel, Elaine would settle for a light-eyed camel instead—which wasn't much easier to come by, of course, but they could, with a little movie magic, make one appear blind on-screen. Blank check in hand, crew members set out on a mission: Find one perfect camel—and a few more stand-ins just like it. They lucked out; the first one they encountered had it all, and at $700 was a steal. They hesitated. "We had lots of time to spend, and lots of money. We didn't want to go back to the office and say, 'Elaine, guess what. We bought the very first camel we looked at!' We figured what the hell, we'd keep looking. We told the camel dealer, 'Thanks a lot. We'll get back to you,'" they explained. Onward they searched, but hey, you know a star when you see it. None of the subsequent camels they looked at had the *it* factor of the first one. They returned to the dealer only to be told they were too late. It had—allegedly—been eaten.[28]

That kind of paralysis would creep across the rest of the shoot.[29] Mounting tensions in the region would have made any other director hurry up and wrap early to get out of there as quickly as possible, but not Elaine. "Elaine May is a woman of many words. However," a source said, "the word 'cut' does not happen to be among them."[30] Though she managed to stay on schedule during the shoot, true to form, she stuffed as many long takes into that time as she could. "The camera would start and the scene would go on," one production member recalled. "And it wouldn't stop until the cameraman would say, 'We're out of film.' By that time, Warren and Dustin would have forgotten their lines a long time ago. So they'd just stand there, trying to improvise. Only Warren wasn't too good at improvising. Anyway, it would go on and on. And some of us would wonder when the heck it would end. But until Elaine May says 'Cut,' you do not stop the cameras. And most of the time, she just let the scene go until the film was gone."[31] The issue with Elaine overshooting was not that it was expensive, but that this time it didn't get the new, exciting performances she was often chasing. With her actors on different wavelengths, with different methods of working, it just got her diminishing returns. "Warren would never learn his lines," Hoffman said. "He would be getting warmed up by the time I was running out of gas. We'd be shooting—forty takes—it was brutally hot, and he'd be learning the script on camera. Which would have been fine if I wasn't there, too. It was hard, but there was nothing I could do about it."[32] Sending all the footage off to Rome to be processed, where it would come back twice a week instead of every day, only added to the backlog. "My crew couldn't really keep up with it, so I would end up having to sync dailies, also," editor Stephen Rotter says. Elaine would watch and take her notes, none of which he ever saw. He was swimming in footage, barely having any time to make rough assembly cuts for the cast and crew to watch and respond to as they moved through filming. "I was a little panicked that I was so far behind, but it didn't seem to bother her. But it certainly bothered me."[33]

And then there were the dunes. You know about the dunes. You've heard the story. The one that somehow, by the sheer insanity of it, managed to be the one that stuck when the story of *Ishtar's* production history stretched to mythic proportions. The one about the sand dunes in the middle of the desert that Elaine asked to flatten. The one that's probably not true—just watch the movie for yourself and you'll see that dunes abound—but stands to represent the kind of chaos the film's Moroccan shoot would entail.

Here is what Paul Sylbert says: Elaine had talked nonstop in preproduction about wanting to shoot in a desert with dunes, and he had finally found the perfect spot. "There were these great coastal deserts. Perfect. But Elaine was not prepared to use them. With all the talk of dunes, her idea of the desert was Brighton Beach. . . . On the way back from seeing the fabulous dunes—me, Warren, and some others, we knew we had found our location—she suddenly said, 'Dunes? Who said anything about dunes?'"[34] To please her new whim, he leveled eleven bulldozers' worth of sand.[35]

And here is what Phillip Schopper says: "That didn't happen. The only place I can think of where that *sort of* happened is there's a scene where they're crawling at the desert. Where we were, the desert itself, the floor is hard and rocky. You can't have a whole movie where it's nothing but dunes and now we're in this desert movie; you can't have them crawling along and they're not in sand. It just looked too weird. So we got a truck and scooped up a bunch of sand in it and, in an area of about thirty square yards, dumped that sand and spread it around, and that's what they crawled on. That became, 'Elaine May didn't like the way the desert looked, so she changed the desert.' I mean, it's silly. It's just stupid. I mean, if we had left them walking on ground, we would say, 'Where are they? Weren't they just on sand dunes?' It's crazy."[36]

And here is what Elaine says: "The fact that we kind of feel that we can choose the truth, it really . . . A friend of mine called today and said, 'I read a story that when you made *Ishtar*, you got to the desert, and you said, "What are those hills?" and they said, "Dunes," and you said, "Flatten them."' And I said to him, 'Well, do you believe that?' And there was a long pause, and he said, 'Well, no, but it's such a great story!'"[37]

MAKING A FILM is a team effort, but Elaine didn't trust many aside from Schopper, who acted as her translator and buffer, much to the rest of the crew's annoyance. "Wherever she was, I was, pretty much," he says. "So they mostly resented me, because they knew if I was talking to Elaine about something, something wasn't going right and there was going to be some issue."[38] One of her biggest issues would be with Storaro. Clashes with him over shots became a constant. "Poor Vittorio," Schopper says. "I would have to come up with things to pretend to talk to Elaine about, to pull her aside to say, 'Look, you can't do this angle or this light . . .' so we could discuss it. At a certain point, Vittorio started catching on, so he would come running over to listen to every conversation."[39] Elaine composed her shots with comic effect or painstaking realism in mind; the technical practicality was an afterthought. If she had her way, she would shoot Hoffman and Beatty scaling a different dune in each take, light a club so dimly you could barely make out the faces of extras in reaction shots. If it didn't work when she saw the footage in edit, she would salvage it in her own DIY way. But try telling that to one of the most esteemed cinematographers of his time. Every shot he set up, she disagreed with, until eventually, he figured out how to outsmart her: He began to put the camera opposite where he actually wanted it, then waited for her to object.[40] It wasn't unusual to see him moving the key light himself when Elaine decided to change a shot halfway through shooting a scene.[41]

The madness seeped into everyone. Williams, who spent the shoot making up for the hard drugs he couldn't take into Morocco with booze, decided to adopt a Method-like approach to writing for Chuck and Lyle. "I want to experience this," he said when given an assignment to write something for the pair to sing while lost in the desert. "So they're shooting out in the middle of the dunes and the sun comes up in the morning and I'm knocking on Dustin's door in tears because I spent the night in the desert."[42]

By the time the film wrapped in Morocco and returned to New York to finish filming, the only one with any pep left was Elaine. "It was a very hard shoot, but I really liked it," she insisted. "I actually have an affinity for the desert."[43]

SOMEWHERE OVER THE Atlantic Ocean, in the plane back to New York, Elaine decided to quit smoking.

A father and ex-husband dead from heart attacks and a mother dead from lung cancer[44]—heavy smokers, all of them—had scared her. She had tried to cut back, tried swapping out cigarettes for cigars, but she still worried. Making movies wasn't working in the emergency room or doing hard manual labor, but it wasn't an easy job. The stress of it all—plus her outlet for handling it—was catching up to her. She was in her fifties now. She had only so much time left, and she wanted to stretch it out as long as possible.

She felt, she said, like the business was making her kill herself. "I'm not going to let them do that to me," she thought. When she returned to New York, she quit cold turkey.[45]

WHATEVER MADNESS WENT down in Morocco came with them to New York, where they'd need to not only shoot the New York side of the story but also make up interior shoots they ended up skipping in Morocco to get back two weeks early. The production, forced by New York union rules to hire a local camera crew to be on standby for its Italian, Storaro-led one, was hemorrhaging money.[46] The shooting hours were so long, they gave up trying to watch the dailies.[47] To suggest, at midnight, wrapping a sixteen-hour day spent shooting 30,000 feet of extras—now falling asleep on set—was to risk an explosive reaction from Elaine.[48] Trying to keep away from her cigars, Elaine ate constantly, "like a rabbit." One day on set, she blindly picked up a special effects smoke cookie—a charcoal-like disc in a steel tray—and took a bite.[49] Making any movie can get nutty. Making *Ishtar* was like spending every day at the circus.[50]

"Okay," Elaine told Hoffman and Beatty. It was late in the second day of shooting the same scene, over and over and over again. "Let's do it again. We didn't quite get it."

Beatty sighed. "Elaine, we got it before lunch."[51]

There was no use in fighting. The crew had gone into the shoot, "eyes wide open," production manager G. Mac Brown says. "Knowing she's stolen the negative before, are you kidding? You're up against it here. So you need to stay partners somehow."[52] Still, she managed to surprise and frustrate them with her at times perplexing and seemingly inefficient method of working. The crew may have shown up and committed to the work day in and day out with the best intentions, but they certainly groaned while doing it. Elaine wasn't the kind of director whom they could schedule meetings with to troubleshoot their problems or to get more information. In order for Brown to do his job and get a decision out of her on one thing or another, he'd often have to trail behind her as she meandered the set trying to avoid him. It wasn't unusual to hear complaints of "I can't do my best work" or "This fucking broad's crazy!" from the old-school New York crew.[53]

At this point, it was clear: You could not persuade Elaine to budge from her vision, could not strong-arm her into practicality. How charmingly naive for any of them to have once thought they could. She had a way of waiting them out, wearing them down until it was just easier to let go and give in. Elaine was going to make the movie she wanted to make, and they would all just have to live with it.[54]

IT'S ALL WELL and good for Elaine to get a chance to challenge herself to aim higher and play in a larger sandbox (literally). Elaine could write bigger, but writing was pure imagination, playing out something in your head. Anything is possible on the page; in the real world, it's another story. A film of *Ishtar*'s size and scale would require organization, a firm structure, and a director who excelled not just at coaching her actors but at giving marching orders to her crew as well. In short, it required a leader. Something Elaine never had been and never would be.

Elaine's method of making a film was, more or less, improvising. The objective was only to make a great movie and make it as she went along, worrying not about keeping to a budget or a schedule but simply about making something great.[55] It was a method that worked—reasonably well, at least—on smaller films, but was antithetical to the well-oiled machine of a big studio feature, where a director tells their collaborators what they want and all parties go out and try to best achieve it. "It was about creation for Elaine," said Hoffman. "She loved process. Those are dirty words when you're shooting."[56] In Elaine's world, directing wasn't a dictatorship; it was a democracy. Rather than tell her crew what she wanted, she'd leave it to them to move organically through the creative process, then come to her with their ideas to discuss and figure out from there.[57] But it wasn't always effective. Elaine directed by "I'll know it when I see it"[58] and "Let's do it again,"[59] speaking in a directionless vortex of feedback that could take time to adjust to if you weren't one of her frequent collaborators.[60]

"She knows exactly what she wants, but you have to know her," Jack Weston said. "There's one scene, behind the credits, where Dustin is trying to hire me. Elaine walks up, and if I didn't know her, I'd clutch. She says, 'In order to do this scene . . . I don't know . . . it depends on how you feel . . . there's a way of doing things . . .' I think: Aha, I'm doing it too slow—she wants me to pick it up, without losing what I've already got. It's hard to explain. I know this sounds like gibberish, but it's true."[61] Charles Grodin agreed: "Elaine doesn't talk much about how scenes should be played. She says virtually nothing, a sentence or two, a word. It's more like nudging. There's more to moviemaking than storyboarding. Elaine is wedded to nothing. There are no markers on the floor. She'll make the cinematographer adjust to the life of the scene. Any scene can be changed. She shoots a scene as it was written, and then in other ways."[62]

Even if her way of directing often resulted in unexpected and brilliant performances from her actors, it wasn't as if she didn't exhaust them first. By the end of the shoot, everyone was testy: "Look: Just tell me my moves, okay?" Beatty asked as he struggled to get through a scene with timing troubles. "Read the fucking script," Hoffman told him. "*I* don't read fucking scripts," Beatty shot back, unable to hide his evident aggravation even as he attempted to make a joke.[63]

"I was in the later stages of my alcoholism by then," Williams explains. "It didn't interfere with my discipline, but I certainly didn't waste a lot of time sitting down to think like, 'What is appropriate here?' I mean, if I write songs for a movie, I usually write them and show them to the director and they say, 'Those are great. That's fabulous,' or, 'I liked that one better than that.' And you make the adjustments and you may never be on the set. This entire production felt like a living, breathing exercise. The creation—it felt like it was on all of us."[64]

This is not to say that Elaine's behavior was completely off-the-wall or unusual; making a film is a team effort in every sense of the process, after all. In some ways, Elaine's hands-off approach encouraged and was respectful of her colleagues' creative process, making everyone feel like they had meaningful creative ownership of and input into the final product. "What she does that looks like an inability to make a constructive navigation for you is in fact her honoring a process that she's willing to wait for," says Williams.[65]

But there's a price to pay for every day that passes while you honor that process. Making a movie is slow and expensive, even if it comes in at budget and on time. Making an Elaine May movie on this kind of timeline? It may never be released. There may be more to directing than storyboarding, but that's certainly part of it. Elaine's process may have worked for the movies she had made before—smaller movies, "indoor movies" about human relationships that are big on chat and light on moving set pieces—but it couldn't work on something of this scale. As Paul Sylbert put it at the time: "That woman had not made a movie in ten years. And then the first thing she had to do was paint the Sistine Chapel."[66] The stakes were too high, and there was nothing more dangerous than being wedded to nothing. Once the time arrived to shoot *Ishtar*'s action scenes, with Elaine's evident fear casting a shadow over everyone, something had to be done if they wanted to stay on schedule. It was *A New Leaf* all over again: She was in new and unfamiliar territory, and the less in control she felt, the more insular and fearful she became, until indecision seemed like a better option than asking for help—even from those she seemingly trusted most.

Although the production may not have ended up being as much of a runaway train as it was often depicted as being, it certainly wasn't an efficient one. In an ideal world, Elaine's allies would have stepped in to make up for in practicality what Elaine lacked, allowing her to focus on her strengths—directing her actors through games and finding the best way to play each scene—while they handled the day-to-day decisions. But instead, too nervous, they all became patient yes-men, hesitant to overstep even when she herself couldn't make up her mind. Beatty, who had started the shoot insisting on being the strong support she had always lacked, saw that his idea of support—encouragement—wasn't working. "God bless Warren," Williams remembers. "Even on the set and shooting and filming and wearing down the lines, he was totally supportive and would say, 'You're directing. You're the director. You're the screenwriter. You're the director.' And he let her go."[67] In a way, he had no choice but to give in to her whims. Taking over the picture was never an option. "There were no arguments," Stephen Rotter says. "It's just that she was stronger than everybody else. She just had that power. They just so respected her talent that, literally, they just didn't stand up to her and she just got her way. She really knew how to handle these people."[68]

FILMING ON *ISHTAR* was completed on March 25, 1986, somehow, in spite of everything, reportedly three days under the original schedule and on budget.[69] The shoot had felt so close to the precipice of stretching out into infinity that the crew had placed a bet on the exact time and date of the wrap; the fact that the production accountant was the one who guessed right just seemed anticlimactic after all they had been through.[70] With her eye on a Thanksgiving 1986 release, Elaine headed into her edit suite at Sound One—occupying an entire floor of the Brill Building—to make a movie out of her 650,000 feet of footage.[71] "Not to worry," she told Rotter, whom she would gnash gum beside for months on end. "You and I will go through every frame of the movie."[72] She wasn't joking.

Anyone would have thought Elaine learned her lesson about getting in too deep in endless cutting with *Mikey and Nicky*. But no. The only thing that had changed since *Mikey and Nicky* was that she had more manpower at her disposal—though often she'd just sit down and start splicing film herself[73]—which she would put to tireless work over the next eleven months. Elaine's madness in postproduction took a while to get used to; an unwillingness to flex beyond the typical conventions of your job usually resulted in your being shown the door.[74] "A lot of people found her very difficult to work with because she would not follow convention if it didn't suit her," says Brad Fuller, who was hired to work on *Ishtar* as an ADR editor despite his inexperience. "It wasn't like she was deliberately unconventional, but she wasn't concerned with it if it didn't suit her goals."[75]

Elaine could get lost in the details: the rhythm of a line reading here, the landing of a pratfall there, all the way down to the sound of a camel's footsteps, each of which was recorded individually,[76] and only after the sand in the Foley pit had been changed multiple times.[77] She was locked into all the potential the story still held as they went along. Ever the writer, she edited by sound, so hyper-tuned to it that she could cut together an entirely new sentence word by word, arranging it like a puzzle, noting the better takes down to the slightest inflection. "She has better ears than I do," the sound supervisor would marvel.[78] It was the sound and dialogue, she insisted, that mattered more than anything happening on screen.[79] Sloppy visuals she could deal with; a line of dialogue that was even the least bit off she could not. There was nothing she couldn't rewrite and find a way to cheat into the film; an idea for a new way to shape a scene could come to her at a moment's notice, and she and Schopper would go off to experiment with it. A close-up from an entirely different scene could become a reaction to cut to another. A line of dialogue could be rewritten and dummy dubbed in with a cassette recorder over and over until they found a satisfactory version. "There is no later," she would often say.[80] You had to try everything now, while it was fresh, had to take every side road you stumbled upon en route to the destination. Who knew what you'd miss if you didn't? Getting too comfortable with a plan was a surefire way to find yourself stuck later. For Elaine, a film wasn't something meticulously planned out so much as sculpted from the material she had at hand. There was always an opportunity for spontaneity, for the story to unfurl itself for her in a way she could have never anticipated, for there to be magic somewhere buried in all the footage, nearly every frame of which she could remember. No stone was left unturned. "Once I had sort of semi-concocted an airplane scene, and she said, 'Oh, no, no,'" Rotter says.

"And then about six months later she said, 'Do you remember what you did with that? Could you put it in there?'"[81]

Sound One hummed around the clock to keep up with the grueling demand. Editors' hours stretched all day, from eight a.m. to ten p.m., six or seven days a week. "But on the sixth and seventh day, we would quit after eight hours," Rotter says. "So it was like a vacation."[82] *Ishtar's* release date moved from Thanksgiving to Christmas. Then, as trailers for the film played in theaters across the country, Christmas became May of 1987.[83] People came and people left. Rotter's friends complained about the sorry, exhausted shape he was in.[84] On his first day on the job—months after the edit had begun and still somehow months before it would be finished—sound editor Ira Spiegel remembers another editor (there were a total of eighteen people in the sound department alone) telling him, "For every day that I work, you're gonna have to work two or three days. So you better be prepared to work long hours and come in on the weekends to meet my and our standards." Just as Elaine never knew what she wanted, neither did the post team. She could come in at five p.m. and request a new cut ready by seven, just to see it.[85]

"Elaine had a coterie of people taking care of her," Rotter says.[86] When Elaine was engrossed in the minutiae of the job, basic functions of day-to-day life fell by the wayside. Her mind was suited for certain things, she would say. Filmmaking was one of them, but a lot of others were not.[87] "What do I know?" she'd often ask. "I never graduated from high school."[88] People were tasked with putting her in cabs and making sure she got to and from work all right,[89] though she was still often late.[90] Her appearance could most generously be described as unkempt and unruly;[91] sometimes she'd show up in two different-colored socks.[92] She had to be reminded to eat, and it wasn't unusual to see someone picking macrobiotic food out of her hair later as she focused on the work in front of her, oblivious.[93]

She lived on health food, heaps of greens, salads served with vinegar on the side and nothing else. "Elaine, your meadow has arrived," someone would call out when her takeout was delivered.[94] Giving up smoking was an impossible task,[95] so instead she deepened her long-held fixation on controlling the food she ate. "I can tell you about fat grams and vitamins and what they do," she said years later, "because I was a smoker and I thought, 'I'll never give up smoking, but if I can just learn everything that's right to eat, perhaps I'll live.' So I really studied food and everything to eat and then I gave up smoking. But I knew so much that I could never again eat anything I liked."[96] It was a need for control that she would carry with her relentlessly for the rest of her life. "She's unbelievably insistent on being in shape," Caroline Aaron says. "She really doesn't understand when people let themselves go. She just doesn't understand it. She thinks it just doesn't make any sense."[97] She would take trips to the infamous Arizona wellness resort Canyon Ranch to study Pilates,[98] keep exercise mats in edit rooms so she could get in workouts between cutting,[99] sing the praises of working out with a trainer in her sixties.[100] Good luck if you happened to be her dinner guest. Sticking strictly to the Pritikin diet, she picked fights with people with differing views on nutrition, told anyone who would listen that oil was the enemy, and claimed to be allergic to salt. And she wasn't at all shy about requesting special accommodations or sending dishes back. "No salt in the spices, no salt on the grill, and no salt on the plate. This was extremely important, she said, because salt was very dangerous for her," Doris Roberts recalled her once ordering a waiter.[101] "Look, look. You can see what the salt is doing," she would say if she thought the slightest bit of it made its way into her food. "It's puffing me up."[102]

Any attempts to avoid conflict on the shoot had dissipated; Beatty and Hoffman began showing up often as the edit stretched on. They may not have been able to have much say while still filming, but what made it into the final cut—which had to be agreed upon by all of them—was going to be different. Suddenly, there were not just Elaine's notes to execute, but ones from Beatty and Hoffman, too. Even if few things were radically different—a request for a vanity close-up of Hoffman here, a more generous take of Beatty's girlfriend Adjani there[103]—they fought bitterly, bringing in Bert Fields to arbitrate.[104] Not that it really mattered. "Elaine got everything that she wanted," Rotter says. "It just worked out that way. There was nothing that she disagreed with. I mean, you just couldn't defy her. It was impossible."[105] As always, the film was parted with more than it was finished; they were still cutting the negative the night it needed to be turned in. "It had to be ready by midnight and we just made it," says Rotter. "Everything we could do, we did."[106]

The *Ishtar* floor at Sound One looked like a ghost town when the film finally wrapped. Unused cutting tape and magnetic film, rolls of fill leader and china markers, all left behind without a thought. "You know, on my first day starting on *Ishtar,* I was told 'whatever you want,' in terms of equipment," Fuller remembers. "'You can have it. Just order it.' No one's ever said that to me on a film."[107] It was all sold to the *Ishtar* crew, and it was all deserted by them, left to be gathered up and rented to some other film, hopefully one that would have fewer stories to tell down the road. Making this film was, by most accounts, the most nerve-racking, exhausting, harrowing, "nightmare"[108] experience they had ever had. But they'd also admit it was one of the most rewarding ones. Despite everything Elaine had put them through, they couldn't help but still love—no, *worship*—her. "Every movie is like a war," Beatty said. "But if the movie comes out and people like it, the wounds of battle heal very quickly."[109]

SOMETHING WAS WRONG. Elaine was used to bad press by now, but things were different this time.

"When the movie came out," Elaine remembered, "we had three previews, and they went really well. And [former Columbia owner] Herb Allen said, 'This is fantastic! Thumbs up!' So I went to Bali, because I thought everything was fine. I hit Bali, and Warren calls and tells me that the day the press came, an article came out in the *Los Angeles Times* in which the head of Columbia wiped us out."[110]

There it was, barely a week after her new movie finally opened, in print. It's true that the *Los Angeles Times* ran a four full-page spread called "The High Cost of *Ishtar,*" full of every damning possible thing you could say about the movie. The budget, the star-power ego trips, Elaine's on-set and postproduction antics, you name it. There he was, the new head of their studio, David Puttnam—a man who happened to hate Warren Beatty, Dustin Hoffman, and big-budget Hollywood, in that order—coming out against the film, without having even seen it.[111] Kind of incredible, considering just the day before, the paper's arts editor criticized the industry's predilection to speculate over and criticize the budget and not the finished project.[112]

But the *Los Angeles Times* wasn't alone. There was Peter Biskind's feature in *American Film* that May, on the heels of a *New York* magazine piece published in March, where Puttnam firmly distanced himself from the film: "It was agreed prior to my joining Columbia that I won't involve myself in the release of this particular picture. It's all too common in this industry for incoming heads of the studios to take the credit or blame (!) for work negotiated by their predecessors. I don't want to be guilty of this."[113] While both pieces attempted to come out on the positive side, insisting the movie would be funny, they were so stuffed with dishy anecdotes from production crew defectors that they couldn't help but add fuel to the gossip fire.

All this was happening while the film was still in edit. Morale was uneasy. Either you pretended it wasn't happening, or you watched helplessly, like knowing you were in a car destined to crash and couldn't do anything about it. "It seemed tainted," Spiegel remembers. "By the time I came onto it, it had already gotten a lot of negative press. It was almost a sense, for some of the people working on it, not so much an interest in the film but the kind of voyeuristic aspect of just working on a film that was gonna bomb or that was going to be sensational. When we were working on it, there certainly was an awareness that Columbia felt [Elaine] was spending too much money and she was being too kind of neurotically attentive to details that didn't matter. Yeah, that was already palpable."[114]

In recent years, the truth of most stories that have circulated about the making of *Ishtar*—and all that talk about the budget, the budget, the budget—have been disputed. For some, including Elaine, it was too much negative advanced publicity—and too *specific*—for it to have been anything other than sabotage. "This film was political and it was satire, but it was my secret. When these articles started coming out, I thought—only for five minutes—'It's the CIA,'" Elaine said. "I didn't dream that it would be the studio. For one moment it was sort of glorious to think that I was going to be taken down by the CIA, and then it turned out to be David Puttnam."[115] Elaine, and those who remain close to her, have pointed to a host of reasons to justify why a studio would go so far as to sink their own film: For starters, Columbia had changed leadership in the middle of production—nothing Elaine hadn't seen before—and inherited a property they no longer approved of. Guy McElwaine had been replaced by David Puttnam, who had a desire to make good on his promise to end rampant overspending. Puttnam had a feud with Beatty dating back to the 1982 Oscars, when *Reds* rivaled Puttnam's film *Chariots of Fire* ("Warren Beatty should be spanked in public," he told gossip columnist Marilyn Beck),[116] *and* with Hoffman after he walked off a film Puttnam was producing. Even supposed financial suicide could be explained away: Coke could just write *Ishtar's* failure off. (And they did, for $25 million, less than two months after its release.)[117] Seems like an easy way to assert power, get revenge, and avoid losing too much money all at the same time.

Their allegations aren't baseless. Even if a new studio head would want to take a public stance of "this is not the way we'll be doing things from now on," Puttnam's publicly divisive behavior and his disdain for *Ishtar* were excessive. And it's true: The appearance of such damning stories in the press just months before your film finally opens or during your opening weekend does not bode well for getting butts in seats. But they're not the entire story. Turning *Ishtar's* failure into a simple victim and villain narrative would be easy revisionist history; the whole truth is far more complicated. Columbia wasn't the only one to blame for *Ishtar's* failure; prior to Puttnam's tenure, they had been as vocally supportive as they could have possibly been.[118] A few months of very bad press isn't great, but it was a drop in the bucket when the well was poisoned all along. The truth is that *Ishtar* wasn't killed by one person; it was death by a thousand cuts.

By the very nature of who was making it, *Ishtar* was always going to be a highly talked-about film. Even when it was still unconfirmed and "kept so highly secret that news of it has not even reached most Columbia executives," people were desperate to find something to talk about.[119] You can see the breathless yearning for something—anything—to go wrong as early as the reports of Columbia's official announcement. Look at how high the house of cards was already stacked: A studio comedy shot in Morocco! The teaming up of three of Hollywood's most notorious perfectionists![120] Two stars commanding a then high of $5 million each—plus a gross of the profits—together in the same film *and* playing against type![121] A director of a scant three small films, two of which were famously held up in litigation, and the last of which was made nearly ten years ago, netting $2 million for herself and refusing to talk about it! A budget reportedly more than $30 million—and that's *before* marketing and advertising and the inevitable overscheduling![122] All signed off by an executive rumored to be on the verge of getting fired! There was something so brazen—even by Hollywood's standards—about it, particularly in the wake of the big-budget 1980 disaster *Heaven's Gate,* to which it often found itself compared. "Memory does not immediately yield a film for which so many critics, reporters, and industry members were lying in wait, avid for signs of terminal weakness and early demise," the *Los Angeles Times* critic Charles Champlin wrote in his defense of the film.[123]

All of this was happening in an era of high-concept blockbuster madness, when movies were beginning to cost more and chase higher returns. But who really got to participate in the blockbuster genre—which typically bends toward comedy or action—and who got shut out, once again, by an industry that was against them from the start? More women were making films in the studio system than the last time Elaine had directed, but it's not as if they had high budgets at their disposal. Barbra Streisand's *Yentl,* a film just as extravagant and arduously developed as *Ishtar,* was dropped from or turned down by multiple studios for its comparatively humble $14 million price ticket. The first two films Penny Marshall directed were ones she came into after men dropped out. Of the top-grossing movies of the 1980s, only one directed by a woman—Amy Heckerling's 1989 film *Look Who's Talking*—cracked the top fifty. For all its intentions of emulating a *Road To . . .* movie, *Ishtar* was never going to be as simple and high concept as most of the box office hits. That, coupled with Elaine not only being *Elaine* but being a woman in charge of a picture that cost anywhere from $30 to $57 million—depending on who you ask—was simply too audacious to accept.

This impression that everyone was out to get them swirled around the whole production, so it's no surprise that a circle of paranoia and distrust surrounded *Ishtar* as a twisted form of self-protection. It's why the set remained all but closed,[124] why Beatty and Hoffman gave so few interviews, why Elaine, when contacted by one magazine to comment on an in-depth feature on the film, said simply, "If you can, I'd appreciate it if you didn't mention my name in your article."[125] Shutting off access to the truth doesn't limit the lies that can spread; it just makes it easier for people to say whatever they want, truthful or not, instead. All through 1986, the bad press piled up. The *Los Angeles Times* had gotten its hands on the script in February—while *Ishtar* was still shooting and planned for release that year—and published a detailed summary, calling the plot confusing, the mid-eighties equivalent of spoilers showing up on Wikipedia.[126] In April, Charles Grodin spoke to reporters in *Ishtar*'s and Elaine's defense: "Given the group, and the exotic locale, it was hard to believe we weren't actually on a sound stage in Hollywood. And if Elaine gets misinterpreted as a director by outsiders, it's because of the way she works. If you visited the set, you wouldn't know she's the director. She's highly imaginative, but she's also low key; she permits things to happen."[127] They had wrapped filming only a month before and were already on the defense, doing damage control.

A HANDFUL OF successful preview screenings[128] wouldn't be enough to save the film. The tidal wave of gossip stuck. They held a star-studded Camp Ronald McDonald benefit premiere,[129] and Elaine skipped the press outside, refusing to have her photo taken even at the party for the film she had spent the past two years of her life working tirelessly on. Two days later, *Ishtar* stumbled into theaters, dead on arrival. The film had a few allies at the time, critics who didn't ignore its fumblings but highlighted its strengths, like John Powers at the *L.A. Weekly,* who called it "often hilarious and never less than amiable,"[130] and Janet Maslin at *The New York*

Times, who wrote that "the worst of it is painless; the best is funny, sly, cheerful, and here and there, even genuinely inspired."[131] But its critics were a far louder and more gleefully vile bunch.

Ishtar was everything they had thought it would be: "a kind of perverse joke,"[132] a "runaway ego trip,"[133] and "colossally dunder-headed."[134] "It's not funny, it's not smart, and it's interesting only in the way a traffic accident is interesting," Roger Ebert wrote in a devastating pan.[135] They homed in on its budget, eager for the expected payoff to the yearslong rumor mill. "An expenditure of $45 million or more on a joshing Bing and Bob *Road to Ranchipur* movie is crazy and even vaguely disgusting," said one review,[136] while another called it "a skimpy excuse for an epic-comedy. It's a piffle with a $40 million-plus price tag."[137]

"There was true indignation about the fact that there were two stars. Even after they laughed," Elaine reflected. "That's the interesting thing—you'd think, surely that laughter will make a friend of you, won't it? But no, it won't. They just were pissed."[138]

She was more diplomatic in her disappointment than Grodin, who argued for decades after its release, "Why should the public be concerned what the budget of a movie is? Coca-Cola financed the movie. It's not as if Coca-Cola was going to give that money to the people of America rather than spend it."[139] Grodin has a point: Who cares? Yes, finding entertainment in the misfortunes of those with or responsible for enormous fortunes has long been a simple, primal pleasure of the average working American. When something seems too big to fail, the natural reaction is to root for its doomed collapse. But critics' and audiences' "eat the rich" fury was misdirected. There's plenty of blame and resentment for high paychecks to go around, but the majority of blame for waste and greed in Hollywood lies more with its corporate overlords than it does with its artists. And even then, is it really fair to judge art based on how much it cost to make it? Maybe it would be an easier argument to make if anyone on *Ishtar* at least owned the fact that they did indeed make a very expensive movie at the time, without mentioning in the same breath that its budget quickly became the norm. If anything, it's like Elaine hiding her *Mikey and Nicky* reels.

Losing such an incredible amount of corporate America's money—which, let's be honest, is about as real as Monopoly money—in the name of creative freedom is the exact kind of bad behavior that has come to be lauded for its irreverent badassery. Instead, though, they've chosen to play the scorned victim, pass the buck, or spout an oblivious alternative history: "Right after that, Stallone did his next [*Rambo*] and he got $750 million or whatever it was for doing that movie," one source argued. "When *Rain Man* came along, the budget for *Rain Man*—shot entirely in America—ended up being somewhere like $80 million or $90 million. [*Ishtar*] cost $36 or $37 million."[140] The budget for *Rambo III* was $58 million, while the budget for *Rain Man* was $25 million. Who's to say what *Ishtar* finally ended up costing—the filmmakers themselves give a different number every time, including a claim that "no one could ever agree upon a budget, so there just wasn't a budget"[141]—but it is estimated that the projected $30 million ended up wrapping at around $51 million.[142]

But there was more that *Ishtar*'s critics took issue with than just the budget. Hoffman and Beatty playing against type was unbelievable and seemingly masochistic as they "[act] out their worst anxieties about themselves, parading their fear of impotence on a royal scale."[143] And Elaine was simply too timid and too strange for this type of film, completely inept at "staging a large-scale comedy."[144] Hatred of *Ishtar* became ubiquitous. *The Village Voice* would run two pans in a span of a single month, calling it both "so dead you think vultures will start circling the theater"[145] and "even worse than its worse pans . . . The directorial incompetence crashes through the camera lens as demented insolence."[146] Though he would apologize for it decades later, one of Gary Larson's most popular *The Far Side* comic strips depicted "Hell's video store" as a place where the shelves hold nothing but VHS tapes of *Ishtar*.

The damage was done. *Ishtar* would walk away with just over $14 million in box office grosses. A soundtrack planned to coincide with the release was delayed over cover approvals and track delivery.[147] Positioned as Rogers and Clarke's *Greatest Hits* album shown at the end of the film, with full-length versions of each song that

Beatty and Hoffman recorded with James Taylor's band,[148] it was shelved indefinitely once Columbia looked at the beating the film had taken. In 1989, Elaine, Beatty, and Hoffman would sue Columbia for at least $8 million in back fees, expenses, damages, and interest, claiming that they didn't fully receive their promised pay, and that Columbia didn't do enough to promote the film.[149] *Ishtar* became an easy and lasting punch line, shorthand for box office disaster. "If all the people who hate *Ishtar* had seen it, I would be a rich woman today," Elaine quipped nearly twenty years later.[150]

She would get her revenge eventually, but it would take a while. Slowly but surely in the years between *Ishtar's* spectacular crash and Elaine's joke about it, the film would find a home as a cult classic, first in the home video market, then later, as the aughts got underway, as a prescient commentary on the increasingly idiotic world in which we live. It was an indictment of things that were just simmering then, things that would reach a boil or come back around again: the man-children Judd Apatow would center in his films; *American Idol* and the thirst for fame in spite of any real talent; the continued fumbled overstepping of American diplomacy in the Middle East. And not only that, but it was funny. *Really* funny. It wasn't a perfect film, and certainly not one without its fair share of faults or (at times, racist) misfires, but it was far from the "worst movie of all time" that it had been positioned as. At its best, particularly in its wonderful first act, it shows glimmers of the kind of films Elaine could have continued to make had she been given the chance. Maybe she would have thrived in the last gasp of a golden era of cinema, where James L. Brooks and Rob Reiner and Nora Ephron were making intelligent R-rated comedies, talky indoor movies that sharply examined human relationships. Hers would have been the darkest of them all, no doubt, but the audiences were there, if she had been given another chance to reach them.

ELAINE'S REPUTATION WAS buried somewhere in the Moroccan sand. She had gotten her second chance and blew it. She didn't stop to acknowledge that Beatty didn't have too much trouble bouncing back from the disaster, that most male directors in her position were afforded an endless string of second chances and were rarely called crazy. She could see the times where she was an outlier in the system before, but not this time. Her pattern of bad luck had to have been because of something else. She would stammer her way through bluntly asked questions about it that held the mirror up a little too closely. "Being a woman in Hollywood, I mean, it's very hard to know that, as a woman in Hollywood . . ." she said on one occasion, in a rare appearance at a screening of the film nearly twenty-five years after it bombed. She trailed off, struggling to articulate her feelings about the situation. Was her experience on and punishment after *Ishtar* exaggerated? Had she really been treated differently than a man would have been? The improvising legend was stumped. "I don't know that you're *different*, being a woman in Hollywood. I mean, it could be, but there's no way to compare, if you're directing, because you're not on another director's movie. But there's been enough misfortunes with movies that you think you just have to be, you know, not a studio head in Hollywood to have a lot of shit happen to you. There are guys who really get away with it, who Hollywood executives respect, really, as fans do. Clint Eastwood, I think, could do anything because he's tall and they respect him. And in that way, it's better to be Clint Eastwood than a woman in Hollywood. But a lot of guys are considered women in Hollywood, in a funny way."[151]

The blowback from *Ishtar* went beyond the same old kind of studio bullshit she had dealt with before. It was too great for even her to fully understand. "I kind of like *Ishtar,* and the seven people who saw it liked it, so I really don't know. I wish I could give something astute like 'It was before its time,'" she said a decade later, when the disaster was still a relatively recent memory and its future reclamation seemed like a pipe dream. "But no, it's just this pleasant, sloppy comedy that people—no, actually, the media—just loathed . . . I don't know. I'm really not being coy. I actually have no idea. I can tell you why other things of mine failed. But *Ishtar* . . . I understand why it failed. Why it failed *so big* is actually difficult to figure out."[152]

She'd had enough. "I was very upset after this movie—and so

was everybody else," she said.[153] She would never direct a feature film again.[154] She went back, once again, to what was safe. "I'll write," she thought. "That was probably what being a woman in Hollywood is," she finally realized, the answer to the earlier question finally coming to her. "I probably should have kept making movies. So for all you women here, let that be a lesson. Just don't stop."[155]

CHAPTER 10

There's No Prize, Just a Smaller Size

1988–1996

Elaine likes to play games. It doesn't matter if they're physical, like the frantic back-and-forth sprints that running charades require, or mental, like word puzzles that take all day to solve. Give her the puzzle-on-top-of-a-puzzle that was *The Nation*'s weekly crossword or the arduous Sunday *Times* crossword, the completion of which became a weekly ritual for her and Schopper. It was all but inevitable that she would absolutely steamroll you at Scrabble—which she rarely played without scoring a near-impossible 50-point word— but you'd play against her anyway, partly for the thrill of watching her win. They all had the same thing in common: They were the most demanding games she could find, or the versions where the level of difficulty was jacked up to 11 and stayed there, games so tough only someone truly insane could possibly enjoy them. "Those are the only ones worth playing," she would say. She was wildly competitive and always out to win. She couldn't be bothered by feelings of guilt or generosity toward any opponent she was trouncing again and again. "No, no, no. I love it," she would say. "I love to see you get upset over it." Better them than her.[1]

Maybe part of it was about ego, a not-so-subtle reminder to those around her of her intelligence, particularly in moments of doubt. Or maybe part of it was just that Elaine had been challenging herself for so long—whether a necessity demanded by easily bored genius or by the nature of having to hold her own in an uneven playing field—that she was simply incapable of choosing the easy option. It could have been that this was how she got her thrills or how anything was qualified as valid and good in her book. Maybe things were fun only if they were hard, but maybe being hard was the only way they could be worth something, too. God forbid anything be easy. Easy was cheap, easy was lazy, easy was soft.

She had failed at the game that was making a big-budget block-buster. But rather than let herself stoop to easy, her next move would instead be to try her hand at the opposite extreme: Could she succeed at making a movie that cost next to nothing?

AFTER THE UPROAR over *Ishtar*'s budget, Schlossberg, Schopper, and Elaine were feeling if not resentful, then defiant. An attitude of "we'll show *them*" permeated the trio; they decided to prove to the world that they could make and distribute a movie with stars, independently and on a shoestring budget.[2]

They would take a screenplay Jeannie had written with her friend, Laurie Jones, and turn it into an odd-couple buddy comedy about an uppity snobbish sophisticate and an astrology-citing New Age kook called *In the Spirit*. Schlossberg would raise the money to finance it himself, and they would pad the cast with their inner circle. Elaine and Marlo Thomas would costar as the reluctant friends, and Jeannie and Peter Falk would take on supporting roles. Some members of the crew and postproduction staff on *Ishtar* who hadn't been put off by its chaos stayed on with Elaine for its follow-up, including Brad Fuller and Ira Spiegel. Newcomers abounded. Acting coach Sandra Seacat would direct her first—and only—feature. Many of the crew members' careers were in their infancy; they came cheap and saw the small production as an opportunity to get a foot in the door. "They were giving people a step up, knowing that there were other people who have a lot of experience, like Elaine and Phillip, around who could oversee things at the same time," Fuller said.[3]

The year was 1988, and although some of New Hollywood's most original directors, like John Cassavetes and John Waters—as well as its most prominent female filmmakers, like Claudia Weill and Joan Micklin Silver—had been working outside of the system, the studio still reigned supreme. A veteran in her late fifties, Elaine was a far cry from the majority of mostly young filmmakers working independently at the time. She lived in the San Remo and palled around with Warren Beatty; she could never live the life of young, punkish twenty-somethings living in Lower East Side walk-ups making dirt-cheap experimental films and earning next to nothing. In a year, Steven Soderbergh's *Sex, Lies, and Videotape* would take the increasingly popular Sundance Film Festival by storm, win the Palme d'Or at Cannes, and go on to a triumphant theatrical run, its success ushering in a boom of American independent cinema that would dramatically alter Hollywood power structures for the next decade. In time, stars of Elaine's caliber would step away from big-budget productions to work on smaller films in the name of creative challenge or artistic fulfillment. But for now, following a Hollywood blockbuster with a scrappy independent couldn't have been seen as anything other than a humbling and humiliating sign of defeat.

Not that any of them thought of it that way—at least, not publicly. They would spin the narrative, make it seem as if they were making a statement on an inherently sexist film industry that increasingly put profit before art. "A movie shouldn't have to make $100 million in order for it to be made," Marlo Thomas said. "The big money-makers are male-driven adventure films like *Indiana Jones*. There's a place for such movies, but there's also a place for smaller pictures about women. It's a little disturbing that more pictures aren't being produced with modest budgets dealing with relationships and social questions."[4] They weren't wrong, but in martyring themselves for creative control, they weren't saying the unspoken truth, either. Producing their own film wasn't just an underdog's courageous attempt; it was that they didn't really have any other choice. Schlossberg alleges that claims Elaine was blacklisted from directing after the twin debacles of *Mikey and Nicky* and *Ishtar* were exaggerated, that she *had* been offered plenty of directing gigs, but chose to pass on every one.[7] Phillip Schopper disagrees. "She in effect couldn't work again. Except she did. She worked an enormous amount, but it's kind of off the record," he says. "But she wasn't ever given another movie to direct, or anything like that."[8] But hard work and a seeming dedication to spiting those who wronged you rarely results in compelling art—especially when so much of its creation is put into the hands of those without the experience to do it right—and they'd inevitably pay for it down the line.

If the eight-week-long shoot in the spring of 1988 seemed uncharacteristically speedy for an Elaine May film,[5] *In the Spirit*'s drawn-out postproduction would be a familiar return to form. There was an inordinate amount of work to do, and it wasn't just Elaine's typical kind of relentless refining. Structurally, the film was a mess, and everyone knew it.[6] It had started out as a comedy of manners, and somewhere along the line took a turn into the realm of murder mystery, a genre that none of them had any real expertise in. Seacat, having never seen a movie through a fairly uncomplicated edit process, let alone one that would become so involved, quickly exited. Elaine took the reins, and for all intents and purposes, *In the Spirit* would unofficially be her fifth film as a director. Whether it was an intentional choice in place from the start—with Seacat serving as something of a front, there to help them avoid bad press from those hoping for another train wreck and ensure funding from private investors hesitant to back an Elaine May film—or something brought on by the situation they found themselves in as it wrapped is uncertain. But the fact is, by the time the edit was underway, "there was never any other understanding but that this was Elaine's film."[9] She would do what she did best: steer another film away from crisis while refusing to be known as its savior.

Not that Schopper or Schlossberg will admit to that much or acknowledge the film's messier-than-industry-norm postproduction, or that Elaine used it to essentially not only ghost rewrite but ghost direct the film. Schlossberg describes her work in the vaguest of terms: "When you do a low-budget film, you have to cut corners," he diplomatically explains. "And when you have to cut corners, you have trouble making a movie, putting it together."[10] Elaine, he says, "was helpful to me in every aspect of the film, including the editing."[11] To acknowledge the fact that her behind-the-scenes work— which went far beyond that of a star, which is the only credit she has on the film—was more involved and complex than that she simply "came in and helped" would mean publicizing the fact that they went into production knowing they had a weak script and an inexperienced director, but moved forward with shooting it anyway.

And whether they did so for the sake of stubbornly committing to the game of it all or because they needed someone willing to shield Elaine or out of a sense of familial loyalty didn't matter. For Elaine to get credit for salvaging what was a deeply flawed film, someone would have to be thrown under the bus, and each of the potential victims was simply too close. She couldn't betray any of them like that. Not Seacat, not Schlossberg or Schopper, and certainly not Jeannie.

Putting together a cut of the film would be "an arduous task"[12] that ate up the rest of the following year. As 1988 stretched into 1989, Elaine did more than simply help; she, Schopper, and company embedded themselves at New York's Magno Studio, where they would spend the next several months pulling from their go-to bag of tricks full of dialogue replacements and repurposed shots to make a cohesive whole out of parts. Though the process was at times exhausting, involving long hours and intermittent chaos, unlike Elaine's past productions, the atmosphere was far from stressful. It was pleasant, if not downright fun. Since the group had no studio breathing down their backs and no real deadline in sight, the Magno editing suite became its own safe, insular world, a clubhouse where "it felt like a family play," one postproduction staffer recalled.[13] Thomas and her husband, Phil Donahue, would often drop by, hang out, and weigh in on scenes; Schopper and Schlossberg were always around, as was Jeannie. If she harbored any resentment toward her mother for taking control of her work, she didn't let it show. "Jeannie was like her assistant in her cutting room," assistant editor Michelle Gorchow Sobel recalls, whether that meant rigging a flatbed editing table so Elaine could eat popcorn, wipe her hands, and cut film at the same time or tracking selects during screenings of the dailies. "Isn't that great?" Elaine joked on one occasion. "That's why you have kids: To log your dailies."[14]

Surrounded by her support system and working without any real stakes, Elaine was in her ideal environment to experiment. She worked on her own edit flatbed alongside Fuller and Schopper, manually pulling film and splicing scenes with laser focus. Even when she got stumped, she didn't stay that way for long. She would arrive at the suite the next morning with a burst of inspired gusto: "I just figured out what to do with that scene," she'd say, plowing right into the work.[15] She was a fount of ideas; new ones flowed from her in inexhaustible abundance. Often "she'd come in and she'd look at stuff and she'd put her hand on your shoulder and go, 'This is going to sound crazy, but—' and then say something and it'd be a good idea," says Fuller.[16] Only occasionally were her suggestions on the nutty side, and even then they were still worth trying, but experience had taught her to exhibit a self-deprecating sense of self-awareness. Gone was the "scarifying lady" of films past; age or experience or maybe just the present company had softened Elaine. Spiegel remembers one occasion in which, left without child care for the day, he brought his seven-year-old son along with him to Magno. "We were going up to the screening room in the elevator, and it was very packed. Elaine was talking with Peter Falk, and Elaine said, 'Yeah, this scene is really fucked up. We've gotta do something about it. It is just so fucked up.' And my son tugged on my hand and said, 'Daddy, that lady said a bad word.' Elaine had heard him and leaned down, I think got down on her knees, and put her hand on his cheek and said, 'That's right. This lady said a bad word. And sometimes this lady says bad words. And when you are around, if you ever hear her say bad words, just tell her not to say them,' and apologized to him. She was just so sweet, the way she did it."[17]

Or . . . maybe not gone *entirely*; she wasn't suddenly without her neuroses (if someone had a cold, an assistant would be tasked with methodically spraying down surfaces in each room) or high standards ("Just because someone isn't being paid is not an excuse for doing shitty work,"[18] she said as justification for firing an intern).[19] Nor had she gotten any more organized or less distractible; the longtime New Yorker was not above asking for directions home from the studio at night, stepping out onto the street and requesting her companion point her north.[20] "Because she was on nightclub hours, she would wake up late and come in late," Fuller says. "But once she came in even later and she said, 'I'm sorry I'm late. It was such a nice day, I decided to walk.'" Rather than take the straight shot down Central Park West from her apartment on West 75th Street to Magno on West 49th, she decided to walk through Central

Park's winding paths, and in doing so, ended up some forty blocks north in Harlem.[21]

But there was a cost for all that freedom. Because Elaine was surrounded by yes-men and rarely challenged with "enough is enough," the prevailing mood among crew was that the film would simply never end. Scenes became overworked and overthought. Seeing every possible permutation of a scene didn't always work, "because sometimes when you take off the belly button, the ass falls off," she admitted.[22] She knew that you could make a good movie great in edit, but you couldn't make a great movie out of something that was just okay. But that didn't mean she wasn't going to at least try.

Eventually, in April of 1990, two years after it was filmed, *In the Spirit* was released to limited theatrical audiences. She had done all she could to help her own daughter's first produced screenplay succeed, save for doing any real publicity for it. Whatever distrust of the press she harbored before had been exacerbated by the *Ishtar* debacle. No, she would not do press. The press were the enemy. They were rooting for her to fail. And wasn't she already giving them an easy shot with this step down from the big leagues? Why should she give them anything more, let alone any of herself? If she couldn't keep a viselike grip of control on how she would appear and be perceived by the public, she didn't want any part of it. Nearly all advance publicity for the film was written by Elaine herself. A "conversation" with Marlo Thomas appears in *Interview,* with Marlo needling her for more than just the one-word answers she'd grudgingly provide.[23] And a "profile" of Schlossberg in *The New York Times* belittles the form, her animosity for journalists on full display:

> There has been a great deal written lately about the failure of journalists to remain "dispassionate observers." Interviewers have been accused of deliberately creating situations to gain a subject's trust, such as doing "buddy" things with him, or moving into the same apartment. These kinds of overtures, of course, arouse expectations of a favorable interview even though the journalist already knows he is going to do a smear job. So I was well aware that Mr. Schlossberg might expect a "puff piece"

because of my connections to his movie. If so, he was going to be surprised.[24]

And in lieu of a trailer, she wrote and directed a promo clip at Schlossberg's request. She had no idea what a promo even was; he arranged for studio samples to be sent over for her to reference. "She called me up and she said, 'What a bunch of crap! These people are just talking about how great it is and how much fun they had. It's grueling most of the time!'"[25] She agreed to write a promo, but she'd do it her way, satirizing modern-day self-promotion. No one was spared from mockery, not even herself: "I'm willing to talk about [the film]," she says in the clip, her silhouette obscured in shadows, "but I don't want to be identified."[26]

The final result of the countless hours that went into it is a film that is not good in any objective sense of the word, although it does have its share of redeeming, enjoyable aspects. Elaine's and Thomas's long, close friendship translates well on-screen; the duo crackle with effortless comedic chemistry. The first forty minutes are a clever mockery of New Age eccentrics and Manhattan's wealthy upper class that presents them as more alike than dissimilar in their supreme level of disconnect from reality. And Elaine turns in a winningly deadpan performance as the straight woman countering Thomas's Marianne Williamson send-up. It could be by virtue of the fact that she so rarely appears on-screen, but as a performer, Elaine doesn't seem to have a truly *bad* performance in her. Her presence alone manages to elevate even the weakest of scripts. But a well-made mystery-action film that "could have been written for Paul Newman and Robert Redford as a male buddy picture," as Thomas positioned it at the time, it is not.[27] As the film progresses, the seams begin to show. Its fragments are held together with little more than spit and duct tape: over-the-shoulder reaction shots to accommodate overdubbed lines abound; seemingly significant characters pop up in a scene here and there, only to never appear again; it often dissolves into just plain illogical silliness. Its strongest moments give hints that everyone involved is capable of something far better, making you long for that movie instead.

The fear Elaine harbored toward critics was maybe more intense than it needed to be. While they acknowledged the film's evident faults, they were far more diplomatic in their critiques this time around, leaving their pitchforks from the days of *Ishtar* firmly planted in the past. There was a decent film in there somewhere, with "hilarious performances" from its stars,[28] but it was obscured by Seacat's "lame direction."[29] Elaine's bag of tricks may have saved the film from being a fiasco, but they still made for a fairly confusing few hours. "The camera is treated as if it were radioactive," Janet Maslin observed in her review for *The New York Times*, "never being allowed to linger where a performer might be heard clearly or shown off to good advantage. A telephone receiver covers the mouth of the person speaking; hair gets in the way of faces; back-of-the-head shots abound. The editing"—*Elaine's* magic-trick-laden editing—"is so bizarre and unpredictable that it seems just plain irrational at times."[30] In the end, *In the Spirit* was more dud than disaster, "an unexpectedly mundane caper story" that "[wasn't] often funny or fresh."[31] It departed theaters just as quietly as it arrived, left to spend the rest of time lingering in relative obscurity, the least known of any of Elaine's films.

They played the game through to the end, refusing to forfeit. The postmortem would be that it was a fun experiment, but far too difficult an endeavor to try again.[32] It's not like Elaine was really sweating it. She was already on to the next project, even more averse to being pigeonholed than ever. So maybe *Ishtar* had gotten her all but kicked out of Hollywood and *In the Spirit* wasn't exactly a ticket back, but what if it was better that way? Had either been great successes, Elaine would have been shoved onto the grueling industry conveyor belt, faced with the demand to churn out movie after movie, whether she wanted to or not. Instead, theater—her first true love, and the place where she still had a few lives left—and writing would dominate her focus. In taking that path, forced or not, she had the freedom to follow her whims and do precisely what she wanted. She didn't have to think about the rationale or strategy behind each career choice; she could take on a project for no reason other than that it seemed like a fun thing to do, like the time she wrote a short novel and shopped it around—unsuccessfully—under a pen name. ("She didn't want the novel

to be published just because it was being written by Elaine May,"
Phillip Schopper says. "She wanted to see if anybody was interested
in whether this was a good novel or not.")[33] So she'd have to take
money gigs every now and then to make up for it—try, if you can,
to imagine Elaine on a cruise ship in the South of France, lecturing
a bunch of bloated billionaires about the art of filmmaking[34]—but
really, what else was she supposed to do?

FOR THE NEXT four years, theater became the center of Elaine's attention, starting in the spring of 1991, with *Mr. Gogol and Mr. Preen,*
an *Odd Couple*-esque comedy about two New Yorkers directed by her
friend Gregory Mosher. Its premise—a chance encounter between a
lonely recluse living in squalor and the vacuum cleaner salesman
who appears at his door that turns into a hostage situation—seemed,
though not a particularly original idea, one that was ripe for deep-
ening by the kind of psychologically charged, banter-heavy black
comedy Elaine excelled at. But like so many works of hers before
and many to come, it was little more than a sketch stretched past
its limits. Reworked and rewritten in previews so much its Lincoln
Center opening had to be delayed a week,[35] it was a strong sketch,
but a weak play with little steam. Because it got the biggest laughs
and made its point about urban isolation early, the impact of the
heartbreaking sentiment of its twist ending was diminished by the
vacant, meandering path that it took to get there.

Her anticipated comeback to the New York theater world after
a decades-long absence, it was met with universal disappointment.
"There are glimmers of her special talent," Mel Gussow wrote in
his review for *The New York Times*, "but not enough to justify the
fuzziness of the effort."[36] "Its actors and director never fail the playwright, but sometimes she fails them," one review assessed,[37] though
its director looks at it differently. "It was a good play," Mosher says.
"It was funny. If it wasn't, that was probably my fault. It might have
been funnier on the page than eventually it was on the stage."[38]

If the play's poor press and short run—closing just barely a
month after opening—bothered Elaine, she didn't let it show. No,
she insisted that she didn't care about any of that. To her, the purpose of staging the play in the first place was not for reception or

accolades, but simply for her own enjoyment. "Sometimes you do theater because it's fun," Mosher reasons. *Mr. Gogol and Mr. Preen* was never intended to be anything more than that. "It wasn't like, 'Oh, let's try it out and then move it to Broadway.' We didn't think in those terms, ever."[39]

Turning sixty in the spring of 1992, Elaine entered her third act with a ravenous hunger for work. Maybe it was like food after a fast, and she'd gobble up every last crumb. Maybe it was a resurgent spark of her manic youth; free of the limitations of being a wife and mother or a cog in the Hollywood machine, she was still the same girl who could write prolifically with no end in sight. Maybe she was staring down her own mortality, looking around at her aging peers, wondering how much time she had left; she had finally kicked smoking for good, but who knew what kind of damage it had done. Or maybe it was just that working so much was second nature by now, and she didn't know how to stop.

ELAINE AND GENE Saks were performing at the Williamstown Theatre Festival, both marking a return to the stage after long absences, and it was a disaster.

Ever since Elaine had directed Saks in a production of Herb Gardner's *The Goodbye People* at the Berkshire Theatre Festival in 1971, the two friends had been looking for a reason to work together again. Elaine finally found it: four plays they would pare down and perform as an evening of one-acts. Once rehearsals began, though, it became clear that they had bitten off more than they could chew. Now here they were, Saks and Elaine, performing a significantly abbreviated version of the night, and Saks was grasping at the cool summer air that surrounded them in search of his lines. It was up to Elaine to carry the show for the both of them.

It wasn't supposed to be like this. That summer, the pair of actors turned directors had shown up to much fanfare in the small Massachusetts town. There was no keeping their return to the stage quiet; press invaded the town in hopes of getting some semblance of a scoop. "They were wandering around the grounds of Williamstown with their cameras and their microphones and all that," director David Saint remembers. "And if she saw them anywhere, she would run the other direction." Elaine would fly through the mountain trees, up a hill, down the road—"like a little gazelle"—anything to avoid being seen.[40]

Any sight of the shy and slight woman offstage was "like getting a rare sighting of a splendid yet mysterious bird."[41] Had they gotten a chance to truly observe her, it's possible they would have characterized her as less like a rare bird and more like an absent-minded professor, unkempt in plain utilitarian clothes.[42] Maybe they would have spotted her, like Saint did one day, happily power walking the rural Massachusetts roads on her way to rehearsal. Arms swinging to and fro, striding confidently as if she were queen of the world—blissfully unaware that she was headed in the wrong direction, just a few short miles from ending up in the hills of Vermont.[43]

Or maybe they would have caught her at rehearsal, where she made one seemingly cockeyed choice after another, trying to plot out a path to the truth. Maybe they would have seen her sense of loyalty at work, refusing to replace Saks despite his struggles and doing all she could to help him feel at ease. Perhaps they would have noticed her creative process, which was often a mental journey that seemed to meander until she suddenly arrived at her point and everything made sense. She knew exactly where she was going the whole time. "The shortest distance between two points for her is all around the world," Saint says. "She doesn't care about the shortest distance between two points. She wants to find what's most interesting about the little paths along the way."[44]

But instead, they only saw what was onstage: Elaine's eyes darting back and forth nervously, hoping that playing her character's unwritten anxiety for laughs would draw attention away from her struggling costar. They saw, as Saks's pauses grew longer and audiences began walking out, that she was capable of only so much.[45]

"Rarely has so much talent been expended for so little return," one critic wrote, bewildered at how the two titans suddenly seemed like inexperienced novices.[46] If their goal was to bring the show to New York,[47] they still had a lot of work to do. For now, the "self-indulgent" piece was simply "a labor of love that winds up more labor than love."[48]

Elaine refused to give up on it before she could figure it out, before she could dismantle and reassemble it again and again until it either worked or could be proved unfixable. They would restage it the next season, once again to mixed reviews. The show would not survive, but it wasn't a total waste. "If her life depended on it, Ms. May would not know how to be uninteresting," *The New York Times* wrote.[49]

IT WOULD BE Elaine's third theater outing this decade that proved to be the charm. *Death-Defying Acts,* a series of three Off-Broadway one-acts, held the perfect recipe for Elaine's success. Working with longtime friends (David Mamet and Woody Allen) who were more than happy to draw attention away from her and under the wing of her trusted producer (Schlossberg), she was free to write what she wrote best (a true one-act) the way she best knew how (which was to say: rewriting). Not that this meant it was going to be easy.

Hotline was initially staged more than a decade before, in 1983, sharing a bill with one-acts by Mamet and Shel Silverstein that the trio staged with Gregory Mosher for a four-week-long Chicago run. It was, like so many of Elaine's works, self-referential, a black comedy about a suicidal woman and customer service ineptitude, harking back at once to both *Not Enough Rope* and the Nichols and May classic "Telephone" sketch. This time, though, it was the darkest and most obliquely personal version of her reliable premise.

Hotline's protagonist, Dorothy Duval, is a caustic New Yorker desperately trying to call a suicide prevention hotline before she kills herself, hitting roadblock after roadblock: an operator who can't speak English, a busy signal at 911, and a directory listing for the Suicide Center that is, inexplicably, a coffeehouse. It's when she's finally connected to Ken, the green phone counselor, and the play becomes a series of lengthy dialogues, that it becomes increasingly easy to see the connections to Elaine herself. Dorothy is cynical, neurotic, and unpleasant, sure, but there's an undercurrent of sadness to her unpleasantness, a justification for it. Unlike so many of Elaine's characters, Dorothy isn't an idiot; if anything, she's *too* smart to function in this world. Life, to Dorothy, is something best suited for the truly stupid and ignorant; it's nothing more than an endless string of disappointments. Better to get out early, she reasons, once you realize that "after nothing happens for long enough you know that this is the nothing that's going to happen for the rest of your life, so why stay around and watch it."[50] There's a vulnerable, hurt person in there; she's just hidden beneath the shell she consciously dons to protect her from the cruelties of reality.

In Chicago, away from the center of attention and under the supposed veil of a media blackout she insisted upon, and with friends like Warren Beatty and Mike coming out to help, Elaine would play the part opposite Peter Falk. This was Elaine's first written work with her name on it since *Heaven Can Wait* and her first time onstage since David's death; the similarities between the character and the woman playing her were difficult to dismiss. When Schlossberg said Elaine wrote through the loss of her third husband, it's easy to imagine that this was what came out. Here she was, making good on her philosophy that "you can take almost any really tragic situation, and simply by dealing with it the way you would in life, you can turn it into a comedy." Don't wallow. Don't think too much about it. Spin it into an amusing story, and it can't hurt you. "You don't even have to be funny. You just have to be accurate."[51] It's no wonder why, twelve years later, she neglected to play the part again. It was safer on the outside, controlling this version of reality, manipulating it to her desired outcome, playing God. Better to let someone else revisit that dark place. Someone who wasn't her.

Polishing the play for its Off-Broadway debut wouldn't be an easy task, though. In director Michael Blakemore's diary account for *The New Yorker,* Elaine blows through the difficult production like an agent of chaos from her very first appearance: "Her talk is full of witty indirection and relentless comic shaping, not all of which I always get," he wrote of their initial meeting, "probably because I sense that it's a smoke screen from behind which I am being sharply assessed."[52] She had no qualms about giving her notes directly to the cast, ignoring whatever boundaries between playwright and director were supposed to exist;[53] made so many cuts and revisions that it was impossible to keep track of them all; could be found trying to create elaborate additions without any regard to practicalities of having the right number of actors or crew to pull it off; and often called upon her slew of friends for opinions, many of which she tried to implement, no matter how crazy-making or eleventh hour they seemed to be:

> [May] already had a message from Mike Nichols. "Mike thinks the play could be a real crowd pleaser but thinks we should turn Dorothy's monologue into a proper phone conversation with Ken saying things into his phone on the other side of the stage. I could easily write that." *And* add 20 minutes to the length of the play. *And* expect Gerry Becker to master in a few days material he's had trouble getting the hang of in six weeks. *And* have Linda walk off the show because it's no longer the play she first accepted. More madness.[54]

But her tinkering would pay off in the end. You could never accuse Elaine of being gentle, but time had sanded down her rough edges a little and drawn out her ability to expose the tender interior of something a little better. It was something she had always been capable of, but had shown audiences in small fits and spurts, there only if you looked close enough. This time, though, you didn't have to squint so hard. The girl who wrote *Not Enough Rope* had a worldview that was all cynicism and anger; the woman who wrote *Hotline* had an expanded perspective, the kind colored with insights into humanity that come only with living life longer and experiencing more loss, both personal and professional. Critics would pick up on this shift: *Hotline* may have had a familiar setup, but Elaine transcended it as only she could, following the kind of biting one-liners she was known for with "a lingering sadness that follows us up the aisles at intermission."[55] In "delving into the absurdities of loneliness and the triumph of real human caring,"[56] she had finally been able to achieve what she had chased for so long: "a recognizable sense of truth—heightened truth, to be sure, but truth nonetheless."[57]

That's not to say *everyone* got it, though. Even *The New York Times* critics found themselves split. Margo Jefferson derided it as a "banal" work reminiscent of "a talking cure in which the talk gets duller and duller and the cure farther and farther away, until we long to bring a curtain hurtling down on the whole thing."[58] But Vincent Canby called it as "alternately desperate and hilarious," and praised her playwriting for its economy of detail—a commendation that was a first for Elaine.[59] For others, the issue wasn't its structure but its subject: the New York *Daily News* viewed its treatment of a subject like suicide as little more than a "sick joke," centered on a protagonist she "delight[ed] in making . . . so repellent" you almost wished she *would* just get it over with already.[60]

Not that it really mattered what they thought—any of them, good or bad. If you saw *Hotline*'s humanity, you were an idealistic sucker. If you didn't, you were probably just a bitter son of a bitch. Either way, she'd laugh all the way to the bank. After she got done complaining, that is. It didn't matter what the critics said, as long as a show turned a profit. And the money was more than there; less than two weeks after opening, *Death-Defying Acts* amassed more than $800,000 in advance ticket sales—the highest to date in Off-Broadway history.[61] It wasn't a clean win, but it was a win she desperately needed, even if she didn't give a shit. Her mind was already in Miami Beach, where she'd get to work on the project that would be her biggest triumph yet.

CHAPTER 11

Don't Call It a Comeback

The Birdcage (1996) and *Primary Colors* (1998)

A funny thing began to happen around the beginning of the decade: Thirty years after they had made their first splash in New York, Nichols and May were once again the toast of the town.

Such is the nature of celebrity, of course; if you keep your hand in the game, live long enough, and survive all the inevitable fallow periods, you'll find that time is circular. Things always find a way to come back around to the center of the spotlight again, people included. Little by little, you graduate through the levels of notability until you find yourself standing with the other elders in the room, heralded with a retrospective view for your position as a tastemaker or a trailblazer or some other terribly indulgent—even if true—title. Eventually, even you begin to enjoy rubbing elbows with the kind of company you once ridiculed, begin to view success as a hard-won gift, not a by-product of selling out. You begin to—dare you say it—enjoy the attention you once shied away from. There they were, Nichols and May, in that very position. Together again, older and softer—who would have ever predicted *softer* of all things!—than the catty twenty-five-year-olds they once were, finding themselves at retrospective celebrations and serving as event honorees left and right.

There was the fete thrown in their honor by the Museum of Television and Radio at the Waldorf Astoria, where New York's finest watched the two reunite to perform five of their classic sketches.[1] "I'm truly phobic about this," Elaine nervously told a reporter as she eyed the photographers eager to snap photos of the rarely seen star on the red carpet. "But I'm not scared to wing it onstage."[2]

Moments later, she would stand in front of the eight hundred celebrity guests and open with a bit about how she'd weighed 250 pounds just two months prior "because I hadn't done well since the act broke up. But when I was called and told this evening was going to take place, I went on a sensible diet and soon had lost so much weight I was able to make money from sex, but only from the guys who live in my building."[3] Screenings of some of their best television appearances ran for a ten-day retrospective hosted by the American Museum of the Moving Image (pointedly, it's worth noting, dedicated to Mike's career).[4] And when they weren't being honored, they could be coaxed from retirement (however feigned that was) if the cause was good enough, whether it was joining Simon & Garfunkel for a one-time-only benefit show,[5] performing at the annual Promise Ball fundraiser for juvenile diabetes,[6] or performing for the New York Public Library's annual black-tie fundraising gala, where they scrapped a previously planned, staid reading of Nabokov for an impromptu performance of "Mother and Son."[7]

They weren't *so* defanged that they wouldn't refer to most of these rich-and-famous-only nights as "ratfucks,"[8] but they were considerably less angry now, even though they had far more reasons to be angry than they did back then. "I think that we were hostile because we could hear people's thoughts," Elaine reasoned. But, she added, "we got much nicer. But we're also richer and more successful. I don't know what we'd be like if we weren't."[9] They were worn a bit—thirty years on the up-and-down circuit of Hollywood will do that to a person—but weren't weary. They would dutifully show up and allow themselves to be toasted and sip champagne with the power players opening their pocketbooks before performing one of their greatest hits for the umpteenth time. They would *enjoy* it.[10] "The old sketches are still as funny for us," Elaine said. "I still find Mike so funny—what he says, even his expression when he's not speaking. That hasn't changed one whit, tittle, or iota."[11]

They were good together again, had rebuilt their rapport. "Somehow all the problems we had in the middle, when our act broke up and we were abrasive to each other and we were both strange and difficult people, all that has burned away," Mike said.[12] They were always finishing each other's sentences, always improvising. They

couldn't *not*; it was like a tic, a skill that had become deeply embedded in their DNA, a second language whose fluency came right
back no matter how long it had been out of practice. Occasionally,
they would wish aloud that they were still actively performing new
material. There was simply too much going on in the world just
begging for their satirical take. Something as simple as a dinner conversation about the advent of multiline business phones could turn
into a bit: "You have reached the emergency room," Elaine would
riff, adopting her old operator character. "Press one if you're bleeding profusely. Press two if your arm is broken." "Ingrown toenail,
press three," Mike would chime in, without skipping a beat.[13] The
sum of their whole, they came to realize, was better than their parts.

When Mike called Elaine desperately in need of help on his next
film, *Wolf*, it was clear that she would be the one to save the day.
Prioritizing plays hadn't diminished her exalted position on major
film studios' short lists of the best "top tier" script doctors.[14] In recent years, she had been rumored to have worked on Warren Beatty's *Dick Tracy*[15] and updated *A New Leaf* for a potential remake with
Bill Murray and Meg Ryan;[16] she scripted a remake of the German
film *Men* for Dustin Hoffman and Bill Murray that, after years of development hell, went unmade;[17] and she did a major script rewrite
of an early version of *Runaway Bride* when it was set to star Harrison
Ford and Geena Davis.[18] And anyway, Mike would still ask for her
opinion even if her recent résumé was lacking. "I never once made
a movie without first showing Elaine the script and listening to her
ideas or bringing her in to talk to the writers," he said.[19]

But *Wolf* would end up needing far more serious help than a dialogue polish or a scene or two reworked. An ill-conceived concept
Jack Nicholson and Jim Harrison had developed about a man whose
masculinity is reawakened by becoming a werewolf, it had already
gone through several rounds of fruitless rewrites. "It seemed like
once a year she would get a copy of *Wolf* and it was bad," Schopper remembers. "Elaine was pretty surprised that of all things, this
script that she's seen a few times now is back in Mike's hands and
he's saying, 'Can you rewrite this?'"[20]

She spent a confounded weekend with it. What was it he saw
in this dud? There were no stakes, the plot was inconsequential,

its characters were flat. Was it trying to be a literal horror film, in which Nicholson really *does* turn into a wolf, or was it intended as a highbrow metaphor for the intersection of predatory behavior and masculinity? No one really knew. "I read it and thought, *I can't lick this*," she recalled. "To want to be a wolf—to give up thought and human nature—what kind of a cluck would do this? 'Oh, good, I'm becoming a wolf' is not a story, and a movie almost always has to have a story. A play doesn't, but a movie does. But it was going to be made, so he was stuck with it."[21] And if he was stuck with it, she'd do her best to steer him away from complete failure.

She would rewrite the female lead, lending the character a deeper backstory and enough of her own fiery wit and biting comebacks to convince Michelle Pfeiffer to sign on. And when Mike shifted the setting to a publishing house, she filled out the world with ease. (One of her earliest additions, a line of party dialogue that would eventually be cut: "At first I thought, *Not another Holocaust book,* but it's selling. It's selling.")[22] When the "find your way around" script hit another block around how to explain the reaction to Nicholson's transformation into a wolf while filming, Mike brought her out to L.A. to work it out.[23] There, she floated the idea of getting her driver's license—which elicited a strong *oh, Jesus* reaction from everyone on production as they envisioned where her head would be while her body was behind the wheel—and swiftly wrote Mike a scene that in one swoop explained the unexplainable, a task that had stumped them the entire time.[24] "It's like some Taoist thing with her," Jim Harrison said. "Very mysterious. Come in, do the work, take the money, leave no tracks."[25] But it was a patchwork remodel on a house with a rotted foundation. As assistant director Mike Haley admits, "even Elaine couldn't save that." The best she could do was "at least put the right ingredient into something that still wasn't gonna turn out to be a very good cake. She got us through a piece of it."[26] Her work on *Wolf* didn't just get Mike through an otherwise disastrous production; it made him realize that they could work together on a deeper level than they had in years: "We rekindled something we hadn't done—except for inaugurations and stuff—for 35 years. That was very emotional for us. And very exciting."[27]

Pfeiffer, impressed with her work, sought out Elaine's help with her next film, *Dangerous Minds*. Based on a true story, the movie follows a retired U.S. marine who takes a job teaching English at a Los Angeles high school in a low-income, racially segregated district, and finds herself using unconventional methods to reach her troubled and apathetic students. Elaine would put at least two months of work into transforming the film, working quickly, sometimes faxing John N. Smith, the director, rewrites at four a.m. for scenes they were planning to shoot that day. "She had a very, very, very fast brain," Smith says. "She would be spilling out ideas, some of which would work and some of which, as we would talk more, didn't really go in the right direction, so she would come up with something else. She was a major reason that the film was so successful, because she really honed in on the important thing, the story about the teacher and the kids."[28] As usual, she refused credit.

WHEN MIKE SAW the 1978 film version of *La Cage aux Folles,* he knew almost immediately that he wanted to bring the comedy of deception to American audiences—and he wanted Elaine by his side to do it. He hadn't expected it to take fifteen years, but when the rights finally became available to him in 1994, he called Elaine. "Are we still interested?" he asked. "She said, 'I sure think so.' We talked about it for a day and said, 'Yes, yes. This is a great time for that plot.'"[29] Their adaptation would be decidedly true to the original: Two gay drag club owners scramble to hide their true identity when their son brings his fiancée and her conservative parents home for dinner. "I just thought the original was so funny that I just couldn't fail," Elaine joked.[30] But the reason she wouldn't fail wouldn't be through a faithful retelling; the film would be made hers by the way she tilted her head to look at it.

It was the mid-nineties and the AIDS crisis was raging on, unchecked; in 1994, when the film was first announced in the trades,[31] the disease was the leading cause of death for all Americans from twenty-five to forty-four.[32] Meanwhile, the gay community was being demonized by a Republican Party that was creeping even further to the far right as ultraconservatives who built their platforms in evangelical religious spheres began to move into the mainstream media (not to mention Congress). "I thought it was perfect for America," she explained, "because it was such a righteous piece. It had so much to do with people who thought they really knew what was right."[33] Elaine knew that an Americanized *Cage* could not exist in a vacuum; it had to meet the moment and reflect it in all its ugliness. "Elaine's triumph," Mike said, "was to ask the question, 'How would it be if this happened right here, right now, in today's society?'"[34] It would be a high-wire balancing act. Not only would she have to skewer the prejudice and hypocrisy of right-wing politicians and acknowledge the cruelty the gay community faced at their hands, but she had to do so without losing the original's light touch—all while skirting it all around a nervous studio system that had yet to release a major motion picture with two gay characters as the leads. ("If it had been about a man and a woman, it would have been a sitcom on nightly television every night," she noted.)[35] Oh, and she had to make it seem effortless, too. This wasn't a message movie; it was a studio comedy. At least that's the line those involved making it would push in their defense. It wasn't political; it was about family. "Family values is an idea that can't belong to any one group, because everyone has families," Mike argued at the time. "*The Birdcage* is a comedy about what constitutes a family and the lengths to which people who love their family will go for them."[36] Of course, the very premise of what constitutes a family—particularly in an era before the legalization of gay marriage, which would become a substantial detail in Elaine's version—was political in and of itself. But they didn't dare say it out loud. Not if they wanted to collect United Artist's money to make the film, and not if they wanted, down the road, to convince audiences all across the country to sit down in a theater and watch it.[37]

Elaine got to work. She gave both sets of parents—the ultra-conservative Keeleys (Gene Hackman and Dianne Wiest) and the drag club owners Armand and Albert (Robin Williams and Nathan Lane)—more detailed identities. The Keeleys would become a prominent right-wing senator and his Wasp wife, while Armand and Albert would be Jewish. Moving the film from the French Riviera to South Beach—at the suggestion of Bo Welch, the film's production designer, after he, Mike, and Elaine toured drag clubs in Chicago and Savannah—allowed for another layer of specificity that lent itself to material riffing on the geography and, by association, wealth. "We started not really knowing the where of it all," Welch remembers. "The strength of a great writer, I think, especially in comedy, is specificity. So she really embraced this and really dialed it in for that locale."[38] And she would, despite claiming there was no political bent to it, make sure its leanings were known, filling the script with digs at anti-Semitism, Don't Ask Don't Tell, and the growing trend of politics as entertainment. In the film's climactic dinner scene, as the ruse begins to unravel in a spectacular fashion, Albert delivers a monologue about the pro-life movement that is equal parts hilarious and horrific. It's lifted nearly word for word from her own life: "These abortion doctors were [being] killed, and I was at a dinner party and there was a guy there who was a pro-lifer," Elaine said. As she watched the argument over abortion unfold, each side rallying back and forth, she couldn't resist chiming in to disrupt the situation and send the evening into disarray. "I said, 'The doctor was just doing his job, and this woman can just go to another doctor. If you really want to stop abortion, why not kill the mothers?' And in the really cold pause that followed, I said, 'Because I know what you're going to say: If you kill the mothers, you'll kill the fetuses. But you know, they're gonna kill the fetuses anyway. They're gonna go down with the ship. So why not do it this way and really teach people a lesson!?'" It was, she admitted, ill received: "People, needless to say, that I never saw again." But when the time came to write *The Birdcage,* she thought about that evening, how perfectly ridiculous it was, and how easy it would be to simply slip it in verbatim. When the studio called to voice their concerns about the potential offense, she leaned on the family angle: "This is a story about two homosexuals who live together and raise a son. It's going to offend people anyway. We might as well."[39]

Mostly, though, she worked toward her philosophy that comedy wasn't about the big, easy laughs. It was about the small, ordinary, everyday things that people care about most. "Most of the time," she explained, "writing something funny has to do with balancing something horrible with something absolutely mundane, and the mundane thing will take precedence."[40] What made the dinner scene so funny wasn't just that Albert's abortion tirade was an outrageous thing to say; it was the underlying, average, relatable stakes that the scene itself sat upon. The goal of the scene was simply to have dinner—"some small social ritual that's terribly important"—go well enough that all the characters involved could avoid humiliation,[41] and after several near misses, Albert had all but blown it.

The resulting script is her strongest and sharpest comedy, even if she handed it off to Nathan Lane with a feigned exasperated profession that "I did the best I could."[42] It's also her most humane, full of genuine affection for each of the characters. "You come away with a sense that there's love and dignity to all these characters, however eccentric they are," Christine Baranski noted. "Love levels things; unconditional love can normalize any situation."[43] But that love didn't keep her from naturally hitting stumbling points. For the first time in her career, it seemed, she wasn't entirely in touch with the current cultural climate. In early iterations of the script, as in the French film, Albert and Armand's maid, an aspiring drag queen, is written for and played by a Black actor. When Mike met with Adrian Lester to discuss the part, Lester presented him with feedback that "it feels like the lines don't give him enough depth for us to see past the slapstick elements, and it starts to be a bit negative."[44] Aware of the racist implications the role would have, Mike had Elaine merge the role with Albert's dresser, Agador, instead, who would be played by Hank Azaria.[45] But even that was a short fix; Agador's relative flatness, at times, relies upon Latin clichés in lieu of characterization. Confusion over Albert's own political leanings persisted; while his interactions with the Keeleys can be read as putting on the pretense of being a Republican to win their affection, Lane recalls that "the notion was he seemed to be as conservative as Senator Keeley, and that he was sort of a Republican and agreed with him on a lot of things"—a choice that doesn't entirely seem consistent with his identity.[46] Williams was told to refer to Albert as his wife—Mike "wouldn't allow him to say partner or husband, because Robin asked about that"[47]—and then there was the "fag" of it all. The word was a constantly relied-upon punch line,[48] a detail that Nathan Lane remembers causing enough personal discomfort in one scene that he finally told Mike, "There must be another way of saying 'Alexander the Great was a fag' without saying the word *fag,* because it makes me feel uncomfortable. It's a powerful word, and it's a really unpleasant one, especially if you've been called a fag. And as the only fag in this scene, I want to tell you, it's making me uncomfortable," he says. While Mike let him run through other options, the take doing the line as is was what ended up in the final film. "It was a weird thing. Both Mike and Elaine came from a generation where fag was a punch line," he says. "As great and sophisticated as they were, they held on to that."[49]

While the presence of people of color in her life was arguably lacking, at least publicly, it's not as if she and Mike weren't close with any gay people, or that they were uncomfortable with or prejudiced toward them. But theirs was a humor, and a point of view, that had come of age in a different era, one that didn't think to interrogate which people were consistently relegated to punch lines and why, or who was telling the joke. And they certainly weren't questioning whether a story so strongly tied to a certain experience not their own was theirs to tell. Despite Elaine's heightening of the universality of Armand's and Albert's relationship—driving home a "Gays! They're just like the straights!" argument for equality common for the time—with good intentions, it's flattening in the process. She could do all the research she wanted, whether that meant interviewing drag performers backstage after shows[50] or imbuing her characters with traits taken from men she knew in real life—but research could take her only so far, could only place Band-Aids over the script's inherent flaws. Mike was the sensitive one, the one who thought twice about punching down or portraying negative stereotypes, not Elaine. Political correctness was the latest thing, and not only did she not quite trust it, but she didn't like what it was doing to comedy. "We do tend, in this country, to take a precedent and make it silly. We take it so far out and there's nothing you can say. I suppose the thing about political correctness and what it does to comedy is it's a terribly respectful thing," she lamented.[51]

* * *

MIKE'S RELATIONSHIP WITH his screenwriters was always a faithful one. Mindful of the care and attention they had put into their work and conscious of staying true to their words, he often involved them in part of the production process some way or the other. But Elaine wasn't any writer. As *The Birdcage* moved into production, he treated her as his equal. She was constantly by his side, making creative decisions on everything from the set design (on one occasion she realized Albert and Armand's home "was more a gay set than a family house" that told a "visual story that they had orgies here while the kid was growing up")[52] to the actors' choices in rehearsal.

Elaine didn't trust many people with her work, but she trusted him. "If you're a writer," she would say years later, "you really want Mike to direct your screenplay. Because you know that every shot and every costume and every piece of furniture and every shoe and everything you see is going to tell your story, and never give it away."[53] If Elaine's greatest triumph was translating the story to the current setting, his was giving her the amount of control and security needed to keep her name on it when all was said and done. On set, he insisted everyone have the same kind of reverence for Elaine's script that he did. "You have to know the words," Mike urged his actors. "Each word is important, and somebody has thought about this and I expect you to be able to deliver that."[54] Improvisations and ad-libs would be allowed during the three-week play-like rehearsal period, but they would all be noted by Elaine, who would choose which would be adhered to come shooting. Not even Robin Williams's most memorable moment—a spontaneous brief history of dance from Bob Fosse to Twyla Tharp to Madonna—was improvised entirely on the spot. It was born from the rehearsal period— and was one of few big laughs that didn't come from Elaine's pen.[55]

They were the elder statesmen on set now, no longer just surrounded by their peers, a close-knit working family that had come up together, but with younger people who had grown up listening to Nichols and May records. Early in production on all his films, Mike would assemble the crew's stakeholders at a meeting at his office in Midtown, where they would discuss the film, their collective vision for it, and the plan to move forward. The early meetings were always a treat, a chance not just to work, but to bask in Mike's presence. Because Mike made you feel good, made you feel wanted. On *The Birdcage,* the experience was heightened even more. You walked into the room and the realization would hit you: You were working with Nichols and May.

And to work on a Nichols and May production "was like being invited to an amazing cocktail party without cocktails," says Bo Welch. "It was almost like a salon, in a weird way, and insanely fun because it's work, but it was almost a party. [Mike] would direct by telling stories, basically, and someone like Mike and Elaine were just full of stories that you were riveted by."[56] It was an indescribably thrilling feeling, like you were one of the chosen few smart enough for the moment. "Lucky to be invited to the party," as Lane puts it. And yet you would also be wildly intimidated,[57] as if every single original thought you ever had suddenly floated out of your brain, though even if it hadn't, it couldn't possibly compare to their unparalleled intelligence and wit, and so you could do nothing but sit—stupidly, happily, wordlessly—and watch. "If you want to feel dumb, get in a room with Mike and Elaine," Welch says. "When you get in the room with those two major brains and they're bouncing off each other and talking and laughing and reminiscing and talking about what we're going to be doing, it's a whole other level of something."[58]

You would watch them finish each other's sentences like they spoke their own secret language. Most of what they said would go over your head, but you'd still find yourself laughing almost as if on cue—not only a witness to history but a participant in it, since they were cracking themselves up, too. "There's a way in which [Mike] would start laughing when he and Elaine did their improv routines at the beginning of their careers," Mary Bailey, who served as script supervisor on several of Mike's films, including *The Birdcage* and *Primary Colors,* remembers. "Sometimes he would crack up first, and it was just the most wonderful thing, that laughter when it then became the two of them laughing. I saw that happen a number of times. That was a good day to have gotten up."[59] You would sit like a sponge and soak it all up, let their jokes and their stories seep into your pores and hope you'd become smarter and better by pure osmosis. You would find yourself fascinated by the sight of Elaine pecking at a muffin from craft services, oblivious to the fact that more of it was going on her blouse than in her mouth, and notice the learned gentleness with which Mike would brush the crumbs away.[60] "That was one of the one or two happiest times of my life, making *The Birdcage*," Mike would say.[61] And those on set could tell: "He was just so happy to be working with her again, to be reunited on something that they had wanted to do for a long time," Lane says.[62] They were right; the film *was* about family.

THE BIRDCAGE PREMIERED in 1996 to critical and commercial acclaim, winning its opening weekend and continuing to hold the number one spot for the next three weeks.[63] Critics and audiences were taken not only with the humor of the film—which was expected—but by its level of warmth and affection—which was not. The mean boy and the mean girl made a film that wasn't very mean at all. At least, not to the people who didn't deserve it. And even then, there are no real villains, not in a Mike Nichols movie, anyway. They're just flawed people trying their best. "Manipulative as it is, *The Birdcage* is funny and touching, and Mike Nichols . . . directs it with a warmth of feeling that I've never noticed in his work before," David Denby wrote for *New York,* adding, "Elaine May's screenplay is satire leavened by affection."[64] In a rave for *Variety,* Todd McCarthy called *The Birdcage* "a riotous comedy whose irreverent topicality is one of its most refreshing components," calling out its "expertly judged sense of farce, surprising humanity, success at sustaining a manic high-wire act and sheer self-confidence."[65] It's that strength of farce that was enough for many to overlook its weaker moments, notably their skewed vision of their characters' reality. In an otherwise warm review, *The New York Times*'s Janet Maslin acknowledges that theirs is an "AIDS-free universe where homosexuality simply means wacky fashion sense," where "the gay nightclub setting is watered down with shots of a heterosexual audience, and Armand and Albert seem even less like actual lovers than their French predecessors did."[66]

Not everyone was a fan, though. Despite a ringing endorsement from the Gay and Lesbian Alliance Against Defamation (GLAAD),[67] *The Birdcage* would find its toughest feedback from gay artists and critics who felt that the film made *them* the punch line. "Among the specific offensive elements in this treatment are the vastly different ways Elaine May's script treats the club owner's hiding of his homosexuality and his Jewishness—invented for this film—as tossed off with a gag, in yet another example of a script full of self-loathing penned by a Jewish writer," seethed Gene Siskel in a sweeping pan.[68] And essayist Bruce Bawer penned an essay in *The New York Times* titled "Why Can't Hollywood Get Gay Life Right?" in which he argued that the film "doesn't 'get' gay life or relationships; its treatment of them is strained, awkward, synthetic" nor does it "understand that Armand and Albert's charade is not admirable, that what they offer up for Val is nothing less than the integrity of their openness."[69] But the film had already won enough audiences over; the essay was promptly met with a series of letters to the editor from people disagreeing with his interpretation of the film's intent.[70] "As a gay man who also happens to be a parent, I want it to make it clear that Mr. Bawer does not speak for me. Having said that, I confess that I approached *The Birdcage* with trepidation," one wrote. "I laughed for two hours. What struck me this time is that the film is really not about gay parents. It's about the crazy lengths all parents will go to out of love for their children."[71]

Both things can be true: *The Birdcage* is a progressive landmark. It is also inherently flawed in the way it came together. Although *The Birdcage* was a massive step forward for representation at the time, that step forward came with a giant caveat. How representative can a film about the queer experience be if it could get made only by two straight people? In many ways, though, *The Birdcage* was a product of its time. Ellen DeGeneres's groundbreaking *Time* cover was still a year away. Queer stories weren't at the forefront of mainstream studio films; they were relegated to the independent, art-house space. Even Oprah all but outed Nathan Lane—who, as an emerging star at the time, was "not in the closet to family and friends, but not 'out'"—during the film's publicity tour.[72] The culture was shifting, but ideal representation was further in the future.

To get there, people would have to take incremental growth like *The Birdcage*, films that are not perfect, but are shepherded to the masses by allies trying their best.

At the end of the day, any studio head who had lost sleep worrying that the story of two men and their son would alienate audiences was proved wrong. If critical and awards success wasn't enough—the film's cast won a collective Screen Actors Guild Award, and Elaine earned a Best Adapted Screenplay nomination from the Writers Guild of America—the money was there, too. Grossing $125 million,[73] the biggest hit either Mike or Elaine had seen in decades, *The Birdcage* proved that a studio film could feature two gay men as protagonists and be a success. And broader than that, it served as reassurance that the movies they made—intelligent comedies that were targeted more toward adults than the current youth—were still very much in demand.[74] The industry had been ready to write Nichols and May off, but they weren't done yet.

QUICKLY, THEY BEGAN to plan their next steps together. They would embark on three films together: an original script by Elaine for Emma Thompson, about a woman who kidnaps a politician and abandons him in a field,[75] an adaptation of Cormac McCarthy's *All the Pretty Horses*,[76] and *Primary Colors*, an adaptation of Joe Klein's then anonymously penned buzzy roman à clef about Bill Clinton's 1992 presidential campaign. Of the three, only *Primary Colors* would come to fruition.

Mike had been chasing *Primary Colors* before *The Birdcage* even opened, going so far as to win the auction for the film rights with his own money for $1.5 million before selling the property to Universal Pictures for $8.5 million.[77] It wasn't only a gamble financially, but thematically as well. There was room for dry satire, but the material was far from comedic. Mike had handled more serious work before, as had Elaine, but neither—especially not Elaine—had ever attempted such a blatantly political film. Mike, though, would sell the pair not on the strength of their Beltway knowledge, but on their keen eye for the story underneath it all, the one that would sell it to mainstream audiences everywhere. No movie is about *just* one thing, and *Primary Colors* was no exception. As Mike described it as he pitched himself to Klein, it wasn't a film about the Clintons; it was deeper than that. It was a film "about honor."[78] (Lest it sound *too* self-serious, he pitched it to Elaine as "secretly *Seinfeld*. It's about the fun friends have together in what turns out to be the happiest time of their lives.")[79]

"I didn't fully know what to do with it, but I think it had a story by the time I was done," Elaine said.[80] She dutifully spent several months finding the cinematic arc of Klein's text. Eschewing some of the extraneous subplots, she focused instead on using the characters as vehicles for a story that was less a salacious retelling of a real-life scandal and more an examination of power dynamics, loyalty, and morality that questioned how much truth we should expect from our leaders, and whether we are justified in those demands. In short, she turned it, subversively, into something right up her alley.

When the film moved into production in the spring of 1997, Elaine was once again a constant presence on set, there not only to handle quick rewrites and adjustments during rehearsals,[81] but also to serve as Mike's creative partner. Throughout the making of the film, they lived in adjoining houses and drove to the set together every morning,[82] where they proceeded to tell each other the story of the movie. "They would go, 'This is a movie about a man who wants to become president, and he is a master at being a totally sincere and interested person in your life and your plight . . . And you see how he wows the crowd and then how he wows the little group and how he sleeps with the teacher . . .'" says Mary Bailey. "And they would do the whole movie like that."[83] "*We* know the end of the story, but nobody else does," Mike stressed to his actors. "You have to think of this as, 'We don't even know if this guy's going to get the nomination yet. He's just an unknown hick from the Midwest. Who is this guy?"[84] If there were hiccups in that understanding, a step they couldn't remember or something off in one scene that wasn't setting up the next in an organic and interesting way, "that was a problem and it would be addressed."[85]

Elaine wasn't the most social person on set, but being around Mike, free from the pressure of running things, gave her the security she needed to open up a little. She was friendly, even downright approachable, talking with Robert Klein about their shared Second City connection[86] or trying, with Mary Bailey, to find a good club to go out dancing.[87] Mike's role as the leader-as-director she had needed on her past productions allowed her mind to focus on the more minute details that made up the bigger picture. "There was a scene at Thanksgiving and we were all gathered together and it was assumed that [my character] had met the character played by Adrian Lester before," Caroline Aaron remembers. "I went up to Elaine and I said, 'Elaine, what is my relationship to him? Have I met him? Have we spent time together?' She didn't really respond at the moment. Then she came back and she added a line. She said, 'When you go meet him, just go up to him and say, *I marched with your father.*' All of a sudden, it was all cleared up, and all of a sudden, I knew what to do. Her economy was incredible, just incredible, of being able to tell a story in the most efficient way possible."[88] The solution may have been economic, but the same couldn't always be said for the path to it. "I learned with Elaine that you do not ask [something] as if it is a simple question, even though it will seem like a simple question to you," Bailey says. Questions about continuity—things like *When does this scene happen? Is this the same morning as the scene before? The next day?*—were never met with quick answers. "Asking Elaine one of those questions would involve a great deal of further thought, just because she was careful and strict and relentless about certain kinds of dramatic logic. And I would always think, 'This doesn't seem very complex,' but it would be."[89]

Together, Mike and Elaine treated each other with the same careful and protective love they had honed on *The Birdcage*. "They were the head of the fan club for each other," Bailey says. "They were great appreciators of each other's talents or opinions or menu selections—and that's not an unimportant part of a Mike Nichols movie. Respectful, and never 'I'm sure this will be okay with Elaine' or 'Michael will see that this is so.' There would be no assuming a greater degree of collaboration than they had already discussed."[90] (Although that didn't stop John Travolta from attempting to play the two against each other. "If I couldn't convince [Mike] of something, I thought, 'I'll go to Mom.' Once she'd agree with me, I'd tell

Mike, 'Elaine said I could do this.' And Mike would go, 'She did? Elaine! Is this true?'"[91]) The two worked as a team, so it wasn't unusual to see Elaine sitting next to Mike behind the camera, chiming in on each take. "They very often, in my view, parlayed only semi-secretly," Klein remembers. "They didn't make any great attempt to whisper. I'm not an expert on the dynamics of their creative relationship, but I'm sure they were on the same sort of wavelength and I couldn't think of anyone better to be next to the camera."[92]

Sometimes their conversations would result in an on-the-spot line change or sometimes Elaine would play the dry and unsentimental co-director when Mike was overcome with emotion. "We'd been doing a particularly emotional scene," Emma Thompson said, "and Mike would be standing behind the video monitor, these huge tears rolling down his cheeks. And Elaine would be right behind him, staring balefully at the monitor. And when the scene was over, Mike would be wiping his eyes and Elaine would say, quite impassively, 'For the next take, I think [the actors] should move slightly to the left.'"[93]

YOU PROBABLY KNOW the image, the one of Bill Clinton standing in the Roosevelt Room of the White House with Hillary by his side, staring straight into the camera. You can hear the words, too—you've heard them a million times. Nine words—"I did not have sexual relations with that woman"—would come to dominate and define the rest of 1998. To Mike and Elaine's great misfortune, those nine words happened to be uttered fifty-three days before their slightly fictionalized version of another Clinton sex scandal was to hit theaters. "This girl went down on him in the Oval Office, and just like that, it became a tame movie! That was really all we thought," Elaine said. "You couldn't wait another two months?"[94]

They went on defense, digging further into the party line that it wasn't a movie about politics—and it especially wasn't about the Clintons. "It's about us more than them," Mike insisted. "It's not about Clinton, but about the 'Clinton thing.'"[95] The audience, they believed, shouldn't be underestimated. They would be smart enough to understand that they weren't watching a dramatization of the news; they were watching a complex, fictional story. "And it's a story that asks a lot of questions about honor and morality and selling out and the compromises leaders must make and the compromises we, the people who are electing them, must make," Mike said. "And in the end, isn't that a little more interesting than what the president did with a White House intern?"[96] But they knew they were fucked. As if it wasn't hard enough to be sandwiched between two other topical genre films—Barry Levinson's *Wag the Dog*, which had just picked up two Academy Award nominations, and Warren Beatty's forthcoming *Bulworth*—both of which not only focused more on the broader political game than the specific players but had release windows that would spare them the immediate shadow of the scandal. Mike and Elaine had made a movie that, despite their protests otherwise, was about the center of the storm that had just hit—and it was decidedly soft on it.

You can't socialize with the people you're skewering. They knew this. Didn't they know this? Elaine, at least, had known mixing friendliness and satire was a recipe for disaster as far back as their Kennedy birthday performance. "We shouldn't have done it, because we were satirists, and it's dangerous to have a satirist on your show if you were a really serious president," she'd later assess.[97] But now their social lives would put them in a tricky predicament as the real-life controversy grew. Mike not only socialized several times with the Clintons on Martha's Vineyard with his wife, Diane Sawyer;[98] he considered himself a *fan* of Bill's.[99] And the two of them had reunited to perform at a Clinton fundraiser in 1992.[100] They would deny reports that the film was being reshaped at the First Family's request, but even if it wasn't, it was still undeniable that winning their approval—or at least avoiding their offense— was an objective,[101] even if in the lowest depths of their subconscious. But that's the thing about satire; you can do your best to avoid genuine harm, but you can't be honest, can't truly go *all the way* with it, if you're worried about what people are going to think.

ELAINE'S SCREENPLAY IS, in many ways, a triumph. Its characters are rich and nuanced—particularly Kathy Bates's Libby Holden, the ball-busting but mentally unstable operative, for which she'd receive an Academy Award nomination—and are often granted a deeper feeling of insight that isn't always present in the book. Her dialogue blends her wry brand of one-liners with unexpectedly (from her, at least) poignant monologues and the kind of snappy, rat-a-tat strategy-laden discussions that give Aaron Sorkin a run for his money together within an airtight structure.

But it's also a disappointment. Whether it's by nature of Mike's cautious handling of the material or Elaine's new kinder, mature worldview, it's missing the kind of dangerous, scathing wit with which her voice is commonly associated. *Primary Colors* is a sincere film, and it's jarring to see Elaine do sincere. She pulls it off, but with so few screenplays credited to her name to see her full range, it begs the question: Is this Elaine's real voice, or is it Elaine shape-shifting, not unlike her work as a ghostwriter, to imitate someone else? Even her cynicism is seemingly misplaced; it lies not with the career politicians you would think it would lambaste, but with the political process, and most notably, the voters themselves. "It's your own dumb fault it's like this," she seems to say to the audience, sympathizing with politicians who sell themselves with buzzy sound bites because the general public won't pay attention to anything more detailed than a thirty-second TV spot. The film was now without the buzz of unmasking the book's now-named anonymous author and was overshadowed by the drama unfolding in real life. When viewed next to *Wag the Dog* and *Bulworth,* her choice of targets, and the softness with which she hits them, *Primary Colors* is a shrug. Those films took big swings to say *something; Primary Colors*'s boldest argument is that we shouldn't care who our president fucks.

With fiction separated from reality—and particularly many years and many far more insane presidential scandals later—*Primary Colors* holds up on its own as a solid work, but it's understandable why it limped into theaters in March of 1998. While the reviews were largely positive, they were only modestly warm at best. "*Primary Colors* has more serious ambitions to capture something important and disturbing about this era's political atmosphere," Janet Maslin wrote. "Sometimes it does."[102] Despite general praise garnered for Bates's and Thompson's performances, the film's "telling back-of-the-bus, inside-the-motel feel,"[103] and the "slightly subversive pungency of May's sharp and sarcastic script, which includes many of the book's better speeches and knows how to improve on them,"[104] it was met with an uninterested audience. It would pull in only $39 million in the United States, which, combined with the $11 million from global audiences, wouldn't break even on its $65 million budget.

Still, it wasn't a total loss. For her screenplay, Elaine snagged her second Oscar nomination. At the ceremony the following year, she skipped the cameras and the red carpet, sneaking into the Dorothy Chandler Pavilion undetected.[105] If you were viewing the ceremony on television at home, it was as if she wasn't even there.

CHAPTER 12

We Adapt Very Quickly

1998–2014

The Birdcage and *Primary Colors* were the last feature films Elaine May would ever make. How, after her two biggest hits, one a commercial smash and the other an Oscar nominee, could her comeback stall out? Well, first of all, let's reconsider the word *comeback*. Yes, Elaine was making movies again, but it required a man to pull her back up to the surface. And even then, she had to relinquish some sort of control in the partnership, had to take a back seat as just the screenwriter, become half of a whole. Whether it was her choice or not, she didn't have the power to call the same kind of shots she once did, if she ever really had that power at all. Still, though: Why was 1998 the end of Elaine May's film career?

Comedy, and the standards to which it was held, was changing. Of course comedy was changing. Change is an inherent part of the form; the same thing cannot be funny forever, and what's in favor is often dictated by the very young. Elaine knew that; after all, that was how she had made a name for herself in the first place. But now she was truly on the outside of it, unable to bridge the widening generation gap. Of course she was revered and respected, with her influence everywhere—whether people knew it or not— but she was no longer the tastemaker, or even the tastemakers' secret veteran consultant. There was a new young crop of outcasts not unlike the University of Chicago crew she had come up with, and she couldn't be as edgy or irreverent as they were. Nor was she willing to bend in the direction of lame, sanitized corporate-friendly sitcoms. (Not to mention the sophomoric fart-joke humor perpetuated by the Frat Pack.)[1] First in the relay, she had passed off the baton years ago and stuck around long enough to see the third and fourth members of the team run with it now.

And good luck to them, because as far as she saw it, satire was heaving its dying last gasps. "*Saturday Night Live* and Second City are doing satire, but sometimes today, it seems that reality is beyond satire," she said. "And language has so deteriorated in this country—it takes four words for one, and people use phrases like 'vertically disabled.' A kind of newspeak takes over. That may have an impact on satire."[2] At a speaking engagement in 1997—one of a few she would make in the late 1990s in which she lectured or participated in discussions about her work[3]—remarks about the intersection of political correctness and comedy began as a joke only to turn sour, her irritation just barely concealed. "I've noticed that you can't make jokes about—I actually made a list of it. You can't make jokes about violence, poverty, drug abuse, women, children, spousal abuse, sick people," she said. "You have to call somebody who has one leg physically challenged or vertically uneven or whatever it is. And people are really firm about this. I mean, really outraged. And you read letters in *People* magazine in which they say 'Enough of these letters about parties and movie stars! Give us more about the people in the trailer park who save this world.' And you think, This kind of respect in a country that's pretty high up there in records of drug abuse and child abuse and racism and violence and bad education. Affirmative action has not been passed and the Equal Rights Amendment wasn't passed. Health care hasn't been passed and education isn't doing so well. You think, Really, this political correctness is instead of the money."[4]

Ah, the money. It wasn't just comedy that was changing; Hollywood was in the throes of transformation, too. Elaine's career had spanned an entire arc of change across film, from the end of the classical studio system as New Hollywood emerged to the rise of the blockbuster and early indies, and now to the return of a studio system under the influence of Wall Street and more interested in selling stuff than telling a good story. *The Birdcage* would be a highwater mark across all mainstream adult comedies; by the late 1990s and into the 2000s, the adult R-rated comedy would slip away. Studios, eager to cater to teenage boys, were less than eager to give

Elaine—or many other women writers or directors—the financing needed to make any film that wasn't a sci-fi fantasy, an action flick, or a children's movie with built-in brand recognition.

Then there was the age thing. Hollywood has always been a youth-obsessed industry. Its 1960s youthquake is how she got pulled into it; its shake-up during the 2000s would be how she got pushed out. The fact is, it didn't matter if Elaine was a genius. Brilliant or not, she was a seventy-year-old woman with a reputation for being erratic that still preceded her. Even she was the first to admit that "a lot of people in the movie business think I'm crazy, but"—obviously there had to be a but—"I'm a *sane* closet person. A lot of people in the business think you're sane, but you're a crazy closet person."[5] Sane or not, she was far from anyone's first choice to direct a film meant to reflect the current culture and steer it forward. And it wasn't just Elaine getting pushed out. Her peers, those select few she'd trust to direct one of her scripts if she wouldn't do so herself, were also feeling it. In the early 2000s, Mike was moving on to HBO, Nora Ephron was little more than a hired gun, and Warren Beatty was embarking on what would be a fifteen-year hiatus. No one was making the types of movies they made anymore. At least not the big studios, and the smaller ones they could go to instead would never be able to provide them with the kind of budgets they were used to, the kind that would allow a certain amount of comfort and time that were increasingly becoming a luxury. Elaine had tried doing an independent film before; it was not for her, and she wasn't exactly keen to do it again. She wasn't a kid anymore. A guerrilla-style film production full of sixteen-hour days is grueling enough when you're young; at seventy, it's brutal. If Hollywood was divided between those with power and prestige and those without, Elaine and company fell somewhere in the middle, still somewhat beholden to the studio heads for their paychecks. Like the rest of America, Hollywood's middle class was slowly but surely disappearing, too.

But what if we ignore all of that? What if all of that is just gravy? What if Elaine simply decided that she didn't *want* to make more movies? Maybe the creeping decline of the film industry was just a happy coincidence confirming that the theater was what she really enjoyed and where she really belonged. She had done the Hollywood thing, and it wasn't even all that fun. It was, barring a few exceptions, unfulfilling and soul-crushing at every turn. Why bother? There were softer walls to beat her head against. Over the next decade, Elaine would burrow into her identity as a writer of witty and offbeat Off-Broadway plays, to varying degrees of success.

THE WAY ALAN Arkin tells it, he was never really intending to write a play. He was only trying to "work out the bugs" on a new scriptwriting program his wife had bought. But troubleshooting led to typing, and typing led to writing a play, and before he knew it, Elaine was sitting in a reading of it that Julian Schlossberg had organized.[6] There in the audience, watching the play Arkin had written for himself and his son, she realized her next project. "That's so nice," she thought. "Why don't I do that? Why don't I write something for Jeannie, and maybe we could all do it together?"[7] When she approached him afterward, her mind was made up. She wasn't asking him, she was telling him, Arkin recalled. "I had no specific expectations from the reading," he wrote in his memoir, "but this train had already left the station."[8]

Elaine wrote a one-act for herself and Jeannie, then, to round things out,[9] another for the four of them, both of which subtly examined the nuances of power, with Arkin directing the entire evening. In the opener *The Way of All Fish,* a late night at the office leads an intimidating businesswoman and her meek secretary (well, assistant, but the boss refuses to give her any dignity beyond "a word which originally meant desk") to share dinner together, which turns into a game of psychological chicken when the secretary reveals her fantasy of finding fame by killing someone important. And balancing the other side of Arkin's *Virtual Reality* was a finale featuring the quartet, *In and Out of the Light,* a boisterous farce in which a married dentist's plot to have an affair with his over-the-hill sexpot assistant is foiled by the arrival of his son and an emergency from a neurotic patient.

Together, they're two of her most uproarious works, deftly ping-ponging from clever wordplay to broad slapstick and back. As a performer, she fully inhabits both characters, finding humor in the unexpected approach to how a character comes across on the page (particularly with Ms. Asquith, the businesswoman in *The Way of All Fish,* whose power Elaine portrays as more paranoid than chilly). So, too, does she inhabit her characters as a writer. The text gives away moments where her habit of writing a version of herself makes itself known, instances in which she's mined her own life and personality for character traits. Remember the absent-minded dishevelment of *A New Leaf*'s Henrietta, the put-upon and fed-up wife of the Mike-like character in *A Matter of Position,* the bitter resentment of *Hotline*'s Dorothy.

"The genius about her is that she puts a little bit of herself in everything, and that little bit of herself is a mountain to other people," Billy Crystal once said.[10] Looking at the few female characters in her oeuvre, you can see where the little dosage of herself is a little higher, where the line between reality from fiction blurs a little bit more, if you squint just right. No character she writes, male or female—and certainly none she portrays—is exactly *her,* but they're all infused with pieces of their creator, be it behavioral tics or backstories or philosophies. "I'm pretty sure her real life had to—how could it not—color the work. I mean, it's all we have to draw from, is our real lives," Phil Rosenthal observes. "You can't write about real life unless you have one."[11] It's through these onstage doppelgängers that the private, evasive, timid, rarely on-the-record Elaine speaks.

Take, for example, the views of her executive character in *The Way of All Fish.* In real life, Elaine all but physically ducks whenever someone lobs the "What's it like to be a woman in a male-dominated industry?" softball at her. She gives a polite but elliptical response, if anything. And spare her the invitations to panels discussing women in film, please; she's too shy—nervous, even—to be as blunt as she would be within the safe company of her friends. But onstage, behind the mask of Ms. Asquith, she finds another form of security. She pulls no punches: "The appearance of strength is the appearance of power. Do you know the real difference between men and women . . . Strength. Sheer physical strength . . . It's not whether you're a man or woman that determines whose world it is, it's how strong you are that determines whether you're a man or a woman. Metaphorically, of course."¹² (Driving the point home, she would get down on the floor and, at sixty-six, bang out twelve perfect pushups night after night with ease.)¹³

And what about her marriages? Good luck getting her on the record on any of that. But Ms. Asquith can give you some insight if you're looking. Elaine writes what she knows, and what she knows is this: "I don't really notice people unless they're directly in my line of vision, part of what I'm focusing on." That sounds a little like another hyper-focused to the point of ignoring everything else, even her own basic needs, person we know, doesn't it? Anyway, she continues: "That was one of the reasons for my divorce. . . . I'm very insensitive. And everyone has to forgive me. Until they don't. It's a shortcoming—being blind to others. Power in a relationship belongs to whoever wants to leave first—and you can't anticipate that unless you notice the other person."¹⁴

As for the persona of Elaine May protecting the "vulnerable" woman underneath? Ms. Asquith has thoughts: "I can't tell you how much I hate that word. I have no idea why everyone thinks it's so special to be vulnerable. It's a self-pitying, time-consuming preoccupation and everyone has it."¹⁵

Elaine manages to instill bits and pieces of herself in both the female characters of *In and Out of the Light.* There she is in Sue: seen by others as daffy but actually deeply perceptive and incredibly restrained, maybe even to her own detriment: "I'm a very private person," she says, "and that's made it difficult to talk about my marriage or divorce, so I've never really had any closure."¹⁶ And there she is in Wanda, the hysterical patient whose neuroticism leads everyone else to perceive her as crazy—and well, she is *a little*—but is actually revealed to be a gifted psychologist. Elaine may not own her contradictions, but Wanda does: "Why is that so surprising? Because I seem like an idiot in this chair? Everyone seems like an idiot somewhere. It just means you have imagination, you can see past the moment to the end, past the flesh to the skull."¹⁷

The work itself couldn't have been more ideal. Arkin was a likeminded director, Schlossberg a trusted producer, and Jeannie an effortless scene partner. She didn't even have to venture far from home; every day that summer, she could walk the four short blocks between the Promenade Theatre and her apartment, as if it were a little family play they all put on every night after dinner. The show was an easygoing, well-received hit. Critics noted the unevenness of the three plays, acknowledging that it was a stretch to even call them that when they were more like sketches. But all that (and the blatant nepotism at work, too) could be excused by the alchemy of talent, wit, and star charisma that melded to make the evening so thoroughly enjoyable. "The mere presence of Elaine May on a New York stage is worth the trip," one review noted. "Her return is an event, and a hilarious reminder of what a unique comedic talent she is, with or without Nichols."[18]

The New York Times was especially praiseful. Film critic Vincent Canby gave it one positive review,[19] while the tough-to-please *New York Times* theater critic Ben Brantley gave it another: "What Ms. May and Mr. Arkin have done is retain the primal appeal of a classic comic situation while spicing it with subversive details that keep catching you off guard." Even with the stumbles, the plays "percolate with actorly inventiveness and a willingness to pursue a warped logic step by step into the land of absurdity."[20] It was such a hit she had the luxury of choosing when to bow out. "We opened and we ran and ran and ran, and Alan would say to me, because he really doesn't like to do things over and over, nor does anyone, he said, 'I'm going to kill myself.' And we finally left the show . . . and I left Jeannie in it. She never forgave me."[21]

If only her next collaboration with Arkin was that fortunate.

Aside from the idea that she and Arkin could work together again, nothing else about *Taller Than a Dwarf* could have possibly seemed like a good idea. Nearly thirty years after her first disastrous attempt, Elaine was set to finally make her official Broadway debut as a playwright. But the play she was doing so with was the one she had already tried to take to Broadway before. Twice, actually, the first attempt at which was nothing short of a career-paralyzing catastrophe. What could have possibly possessed Elaine to think that this time would be any different, that the third staging of *A Matter of Position* would be the charm? Was this the same woman who had once insisted that the only thing safe was to take a chance? There's not giving up on a play, believing in its potential enough to keep working on it. But then there's beating a dead horse, relentlessly holding on to the idea of something beyond salvage long after it's time to let go, to the point where you have to ask yourself: *What am I doing this for? Is it to prove something, whether to myself or my critics? Am I resting on my laurels? Or am I resting on the efforts of others involved, hoping their fresh perspectives can make sense of the garbled knot I've tied?*

It's possible that *Taller Than a Dwarf* looked like a sure bet on paper. It had star power in its leads—Matthew Broderick and Parker Posey, in her Broadway debut—and its director, Arkin, with a solid supporting cast of veteran character actors like Joyce Van Patten and Jerry Adler. It would premiere at the Longacre Theatre, produced by Schlossberg, who had shepherded *Power Plays* to a successful run. You would think, given the slump Broadway was in, with such a dearth of new plays[22] that it had been declared "a forum for automated theme park shows,"[23] that a new comedy—the *only* new comedy that season—by one of America's greatest voices would be a much-appreciated hit. So how could it have possibly gone so wrong as to have been called "painfully unfunny"?[24]

Well, because, for the first time in her life, Elaine's writing was lazy. *Taller Than a Dwarf* positioned itself as a play about Selma and Howard Miller, "an average couple during the millennium learning the new rules of the American dream,"[25] but there's hardly any millennium to it. According to Schlossberg, Elaine's desire to stage the show led her to give it another rewrite "to get it to the point that we were excited about doing it,"[26] but the rewrite that would come to be known as *Taller Than a Dwarf* was virtually unchanged from *A Matter of Position*. Entire chunks of the original text reappear, the colloquialisms of 1962 woefully out of place in 2000. Its updates amounted to little more than ham-fisted amendments tacked onto the opening and ending: a television playing news bulletins about internet millionaires; moments where each character indulgently shares their backstory directly to the audience; a few heavy-handed asides about current events; and more than one deeply problematic racial stereotype, including a child neighbor who has been rewritten as Black, for no real reason other than to make him a caricature with cheap attempts at Ebonics and one astoundingly regrettable rap verse.[27] A half-baked reheating, it's dated, and its humor is appallingly stale, bordering on outright offensive.

"They were kind of insistent in doing the script the way it originally was intended to be done," Jerry Adler says. "When I first read it, I would say, 'Oh my god, this is not going to work. But I'm sure with Alan Arkin and Elaine May, they're going to do a lot of work and it's going to come out fine.'"[28] But because the foundational text was no good, no amount of work they attempted (including calling in Mike, the star of the ill-fated original, for his thoughts)[29] could keep the entire play from collapsing in on itself the same way Selma and Howard's bathtub finally crashes through their waterlogged bathroom floor.

Like most productions she had been involved in, Elaine was constantly around, but unlike other productions, she hung back to allow Arkin to take the lead. "She kept to herself so much," says Adler. "She worked a little bit with Alan Arkin, but they were kind of secretive."[30] Rehearsals and Boston tryouts proceeded without significant changes while the producers moved forward with full confidence. "I really liked it. I can't tell you what was wrong, because if I knew what was going wrong, I would've tried to stop it. I mean, I was having a good time," Schlossberg says.[31] Morale among the cast sank. They would band together, try to figure out solutions, changes they could implement to their own roles, possible ways to fix it. But only Elaine—the playwright, who knew her story inside and out—could do that, and she was MIA, and while Arkin was good with the guys, his approach with the women in the cast—particularly Posey—was often unproductive.[32]

"Parker needed a lot of work," Adler says. "She needed a lot of strengthening up, more than anything else. It was her first show, and she just needed somebody to be good to her."[33] In Arkin's abandonment, Joyce Van Patten took up the mantle of trying to bolster Posey's confidence and guide her performance,[34] but it was a near-impossible task when the part on the page was so underwritten. "I think it was hard on Parker," Cynthia Darlow, who played the super's wife, remembers. "It wasn't really her fault. I think it was in the script that it just never got fully fleshed out somehow."[35]

Taller Than a Dwarf opened in New York on April 24, 2000, to reviews that were uniformly bad—and utterly confounded. It was "jaw-droppingly unfunny" to the point of containing "the moral low points" of Elaine's lifetime of work.[36] The premise was illogical, and Arkin and the cast didn't "have the skill and panache to pull off the play's generous helpings of slapstick."[37] It wasn't a play; it was an assemblage of "gag-based scenes, dialogue that seems to have been written with a laugh track to be inserted later and characters whose motivations for saying and doing anything are either trivial, contrived or entirely obscure until it's too late to care."[38] (Ironically, exactly what she feared the play would become when faced with the request for cuts from Arthur Penn back in 1962.) The feedback was unanimous: "May can and must do better than this."[39] But how could she when there was no accountability from those she had surrounded herself with, who held fast to the idea that the flaws were not within the work itself, but in the eyes of the critics? "This is always the sad part about Broadway," says Schlossberg. "The audiences often in previews are standing and cheering. Then the reviews come out, and all of a sudden they're not standing, except to leave. It's very funny to watch how the critics, especially twenty some odd years ago, could turn a play."[40] The staggering misfire made it seem as if Elaine's tilted insight was no longer portraying reality.

It was a kind of flop so bad that it was known even by the general public, those who weren't the small subset of the population—industry insiders and *New York Times* arts section fanatics—who usually paid attention to the latest Broadway news. "It's a drag when your reviews are bad," Parker Posey said, "and you go to your corner deli for coffee, and the guy says, 'Ahh, flatter than a matzo!'"[41] The play didn't even last two months; it closed in early June after fifty-six performances.[42]

Elaine pressed on, accepting its fate with shrugging, laugh-it-off nonchalance. "You just dodged a bullet," she told her friend Caroline Aaron, who had turned down one of its roles with some reluctance. Elaine reduced *Taller Than a Dwarf*'s failure down to the simple fact that it was a Jewish play with gentile actors who didn't quite grasp their characters.[43] Whatever the reason for people not liking it, it wasn't any of her business, and it wouldn't stop her from sharing her perspective. "She logically feels that 'the only thing I have to offer is my own voice.' You're so welcome to not agree with it, to not see it the same way she does. She just can't cut the suit to fit the fashion. She's literally incapable of it," Aaron says. "You just want to suck on a gas pipe when you get a bad review or something disastrous happens, or you think you're finished, or whatever it is. I don't see that in Elaine. I just see her being creative. It's like the weather. She can't help it."[44]

She was approaching an age where most would be contemplating retirement, delicately choosing final projects that would lend themselves to their legacy and ensure they ended things on a good note while they stepped back from their work. Step back from her work—ha! As if that was something Elaine could ever be capable of doing. Slow down, sure. Reprioritize things, yes. Make her circle of collaborators even tighter, ensuring that the only projects worth her time were ones made in the company of dear friends and family. But stop? Retire? Absolutely not. She couldn't turn it off if she wanted to. There was always a new project on the horizon to be excited about.

STANLEY DONEN WAS having a little bit of a moment, you could say, when he and Elaine got together at the turn of the new millennium. A consistently underrated and written-off filmmaker in his active years, Donen shared with Elaine the unique experience of having a career cut short by Hollywood's obsession with the numbers. He had not directed a film since 1984's *Blame It on Rio,* and his attempted comeback, a Broadway musical production of *The Red Shoes* in 1993, opened and closed within the same week. But everything gets reevaluated at some point, and he was no exception to the rule. Even if he wasn't making new movies, his oeuvre, at least, was beginning to be revisited by critics in a more positive and appreciative light by the late nineties—and Donen looked like he was enjoying every minute of it.

And what better way to enjoy success than with a new girl by your side to share it with? One night, Elaine and Donen found themselves at the same dinner party thrown by Julian Schlossberg. Donen was smitten. The next day, he called Schlossberg and asked, "Do you think she would go out with me?"[45]

It wasn't long before the two were linked as a new couple in 1999.[46] Less than a year later, in April 2000, the New York rumor mills were reporting that Donen had proposed by singing Elaine a love song he had written just for the occasion.[47] Sure, the news of their possible engagement happened to appear curiously close to the opening of *Taller Than a Dwarf,* part distraction from the rumblings of trouble and part free publicity. And all right, she didn't say yes; he estimated he asked her at least 171 more times over the next twelve years.[48] But this simple fact is unimpeachably true: They were wild about each other. Donen's eyes would grow bright with adoration anytime her name was mentioned. "She is simply, in my opinion, the most gifted person I've ever come to know," he said. "She's funnier than anybody on earth."[49] Elaine returned his affections with a dog tag engraved with the words: "Stanley Donen. If lost, please return to Elaine May."[50] He wore the large silver medallion around his neck for the better part of a decade. Donen could be prickly and demanding—"Stanley did not suffer fools. He could be really, really mean," says producer Ben Odell[51]—but so could she, which was part of the attraction. They came from different generations and filmmaking experiences—he in the golden age of the studio system, her in the maverick New Hollywood era—yet "he was not threatened at all by her talent. I think he found it very sexy that Elaine was her own, that she was a self-possessed woman," says Mary Birdsong, who worked with the pair on their play *Adult Entertainment.* Even as a self-possessed woman, Elaine still liked to play the role of doting girlfriend, more than happy to tend to his needs with care and put him first. "She wanted very much to prop up Stanley," Aaron says. "I always felt like when I was around them, that her priority was to make sure that he was well attended to, he was okay. She took very good care of him when he got older whenever I would see them out socially."[52]

And socially, they were everywhere, the It Couple of the uptown geriatric literati. If they weren't at one of Marlo Thomas's frequent parties,[53] they were out on the town, the sight of Elaine working the social circuit a feast for Liz Smith after decades of crumbs. There they were at Amy Irving's fiftieth birthday, holding court with a host of A-listers,[54] and noticeably swooning at each other in Café Carlyle while Maria Friedman sang "The Way You Look Tonight."[55] On one New Year's Eve, they showed up to a party at precisely midnight and held everyone hostage until two a.m. with their riffing.[56] Running into Robert Klein outside Donen's apartment building, Elaine relished the chance to sing the news of her boyfriend's recent Venice Film Festival Award to anyone within earshot, girlishly ebullient.[57] Before, she had been discreet, never keeping her relationships secret but not exactly parading them around either. Stanley, though, Elaine was more than eager to show off.

It was Elaine who convinced Stanley to return to the theater, enlisting him to direct her attempt at a palate cleanser in 2002. This time, she lowered the stakes to fix the things that had spelled death for *Dwarf* from the get-go. It was a new play this time, and it steered clear of the bright lights and big expectations of Broadway, playing instead downtown at the Variety Arts Theater in Union Square. (Lucky for them, Off-Broadway was the place to be post-9/11, where the stars who wanted to make good theater regardless of profit and producers looking to cut costs and save money in the face of a ticket sale slump could coexist.) Called *Adult Entertainment,* it was a spoof-filled show within a show about a group of small-time, local public access TV porn stars who decide to make a "prestigious" film together and enlist the help of a recent Yale grad to write it. The show played up the title's double entendre, poking fun at the ways in which the lowbrow adult and highbrow art-house film industries weren't entirely all that dissimilar.

Taller Than a Dwarf showed that maybe Elaine had lost touch with the reality of everyday people. Better, then, to write about her reality: show business. It didn't matter if the extent of her knowledge of the adult film world appeared limited to *The Robin Byrd Show* and the easy laughs that came with character names like Frosty Moons and Heidi-the-Ho and fake film titles like *Saving Ryan's Privates.* Nor did it matter all that much that her idea of a realistic reflection of it was astonishingly chaste, with no nudity and only "a few sketchy rehearsals of simulated sex."[58] (Paradoxically, it actually kind of helped. "I thought we were going to get some people who were going to storm out of the theater and say, 'This is an outrage and I'm not going to be a part of it! We get one or two but not a lot," Donen said at the time.)[59] It wasn't so much about the content as it was about the ecosystem of show business, and she had more than enough knowledge in that area to get by. *Adult Entertainment* was the kind of high-concept satire that she was good at, and the pair filled the cast with seasoned pros—like Danny Aiello and Jeannie, whom, by now, Elaine seemed to write exclusively for—and new talents alike who were enthusiastic to play. (They even went so far as to seriously consider auditions from actual adult film stars. Give it a little more truth, you know.)[60]

Stanley and Elaine worked well together as a team, more like a pair of co-directors than writer and director. "It was almost like macro and micro," Mary Birdsong says. "Stanley seemed to be more movement and big picture, and also musical numbers within the play, whereas Elaine tended to be more the meat and bones of the acting in each scene and the dynamics and relationships between the characters."[61] They cultivated a kindhearted family-like atmosphere that centered around the shared reverence the cast had for the pair. "They were very much Mom and Dad in certain ways to me, of just wanting to please, wanting to do a good job for them," says Birdsong. Elaine, in particular, was held in high esteem. They had known of her legend before they even knew her as a person, and while she more than lived up to her reputation as a brilliant and decisive "tough Broad with the capital B,"[62] her air of fragility had only grown over time. You couldn't help but feel protective of the wisp of a woman who was constantly eating rice cakes and misplacing her glasses and who rarely, if ever, raised her voice; couldn't help but want her approval without making it obvious that you wanted her approval. Even Stanley deferred to her, delighting in her genius and happily allowing her to be the boss.[63] The warmth was evident in the pages, too. *Adult Entertainment* had the potential to be mean or cruel or judgmental, and it wasn't any of that; it wasn't even all that mocking, perhaps a first for work from Elaine. No, it was "satire with a heart," a play in which her fondness for her characters was well known.[64] Critics wouldn't be able to accuse her of heartlessness or a loss of morals or whatever else they wanted to throw out. She would give them goofy, giggly, positively silly. A lighthearted good time.

That is, until the show hit the second half, at which point, the characters, fixated on the philosophy behind their required readings, take the show somewhere else entirely. As the play grapples with the struggle to make good art in a world that commodifies mediocrity, it switches from presenting a light spoof to attempting to convey a deeper message, though who, exactly, that message was for was unclear. The tonal disconnect was evident as tryouts in Stamford got underway in November of 2002. Throughout rehearsals and tryouts, the script remained a work in progress, being shaped and reshaped in real time. Elaine watched as the actors improvised their way through the pages, using their work as a litmus test. "If we got up on our feet and improvised a scene that we had just read through and we forgot a big chunk of information, she would know that she hadn't made that clear in the writing. That would show her that something was not quite there yet, or it would show her that maybe that part wasn't even necessary, the part she had on the page, and that she should lose it," explains Birdsong.[65] But as a work in progress, it was savaged upon previews as "endlessly gabby" and "not so much written as thrown together,"[66] a comedy that "proceeds bumpily and grindingly under the direction of Stanley Donen."[67] It was overlong and overplayed, and ultimately, "mostly boring."[68] Yikes. They had been having such a good time playing with it, but neither Elaine nor Stanley could afford a fuckup of *Dwarf* proportions. As they convened to figure out how to fix it, they bought time by courting public distraction. Like the conveniently timed blind item about their new relationship when *Taller Than a Dwarf* was faltering, a new piece of gossip found its way to the papers: "Hmmmm . . . NO one will return our calls to confirm or deny whether *Charade* director Stanley Donen and fiancée Elaine May have finally wed. Donen directs the brilliant comic's play *Adult Entertainment,* which opens at the Variety Arts Theater Dec. 2 . . ."[69] For someone so intensely private as to rarely, if ever, share information about herself with the press, Elaine sure had a knack for showing up in the gossip pages when she had a new play to promote.

Meanwhile, the producers pushed the opening back by a week and a half[70] and quietly slashed ticket prices for the first ten days[71] while Elaine brought in Mike to take a look at it.[72] Everyone was in agreement: the show needed to be "tightened and shortened."[73] But how much tightening and shortening could they do before there was no play left at all? What Elaine had were two concepts: the first half, an extended sketch; the second, a meditation on the intersection of art and commerce in the modern age. She couldn't have one without the other and still have a show, but neither was really connecting. She had only so much time. It would have to work.

By its official opening, the most jarring kinks had been worked out, though not entirely scrubbed. In a fairly favorable review, *The New York Times* assessed that its first half was "so fat with hilarious earnestness that you may feel you're overdosing on laughter," but that "the sentimental second half . . . feels malnourished."[74] It was fine, "competent but unremarkable," as one review called it.[75] It's as if, in their lukewarm reviews, critics had lowered their expectations for Elaine to consistently live up to her genius. (Well, most of them. *Variety*'s Charles Isherwood challenged: "Perhaps only a certified comic genius would conceive of stretching two and a half jokes out across two and a half hours of stage time. Certainly only a certified comic genius would be allowed to. The genius in question is Elaine May, whose certification may soon be in need of revoking, at least if 'Adult Entertainment' is proffered as exhibit A.")[76]

So what if Elaine was "always a first-class sprinter" who "tends to flag at longer distances"?[77] Age had bought her some forgiveness. The fact that she was still able to pull off part of the race at such a clip was a small wonder in and of itself. And, anyway, her less-than-stellar offerings were still better than a lot of others' best efforts. The show was a modest success—thanks in part to a small boost in ticket sales in the middle of a Broadway strike[78]—before closing four months later. *Adult Entertainment* made its point: Not all art has to be genius; sometimes all we can ask from it is that it gives us a fairly good time. Sometimes that's enough.

FILM HAD OFFICIALLY taken a back seat, a medium in which she could have some fun, casually keep her skills in shape—use it or lose it—and lend a friend a favor more than anything else. Such was the case with *Small Time Crooks*, the 2000 class comedy by Woody Allen, who had written the part of an enthusiastic but dim-witted woman—aptly named May—with her in mind. "I wanted her for *Take the Money and Run* years ago, and she said, 'You wouldn't wanna lay eyes on me. I'm wearing a neck brace.' She wasn't wearing a neck brace; she was just hard to get for the movies," he said. To his surprise, when he sent her the script for *Small Time Crooks*, she said yes.[79]

Allen's career had always been defined by peaks and valleys; with the just okay *Small Time Crooks*, critics heaped much of their praise on his sheer triumph of getting the reclusive actress up on the big screen again.[80] And oh, what a welcome presence she was when she was up there. Playing the character with natural ease, she seemed to be improvising the entire thing. In her breezy sixteen minutes of screen time, she managed to "commit an act of screwball larceny, smoothly wrestling every scene she is in from such comic titans as Woody Allen, Tracey Ullman and Elaine Stritch,"[81] walking away with an award for Best Supporting Actress from the National Society of Film Critics for her efforts.

As a writer or director, though, she couldn't grab on to the same kind of luck. The remake of *Kind Hearts and Coronets* she and Mike had long talked about, the one that had gotten the interest of Robin Williams and a soft yes from Universal, was dead. The studio wouldn't fully greenlight it until it saw a rewrite,[82] and the failure of Mike's most recent film, *What Planet Are You From?*, didn't help their cause. Perhaps it was for the best. Elaine's 2001 draft, written with Will Smith in mind to play the poor distant relative of a wealthy duke who sets out to murder the eight other heirs ahead of him in line of succession,[83] updates the story to center on a Black man born to a white, blue-blooded woman. Elaine plants both hands firmly on the same third rail of "is this the best person to tell this story?" offense she had merely grazed in *The Birdcage* in her attempt to write a comedy about race. The script is shockingly unfunny; if Elaine's guiding principle was to be relentlessly truthful, this—with its racist caricatures and clunky dialogue full of minstrel clichés—didn't even come close.[84]

Then there was the adaptation of *Skinny Dip,* Carl Hiaasen's comedic caper about a presumed-dead heiress and an ex-cop who team up to screw with the heiress's husband—the man who tried to kill her. Mike, so sure of the bestseller's film potential—and in his and Elaine's ability to translate it—had purchased the rights to it himself in 2004.[85] Ever loyal to writers, they invited Hiaasen to New York to be involved with their process of condensing the novel into a traditional three-act film script. "I wasn't starry-eyed so much about the possibility of the movie as I was just being able to meet Mike and Elaine. They were legendary, and when you saw them together, shooting ideas back and forth, it was worth it, you know?" Hiaasen says. "These are two talents that I had, when I was a kid, watched on television. And to be sitting in the same room with them, it just seemed a little surreal."[86] Elaine completed the first draft, but she became seriously ill as negotiations with its potential star, George Clooney, were drawn out. By the time she recovered, Mike had moved on to *Charlie Wilson's War,* and the project faltered.[87]

The project that would take the most of her time and focus was her intended gift for Donen: *Bye Bye Blues,* a screenplay for an original musical she hoped he would direct as a triumphant return to the screen and his swan song. Set to music and lyrics by the famed John Kander and Fred Ebb,[88] the duo behind the music of *Cabaret* and *Chicago,* the story told a heightened version of their current predicament: A legendary director who wants to make a musical about an architect—who is more interested in building beautiful things in a world that prioritizes commerce—can't get funding for it because the industry has put him out to pasture in his old age. So he decides to make it independently on a shoestring budget, enlisting film school students as his crew and playing the lead himself. But when Harvey Weinstein comes on board to distribute it, he gives him an ultimatum: When the architect overdoses on heroin and dies at the end of the film, the director playing him *actually* has to die, too. (It's a juicier marketing angle.) If that wasn't meta enough, it gets even more brain-melting: They decided that Donen should also play the fictional director, and—given the lack of production options they had in real life—they should make it with a student crew, too.[89] How hard could it be?

Incredibly, actually, according to Ben Odell, who came on board the project as a master's student at Columbia University in 2003 and would work—without pay—as a producer on the film. "He wanted to shoot the actual movie with film students. It was a time when the digital revolution was happening, kind of [the] beginnings of the 2000s where you had a bunch of these little movies that were being made for hundreds of thousands of dollars and going to Sundance," Odell explains.[90] But as much as Donen tried to engage in the new way of making movies from a technical standpoint, he couldn't get on board with the new way things were done politically. These days, if someone is dangling a check to pay for your movie, it's not unusual for them to assume that their cash automatically buys them a producing credit, too. This pissed Donen off. Credit without work? That was bullshit. "Are you going to carry the fucking cables?" he challenged one would-be financier. "I'm going, 'What? Carry cables? He's financing the movie. What are you doing, Stanley?'" Odell recalls. "And he just sent him out. Stanley didn't like him, so he was like 'I don't give a shit if he writes a check for my movie or not.'"[91]

For five years, Odell met often with Donen, running budgets, seeking out investors, pitching a "making of" documentary to HBO, working out of his office overlooking Central Park or occasionally at Elaine's apartment, which she now shared with him, nearby. "Everybody wanted to talk to him about *Singin' in the Rain* and his career, but nobody wanted to give money to make a movie," Odell says.[92] They could have been scared away by the student crew part of the equation, or by the script, which "was amazing but insane," says Odell. "It was funny and satirical and pointing to things that we suffer from in the art versus commerce world we live in, and crazy and daring."[93] But Hollywood doesn't *want* to be told what it's doing wrong; studio executives don't *want* the public to see depictions of its hypocrisy. Their ages didn't help, either. Stanley and Elaine wouldn't be the first in Hollywood who were respected and appreciated for their past work but deemed too irrelevant to contribute anymore. Hollywood sets money on fire for vanity projects every day of the week; wouldn't it be fair that two aging filmmakers—ones whose careers were cut short in the first place—get a crack at theirs?

The decision wasn't just with a studio or financiers; securing insurance on a film led by a director in his eighties and a screenwriter in her seventies would have been a nightmare. Robert Altman was able to find a work-around by hiring Paul Thomas Anderson as a "standby" director to get his final film made;[94] it's difficult to see Donen or Elaine willing to make the same compromise. "They were only willing to make it under [certain] circumstances," says Odell. The two had their set ways of making movies, their own idea of what they wanted and what their worth was, in spite of the changing times. Either one of them could have financed the movie entirely on their own if they wanted to, but they were too stubborn to admit that kind of defeat. "I think it's a hard thing as you grow older to let go of the idea that your value is still there, and Stanley at the top of his game was a top director," says Odell. "It's hard for that person to accept maybe that they have to play by different rules at the end. And I think that's probably where the struggle was."[95]

As the film slumped along, the seemingly impossible happened: Elaine got good at socializing. Not the "intimate parties with your friends" type of socializing—she had learned long ago how to be more of a person around others and make small talk. No, she got good at the *public* kind of socializing: seeing, and more important, being seen. Elaine's life on the social circuit took off during the early 2000s and would continue on an upward trajectory for the rest of the decade. She had learned the hard way: You spend too much time in hiding, and it's harder to come back. As she moved through her seventies, this fact took on a darker turn: Spend too much time away, and people may assume you're dead. Better to get your name out there, insist on your relevance in an industry that glorifies wunderkinds, and talk up your new project to the rich fucks who might be willing to give you their money. "They were constantly plugged into the New York scene," Odell says. "They had so much hunger to be alive and in the world and participating."[96]

Suddenly she was showing up at Broadway plays and benefits,[97] previews[98] and premieres[99] and after parties,[100] even hosting—Elaine, of all people, *hosting!*—screenings of films.[101] And so much for the firm "she hasn't done an interview since 1967" line. Not only was she answering the Proust Questionnaire with cheeky aplomb ("*On what occasion do you lie?* When answering questionnaires")[102] and being profiled alongside Mike in the pages of *Vanity Fair,*[103] but there she was, sitting on panels[104] and Q&A sessions[105] and traveling to festivals across the country to speak about her films.[106] Search her name on Getty Images and you'll find image after image of her beaming comfortably in front of a step-and-repeat, looking impossibly chic, hair blown out in a long, shaggy chocolate bob, wearing some vintage dress she had for decades and pulling it off with surprising grace. But look closer, zoom in a little, and you're bound to discover that something is off. Which, of course, is how you know it's Elaine, and not just some very good impersonator. Crumbs or stains all down the front of her blouse; a ragged old purse with a mess of papers spouting out of the top clutched tightly to her chest; lipstick that extends past the confines of her mouth and drugstore eyeglasses with the price tags still on—"That's how I know they're mine"[107]—dangling on a chain around her neck, sometimes overlapping, a second pair tossed on with absent-minded forgetfulness of the first.

The woman who had spent so much of her life trying to disappear was now fighting for visibility. Perhaps the ordeal with *Bye Bye Blues* made her realize that she had used up the currency that *The Birdcage* and *Primary Colors* had afforded her, and now her worth in a town where she hadn't made a film in years was tied directly to her participation in its bullshit extracurriculars. Or maybe she looked around at her peers playing the game—the ones whose work she had made better, and to whom she was now toasting at lifetime achievement award ceremony after lifetime achievement award ceremony—and realized that legacy is partly self-made. She had hoped to achieve immortality with her work, but what she had not accounted for all those years ago was that she'd have to be partly responsible for keeping her work in conversation. Things can't become immortal if they're already buried.

Or it could be this: She was willing to do whatever it took to get money for *Bye Bye Blues*. Not for her sake, but for Donen's. And maybe the fact that it wasn't about her made it easier to grin and bear it if it might drag the film across the finish line. Donen had brought her joy and companionship at a time in her life when more relationships had ended than begun. Wasn't this the least she could do for him?

A CONSIDERATION: ALL of Elaine's work as a writer and director in the twenty-first century can be collectively referred to as acts of love. If what Caroline Aaron says is true, if Elaine truly thought "the only thing I have to offer is my own voice," then what if it didn't just apply to how she worked, but how she showed those closest to her that she cared about them, too? And not just in what she wrote, but how and for whom she wrote it. Maybe Elaine knew that there was no real point in writing if it wasn't in service of someone else. The evidence sprouts in her early films: her step-daughter's and mother's appearances in small roles in *A New Leaf*, Jeannie's casting in *The Heartbreak Kid*, the way there was always a part for her friends. Maybe it was because she sought the safety of those she knew and trusted, or maybe it was because she knew that it wasn't much fun if your friends weren't there, too. Or what about this: For so long, her work had been her first and greatest love. What if to be loved by Elaine was to be let inside the world she had created for herself, your inclusion in the work a genuine display of affection and approval from someone who could be unflinching in her judgment and guarded in real life, even around those who knew her well.

The work she rounded out the rest of the aughts with appears to suggest this. It wasn't just *Bye Bye Blues*, an act of love for Stanley. Almost every play she wrote after 1998 had a role for Jeannie in it, who rarely performed on the stage or screen otherwise. And you can see her looking at a string of third-rate material being offered to Marlo Thomas and thinking, *I can give her something better*. She had given up script doctoring. Too much of it had dulled her perspective and compassion—"A producer said, 'Why don't you see it from Hitler's point of view?' and I agreed"[108]—but she always made an exception for those closest to her and was there with thoughts whenever Mike called her.[109] There were younger filmmakers and comedians with whom she was becoming close, too. After *Everybody Loves Raymond* creator Phil Rosenthal introduced himself to her at a performance of *Relatively Speaking* in 2011, the two became fast friends. He would take her to lunch, get her to speak about her work at the Austin Film Festival,[110] and on one occasion, introduce her to self-serve frozen yogurt with slapstick results. "I'm putting my toppings on and I look back, and Elaine is walking toward me with her cup. But there's a stream of yogurt coming from her cup back up into the machine about three feet away. Three feet of yogurt is flowing from the machine to Elaine, who forgot to shut the machine," he said.[111] Some of them, she could see, were in prickly positions not too dissimilar to the battles she had once fought. She became a generous advisor to Kenneth Lonergan throughout his six-year-long battle against Fox Searchlight while making *Margaret*. As the edit process on the three-hour-long film wore on, Lonergan would show her different cuts and scenes for feedback. "She doesn't miss anything," he says. "She said right away, having seen it once, 'Only a teenager could possibly think they would have that much effect on the world,' which is something that hadn't occurred to me in those terms. She just had this very acute sense of what's important and what's not, and what's really happening in a scene."[112] And it wasn't just creative advice; she passed along the suggestion Cassavetes had given her back when she was trying to hold the studio back from *Mikey and Nicky*, the strategy she wished, years later, she had tried: "Get together a screening with the most famous people you can think of, and invite them all, and invite the producers. And after that screening the producers will be scared of you." She knew how things worked: Studio heads loved you until they signed the check. Then you were their enemy, and everything you did with their money was a threat.[113]

Elaine knew better than to sit around and wait for *Bye Bye Blues* to happen. Getting a movie off the ground can take years; who had time for that anymore? Not her. She would round out the rest of the decade with more immediate works in the theater, love letters to those closest to her in the form of one-acts, with mixed results.

In the spring of 2005, she returned to Broadway with *After the Night and the Music,* an evening consisting of three one-acts intended to be about life and love "in the new millennium." But as was true with *Taller Than a Dwarf,* Elaine's idea of the new millennium seemed to be about thirty years behind everyone else's. The evening saw winning moments from its stars, notably Jeannie and J. Smith-Cameron, but they came few and far between. None of the abbreviated plays—from *Dancing in the Dark,* a scene in which an overweight former chorus boy asks a socially anxious lesbian to dance with him, to *Giving Up Smoking,* a series of monologues by lonely people waiting by their phones (which are, inexplicably, landlines), all of which seem to orbit around Jeannie's centerpiece, to *Chelsea Nights, or Take My Wife,* a *Bob & Carol & Ted & Alice* riff—felt even close to current.

They were limp and lifeless, "terminally torpid," as the *Times's* Ben Brantley put it. From what sitcom did she swipe the banal setup of a schlub who can't get girls and a lesbian who can only lead? What was original about a depressed divorcée waiting by the phone all night for a man to call? Answering machines? A swingers party? *In 2005!?* You had to hope that these were just old, unused plays Elaine had written in the seventies, and not that the sharp knife she had always used to cut into tales of neuroticism and human selfishness was now dull. "Elaine did not want to put a time frame on the play in the program, like, 'This takes place in 1970' or whatever. I think she left that open," recalls choreographer Randy Skinner, who worked on staging *Dancing in the Dark.* "I think it was just one of those things where people had a hard time buying into the basic premise because they were so far removed from that part of life."[114] Perhaps the night could have been saved if the production had followed through, giving the audience more context than they assumed they needed and staging the shows in the same manner as revivals of similarly dated Neil Simon plays. But the combination of the careless, uninspired material and the overworked production did not bode well for the evening. It would weather predictably tepid reviews, though most would cut it some slack. The cast was good and deserving and capable of performing better material—which *was* there, in fits and spurts.[115] You could see moments of goodness, small gems, be it a clever punch line or lovely moment of pathos,[116] that could be found buried underneath the schlock. If it was a disappointment, it was only because everyone knew Elaine was capable of so much more. It was still there. She just had to spend more time looking for it.

THE DAYS OF rewarding roles for Marlo Thomas, who was now sixty-nine, were largely in the past. The actress formerly known as That Girl was not immune to Hollywood's babe, mother, or district attorney trope. In recent years she had, aside from a few regional theater productions, shifted her priorities away from acting and onto her work with St. Jude's Children's Hospital and advocacy for women's issues.

Elaine, who had written for her many times over their past thirty-some years of friendship, couldn't resist giving her something creative to do. "She called me and said, 'I've written a play I'd like you to read, and I think you'll just be great for it,'" Thomas recalled.[117] The play in question was *George Is Dead*, a story about Doreen, an aging, spoiled, and newly widowed socialite who clambers into the home of her childhood nanny's daughter, Carla, and her husband, Michael, in the middle of the night, seeking comfort and care in a moment of crisis. It was enough for Thomas to do a double take. A woman who says things like "I don't have the depth to feel this bad"? That wasn't how her best friend saw her—as a dumb and ditzy woman-child narcissist—was it?[118] But she would soon see that the play was more than just a one-note comedy. It was a brutal—but funny—examination of the growing wealth divide, the social and cultural differences between the have-too-muches and the have-nots, an escalation of the kinds of arguments she and Thomas had all the time. See one particular dinner tiff:

Marlo: I wasn't bullied in high school.

Elaine, delighting in the easy setup handed to her: Of course you weren't. You grew up in the back seat of a limousine.

Marlo, not realizing she had taken the bait: I am so sick and tired of you saying I don't have any problems just because my father had money. He didn't have money when I was born! He *made* his money![119]

Doreen wasn't just a dumb sheltered woman who was easy to make fun of; she was a complicated person, one who sounded uncannily familiar in some respects. "On a closer look, she's very frightened and manipulative," Thomas said. "She finds ways to get other people to take care of her, she's very clever. Her guilelessness is one of the things that make her interesting. Her manipulation isn't hidden. She says exactly what she thinks and exactly what she wants, and that's what makes her a child-woman. She's as honest and forthright and manipulative as a child in getting what she wants."[120] Frankenstein had his monster; Elaine had her Doreen, the heightened reflection of her—and Thomas's—biggest flaws. There it was: specificity. The element that set good comedy apart from inferior attempts, the element that had made all of Elaine's best works sing, the detail that she had lost sight of in her recent string of material.

George Is Dead would be given another gift that her other recent outings had lacked: a lengthy rehearsal period. Over four years, Elaine relentlessly honed the play as she tried it out in various theaters across the country. It premiered in one-act form at San Francisco's Magic Theatre, sharing a bill with two other one-acts under the umbrella *Moving Right Along,* neither of which matched its spark. Opener *Killing Trotsky,* by Czech playwright Jan Mirochek and directed by Elaine, was dated and listless. And *On the Way,* written by Elaine and directed by Jeannie, was little more than unnecessary, meandering backstory for *George Is Dead* in which the audience meets the titular George. But *George Is Dead,* with "funny and pointed moments" though "still . . . underdeveloped," had potential.[121]

Two years later, she cut the dead weight, staging the play alone at David Saint's George Street Playhouse in New Brunswick as *Roger*

Is Dead. ("Listen, I can see the reviews now," Saint said as he pleaded for a temporary retitling.)[122] Expanding it to ninety minutes, she directed it with a certain sense of looseness. Discovery, not rigid refinement, was the goal. "She wouldn't map out every moment ahead of time, but she would put a lot of possibilities," Saint says, some of which she didn't know why she wanted until the moment later arrived.[123] Opening the play up would help her find its spine: The rich will always have it easy, at the expense of the middle class, who help to make this so, and the roles we are born into will rarely change over time. But the rest was still muddy. A scene woven in from *On the Way* was a distraction, and by the end, the play lost its momentum.[124] Still, though, an improvement. A year later, in Phoenix, she directed it again, still trying to make it work at ninety minutes, a length at which it became necessary to either trim or flesh out even more, the former being the better option. "Until Doreen's doozy of arrival, *George Is Dead* treads comic water—George finds common political ground with the Dominican driver taking him to the airport, and another scene establishes the relationship between Carla and Michael."[125] For *George Is Dead* to work, George had to actually be dead.

And he was, finally, in 2011, when *George Is Dead*, back in one-act form, premiered on Broadway, under the bill of *Relatively Speaking* with one-acts by Ethan Coen and Woody Allen, directed by John Turturro. *There* was the "sharp satirical touch"[126] of Elaine May that had been feared lost. Finally, redemption in the form of "a delicious study in narcissism"[127] standing out in an otherwise reasonably fine evening. *George Is Dead* was "an angry little class tragedy dressed with mordant laughs"[128] that "puts our passion for ignorance on parade."[129] It wasn't perfect; Elaine makes some uncharacteristically soft choices at the end. Perhaps at this point in her life it was hard to end a play about death on a cruel note. Perhaps she wanted to linger in the sentimental, the maybe-sort-of-happy ending she wasn't sure she'd get in reality. But it was the most fully developed work she had done in years.

ON THE *Bye Bye Blues* front, crickets. Years' worth of them. Progress along the way—sometime around 2005 or 2006, it seemed within reach enough that Randy Skinner was brought in to choreograph and sit in on ensemble auditions[130]—was delayed by Donen's health, and the project wouldn't be resuscitated until years later.[131] Nothing was moving, and none of their famous friends—not even Steven Spielberg—could get it off the ground.[132] The idea that two greats who still felt they had much more to offer were instead supposed to settle into their old-age home, never to be heard from again, was demeaning and depressing, something she had no problem bitching about with Mike, sometimes even publicly.

A conversation between the two at Lincoln Center in 2006 took on the life of an airing of grievances as they complained about money's infiltration of Hollywood and the increased insistence on making "marketable" movies, the steady erosion of art and integrity in the overwhelming modern world. "Look how quickly we all get used to eating shit," Elaine declared. "Really, about seven years ago, if somebody had answered the phone saying, 'We really value your call. Please hold for the next hour and twenty-five minutes,' we'd have hung up. We get used to it very fast. We get used to skim milk very fast. Whole milk tastes like cream. We adapt very quickly to being treated very badly."[133] Their older ages hung heavily in the air, coloring their every exchange even when they weren't addressing it directly, which they did a lot of. Together, they wondered what the future looked like, how they were going to fight for their art when they were no longer young people who could make a movie for a minuscule $15,000.[134] Still, Elaine argued, they had to think smaller, smarter. If the only movies that made $100 million now were movies for sixteen-year-old boys and their dates, then they had to accept the fact that they wouldn't be making box office hits anymore, had to get used to not making as much money, even though that was what everyone wanted. Why not instead band together "all artists who are pissed about this" to buy their own movie theaters to show their films themselves, she proposed.[135]

Mike, with all his acclaim and awards and box office successes, didn't have as much to complain about as she did. Sure, he, too, was going through a slump, but history had shown that he'd find a way out, and if they had been keeping score, he was winning. She couldn't help but point out the obvious: "You also are somebody who, whatever movie you make, is going to find a way for it to be seen and shown. Because you're very famous and very good. But people who are beginning and people who don't have the clout that you have, they have no place to show their movie. And probably only one out of thirty of them is that good, but one out of thirty is not bad. There's stuff you do, all of us do, that we really feel hopeless about."[136]

For someone so protective of her scripts, she trusted Stanley to handle the majority of the decision-making on *Bye Bye Blues*. In all the time he spent trying to produce her movie, Odell spoke with Elaine only two or three times. She spent most of her time in another room of the apartment editing Schlossberg's fourteen-hour-long documentary series, *Witnesses to the 20th Century*. It was never released. When she was around, she was elusive and shy. "She was just so slippery and it felt like she was protecting a lot," he says. "Wickedly smart, wickedly funny, wickedly clever. But you could never get to the center of her."[137]

In a way, it seemed like they *wanted* the film to drag on in perpetuity, simply because it was something that kept them busy, a project to plug in conversations to make themselves feel like they were still relevant. There was a process to always be engaged in, calls to make to agents and producers and studio heads, budgets to assemble and auditions to run. If it remained in preproduction forever, then they wouldn't have to face the vast unknown of retirement. "When you're a workaholic and everything's around your work, what do you do when the work dries up?" Odell says.[138] Ten years after Odell had first been brought on board the picture— five years after he departed—Elaine and Stanley, with Mike now serving as a producer, held a private reading for investors. It felt real this time. They had real actors: Christopher Walken and Ron Rifkin, Caroline Aaron and Charles Grodin and Jeannie—the Elaine May Players. It seemed promising, like they were getting close to the happy ending before the credits roll. But real life is not a movie. Real life doesn't always get the happy ending, with outstanding balances sorted and all loose ends tied neatly in bows.

FADE IN:

INT. MIKE NICHOLS'S UPPER EAST SIDE APARTMENT—
2012—DAY

MIKE NICHOLS and **ELAINE MAY** sit down after lunch.
A REPORTER sits across the large coffee table from
them.

An improvisation. Their last, in public, at least.
Though neither of them is aware of it yet. Or,
rather, they're aware of the *possibility* of it—now
in their eighties, they are well acquainted with
the ways in which age comes for us all, sooner or
later—but they don't dwell on it. They're still
too busy thinking about next times to consider
last times.

CLOSE ON Mike, reminiscing about one of their
great performances of yore. He turns toward
Elaine.

                    MIKE
   Why didn't we stick with the act? It was your
   fault. You wanted to stop. We should still be
                 doing this.

Elaine cannot fight the first rule of improv, the
one she came up with.

                   ELAINE
            We can do it again.

                    MIKE
         It would be different.

                   ELAINE
      We'd have to drop "Teenagers."

The suggestion of such a thing is too much for
their lone audience member—

                  REPORTER
               No, don't!

                    MIKE
    No, certainly not. It would be funnier.

CUT TO some short span of time later. The
memories—good and bad—have been flowing, the pull
of nostalgia is impossible to resist.

> **MIKE**
> *(wistfully)*
> We were fools to give it up.

> **ELAINE**
> *(nods in agreement)*
> We were.

Mike looks at his oldest, dearest friend, the girl who had laughed viciously at him from the front row of *Miss Julie* sixty years ago.

CLOSE ON: Elaine, clutching the reporter's list of questions with a death grip, trembling slightly. Nervous, even after all this time.

PULL BACK TO: Mike leans in, as if he's about to share a secret revelation:

> **MIKE**
> Very slowly, life gets better and you learn that
> there is another way to respond to people.
> You've changed more than anybody I've known
> in my entire life.
> *(beat)*
> You changed from a dangerous person to someone who
> is only benign.

It's true. Heavy hangs the armor of the angry girl. It's nice to let it rest sometimes.

> **ELAINE**
> What a vicious thing to say!

Well, maybe not today.

> **MIKE**
> But it's true! If you can't say anything nice, you
> don't say anything. You never ever attack people
> to their face, or behind their back. You're the
> most discreet person about other people that I
> have ever met in my life. I haven't heard you be
> unkind for fifty years. You have done a complete
> 180-degree turn—don't you know that?

> **ELAINE**
> That's such a horrible thing of you to say.

> **MIKE**
> I'm really sorry—

                         ELAINE
        I feel exactly the same way about you, too.

                          MIKE
                          Bitch!

They break. The sound of their laughter fills the
room. Just like it had so many times before.[139]

A year later, Mike would be dead, and Elaine would
have to figure out, for the second time in her
life, how to be a person without him.

FADE OUT.

CHAPTER 13

What Is Important in Life and Art?

2015–2023

"Luck is very strange," Elaine told Mike before he died. "I'm lucky in that I met the guy who said, Go to the University of Chicago, and I hitchhiked there. Then I met Paul Sills, and then I met you. My few pieces of luck." The way she saw it, your life is not predetermined. Things don't shake out the way they do "for a reason." Life isn't fate; it is just a series of coincidences strung together, some more fortunate than others, that don't care if you are smart or talented or beautiful. Those got you only so far. Luck got you the rest of the way. "One piece of luck spikes to another piece of luck, spikes to another piece of luck."[1]

PAUL SILLS, BERNARD Sahlins, John Calley, Gore Vidal, Peter Falk, Ted Flicker: So many of her friends, gone in the past few years. Now Mike, too. How could it have been her left at the end? How could she survive being the survivor?

Work would be the answer, just like it always was. The work couldn't leave you, couldn't make plans for lunch in a week or two only to drop dead that very night, and before you even got a chance to say goodbye. The work couldn't break your heart, not if you didn't let it. The work had been a good and loving companion when she had needed it most, and it would be there for her again. But maybe this time it wouldn't be a way to bury the grief. Maybe this time, after years spent using work to show her love for those closest to her, it would be a way to process it instead.

Elaine would sit in the director's chair once again, spending the better part of 2015 helming an hour-long documentary on her dearest friend for a 2016 episode of PBS's *American Masters*.[2] And for all those months, it was like Mike hadn't left—because she wouldn't let him. Using a sit-down interview Mike had done with Julian Schlossberg a few years prior as her base, Elaine worked through her grief as she crafted the story of her friend's life in just fifty-four minutes. "I think it was great for her to be able to, in a way, have some sort of closure," Schlossberg says. "A catharsis. I think it was great to go back to go over what happened and what she felt and what she was able to say."[3]

What she wanted to say seemed curiously conventional at first. The first two acts of "Mike Nichols" on *American Masters* follow traditional documentary form: archival stock footage and old stills, friends and collaborators like Meryl Streep and Robin Williams as talking heads, a few jokes thrown in for comic relief (it takes guts to open on Hitler), but nothing out of the ordinary. That is, until you begin to realize that you're seeing Mike more than anything else. There he is, talking to the camera, completely unadorned, the shot holding on him for extended stretches of time, ignoring the obvious choice to cut to another celebrity with an adoring story. "Wasn't he wonderful?" she seems to ask. "Why would you want to hear or see anyone but him?" The result, as *The New Yorker*'s Richard Brody called it, is nothing short of "lovingly obsessive."[4]

It's in the film's final arc where Elaine finally shows her hand: a four-minute-long interjection, nearly all unbroken, as Mike lets criticisms rip. People who "describe our work to us" who "often don't know what they're talking about"; critics who "think expressing an opinion is a creative act"; the "auteur theory" (and how creating "a pantheon of great directors" unfairly diminished his work and others')—they all get served lethal shots of disdain from Mr. Mike Nichols. The man who seemingly had it all, bitter that the one thing that mattered so much—the work—was often misunderstood or dismissed. An airing of grievances, with a chorus of voices joining in his defense, a peace brought forth by candidly speaking his piece. In a way, it's also hers. The views of the pair, parlayed through the microphone of Mike, just like the old days. Never emerging from behind the camera for an interview herself, Elaine appears only in archival footage, a ghostly presence even in narration until the very end. We close not on him, but on her, praising him at his 2003 Kennedy Center Honors ceremony before continuing in the sole voice-over:

> Mike Nichols was so dazzling, so successful that his work was oddly underrated. His work, his best work, is about who we were at the end of the twentieth century and who we were about to become. *The Graduate, Carnal Knowledge, Silkwood, Working Girl*—put them in a time capsule, and you'll see, to your amazement, that every three years, American culture undergoes a complete change. Mike's movies and plays reflect that change, but they're not about it. They're about us.

A team, until the end, and then some.

NO SOONER HAD *American Masters* aired than news broke that she had been cast opposite Woody Allen in his highly publicized new streaming series for Amazon.[5] Two months later, she was next to him on set, running around Manhattan in sixties period clothing. It had been sixteen years since Elaine had last acted on camera. Now here she was, expected to pick up where she had left off, all while the prying eyes of the paparazzi watched.

Did she know then what would become apparent when the series aired later that summer? That *Crisis in Six Scenes*—a show following well-to-do couple Sidney and Kay (Woody Allen and Elaine) whose quiet lives in late-sixties suburban New York get shaken up by a young, on-the-run radical (Miley Cyrus) who takes shelter with them—was, in the most simple and uncomplicated words, a mess? That the writing was dismayingly clunky and remedial, serving a plot that was a sloppy mishmash of previous (better) work, with an arc that was less a narrative series debuting in the golden age of streamers than a two-hour-and-eighteen-minute movie with bathroom breaks? Or that its aggressively white portrayal of the late-sixties progressive movement that never really seemed to *say* anything about it rang stale and toothless in the months leading up to the 2016 election? Did she know, and do it anyway, simply because she was his friend? Did she think she could save it, the way she had saved so many other films before? If we judge by the genuine fun Elaine seems to be having on camera, the choices she makes to breathe life into her relatively flat character, and the kick she appears to get out of acting opposite twenty-four-year-old Cyrus, none of its myriad weaknesses seem to have mattered all that much to her. She was there for a good time, and a good time was apparently had.

Crisis in Six Scenes would be pilloried upon its release in September of 2016. The #MeToo movement was still a year away, but public opinion of Allen was beginning to turn. The writer and director had managed to emerge relatively unscathed from a period of controversy surrounding his relationship with Soon-Yi Previn, his alleged sexual abuse of then adopted daughter Dylan Farrow, and his custody battle with ex-wife Mia Farrow in the early 1990s. But in 2013, Dylan Farrow went on the record in an interview with *Vanity Fair* about her alleged assault, and the scandal resurfaced. Allen was on defense again. This time, he wasn't winning.

Despite arguments to put aside Allen's controversial alleged behavior (which made *Crisis in Six Scenes'* "lighthearted jokes about the relative quality of adoptive daughters awkward, to say the least")[6] and separate the art from the artist, the art was not making a great case for itself. It was, by *Vanity Fair's* standards, "often cringe-inducing, a rickety charade that confirms all of Allen's fears about being in over his head and running on fumes,"[7] and in the eyes of *The New York Times*, "instantly forgettable."[8] Its choice of timing was questionable; to present "a mediocre show that suggests action to prevent social injustice is mostly a madcap folly"[9] as history was repeating itself only exacerbated its flaws. Elaine, at least, would walk away with praise for making the most of it. "If there is a hero in this story, it is Elaine May's Kay, who is the only figure in the entire series that is neither mannered nor precious," assessed *Variety*.[10] At this point, her mere presence was so welcome that she could have read a phone book on camera and received warm reviews.[11] It was nice to see Elaine on the screen again. Really, it was. Beggars can't be choosers—in spite of the show's low points, "as the work that has returned Elaine May to public view, it can only be welcomed, with rose petals and trumpets," the *Los Angeles*

Times argued[12]—but you couldn't help but beg for Elaine to be given better material than this.

ELAINE HAD TRIED to disappear into her work again. Just as suddenly as she had seemed to be everywhere, she was nowhere. Gone were the interviews and panels, gone were the parties. From 2016 to 2019, Elaine made only two photographed appearances.[13] She had settled into a more low-key routine, splitting time between the Upper West Side and the home she and Stanley had purchased in Westchester County, although it was rumored that the pair had broken up around 2016.[14] There were dinner dates with Jeannie and Carol Kane[15] in the neighborhood, and regular gatherings at Marlo's apartment across town, where she was still the same dinner party pariah she had always been, saying things like "I don't get all this about Lincoln. It's not like he wanted to free all the slaves right away. And all that death. Why didn't we just stop buying cotton?"[16] One step in the door and you'd hear her loudly arguing about democracy with Michael Moore, telling him "It's over, Michael. Just stop working so hard at it. It's finished."[17] She didn't watch many movies or keep up with TV. *Breaking Bad*, which she had never seen, seemed "like a great argument for health care" to her. "Oh, 'he killed people,'" she scoffed. "What did he do that was really so bad?"[18] She occasionally went to the theater, but she wasn't always capable of approaching it as simply a spectator, and not an architect of it herself. David Saint recalls taking her to a performance of *Hamilton* early in its lauded run at the Public Theater, where she seemed to be the only person who wasn't enamored with it. "She had problems, and I said, 'What? But he's just following Chernow,' and Elaine immediately said, 'Huh. Chernow? Have you read the . . .' and she mentioned five other biographies of Hamilton."[19] Her life had mellowed out. She was good at not being noticed. She liked it. But what she hadn't accounted for was that disappearing wouldn't be as easy an option this time. The world wasn't going to let her recede entirely from view again.

It's hard to pinpoint exactly when the Elaine May Renaissance started. Its roots could have been planted in 2006, when a Film at Lincoln Center retrospective sparked features praising her short directorial career and lamenting that its abrupt end marked a "great loss for filmgoers,"[20] one that had only widened as her films gradually went out of print. So, too, had she gone missing in a way, "overlooked in virtually every New Hollywood hagiography."[21]

Or maybe it was later than that, sometime around 2013, when President Obama honored Elaine with a National Medal of Arts. She took the stage, both proud and bashful as a military aide read her citation—"with groundbreaking wit and a keen understanding of how humor can illuminate our lives, Ms. May has evoked untold joy, challenged expectations, and elevated spirits across our nation"—letting a half chuckle and embarrassed eye roll slip midway through the effusive commendation.[22]

It could have been 2016, when the Writers Guild of America awarded her a lifetime achievement award, and she actually showed up to receive it, admitting she was surprised to find it was a far larger affair than the small, intimate restaurant party she had assumed it to be. She began her acceptance speech with a warning—"I'm going to let you down in some way"—only to elicit screams of laughter as she put down antisocial writers, inane red-carpet questions, and Republicans in the first two minutes alone. "Writers really work alone," she said in a rare moment of seriousness. "They suffer. I mean, very few loved ones loan writers to their work without, you know, a *little* penalty. And writers don't have a crew. They don't have an AD. They don't have a script. They're just on their own."[23]

It just kept going. Over the next few years, Elaine's career as a filmmaker was rediscovered, reevaluated, and re-appreciated as it was lauded from bespoke apparel brands printing her name on T-shirts to international film festival retrospectives and Criterion Collection remasters. Imagine how many millennials googled her name for the first time when, in 2011, Alec Baldwin's declaration that Tina Fey was "going to be the next Elaine May" after *30 Rock* made the rounds.[24] An appearance on Phil Rosenthal's unscripted Netflix food show, *Somebody Feed Phil,* won her even more fans, ones who got to know of the extent of her career only after they had been charmed by the kooky old woman with food in her hair. "I don't understand," she told him. "I've had a pretty good career.

And the thing that people stop me for is eating ice cream with you."[25] There were always Elaine May stalwarts to be found if you looked hard enough, filmmakers like Martin Scorsese and Quentin Tarantino and legacy critics like Jonathan Rosenbaum, Richard Brody, Janet Maslin, and Carrie Rickey who had long been the few loud voices reminding the rest of us that we had gotten things wrong. But something was different this time. This time, some of the loudest voices belonged to some who had barely even been old enough to understand the *Ishtar* implosion in its time. Up-and-coming writer-directors like Greta Gerwig, Lena Dunham, Natasha Lyonne, and Leslye Headland were singing her praises and citing her influence left and right, spreading the gospel to a younger generation.

By 2018, the reclamation of Elaine May had arrived in full force. History was course-correcting in real time to give Elaine her flowers while she was still around to get them. Whether she wanted to accept them, though, was another story. The spotlight, even as it was diffused across social media—one place where, of course, Elaine had no presence, though appreciation for her there was a constant—was impossible to sidestep, and was only about to get even brighter.

ELAINE WANTED A garbage disposal.

At least, that's the way the story of just how Elaine was lured back onto a Broadway stage for a revival of Kenneth Lonergan's 2000 memory play *The Waverly Gallery* starts. When Lonergan had asked her years before, she had passed on the central role of the gregarious Greenwich Village gallery owner—based on Lonergan's own grandmother who was—gradually slipping into dementia, unsure of what she could bring to the role that would differentiate her performance from Eileen Heckart's in the original run.[26] When the possibility of a revival came up in 2017, Lonergan says, "the very first meeting we all had, we all agreed that Elaine would be our first choice, if it could work out."[27] It was a challenging part, equal parts humorous and harrowing, and it needed an actress who had not only the emotional depth to convincingly portray all aspects of a woman unraveling, but the genius to do so while nailing a technically demanding script. What other actor Elaine's age still possessed the fearlessness to leap into such thrillingly dangerous waters and the wit to soften the landing? But it had been more than fifty years since she had last acted on Broadway, twenty since she had appeared in *Power Plays*. She was nervous. "She's very tough and there's really not a lot she can't handle," Lonergan says. "But she's also extremely delicate and sensitive and shy and she's not brash. She knows how smart she is and she knows how attractive she is and she knows how funny she is. But . . . she's got definitely a shy side that doesn't like to be in the center of the spotlight and is not interested in the glitzier side of show business. And she's been badly burned."[28] It would take more than a polite ask to get her to agree.

So, the garbage disposal. The way the story goes, Elaine ran into Scott Rudin, one of the show's producers—and, coincidentally, one of Elaine's neighbors—near the elevators in their building. "If you can get a garbage disposal installed in my apartment, I'll do the show," she said.[29]

"I don't know if he did or not, but that definitely happened," Lonergan says.[30] Rudin's real persuasive feat was making Elaine feel protected and taken care of well enough to return to the stage. Come August of 2018, rehearsals were underway, and Elaine found herself surrounded by an ace crop of accomplished actors ready and eager to play at her level. Joan Allen, who had started her career performing "A Little More Gauze" at fundraisers for the Steppenwolf Theatre in Chicago, would play her put-upon daughter.[31] Lucas Hedges, a budding talent who had just been nominated for an Oscar for his work in Lonergan's 2016 film *Manchester by the Sea,* would take on the role of Lonergan's stand-in as her grandson. Michael Cera—who, years earlier, had wanted her to voice a character in an animated TV show he was pitching[32]—would play a young artist at her gallery, and David Cromer—a veteran actor and Tony-winning stage director himself—would play her son-in-law. All had one thing in common: a feeling of being floored by their great good fortune to work with a titan they had so admired. To put it in Cera's words: "I desperately tried to claw my way into it, to work with Elaine. I would have, like, taken out the trash on this production."³³ The old warning about never meeting your heroes? Absolutely untrue.

As the rehearsal process progressed, they found that all their lofty expectations were being met. Working with her was "a re-education in the relentless and rigorous exploration of why and how every moment connects to every other moment, a re-education in absolute truthfulness, in utter faith in the principles of true ensemble work," said Cromer.³⁴ She wasn't only *that* good; she was even better than they could have possibly imagined. "I think she's always been a great actress," Lonergan says, "and I didn't realize quite how great until she was in *The Waverly Gallery*."³⁵ Watching her work with director Lila Neugebauer, he was taken with her relentlessly detail-oriented approach to a scene, even if her need to root her performance in concrete reality didn't make things easy. "We couldn't tell if she was being incredibly stubborn or just incredibly thorough, and it turned out it was both," Lonergan says.³⁶ Plays can easily fall into the trap of people sitting around talking; you need to insert movement to keep things visually interesting. But that's stage truth, Elaine would argue. Not the real truth. No, you don't ask Elaine to turn her head when an actor enters the room, or pick up a picture frame out of nowhere, or walk across the room in the middle of a conversation, unless there's a real logical reason for it. "Part of you is like, 'Well, you're an actor, figure it out. We don't need to have a big discussion about it. That's what has to happen, so find a way to do it,'" says Lonergan. "And sometimes she would, and if she wouldn't, she would just very politely, and persistently, but not in an obnoxious way . . . just come back to it over and over again until you finally realize that what she wanted was to have no faking at all at any moment."³⁷ Gladys Green is a hostage in her own mind, slowly floating away from reality as her dementia progresses from bad to worse. "She really brought sort of a frailty and a sensitivity to it," Lonergan said. "It was like watching someone who's already on the edge of a precipice falling over it."³⁸ But it was her *character* who needed to fall off the ledge, not her. Faced with the difficulty of being present onstage as an actor while playing a character who is becoming increasingly lost in space—and the maze of repetition-heavy dialogue, at times with the added challenge of directing it toward or interrupting people who weren't looking at her that came with it—Elaine needed all the physical truth she could find. One day, in the middle of rehearsals, she admitted: "This is as close to hell as I ever want to get."[39]

"As natural and as off the cuff as it seems, she really needs to understand, logically, what is going on in the scene," Allen explained. "And she is dogged about it. She will not let go until she understands, and she will ask questions and ponder it."[40] Elaine would argue that it was the fixation on details, this sinking of a foundation—even if it had once earned her, as she told the cast, the nickname of "Logic Nazi"[41]—that allowed her the ability to become spontaneous and natural in performance. Despite the sociopathic implications of the nickname, Elaine was unfailingly generous, never allowing her concerns to derail the rest of the rehearsal process, always a team player. "She does not get involved in your work and say, 'Oh well, if you do it like this instead,' which is very tricky territory between actors. She never meddled with us. She just played with us," Allen said.[42] She had only one fear: crying onstage. Faced with a breakdown scene in which the stage directions instructed her to cry, Elaine came clean. "I'm not an actor who can do that," she told Lonergan. "I've never been able to do that."[43] They rehearsed the scene. Elaine worried about her line "What's wrong with crying?" She was getting upset, sure, but the tears were still absent. She asked to cut the line. Lonergan hesitated. "If I cut it," he reasoned, "she probably won't cry. And if I don't cut it, I bet you she will, eventually."[44] They rehearsed it some more. Literal tears weren't entirely necessary, Neugebauer suggested.[45] Elaine worked harder. And then, one day, there they were. Soon crying was easy. "I don't know," she told Lonergan. "I don't have to do anything. I just look at Joan's face and she's so wonderful and she's so upset that it just makes me cry and it's not a problem at all."[46]

Fifty-seven years after she walked off the stage at the Golden Theatre, away from young fame and glowing acclaim, she had found herself back in the very same position. But it was different this time. When *The Waverly Gallery* officially opened on October 25, 2018, Elaine showed a part of her range she had long kept hidden, delivering a stupefying performance of a lifetime. Funny and sharp, warm and poignant, heartbreakingly, breathtakingly brutal—and so intensely honest that it was hard to believe at first it was all an illusion. Audiences would often find themselves, early in the play, concerned she was truly having trouble with her lines before realizing that she was just deeply in character. Fifty-seven years ago, a star had been—well, not so much as *born* on that stage as cemented—and now, at eighty-six, one was being entirely reborn.

Giving the show *The New York Times*'s Critic's Pick, Ben Brantley declared Elaine "just the star to nail the rhythms, the comedy and the pathos of a woman who's talking as fast as she can to keep her place in an increasingly unfamiliar world,"[47] while the *Daily News* called her performance "both one of the most beautiful things you'll ever see in a Broadway theater and one of the most profoundly sad."[48] The world, it seemed, had finally caught up to Miss May, although the overwhelming amount of near-unanimous adoration would have likely embarrassed her. No, don't show the glowing reviews to the woman who downplayed her own achievements in terse paragraph-long *Playbill* bio that concluded "She has done more but this is enough" and paired it with a lo-res selfie in lieu of a real headshot. (But even *that* garnered viral appreciation online.) Even the *New York Post* was falling over itself for her, declaring: "The hottest ticket for theater lovers is 86-year-old Elaine May."[49]

They weren't exaggerating. In a strictly limited run, the show was a hit, and Elaine was firing on all cylinders. For years, she had been siloed, examined as *just* a writer or *just* a director, *just* a comedian or *just* an actor. In her portrayal of Gladys, it was evident that she was never just one thing (people rarely ever are), but that each quadrant of her brain intersected, one informing the other over the show's 140 performances. And where so many stage actors lament the trap of getting worse the longer a run lasts, settling into the role so much that the performance becomes rote, Elaine only got *better*. "I saw that show maybe twenty times during the run, and I never saw her do it exactly the same. I never saw her be not absolutely sensational, but she just never had an off night," Lonergan says. "It's not because it was my play, it's not because she's Elaine May, but it was one of the greatest, if not the greatest stage performance I've ever seen."[50] The rest of the cast—which had become, in a way, a family centered around their beloved and revered matriarch—would sit together whenever they were not in a scene and watch her on the backstage monitors, marveling at the new choices she would try, the small ways she would vary her performance.[51] They were drawn to her through her collaborative nature, bonded to her by her unsentimental generosity, and held there by their respect. "She's very friendly, very sweet, very someone vulnerable who you want to help out," Lonergan says. "Everyone fell in love with her and wanted to help and support her."[52]

She had some trouble with her eyesight at the time, but was otherwise far from the frail woman she both portrayed and appeared to be in real life. "She was in such good shape that we'd have to ask her to move more slowly because she looked too strong for the character," Lonergan says.[53] Over the five months of rehearsals and performances, she missed only a single act of a single show near the end. And even then, she had to be talked into missing it, Allen remembered. "She had a really bad cold and she came to the theater anyway and she got through the first act. And our stage manager basically had to beg her to not go on for the second act. It took a good twenty, twenty-five minutes, but he said, 'Elaine, go take care of yourself.' The theater was very chilly backstage and she's a tiny little slip of a thing and she couldn't get warm. He was like, 'Go home. Please.'"[54] Here she was, eighty-six, performing an emotionally draining role eight times a week, and having the time of her life. To her, the schedule wasn't punishing; rather, it was something of a luxury. She loved the routine of it all, knowing where she had to be and when, loved knowing what she needed to do that night onstage, and loved knowing that she'd share a beer with Michael Cera over shoptalk before heading home.[55] Rinse and repeat. "She told me it was one of the easiest jobs she's ever had," Lonergan said.[56] Perhaps it's because doing the show allowed her to stay inside its world. Difficult as it was, it was all pretend. Its tragedy was not hers. When it was over, she had to go back to the real world, back to a life where people wanted things from her and the phone was ringing off the hook, back to a world full of illness and death and all the meaningless tasks to get done in the face of it all. "I'm overwhelmed completely," she told Lonergan when the show ended the following January.[57] Just a month later, Stanley Donen died, a loss that "really, really rocked her."[58] The pair had been together for nearly twenty years; it was her longest public relationship. She was devastated.[59]

As the spring stretched on, Elaine's performance lived, so talked about that it was as if *The Waverly Gallery* had never closed. Its widespread appreciation galvanized those who had long worried she was in the process of disappearing to deliver her the recognition they thought was far overdue. There were appreciations in *Vogue* and *Vulture*; a full-page ad in *The New York Times* ran an excerpt of a piece Lonergan had written for *Variety* in praise of her performance. Elaine may not have given a shit about awards—and she skipped every major ceremony that season despite sweeping her category—but in the eyes of the people who worked with and loved her, one award in particular mattered a great deal. They were going to get her the Tony. It wasn't just that her performance alone was the standout of the season; it was that, after sixty years in show business, it seemed like a criminal oversight that she didn't already have one. It was the least they could do. Truth be told, not even that seemed enough. "I think they should have given her a somewhat larger Tony," Mary-Louise Parker says.[60]

THEY PRACTICALLY HAD to drag her to Radio City Music Hall that June. "She didn't even want to go to the Tonys. She had to be talked into going to the Tonys," Renée Taylor says.[61] But this was one night where all her lack of interest in publicity or fame or accolades—feigned or not—wouldn't stand. She gave in, persuaded that she would be representing the play and the rest of the cast, and agreed to go if Julian Schlossberg would take her.[62]

It was a sort of storybook happy ending to a triumphant theatrical homecoming, the kind of happy ending Elaine would never write herself. In no Elaine May comedy would Samuel L. Jackson and LaTanya Richardson Jackson open the envelope and read her name—just as predicted—as the winner for Best Actress in a Play, the first major acting award she'd ever win. There certainly wouldn't have been a standing ovation from the audience. And she never would have perfectly executed a speech without stumbling or blowing the punch line.

Elaine always insisted that the difference between romance and comedy was that comedy was truest to life, but sometimes life isn't a comedy. It happened, all of it, in the most idyllic fashion possible. Elaine, wearing a simple long-sleeved black gown she'd years ago made her gala uniform, flung her chain of drugstore eyeglasses behind her neck as she accepted her trophy. "I've never won a nomination for acting before. I want to tell you how I did it," she said, then proceeded to acknowledge the brilliance of everyone else involved with the production, simultaneously praise and goad her young costar Lucas Hedges, and spoil the play's ending, all while avoiding any note of sentimentality. "My death was described on-stage by Lucas Hedges so brilliantly," she said. "He described it so heartbreakingly, he was so touching, that watching from the wings, I thought, 'I'm gonna win this guy's Tony.'" The night may not have been a comedy, but she wasn't going to make it any more romantic than it needed to be. Elaine doesn't do sentimental, and she certainly wasn't going to start at this point.

Elaine might have been talked into going to the awards that evening, but she'd be damned if she was going to do anything more than the bare minimum once she got there. Skipping the usual post-win pressroom appearance, she was back in her seat just moments later. The camera catching her during one of the night's comedic bits, likely hoping she'd be mid-laugh, instead found her looking thoroughly unimpressed, ready to go home. It was peak Elaine, as ever on her own terms, norms be damned. There would be no pressroom stop that night, no insights shared with eager reporters wanting to know more about her stunning feat or her thoughts on the current state of theater or how it felt to finally have her legacy recognized after all these years.

ELAINE WAS PRIMED for a gratifying victory lap. So what was she still hiding from? Why the hesitation toward correcting all those rumors and mistruths, toward turning the punch line around? The press wasn't out to get her anymore; the studio heads now running things were, if not fans, forced into admiration by virtue of her stature; more and more people were cheering her on adoringly. Why did she burrow down even more, spurning those who sought to honor her? It wasn't the much-repeated line that she didn't care about success. "Nobody doesn't like being a hit. Everybody does. And anyone says they don't either has quit or is lying, or they're lying to themselves," says Lonergan. "So I'm sure she loved being a big success as she did."[63] But maybe it was that she knew what everyone else knew but wouldn't say out loud: That it was all bullshit. The awards and accolades—what good did they do her now that she was in her late eighties? They made other people feel better about how they had treated her, but they didn't really change anything for her. "I think when she got beaten up enough, she was like 'I don't want to do it,'" Lonergan offers.[64] She hadn't forgotten the discomforting glare of the press. She had been stung, badly, not that she would stand to see herself as a victim. "She doesn't tell bitter stories about anything. I've never heard her really complain about anything career-related," says Lonergan.[65] But all the awards in the world couldn't greenlight a new project or make up for all the ones that had fallen by the wayside over all the years when she wasn't so beloved. "There's a side to show business that is genuinely unpleasant, and phony, and pretentious and ugly. It's always been there. A lot of people have trouble reconciling that with the kind of work they want to do that they really love and think is valuable," says Lonergan. "Everyone likes to be complimented and to make a good impression and to do good work and have people say they like it. And it's a communicative art, otherwise, you require an audience. A play requires an audience. A book requires a reader. But it gets into an area where there are things that are hard to take about it. And also, yet, in order to keep working, you have to."[66] Elaine had made it this far without taking it. Why start now?

In January 2020, shortly before the world came to a grinding halt, Elaine won a lifetime achievement award from the Los Angeles Film Critics Association. Naturally, she skipped the ceremony. Greta Gerwig accepted on her behalf. "Thank you for my lifetime achievement award," Gerwig, by way of Elaine, said. "I look forward to many more."[67]

NOT EVEN COVID-19 could stop Elaine. It wasn't easy that first winter, alone and at risk in her apartment overlooking a desolate Central Park. The empty streets were foreign, the sound of sirens inescapable, the groceries a threat in need of Lysol. The days before pod formations and readily available COVID tests that would allow her to feel safe enough to have dinner on Marlo's terrace were isolating.[68] Outside of Jeannie, who lived with her, and her inner circle, she fell out of contact with many of her friends for the year. Even in normal times, "she's hard to reach," Lonergan says.[69] She wasn't a fan of talking on the phone,[70] she didn't like email ("I polish my emails. It's very hard to be a writer and just dash it off," she once said),[71] and absolutely forget about Zoom. There wasn't anything funny about it. That was the thing. There wasn't any way to quip her way out of it. Not at first, at least. But then, at last, a reprieve.

As the COVID spring turned into a summer of racial reckoning while the 2020 election loomed on the horizon, actors, writers, and directors were finding creative ways to feed their hunger for connection and process the collective trauma. Plays and readings were being produced over Zoom, digital videos were being filmed at home on iPhones, and films depicting the pandemic were already beginning to be produced. *The Same Storm* would be Peter Hedges's addition to the narrative, a series of *La Ronde*–inspired vignettes filmed entirely at home over cell phones, computers, and remote video software.

Although his son had starred with her in *The Waverly Gallery*, Hedges never met Elaine during the play's run. Sending her the script was a whim; he never actually dreamed that she would agree to play the part of Ruth, an elderly acerbic mother reconnecting with her estranged sex worker daughter in one scene and battling COVID in another. "I just thought, 'Well, it's one of those ideas you have to try for and then accept when it doesn't happen. At least we made our best effort,'" he says. The next thing he knew, he got a phone call. "This is Elaine May," the voice on the other end of the line said. "I just have some questions about my part."[72]

She was in. Over Zoom, Hedges toured her apartment full of books and art and antiques with the rest of the crew, Elaine leading the location scout as Jeannie trailed her carrying the laptop. "It was this really intimate process," Hedges says. "You've never met a person and you're seeing their home."[73] Together, she and Hedges worked through the unconventional filming process. The production would send her a computer with all the necessary settings preconfigured and place the assistant director on standby outside her apartment "in a full hazmat suit,"[74] in case of emergency, but for the most part, Elaine had to be her own crew. Not only would she have to perform, but she would have to do her own hair and makeup, costumes—pulling from a closet that appeared to hold every outfit she had ever owned[75]—lighting, and camera operation as she filmed her two scenes herself.

"It was fascinating because you could see how she was trying to understand how this was going to work. She was trying to apply traditional filming strategies to our process, which made perfect sense," Hedges says. "She said, 'How do you do a wide shot?' And I told her, 'Elaine, walk to the far corner of the room.' And she did. And I said, 'There's our wide shot.' And then she went, 'Oh,' and she started walking slowly straight toward the computer. It was a long pause as she walked, she got really close to the camera and the computer and said, 'And I suppose this would be my close-up.'"[76]

The first time she had met Elaine at Mike's apartment, Mary-Louise Parker remembers "being so starstruck and not being able to say anything. Because what do you say? 'You're the most brilliant human being alive'? 'You're every single thing I would ever want to be'? 'Nothing I could ever say will be big enough'? Or, selfishly, 'You're the person I'd most want to impress on earth, aside from Mike Nichols'?"[77] Years later, cast as Elaine's estranged daughter, she found herself face-to-face with her on Zoom, separated by a computer screen but nevertheless getting an up-close view of her intelligence and discipline as an actor, and how giving she was with her scene partner. "I really felt like we fell into that scene, and I didn't have to do anything except listen to her and look at her," Parker says. "That's the very best kind of actor. You're just not at all conscious of them manufacturing anything."[78]

Hedges ran the scene five times. Both actors were *on,* funny and warm, getting laughs from gags one moment and drawing tears the next. He knew he got it in the first or second take, but he wanted to keep going. He'd tell himself that it was out of an abundance of caution—the technology couldn't always be trusted—but truthfully, watching the two play off each other, at times improvising with ease, their chemistry palpable despite barely knowing each other, was too joyful an experience to cut short. And to think they hadn't even rehearsed the scene once.[79] "It looks and feels in some ways effortless to work with her, but what she's doing is not easy or simple at all," Parker says. When it was over, she thought, "Wow. That was one of the greatest experiences I've ever had. I wish I had eighty more scenes with her."[80]

Elaine was eighty-nine, at the mercy of a global pandemic and the limitations of modern technology, and she still had it. "I think it was just a few hours we worked that day, and I remember a sadness when it was over," Hedges says. "It's like one of those scenes that you were like, 'This could play in a loop in my coffin.'"[81] Parker concurs: "I'll say among the top three highlights of my life as an actor was getting to do that scene with her—and it was over Zoom."[82]

ON A FRIGID night in February 2022, Elaine won a PEN America Lifetime Achievement Award. Well, actually, it was the recently established PEN/Mike Nichols Writing for Performance Award; there was something twisted and deeply funny about Elaine, the actual writer of the pair, not only winning a writing award named for her old partner, but not even being its inaugural recipient. When PEN approached her with the honor in the fall of 2021, they came with a stipulation: Its recipient had to be living, and—crucially—had to show up in person to accept it. Elaine, to much surprise, said yes to all of the above with delight.

There was poignancy in the honor, something poetic about stepping onstage at New York's Town Hall once again, more than fifty years after she and Mike played their sold-out run of shows there, to be given a prize in his honor. But as the months leading up to the ceremony ticked by—and the date continued to shift with new COVID surges—the trepidation grew. January came. She was still game. The team pressed forward with plans. February arrived. Elaine was not only still in; she wanted to do a walk-through of the space. As she toured Town Hall one afternoon a few weeks before the ceremony, she made one funny quip after another, equal parts thrilled about an award show dedicated to writers, excited to be recognized for the work that had always been her core, and incredibly, palpably nervous about getting up onstage in front of everyone, according to a source close to the situation. "What do you do if someone talks too long? Do you shoot them?" she asked. Then, just a week before the ceremony, she was out. She blamed COVID—a reliable and understandable fear for someone at risk. Also an easy excuse.

The eleventh-hour fix would be so typical Elaine that it couldn't have *not* been premeditated. She'd direct and star in her own work again, this time as she accepted the award from the comfort of her apartment in a prerecorded bit she cleverly scripted and staged. Complete with people in the background walking through the frame and jokes about an extended twenty-seven-page-long original cut of her speech, it deftly blended commentary on our own lives on camera for the past two years with her life behind it for the past sixty. It took four hours to shoot. (Why start being judicious with takes now?) The final cut lasted just over two minutes.[83]

THE OSCARS WOULD be luckier, but not without some chaos of their own. For months leading up to the 12th Governors Awards, during which she'd receive an honorary lifetime achievement award, no one was certain whether she'd actually show up to accept it. She shunned participating in the accompanying short tribute film while providing a list of people approved to speak on her behalf. Elaine may profess not to care, but she seemed to enjoy pulling the strings on the puppets, controlling the narrative from behind the camera, where she was safe.

And oh, the back-and-forth. One minute she wasn't going to show; then, with the encouragement of Warren Beatty, she reluctantly agreed and flew to Los Angeles. Days before the ceremony, Beatty backed out—and so did she. Then whiplash, again: The day before the show, she was back in. Having counted her out, the Academy was left scrambling to find someone to introduce her.[84]

Then Bill Murray to the rescue, the only one finally able to convince her to go. That night, on Murray's arm, she showed up last and was the first to leave, not even staying long enough for a group photo with fellow winners Danny Glover, Samuel L. Jackson, and Liv Ullmann.[85] Taking the stage to accept her award, she appeared momentarily gripped by terror, staring out at her standing ovation with wide eyes. The once mean and intimidating girl looked so much older than when we had seen her before the pandemic—frailer, less fearless. She looked to Murray, who never left her side, for reassurance, then quipped: "They told me Zelensky would introduce me tonight. But thank god I got Bill instead."[86]

There she was. The Elaine May we knew and loved, steamrolling the evening and taking no prisoners. No one was safe, not even Beatty, whose bailing on her easily landed him under the bus: "Actually, Warren Beatty got me here. He said, 'Go there. I'll give you the award. I'll take you there. You won't be afraid,'" she continued. "And then he never called me again." She joked that a lifetime achievement award should come with the words *for now* engraved alongside it—"because it's really scary if you don't"—and jested with Murray, complimenting him on a speech he prepared in the car but declined to give. Anything to deflect the spotlight from herself when it was most blinding. "I don't know what else to say," she finished, "except enjoy your food. I'm not sure what it is."[87]

It was the highest accolade she had ever won, and her acceptance of it was a bit, all of it. Just like every other speech she'd given before. When Elaine says she doesn't like awards, she really is telling the truth. But maybe it's just a shorthand version of it. Maybe it's not that she's too good for them or that she knows they're insignificant in the grand scheme of things, symbolic of who has the most money for marketing more than who is the most talented. Maybe Elaine hates awards for the very reason that Warren Beatty tried to convince her to go: because she's scared.

There's another thing Elaine May knows how to do well, besides tell a good story: it's how to play a character, fictional or otherwise. There's something terrifying about being in the spotlight, about having all eyes on *you* that Elaine was never able to get comfortable with. To step onto a stage and display some modicum of vulnerability and truth, be the person and not the persona—as acceptance speeches often require—is a trust fall she's unwilling to take. Better to avoid it entirely. Easier that way. And hey, making it funny only adds to the mystique.[88] If we look back at the few accolades she's accepted and the numerous congratulations she's given others in public, they're all performances, every last one of them. She will never skew too personal or too sentimental, never truly reveal herself or her humanity. In an age where we know too much about too many people, Miss May insists on remaining unknowable, seen but never truly seen. She's both everywhere and nowhere at once, just as she likes it.

ELAINE TURNED NINETY years old on April 21, 2022. She hated birthdays almost as much as she hated awards shows. Most years she'd leave town entirely, disappearing without word of where she was going, just to avoid the adulation and attention. But Marlo Thomas wouldn't stand to see the day go uncelebrated. "Just keep talking about Christmas," she told the small group of friends who had gathered. Put the emphasis on the group, not the individual. They sang "Jingle Bells" as the cake came out.[89]

"WHAT IS IMPORTANT in life and art?"

Elaine read the question back to herself. "You know, when I was very young, I thought it didn't matter what happened to me when I died, so long as my work was immortal. As I age, I think, 'Well, perhaps if I had to trade dying right now and being immortal with just living on, I would choose living on.' I never thought I would say that. I feel it's so unethical and wrong."[90]

But Elaine will live on. Of course she will. Her cigar ashes are dusted over the past sixty years of history, and you can't sweep them away.

ACKNOWLEDGMENTS

Here is what Elaine said about writing: "Writers really work alone. They suffer. I mean, very few loved ones loan writers to their work without, you know, a *little* penalty. And writers don't have a crew, they don't have an AD, they don't have a script. They're just on their own."

Here is what I say: This book is the product of three years of time spent alone and a lot of suffering, yes. But a lot of friends and loved ones not only loaned me to this work, but participated in it, too. They volleyed ideas and theories, read early drafts, joined in sleuthing, answered too many anxious "I THINK I SAW HER!!!" texts, filled me with confidence whenever I felt woefully in over my head, and listened patiently whenever I rambled or vented—which was pretty much always—about the latest finding, shenanigan, or hypothesis. Caitlin Bower, Leslie Burnett, Chris and Dorrie Courogen—who deserve additional thanks for allowing me, as a fourteen-year-old, to call watching old episodes of *Saturday Night Live*, taping movies that aired on TCM in the middle of the night, or going to the library to borrow a CD of *Mike Nichols and Elaine May Examine Doctors* "homework"—Caitlin Courogen, Casey Courogen, Chris Frantz, Dylan Hundley, Phillip Iscove, Alyssa LaVacca, Jenny Lester, Lindsey Lewis, Anya Markowitz, Pablo Martin, Katie Philo, Emmy Potter, Caitlin Rose, Tyler Ruggeri, Candace Svoma, Elizabeth Thompson, Carlos Valladeras, Tina Weymouth, Carrie Wittmer, and Travis Woods: I'm so lucky. I'm sure there was some penalty here and there, but you were either so good at hiding it, or I was just so absorbed in Elaine's life, that I never saw it. We can talk about something else now.

This book started, in part, in the spring and summer of 2019 while I was reporting and writing two pieces on Elaine that would run that fall on *Bright Wall/Dark Room* and *Glamour*. Thank you to my editors on both, Chad Perman and Mattie Kahn, for the gift of time and word count. Without those little luxuries, I may never have grown so indignant that Elaine didn't have a proper biography—although I knew why—which then turned into "What if . . . no, I couldn't . . ." Thanks go to Warren Zanes for knowing I was ready before I even knew I was.

More, this writer, and this book, had an amazing crew. I owe them a debt of gratitude, starting with my incredible agent, Nicki Richesin, who emailed me in April 2020 to ask if I had ever thought about writing a book. All I could really say was, "Well, I have this one idea, but it feels too crazy and impossible." She told me to go for it, she stuck with me every anxious step of the way, and I owe this leap of faith to her. Thank you.

At St. Martin's Press, my brilliant editor, Michael Flamini, is owed more thanks than word count will allow (although that's one thing on the list). He believed in this story, gave me the gift of time, pushed me and reeled me back in equal measure. I'd probably still be rewriting this, Elaine with *Mikey and Nicky*–style, if not for him. Claire Cheek tirelessly kept this train on track and consistently reassured me that no question was too small; I hope I did not take too much advantage of that. Clear-eyed feedback from Elisa M. Rivlin, Nancy Inglis, and Michael Clark made this smarter. Danielle Christopher designed a perfect cover. And Dori Weintraub and Michelle Cashman made sure this book found its audience.

Thank you, also, to Marina Zenovich, who opened doors and inspired stakeouts; Sam Wasson, whose encouragement and wisdom made this biography better, and certainly made me feel a little less crazy writing it; and Mark Harris, whose *Mike Nichols* was indispensable in writing *Miss May*, and who so graciously answered my questions and pointed me in the right direction whenever I asked.

Thank you to every person who generously shared their time, memories, theories, and laughs about a woman we both adored and, at times, had the privilege to be made a little insane by: Caroline Aaron, Jerry Adler, Ed Asner, Mary Bailey, Mary Birdsong, G. Mac Brown, Dyan Cannon, Cynthia Darlow, Barry Diller, Jules Fisher, Ted Griffin, Mike Haley, Michael Hausman, Deborah Hautzig, Peter

Hedges, Carl Hiaasen, Judd Hirsch, Sheldon Kahn, Carol Kane, Robert Klein, Swoosie Kurtz, Nathan Lane, Tony Lo Bianco, Kenneth Lonergan, Aasif Mandvi, Todd McCarthy, Gregory Mosher, James Naughton, Ben Odell, Mary-Louise Parker, Jeremy Pikser, Erik Lee Preminger, Cindy Kaplan Rooney, Phil Rosenthal, David Saint, Julian Schlossberg, Phillip Schopper, Cybill Shepherd, Randy Skinner, John N. Smith, Michelle Gorchow Sobel, Ira Spiegel, David Streit, Renée Taylor, Bo Welch, and Paul Williams. Additional thanks to those who shared their thoughts on Elaine with me in 2019 for *Glamour*: Joan Allen, Jeannie Berlin, Alexandra Heller-Nicholas, Natasha Lyonne, and Marlo Thomas. I would be remiss if I did not thank every single assistant, agent, and publicist who wrangled time for me. And in the case of a few particular interviews that came close, but ultimately did not happen: thank you for some wonderful stories to tell over a glass of wine at many a dinner.

This book would not have been possible without archive research, and those who work to maintain these materials—particularly in the height of the pandemic, when they went above and beyond to facilitate remote access—are owed heaps of thank-yous. The entire staff at the Academy of Motion Pictures Arts and Sciences' Margaret Herrick Library and the staff of the New York Public Library of the Performing Arts: thank you. I would live at either institution were it not for such strict hours and food and beverage policies. Thank you to Ayenin Luna-Benitez for taking a million pictures of the University of Chicago archives for me, the YIVO Institute for Jewish Research for the skeleton key, and Andrea Kalas for looking so intently for The May Cut.

And, finally, thank you Brenda DeLellis-Johnson, whose shaping of my writing sensibilities at a pivotal age can make the best argument in favor of a well-funded public school education.

NOTES

CHAPTER 1: I WILL TELL YOU ANYTHING, BUT I WARN YOU NOW, IT'S A LIE

1. "Jack Berlin in Four Mason Appearances," *Hollywood Filmograph* 9, no. 22 (June 1, 1929), 15.
2. Thomas Thompson, "Whatever Happened to Elaine May?" *Life,* July 28, 1967.
3. Janet Coleman, *The Compass: The Improvisational Theatre That Revolutionized American Comedy* (Chicago: University of Chicago Press, 1991), 38.
4. *An Evening with Mike Nichols and Elaine May* Playbill.
5. Helen Markel, "Mike Nichols and Elaine May," *Redbook,* February 1961.
6. *An Evening with Mike Nichols and Elaine May* Playbill.
7. Phil Rosenthal, author interview, October 3, 2022.
8. Elaine May, interview by Mike Nichols, Film Society of Lincoln Center, February 26, 2006.
9. Markel, "Mike Nichols and Elaine May."
10. Jeremy Pikser, author interview, June 23, 2021.
11. Robert Rice, "A Tilted Insight," *New Yorker,* April 15, 1961.
12. "Americans and the Holocaust: How Many Refugees Came to the United States from 1933–1945," United States Holocaust Memorial Museum, https://exhibitions.ushmm.org/americans-and-the-holocaust/how-many-refugees-came-to-the-united-states-from-1933-1945.
13. Edna Nahshon, "The Golden Epoch of Yiddish Theatre in America: A Brief Historical Overview," Museum of Yiddish Theater, http://www.museumofyiddishtheater.org/the-history-of-yiddish-theater.html.
14. Ida Berlin to Rubin Guskin, undated letter (est. March 1942), Guide to the Records of the Hebrew Actors' Union 1874–1986 (bulk 1920–1970), Yivo Institute for Jewish Research, RG 1843, Box I-1:5, Folder 117.
15. Ida Berlin to Rubin Guskin, undated letter (est. March 1942), Guide to the Records of the Hebrew Actors' Union 1874–1986 (bulk 1920–1970), Yivo Institute for Jewish Research, RG 1843, Box I-1:5, Folder 117.
16. Coleman, *The Compass,* 39.
17. Jack Berlin to Rubin Guskin, telegrams, October 6, 1930; October 20, 1930; October 21, 1930; March 17, 1933; April 13, 1933, Yivo Institute for Jewish Research, RG 1843, Box I-1:5, Folder 116.
18. Ida Berlin to Rubin Guskin, telegram, November 23, 1935, Guide to the Records of the Hebrew Actors' Union 1874–1986 (bulk 1920–1970), Yivo Institute for Jewish Research, RG 1843, Box I-1:49, Folder 1516.
19. Ida Berlin to Rubin Guskin, undated letter (est. March 1942).
20. Ida Berlin to Rubin Guskin, undated letter (est. March 1942).
21. Ida Berlin to Rubin Guskin, undated letter (est. March 1942).
22. Ida Berlin to Rubin Guskin, undated letter (est. November 1935), Guide to the Records of the Hebrew Actors' Union 1874–1986 (bulk 1920–1970), Yivo Institute for Jewish Research, RG 1843, Box I-1:49, Folder 1516.
23. Sam Wasson, *Improv Nation: How We Made a Great American Art* (Boston: Houghton Mifflin Harcourt, 2017), 24.
24. Jonathan Rosenbaum, "The Mysterious Elaine May: Hiding in Plain Sight,"

JonathanRosenbaum.net addendum to August 1997 *Writers Guild Magazine* essay, March 12, 2022, https://jonathanrosenbaum.net/2022/03/21700/.

25. Tom Canford (Miller), *A Fever of the Mad* (Sawyerville, Alabama: Hollow Square Press, 2013), 59.
26. "Meet Jeannie Berlin," New York *Daily News,* February 24, 1974; Julian Schlossberg, author interview, March 18, 2021.
27. "Meet Jeannie Berlin," New York *Daily News.*
28. Elaine May, interview with Haden Guest, Harvard Film Archive, November 12, 2010.
29. "Meet Jeannie Berlin," New York *Daily News*; Julian Schlossberg, author interview.
30. May, interview with Guest.
31. Phillip Schopper, author interview, November 2021.
32. May, interview with Guest.
33. U.S. Census Bureau Report (1940), https://www.ancestry.com/discoveryui-content/view/13435950:2442.
34. May, interview with Guest.
35. Schopper, author interview, October 2021.
36. Elaine May, interviewed by Phil Rosenthal, Austin Film Festival, October 25, 2013. Excerpts published in "AFF Panel: A Conversation with Elaine May," *Austin American-Statesman,* September 23, 2018.
37. Peter Feibleman, *Lilly: Reminiscences of Lillian Hellman* (New York: Avon Books, 1990), 290.
38. Coleman, *The Compass,* 111.
39. Michael Braun, "Mike and Elaine: Veracity-Cum-Boffs," *Esquire,* October 1, 1960.
40. Thompson, "Whatever Happened to Elaine May?"
41. Markel, "Mike Nichols and Elaine May."
42. Paul J. Karlstrom, "Los Angeles in the 1940s: Post-Modernism and the Visual Arts," *Southern California Quarterly* 69, no. 4 (1987): 301–28, 305–08, University of California Press, Historical Society of Southern California, https://doi.org/10.2307/41171325.
43. Rice, "A Tilted Insight."
44. Rice, "A Tilted Insight."
45. Markel, "Mike Nichols and Elaine May."
46. Gordon Cotler, "For the Love of Mike—and Elaine," *New York Times,* May 24, 1959.
47. Kevin Cody, "Hermosa's Marvin May Was Inventor, Activist," *Easy Reader & Peninsula Magazine,* February 3, 2015, https://easyreadernews.com/hermosas-marvin-may-inventor-activist/.
48. Schopper, author interview, November 2021.
49. Certificate of Marriage between Marvin May and Elaine Berlin, December 8, 1948.
50. Far more common were marriages of women around eighteen or nineteen. According to a U.S. Department of Health, Education, and Welfare report from 1973, In 1950, 31 percent of all women eighteen to nineteen were married. Comparatively, at that same time, only 7.2 percent of fifteen- to seventeen-year-old girls—and that's just what they were—were married (Alice M. Hetzel and Marlene Cappetta, *Teenagers: Marriages, Divorces, Parenthood, and Mortality,* U.S. Department of Health, Education, and Welfare, Publication No. [HRA] 74–1901, August 1973, https://www.cdc.gov/nchs/data/series/sr_21/sr21_023acc.pdf).
51. Gerald Nachman, *Seriously Funny: The Rebel Comedians of the 1950s and 1960s* (New York: Back Stage Books, 2004), 329.
52. Canford (Miller), *A Fever of the Mad,* 59.

53. US Census Report, 1950, https://www.ancestry.com/discoveryui-content/view /263687019:62308.
54. Thompson, "Whatever Happened to Elaine May?"
55. Kenneth Lonergan, author interview, October 21, 2022.
56. Rice, "A Tilted Insight."
57. Cotler, "For the Love of Mike—and Elaine."
58. Sam Kashner, "Who's Afraid of Nichols and May?" *Vanity Fair,* December 20, 2012.
59. Joseph P. Boon, "Will Jeannie Berlin Win an Oscar Too?" *Bucks County Courier Times,* January 26, 1973.
60. Boon, "Will Jeannie Berlin Win an Oscar Too?"
61. On top of it all, Elaine was barely out of her teenage years. Maybe part of her decision was a desire for youthful adventure. Wasn't she deserving of having some youthful fun when adulthood had been thrust so suddenly upon her?

CHAPTER 2: WHEN IN DOUBT, SEDUCE

1. If we roughly adjust for inflation, it'd be as if you were leaving home with $70 to your name today.
2. Thomas Thompson, "Whatever Happened to Elaine May?" *Life,* July 28, 1967.
3. Gordon Cotler, "For the Love of Mike—and Elaine," *New York Times,* May 24, 1959.
4. John Lahr, "Making It Real," *New Yorker,* February 13, 2000.
5. Beverly Solochek, "Daily Closeup," *New York Post,* November 10, 1970.
6. Sam Wasson, *Improv Nation: How We Made a Great American Art* (Boston: Houghton Mifflin Harcourt, 2017), 15.
7. Elaine May, lecture at Literary Arts (Portland), 1997, https://literary-arts.org /archive/elaine-may-2/ (audio recording)
8. Gerald Nachman, *Seriously Funny: The Rebel Comedians of the 1950s and 1960s* (New York: Back Stage Books, 2004), 324.
9. Jeffrey Sweet, *Something Wonderful Right Away: An Oral History of the Second City and the Compass Players* (New York: Limelight, 1978), 131.
10. Sam Kashner, "Who's Afraid of Nichols and May?" *Vanity Fair,* January 2013.
11. Sweet, *Something Wonderful Right Away,* 131.
12. Elaine May, lecture at Literary Arts.
13. Janet Coleman, *The Compass: The Improvisational Theatre That Revolutionized American Comedy* (Chicago: University of Chicago Press, 1991), 66.
14. Coleman, *The Compass,* 156.
15. Coleman, *The Compass,* 66.
16. Ash Carter and Sam Kashner, *Life Isn't Everything: Mike Nichols, as Remembered by 150 of His Closest Friends* (New York: Henry Holt, 2019), 43.
17. Sweet, *Something Wonderful Right Away,* 96.
18. Sweet, *Something Wonderful Right Away,* 131.
19. Lahr, "Making It Real."
20. Sweet, *Something Wonderful Right Away,* 96.
21. Viola Spolin, *Improvisation for the Theater: A Handbook of Teaching and Directing Techniques* (Evanston, IL: Northwestern University Press, 1963), x.
22. Coleman, *The Compass,* 22.
23. Sweet, *Something Wonderful Right Away,* 73.
24. Wasson, *Improv Nation,* 17.
25. Sweet, *Something Wonderful Right Away,* 73.
26. Cotler, "For the Love of Mike—and Elaine."
27. Wasson, *Improv Nation,* 18, although multiple variations on this story have been told in various sources over the decades.
28. Mark Harris, *Mike Nichols: A Life* (New York: Penguin Press, 2021), 34.

29. Sweet, *Something Wonderful Right Away,* 74
30. Coleman, *The Compass,* 40.
31. Mary Birdsong, author interview, September 21, 2022.
32. Birdsong, author interview.
33. Elaine May, by way of Julian Schlossberg: "No, I don't think that ever happened. I'm sure that Mary's telling the truth, because most likely what it was was, when you're directing, you've got to try to get your point across with actors, and you use lots of different methods, and that might be one of them," Schlossberg says. "Anyhow, as Elaine said, 'Well, if I was gonna be called anything, I'd like to be called Shakespeare,'" voicemail, September 27, 2022.
34. Lahr, "Making It Real."
35. Lahr, "Making It Real."
36. Robert Wool, "Mike and Elaine: Mirrors to Our Madness," *Look,* June 21, 1960, 46–52.
37. Nachman, *Seriously Funny,* 334.
38. Coleman, *The Compass,* 131.
39. When asked by Phil Rosenthal if her and Mike's ability to improvise upon first meeting was because they had "some psychic connection," Elaine laughed. "I have no idea what you just said. Say it to me again. A psychic *what*?" Elaine May, interview by Phil Rosenthal, *Naked Lunch,* July 21, 2022, https://open .spotify.com/episode/30cveCd824JIcwDRe5bnUf?si=3f1a9b54cd3f431e.
40. "Mike Nichols," *American Masters,* directed by Elaine May, aired on PBS, January 29, 2016.
41. Nachman, *Seriously Funny,* 326.
42. Nachman, *Seriously Funny,* 335.
43. Lahr, "Making It Real."
44. Lahr, "Making It Real."
45. Thompson, "Whatever Happened to Elaine May?"
46. Lahr, "Making It Real."
47. Nachman, *Seriously Funny,* 335.
48. Wasson, *Improv Nation,* 19.
49. Coleman, *The Compass,* 65–66.
50. Ed Asner, author interview, February 1, 2021.
51. Coleman, *The Compass,* 66.
52. Asner, author interview.
53. Coleman, *The Compass,* 68.
54. Coleman, *The Compass,* 68.
55. Coleman, *The Compass,* 69.
56. Harris, *Mike Nichols,* 42.
57. Asner, author interview.
58. Coleman, *The Compass,* 72.
59. Asner, author interview.
60. Coleman, *The Compass,* 74.
61. Coleman, *The Compass,* 83–84.
62. Sweet, *Something Wonderful Right Away,* 45.
63. Sweet, *Something Wonderful Right Away,* 103.
64. Sweet, *Something Wonderful Right Away,* 120.
65. Coleman, *The Compass,* 106.
66. Wasson, *Improv Nation,* 27, observed by Sheldon Patinkin; also noted in Coleman, *The Compass,* 182, observed by Larry and Rose Arrick.
67. Wasson, *Improv Nation,* 28.
68. Sweet, *Something Wonderful Right Away,* xxiv.
69. Coleman, *The Compass,* 105.
70. https://www.secondcity.com/media-kit-training-center/.

71. Sweet, *Something Wonderful Right Away*, 68.
72. Elaine May, interview by Phil Rosenthal, *Naked Lunch*.
73. Sweet, *Something Wonderful Right Away*, 67.
74. Sweet, *Something Wonderful Right Away*, 106–7.
75. Coleman, *The Compass*, 198.
76. Nichols and May radio interview, date unknown, though sometime during the run of *An Evening with Mike Nichols and Elaine May*.
77. Sweet, *Something Wonderful Right Away*, 30–31.
78. Coleman, *The Compass*, 109.
79. Sweet, *Something Wonderful Right Away*, 105.
80. Coleman, *The Compass*, 111.
81. Cotler, "For the Love of Mike—and Elaine."
82. Coleman, *The Compass*, 119.
83. Wasson, *Improv Nation*, 34.
84. Mike Nichols, "Life, with a Little Tenderizer," *New York Times*, May 26, 1991.
85. Sweet, *Something Wonderful Right Away*, 106.
86. Harris, *Mike Nichols*, 46.
87. Wasson, *Improv Nation*, 34.
88. Coleman, *The Compass*, 128.
89. Sweet, *Something Wonderful Right Away*, 76.
90. Nachman, *Seriously Funny*, 333.
91. Wasson, *Improv Nation*, 36.
92. *Becoming Mike Nichols*, directed by Douglas McGrath, HBO Documentary Films, 2016.
93. Harris, *Mike Nichols*, 54.
94. Elaine May, interview by Haden Guest, Harvard Film Archive, November 13, 2010.
95. Harris, *Mike Nichols*, 57.
96. Sweet, *Something Wonderful Right Away*, 77.
97. May, interview by Rosenthal, *Naked Lunch*.
98. Lahr, "Making It Real."
99. Sweet, *Something Wonderful Right Away*, 78.
100. Clifford Terry, "Who's Afraid of Virginia Woolf, Richard Burton, Liz Taylor, or even Hollywood, California? Not Director Mike Nichols," *Chicago Tribune*, July 3, 1996.
101. May, interview by Guest.
102. May, interview by Guest.
103. Sweet, *Something Wonderful Right Away*, 83.
104. Sweet, *Something Wonderful Right Away*, 74.
105. "Mike Nichols," *American Masters*.
106. "Mike Nichols," *American Masters*.
107. Sweet, *Something Wonderful Right Away*, 78.
108. Elaine Tyler May, *Homeward Bound: American Families in the Cold War Era* (New York: Basic Books, 1988), 90–108.
109. The Motion Picture Production Code of 1930, as printed in: Thomas Doherty, *Pre-Code Hollywood: Sex, Immorality, and Insurrection in American Cinema; 1930-1934* (New York: Columbia University Press, 1999), 351.
110. Valerie J. Nelson, "Jimmy Boyd: 1939–2009," *Chicago Tribune*, March 11, 2009.
111. Joanne Meyerowitz, "The Liberal 1950s? Reinterpreting Postwar American Sexual Culture," *Gender and the Long Postwar: Reconsiderations of the United States and the Two Germanys, 1945–1989*, ed. Karen Hagemann and Sonya Michel (Johns Hopkins University Press and Woodrow Wilson Center Press, 2014), 297–319.

112. Nachman, *Seriously Funny,* 329.
113. Coleman, *The Compass,* 131.
114. Sweet, *Something Wonderful Right Away,* 87.
115. Elaine May and Mike Nichols in conversation at MoMA, April 18, 2009.
116. Coleman, *The Compass,* 164.
117. Coleman, *The Compass,* 187.
118. Coleman, *The Compass,* 195.
119. Coleman, *The Compass,* 207.
120. Lahr, "Making It Real."
121. Sweet, *Something Wonderful Right Away,* 141
122. Sweet, *Something Wonderful Right Away,* 138.
123. Ted Flicker to "Harold," June 27, 1957, Flicker Collection, USC, Box 2, Folder 5.
124. Sweet, *Something Wonderful Right Away,* 161.
125. Coleman, *The Compass,* 224.
126. Harris, *Mike Nichols,* 67.
127. Wasson, *Improv Nation,* 52.
128. Coleman, *The Compass,* 232.
129. Kliph Nesteroff, "An Interview with Theodore J. Flicker," Classic Television Showbiz, December 3, 2014, http://classicshowbiz.blogspot.com/2014/12/an-interview-with-theodore-j-flicker.html.
130. Coleman, *The Compass,* 236.
131. Paul Sills to David Shepherd, September 27, 1957, David Shepherd Papers, University of Chicago, Box 1, Folder 6.
132. Nesteroff, "An Interview with Theodore J. Flicker."
133. Harris, *Mike Nichols,* 68.
134. "Mike Nichols," *American Masters.*

CHAPTER 3: NICHOLS AND MAY TAKE MANHATTAN

1. Gerald Nachman, *Seriously Funny: The Rebel Comedians of the 1950s and 1960s* (New York: Back Stage Books, 2004), 340.
2. "Nichols and May: Take Two," *American Masters,* directed by Phillip Schopper, originally aired on PBS, May 22, 1996.
3. Nachman, *Seriously Funny,* 340–42.
4. Nachman, *Seriously Funny,* 339.
5. Janet Coleman, *The Compass: The Improvisational Theatre That Revolutionized American Comedy* (Chicago: University of Chicago Press, 1991), 237.
6. Close's biographer, Kim Johnson, breaks down the ways in which his version of the story doesn't align with anyone else's, particularly when it comes to glaring timeline discrepancies, in *The Funniest One in the Room: The Lives and Legend of Del Close* (Chicago: Chicago Review Press, 2008), 57–59.
7. See *Playbill* bio; "Mike Nichols and Elaine May," *Redbook,* February 1961; "A Tilted Insight," *New Yorker,* April 15, 1961; "Mike and Elaine: Mirrors to Our Madness," *Look,* June 21, 1960; "An Evening with N&M Slated This Week at Country Playhouse," *Bridgeport Post,* September 11, 1960; the simplified version appearing in "Mike Nichols: Director as Star" *Newsweek,* November 14, 1966 and "Mike and Elaine: Veracity-Cum-Boffs" *Esquire,* October 1960.
8. Nachman, *Seriously Funny,* 340.
9. Sam Wasson, *Improv Nation: How We Made a Great American Art* (Boston: Houghton Mifflin Harcourt, 2017), 56.
10. Robert Rice, "A Tilted Insight," *New Yorker,* April 15, 1961.
11. Nachman, *Seriously Funny,* 659.
12. Mark Harris, *Mike Nichols: A Director's Life* (New York: Penguin Press, 2021), 71.

13. Yael Kohen, *We Killed: The Rise of Women in American Comedy* (New York: Sarah Crichton Books, 2012), 23.
14. *Variety,* November 13, 1957.
15. Sam Kashner, "Who's Afraid of Nichols and May?" *Vanity Fair,* January 2013.
16. Nachman, *Seriously Funny,* 341.
17. Wasson, *Improv Nation,* 57.
18. How they managed to get away with it, according to Mike: "Each of our mothers thought it was the other one's mother we were talking about." Source: Susan King, "Graduate Degree," *Los Angeles Times,* June 9, 2010.
19. Elaine May, interview by Studs Terkel, May 29, 1958.
20. Robert Shelton, "Mike and Elaine," *American Weekly,* August 7, 1960.
21. May, interview by Phil Rosenthal, *Naked Lunch* July 21, 2022, https://open.spotify.com/episode/30cveCd824JIcwDRe5bnUf?si=3f1a9b54cd3f431e.
22. Wasson, *Improv Nation,* 72.
23. Harris, *Mike Nichols,* 73.
24. "The Knight Watch: Comedy Team Scores at the Blue Angel," *New York Journal-American,* October 24, 1957.
25. Douglas Watt, "Tables for Two," *New Yorker,* December 21, 1957.
26. Nachman, *Seriously Funny,* 332–33.
27. Rollins to Nachman, *Seriously Funny,* 341.
28. Both sketches from that evening can be viewed on YouTube in full.
29. "TV: Suburban Revue," *New York Times,* January 15, 1958.
30. Gavin Smith, "Of Metaphors and Purpose," *Film Comment,* May–June 1999.
31. Harris, *Mike Nichols,* 77.
32. John Crosby, "Strange Things," *New York Herald Tribune,* January 17, 1958.
33. Untitled review, *Time,* January 27, 1958.
34. Charles Mercer, "Mike and Elaine: Insults Did It," *New York Post,* February 4, 1958.
35. "May and Nichols, Comedy Rage, Attract a Lot of Questions, So . . ." *The Courier-Journal,* February 16, 1958.
36. Nachman, *Seriously Funny,* 341.
37. Harris, *Mike Nichols,* 79.
38. They were moving to top billing "at that new night club called Down in the Depths. . . . Ten weeks ago, Mike and Elaine were unknown. Today they're stars." Source: "The Knight Watch: Jots and Dots on Night Spots," *New York Journal-American,* January 22, 1958.
39. Helen Markel, "Mike Nichols and Elaine May," *Redbook,* February 1961.
40. Mike Nichols, "Life, with a Little Tenderizer," *New York Times,* May 26, 1991.
41. Markel, "Mike Nichols and Elaine May."
42. Rice, "A Tilted Insight."
43. Mike Wallace, "Elaine May & Mike Nichols: Are You Scared of Success?" *New York Post,* April 1, 1958.
44. Rice, "A Tilted Insight."
45. Margaret McManus, "TV's New Ad-Libbing Comedy Team," *Baltimore Sun,* August 10, 1958.
46. Markel, "Mike Nichols and Elaine May."
47. Rice, "A Tilted Insight."
48. Markel, "Mike Nichols and Elaine May."
49. Housekeeper information by way of Deborah Hautzig, author interview.
50. Markel, "Mike Nichols and Elaine May."
51. Thomas Thompson, "Whatever Happened to Elaine May?" *Life,* July 28, 1967.
52. John Keating, "From Bistros to Broadway; Nichols and May Give Views on Work in Both Fields," *New York Times,* December 18, 1960.
53. Even to a disastrous appearance on a CBS drama called *The Red Mill* in which they were told, "You don't have to hold to the script—say anything you want,

kids," and at one point, rode a horse onto the set. It was their first gig acting together on television. It was also their last. Source: Harris, *Mike Nichols,* 82.

54. Harris, *Mike Nichols,* 80.

55. Michael Braun, "Mike and Elaine: Veracity-Cum-Boffs," *Esquire,* October 1, 1960.

56. Wallace, "Elaine May & Mike Nichols."

57. Mariana Brandman, "The Trailblazing Women of Stand-Up Comedy," National Women's History Museum blog, September 1, 2021.

58. Edmund Wilson, *The Sixties: The Last Journal, 1960–1972* (New York: Farrar Straus Giroux, 1993), 36.

59. A memo from Alexander Cohen, dated July 12, 1960, to Gilman Kraft includes a bulleted list of deal items agreed upon with *Playbill* publisher Gilman Kraft for *An Evening With . . .*'s advertising, including: "[Kraft] is to furnish us with the names of half a dozen fashion houses who want to dress Elaine May and he is free to photograph her and do exploitation stuff on the dresses for his advertising campaigns." Additionally, a letter from Richard Avedon to Cohen, commenting on the publicity photos he took of the pair, remarked: "I think the complete shape of the sexy one of Elaine is necessary." In all of Cohen's documents, there is no mention of seeking clothes or styling for Mike nor for Mike to participate in his own set of photos or focus on his attractive appearance in any photos he appeared in with Elaine.

60. Kohen, *We Killed,* 17.

61. Rosie Germain, "Reading *The Second Sex* in 1950s America," *Historical Journal* 56, no. 4 (December 2013): 1041–1062.

62. Diller, in 1980: "Women's liberation is never going to change relationships between men and women . . . I'm a third-generation career girl, so I've always been liberated and I take it for granted. And I like being a woman" (Wendy Leigh, "Private Lives: Down-to-Earth Views on Love and Sex," *Washington Post,* March 10, 1980; Elaine, in 1972: "It would be hideous to think that either sex took a script and in any way pushed it toward any point of view other than the author's. I don't think it's important whether you're a man, a woman or a chair." ("Show Business: Behind the Lens," *Time,* March 20, 1972).

63. Caroline Aaron, author interview, September 2, 2022.

64. Arthur Gelb, "Phyllis Diller: A Female Bob Hope," *New York Times,* March 13, 1961.

65. Harris, *Mike Nichols,* 83.

66. Rice, "A Tilted Insight."

67. Joyce Haber, "Elaine May Has a Thing on Not Talking to Press: Nonlinear Interview with Elaine May," *Los Angeles Times,* July 7, 1968.

68. Thompson, "Whatever Happened to Elaine May?"

69. "Nichols and May: Take Two," *American Masters.*

70. They—and Sahl's now-iconic *The Future Lies Ahead*—lost to . . . "The Chipmunk Song (Christmas Don't Be Late)," which is comedy in and of itself.

71. Harris, *Mike Nichols,* 64.

72. Rice, "A Tilted Insight."

73. Harris, *Mike Nichols,* 64.

74. John S. Wilson, "Satirists Heard in Program Here," *New York Times,* May 2, 1959.

75. Wool, "Mike and Elaine: Mirrors to Our Madness."

76. Sam Zolotow, "Miss Colbert Ill; Misses Two Shows," *New York Times,* April 2, 1959.

77. Stephen Farber and Marc Green, *Hollywood on the Couch: A Candid Look at the Overheated Love Affair Between Psychiatrists and Moviemakers* (New York: William Morrow, 1993), 202–3.

78. Farber and Green, *Hollywood on the Couch,* 203.

79. Harris, *Mike Nichols,* 96.

80. Janet Coleman, *The Compass,* 268.
81. "Alexander H. Cohen, the producer of *An Evening with Mike Nichols and Elaine May,* estimates that he has a telephone conversation about business with Miss May every ten or twelve days and that he has one with Nichols three or four times every day" (Rice, "A Tilted Insight").
82. Cohen to Joan de Keyser, letter, June 14, 1960, Alexander Cohen Collection, New York Public Library for the Performing Arts.
83. Review, *Variety,* April 19, 1960.
84. Cohen to Kenneth E. Schwartz, letter, July 8, 1960, Alexander Cohen Collection, New York Public Library for the Performing Arts.
85. Cohen to May, telegram, April 22, 1960, and Cohen to May, letter, April 27, 1960, Alexander Cohen Collection, New York Public Library for the Performing Arts.
86. Harris, *Mike Nichols,* 97.
87. Smith, "Of Metaphors and Purpose."
88. Harris, *Mike Nichols,* 98.
89. "I am listening . . ." Cohen to Nichols, letter, July 25, 1960, Alexander Cohen Collection, New York Public Library for the Performing Arts.
90. Nachman, *Seriously Funny,* 344.
91. Nachman, *Seriously Funny,* 344.
92. Coleman, *The Compass,* 267.
93. Cohen to Gilman Kraft, letter, July 8, 1960, Alexander Cohen Collection, New York Public Library for the Performing Arts.
94. Elaine May to Sam Kashner, "Who's Afraid of Nichols and May?"
95. Howard Taubman, "'Evening with Nichols and May' Opens," *New York Times,* October 10, 1960.
96. A revised contract dated May 24, 1960, in the Alexander Cohen Collection stipulates that Nichols and May would gain 19.5 percent of gross revenue until expenses were recouped, 19.5 percent of the first $22,000, then 24.5 percent of the gross for the next $25,000.
97. McMahon to Alexander Cohen, letter, April 27, 1961, Alexander Cohen Collection, New York Public Library for the Performing Arts.
98. Alexander Cohen's record book of each night's improvisations—the first line, last line, and literary style—for the duration of the show can be found in the Alexander Cohen Collection at the New York Public Library for the Performing Arts.
99. Rice, "A Tilted Insight."
100. Edmund Wilson, *The Sixties,* 36.
101. Phil Rosenthal, author interview, October 3, 2022.
102. "Some Are More Yossarian Than Others," *Time,* June 15, 1970.
103. Wilson, *The Sixties,* 62.
104. Wilson, *The Sixties,* 39.
105. Alice Arlen, "Mr. Success," *Interview,* December 1988.
106. Cohen to Rollins, letter, December 7, 1960, Alexander Cohen Collection, New York Public Library for the Performing Arts.
107. Rice, "A Tilted Insight."
108. Kashner, "Who's Afraid of Nichols and May?"
109. Rice, "A Tilted Insight."
110. Rice, "A Tilted Insight."
111. Cohen to Joe Brownstone, letter, February 3, 1961, Alexander Cohen Collection, New York Public Library for the Performing Arts.
112. Wasson, *Improv Nation,* 73.
113. Wasson, *Improv Nation,* 69.
114. Arlen, "Mr. Success."

115. May, interview by Rosenthal, *Naked Lunch.*
116. Thompson, "Whatever Happened to Elaine May?"
117. Thompson, "Whatever Happened to Elaine May?"
118. May to Cohen, letter, June 1, 1961, Alexander Cohen Collection, New York Public Library for the Performing Arts.
119. Seymour Herscher to Rose Rugg, letter, January 12, 1962, Alexander Cohen Collection, New York Public Library for the Performing Arts.

CHAPTER 4: WHAT THE HELL HAPPENED TO ELAINE MAY?

1. Thomas Thompson, "Whatever Happened to Elaine May?" *Life,* July 28, 1967.
2. Mark Harris, *Mike Nichols: A Director's Life* (New York: Penguin Press, 2021), 110.
3. Gerald Nachman, *Seriously Funny: The Rebel Comedians of the 1950s and 1960s* (New York: Back Stage Books, 2004), 350.
4. The estimate of twenty-five minutes per Judd Hirsch, author interview, March 29, 2021.
5. Howard Taubman, "The Theatre: '3x3'=?; Three Short Plays at Maidman Playhouse," *New York Times,* March 2, 1962.
6. *Not Enough Rope* review dated May 1962, unknown source, New York Public Library for the Performing Arts, Elaine May clippings folder.
7. "Elaine's Play, Marriage End," *New York Mirror,* October 13, 1962.
8. Janet Coleman, *The Compass: The Improvisational Theatre That Revolutionized American Comedy* (Chicago: University of Chicago Press, 1991), 271.
9. "Elaine and I were never married—well, yes, we were, my goodness! It was very unfortunate. She initiated divorce proceedings a couple of months later" (Sheldon Harnick to Mark Harris, *Mike Nichols,* 115).
10. "Elaine's Show Closing Along with Marriage," New York *Daily News,* October 13, 1962.
11. Edmund Wilson, *The Sixties: The Last Journal, 1960–1972* (New York: Farrar Straus Giroux, 1993), 174.
12. Ash Carter and Sam Kashner, *Life Isn't Everything: Mike Nichols, as Remembered by 150 of His Closest Friends* (New York: Henry Holt, 2019), 90, per Maureen Dowd.
13. Coleman, *The Compass,* 271.
14. Harris, *Mike Nichols,* 117.
15. Carter and Kashner, *Life Isn't Everything,* 96.
16. Thompson, "Whatever Happened to Elaine May?"
17. Richard F. Shepard, "Elaine May: Q&A About Her New Play," *New York Times,* September 23, 1962.
18. Jeffrey Sweet, *Something Wonderful Right Away: An Oral History of the Second City and the Compass Players* (New York: Limelight, 1978), 84.
19. Thompson, "Whatever Happened to Elaine May?"
20. Thompson, "Whatever Happened to Elaine May?"
21. Shepard, "Elaine May: Q&A About Her New Play."
22. "On the Phone, Elaine May Tells a Sad Phila. Story," *New York Post,* October 10, 1962.
23. "On the Phone."
24. Thompson, "Whatever Happened to Elaine May?"
25. Sweet, *Something Wonderful Right Away,* 84.
26. Sweet, *Something Wonderful Right Away,* 84.
27. Thompson, "Whatever Happened to Elaine May?"
28. Harris, *Mike Nichols,* 118.
29. Coleman, *The Compass,* 271.
30. Sweet, *Something Wonderful Right Away,* 84.
31. Harris, *Mike Nichols,* 119.

32. "Mike Nichols," *American Masters,* directed by Elaine May, aired on PBS, January 29, 2016.
33. Harris, *Mike Nichols,* 119.
34. Thompson, "Whatever Happened to Elaine May?"
35. Rachel Abramowitz, *Is That a Gun in Your Pocket? Women's Experience of Power in Hollywood* (New York: Random House, 2000), 59.
36. Thompson, "Whatever Happened to Elaine May?"
37. Coleman, *The Compass,* 271.
38. Richard F. Shepard, "TV Plans Study of Racial Crisis," *New York Times,* July 17, 1963.
39. Abramowitz, *Is That a Gun in Your Pocket?,* 59.
40. Sam Zolotow, "Musical to Rely on Fellini Movie," *New York Times,* July 8, 1965.
41. Sam Zolotow, "Gower Champion Takes on New Job," *New York Times,* August 13, 1964.
42. Program for *Name of a Soup,* 1963, Uta Hagen and Herbert Berghof papers, Subseries 3, Box 67, Folder 1, New York Public Library for the Performing Arts.
43. Author interview with Judd Hirsch.
44. Hirsch, author interview.
45. Brenda Murphy, ed., *The Cambridge Companion to American Women Playwrights* (New York: Cambridge University Press, 1999), xiii.
46. Per BroadwayWorld.com's annual catalog of new productions. Two of the three productions that did open in 1962 barely even made it: Seyril Schocken's *The Moon Besieged* closed after its opening night; Alice Cannon's *Great Day in the Morning* lasted a mere thirteen performances. Only Santha Rama Rau's *A Passage to India* went on to have a substantial theatrical run.
47. Luís A. Nunes Amaral et al., "Long-Term Patterns of Gender Imbalance in an Industry Without Ability or Level of Interest Differences," *PLoS ONE* 15, no. 4 (2020): e0229662, https://www.ncbi.nlm.nih.gov/pmc/articles/PMC7112163/.
48. A phrase I'm sure most psychoanalysts would counter with: What *is* normal?
49. Author interview with Julian Schlossberg, April 1, 2021.
50. Hildi Greenson to Stephen Farber, in Stephen Farber and Marc Green, *Hollywood on the Couch: A Candid Look at the Overheated Love Affair Between Psychiatrists and Moviemakers* (New York: William Morrow, 1993), 210.
51. Hildi Greenson to Stephen Farber, Farber and Green, *Hollywood on the Couch,* 210.
52. Farber and Green, *Hollywood on the Couch,* 204.
53. Farber and Green, *Hollywood on the Couch,* 204.
54. Farber and Green, *Hollywood on the Couch,* 205.
55. Farber and Green, *Hollywood on the Couch,* 209.
56. Farber and Green, *Hollywood on the Couch,* 208.
57. Farber and Green, *Hollywood on the Couch,* 205.
58. Joyce Haber, "Elaine May Has a Thing on Not Talking to Press: Nonlinear Interview with Elaine May," *Los Angeles Times,* July 7, 1968.
59. Deborah Hautzig, author interview, September 14, 2022. Allegedly, Susie later ate another dog in the park.
60. Haber, "Elaine May Has a Thing on Not Talking to Press."
61. Dick Lemon, "How to Succeed in Interviewing Elaine May (Try, Really Try)," *New York Times,* January 4, 1970.
62. Hautzig, author interview.
63. Hautzig, author interview.
64. Bernadette Mayer, interview by Adam Fitzgerald, "Lives of the Poets: Bernadette Mayer," Poetry Foundation, September 2010, https://www.poetryfoundation.org/articles/69658/lives-of-the-poets-bernadette-mayer.
65. Tony Hiss, *Laughing Last: Alger Hiss* (Boston: Houghton Mifflin, 1977), 128.
66. Thompson, "Whatever Happened to Elaine May?"

67. Thompson, "Whatever Happened to Elaine May?"
68. Hautzig, author interview.
69. "Amusements for Children," *New York Times,* December 30, 1964.
70. Elaine's adaptation is indeed wacky, and darkly funny for a children's play. The impoverished miller is wanted for tax evasion, he tells the "my daughter can spin straw into gold" lie as a way to keep her safe, and the king and queen have a debate over the legality of keeping her as a slave (Elaine May, *Rumpelstiltskin,* undated script c. 1960–1965, Circle in the Square papers, Series III, Subseries 5, Box 298, Folder 1, New York Public Library for the Performing Arts).
71. Bernadine Morris, "3 Girls Share an Interest in the Arts," *New York Times,* December 26, 1964.
72. Morris, "3 Girls Share an Interest in the Arts."
73. Caroline Aaron, author interview, September 2, 2022: "I don't know if it's because she had a baby so young or whatever it was, but she seemed to skip the years of self-doubt."
74. Thompson, "Whatever Happened to Elaine May?"
75. Sweet, *Something Wonderful Right Away,* 162
76. Sweet, *Something Wonderful Right Away,* 119–21
77. Renée Taylor, author interview, May 9, 2021.
78. May, interview by Phil Rosenthal, *Naked Lunch* July 21, 2022, https://open.spotify.com/episode/30cveCd824JIcwDRe5bnUf?si=3f1a9b54cd3f431e.
79. Stuart W. Little, "Elaine May an Improv. . . . ," *New York Herald Tribune,* April 27, 1964. Part of the headline is missing in this clipping; it ran in syndicated markets with "Sure, Improvise but Keep It Wise."
80. May, interview by Rosenthal, *Naked Lunch.*
81. Little, "Elaine May an Improv. . . ."
82. Mark Gordon to Jeffrey Sweet, *Something Wonderful Right Away,* 121.
83. Mark Gordon to Jeffrey Sweet, *Something Wonderful Right Away,* 121.
84. Little, "Elaine May an Improv. . . ."
85. George Oppenheimer, "Third Ear Gets Hearing at the Premise Theater," *Newsday,* May 29, 1964.
86. Newark *Evening News,* May 29, 1964, via Coleman, *The Compass,* 289.
87. Oppenheimer, "Third Ear Gets Hearing at the Premise Theater."
88. Rube Dorin, "The Third Ear: A New Revue at Premise Theater," *New York Morning Telegraph,* May 30, 1964.
89. Dorin, "The Third Ear."
90. William Glover, "Third Ear Episodes Labeled Little Bores," *Orlando Evening Star* (via the AP), May 29, 1964.
91. Michael Smith, "Theatre: The Third Ear," *Village Voice,* June 4, 1964.
92. Brian O'Doherty, "Third Ear Opens at Premise Theater," *New York Times,* May 29, 1964.
93. O'Doherty, "Third Ear Opens at Premise Theater."
94. Oppenheimer, "Third Ear Gets Hearing at the Premise Theater."
95. Glover, "Third Ear Episodes Labeled Little Bores."
96. Dorin, "The Third Ear."
97. "Once I spent the evening with [Katharine Graham]. I didn't quite know who she was and we talked about our mothers intimately for an hour. . . . About a week later—I can't even tell you about this, it's so painful—Mike gets off the train with this relatively elderly woman, and he says, 'Elaine, you know Katharine Graham.' And I say, 'So nice to meet you.' And he aims a kick at me as he usually did, but sort of misses. And he says, 'Don't you remember, you spent . . .' We leave, and he said, 'Look, I can't go through this time after time. When you meet somebody, here's what you say: ' "Ah, yes." Don't say anything else' " (May, interview by Rosenthal, *Naked Lunch*).

98. Mike Nichols to Sam Wasson, in Sam Wasson, *Improv Nation: How We Made a Great American Art* (Boston: Houghton Mifflin Harcourt, 2017), 99–101.

99. Patrick Goldstein, "They All Have a Secret," *Los Angeles Times*, March 15, 1998.

100. Harris, *Mike Nichols*, 140.

101. Seymour Krim, "U.S. Writers, Actors Protests Vietnam Policy with 'Read-in,'" *New York Herald Tribune*, Paris, February 22, 1966.

102. "Mike Nichols," *American Masters*.

103. "Mike Nichols," *American Masters*.

104. "Mike Nichols," *American Masters*.

105. An excerpt of the sketch can be seen in *King: A Film Record . . . Montgomery to Memphis*, prod. Ely Landau (Commonwealth United, 1970).

106. *The Office* press release, Elaine May clippings, New York Public Library.

107. Lewis Funke, "Robbins Likes 'The Office,'" *New York Times*, November 28, 1965.

108. Tony Lo Bianco, author interview, March 8, 2021.

109. Jules Fisher, author interview, April 1, 2021.

110. Fisher, author interview.

111. Lo Bianco, author interview.

112. Lo Bianco, author interview.

113. Fisher, author interview.

114. Mike Nichols and Elaine May present the "Total Mediocrity Award" at the 1959 Emmys, https://www.youtube.com/watch?v=_dyCXMFDmIQ.

115. Incidentally, her future partner Stanley Donen tried to get her to play the lead in 1967's *Two for the Road*. She declined, and the role went to Audrey Hepburn instead. Carter and Ashner, *Life Isn't Everything*, 54.

116. Thompson, "Whatever Happened to Elaine May?"

117. Thompson, "Whatever Happened to Elaine May?"

118. Marjory Adams, "Film Star Elaine May Is Different," *Boston Globe*, August 15, 1967.

119. Thompson, "Whatever Happened to Elaine May?"

120. Thompson, "Whatever Happened to Elaine May?"

121. Thompson, "Whatever Happened to Elaine May?"

122. Thompson, "Whatever Happened to Elaine May?"

123. Thompson, "Whatever Happened to Elaine May?"

124. Thompson, "Whatever Happened to Elaine May?"

125. Thompson, "Whatever Happened to Elaine May?"

126. Thompson, "Whatever Happened to Elaine May?"

127. Bosley Crowther, "Screen: 'Luv,' Broadway Hit, Begins New Film Life," *New York Times*, July 27, 1967.

128. Andrew Sarris, "Films," *Village Voice*, September 7, 1967.

129. Bosley Crowther, "For Those Who Luv Laughing," *New York Times*, August 13, 1967.

130. Sarris, "Films."

131. Gerald Nachman, "In 'Luv' in Vain," *Oakland Tribune*, August 24, 1967.

132. Sarris, "Films."

133. "It was as a writer that Elaine decided she would achieve immortality," Mike Nichols to Sam Wasson, *Improv Nation*, 24.

134. Adams, "Film Star Elaine May Is Different."

135. Adams, "Film Star Elaine May Is Different."

136. Adams, "Film Star Elaine May Is Different."

137. Adams, "Film Star Elaine May Is Different."

138. Adams, "Film Star Elaine May Is Different."

139. Kevin M. Johnson, "Elaine May: Do You Mind Interviewing Me in the Kitchen?" *New York Times*, January 8, 1967.

140. Johnson, "Elaine May."

141. Thompson, "Whatever Happened to Elaine May?"

142. David Bianculli, *Dangerously Funny: The Uncensored Story of The Smothers Brothers Comedy Hour* (New York: Simon & Schuster, 2009), 99.
143. Tom Smothers and staff writer Mason Williams discuss the controversy at length in a special rerun of the episode with the cut sketch restored that ran on E! in 1993.
144. Judy Stone, "Two Clean-Cut Heroes Make Waves," *New York Times,* April 16, 1967
145. Elaine May, "The Sketch That Couldn't Be Done," *New York Times,* April 16, 1967.
146. Tony Anthony, "'They Are Trying to Bury Me . . . ,'" *Los Angeles Free Press,* December 22, 1967.
147. James Curtis, *Last Man Standing: Mort Sahl and the Birth of Modern Comedy* (Jackson: University Press of Mississippi, 2017), 238.

CHAPTER 5: YOU MAKE THE CREW NERVOUS

1. "Hollywood Company Has Greatest Film Schedule," *Daily Herald,* January 15, 1968.
2. Maya Montañez Smukler, *Liberating Hollywood: Women Directors and the Feminist Reform of 1970s American Cinema* (New Brunswick, NJ: Rutgers University Press, 2019), 78.
3. Florabel Muir, "A Feather in His Cap," *Daily News,* March 18, 1968.
4. Joyce Haber, "Elaine May Has a Thing on Not Talking to Press: Nonlinear Interview with Elaine May," *Los Angeles Times,* July 7, 1968.
5. Salute of the Week: Elaine May, *Cue,* September 20, 1969.
6. Production Notes, *A New Leaf* clippings (digitized fiche), Margaret Herrick Library.
7. Elaine May, interview by Leonard Probst. Appears in excerpts published in Michael Rivlin, "Elaine May: Too Tough for Hollywood?" *Millimeter* 3, no. 10 (1975).
8. May, interview by Mike Nichols, Film Society of Lincoln Center, February 26, 2006.
9. May, interview by Leonard Probst. Appears in Probst, *Off Camera: Leveling About Themselves* (New York: Stein and Day, 1975), 129.
10. May, interview by Rosenthal, *Naked Lunch* July 21, 2022, https://open.spotify .com/episode/30cveCd824JIcwDRe5bnUf?si=3f1a9b54cd3f431e.
11. Nathan Lane, author interview, September 19, 2022.
12. Rachel Abramowitz, *Is That a Gun in Your Pocket? Women's Experience of Power in Hollywood* (New York: Random House, 2000), 61.
13. May, interview by Probst, *Millimeter* excerpts.
14. May, interview by Rosenthal, *Naked Lunch.*
15. May, interview by Nichols.
16. "Inter-Office Communication from A. N. Ryan to Eugene H. Frank, Re: *A New Leaf,*" April 3, 1968 (*A New Leaf,* Production Records, Paramount Pictures Special Collection, File 180, Margaret Herrick Library, Academy of Motion Picture Arts and Sciences Library).
17. Jurgen A. Thomas, "Playwrights Review Season," *Berkshire Eagle,* August 31, 1968.
18. Thomas, "Playwrights Review Season."
19. Thomas, "Playwrights Review Season."
20. Haber, "Elaine May Has a Thing on Not Talking to Press."
21. Kevin Kelly, "'A Matter of Position' Top Comedy, Ready for Broadway," *Boston Globe,* July 21, 1968.
22. Howard Healy, "'Matter of Position' Is No Sketchy Comedy," *Troy Record,* July 8, 1968.
23. Milton R. Bass, "Play Review: 'A Matter of Position,'" *Berkshire Eagle,* July 5, 1968.

24. "Gibson's Play Breaks Box Office Records," *Berkshire Eagle,* August 6, 1968.
25. Terrence McNally, lecture at Literary Arts (Portland), January 19, 2005; https://literary-arts.org/archive/terrence-mcnally (audio recording).
26. Terrence McNally, interview by Terry Gross, *Fresh Air,* June 23, 1993; https://freshairarchive.org/segments/playwright-terrence-mcnally (audio recording).
27. McNally, lecture at Literary Arts.
28. Guy Flatley, "He Won't Kick His 'Bad Habits,'" *New York Times,* March 10, 1974.
29. James Coco, "Elaine May: She Wears Many Faces Well," *Los Angeles Herald Examiner,* October 27, 1969.
30. Patricia Bosworth, "Fat and Forty—And Red Hot," *New York Times,* January 4, 1970.
31. Bosworth, "Fat and Forty—And Red Hot."
32. Coco, "Elaine May: She Wears Many Faces Well."
33. Kevin Kelly, "May, McNally Worth Seeing," *Boston Globe,* August 12, 1968.
34. Milton R. Bass, "Play Review: 'Next' at the Berkshire Playhouse," *Berkshire Eagle,* August 8, 1968.
35. Bass, "Play Review."
36. Bass, "Play Review."
37. Clive Barnes, "Theater: Off Broadway Brings a Happy Double Bill," *New York Times,* February 11, 1969.
38. Walter Kerr, "Elaine May Just Kill You," *New York Times,* February 23, 1969.
39. Haber, "Elaine May Has a Thing on Not Talking to Press."
40. In one scripted scene, a would-be blackmailer explains, "I used to teach dancing. But I made a pass at one of the students who turned out to be eleven. Who knew? She looked an easy thirteen to me."
41. Dick Lemon, "How to Succeed in Interviewing Elaine May (Try, Really Try)," *New York Times,* January 4, 1970.
42. "Inter-Communication from Peter Bart to Robert Evans, Subject: *A New Leaf,*" February 7, 1969, *A New Leaf,* Production Files, Margaret Herrick Library.
43. "Inter-Communication from Peter Bart to Robert Evans, Subject: *A New Leaf,*" February 7, 1969.
44. "Inter-Communication from Bernard Donnenfeld to Charles Bluhdorn and Martin Davis," May 16, 1969, *A New Leaf,* Production Records, Paramount Pictures Special Collection, File 180, Margaret Herrick Library.
45. May, interview by Nichols.
46. May, interview by Probst, *Millimeter* excerpts.
47. Lemon, "How to Succeed in Interviewing Elaine May (Try, Really Try)."
48. At a post-screening conversation more than forty years later during the Austin Film Festival, Elaine would suggest that maybe it wasn't that being a woman was a disadvantage: "The first time I did my scene as Henrietta, this very feminine woman, the entire crew came to my side and then treated the producer with contempt. They'd say things like 'We'll do [the job] when she's here.' I always thought after that, this is the way a woman should direct a movie. Put on those glasses and speak softly. . . . I'm not sure that a guy who knew nothing about movies and wandered onto a set would've been treated the same way. And he'd never get to put a dress on and drop his glasses, so the crew would never get on his side." Thus she both acknowledges that playing into the stereotype of feminine fragility helped her in a way that it would never have helped a man and at the same time takes note of the double standard at work. This troubling anecdote—at once stating point-blank how she was treated differently while framing it as if she didn't have it so bad after all, because hey, a man couldn't have done the same thing—is her own mythmaking at work. Without much effort, she has spun herself as both the victim and the hero of the story, depending on how you choose to tilt your head to look at it.

49. May, interview by Rosenthal, *Naked Lunch.*
50. May, interview by Nichols.
51. Chris Nashawaty, "An Intimate Conversation with Mike Nichols," *Entertainment Weekly,* November 20, 2014.
52. May, interview by Nichols.
53. Andrew Tobias, "Elaine May: A New Film, but Not a New Leaf," *New York,* December 6, 1976.
54. Renée Taylor, author interview.
55. Taylor remembers that she had a newborn and Elaine "would call cut whenever it was time to breastfeed my son on set."
56. Taylor, author interview.
57. Elaine May, interview by Phil Rosenthal, Austin Film Festival, October 25, 2013. Excerpts appear in Stephen Saito, "Elaine May on Almost Getting Away with Murder in *A New Leaf,*" Moveable Feast, January 1, 2014, https://moveablefest .com/elaine-may-new-leaf/.
58. May, interview by Rosenthal, Austin Film Festival.
59. Abramowitz, *Is That a Gun in Your Pocket?,* 62.
60. May, interview by Nichols.
61. "Inter-Communication from Peter Bart to See Below," June 13, 1969, *A New Leaf,* Production Records, Paramount Pictures Special Collection, File 180, Margaret Herrick Library.
62. Stanley Jaffe, interview by Mae Woods, Academy of Motion Picture Arts and Sciences, Visual History, April 21, 2015, from Smukler, *Liberating Hollywood,* 82.
63. Tobias, "Elaine May: A New Film, but Not a New Leaf."
64. Howard Thompson, "Elaine May Spends Her Summer Knee-Deep in Film," *New York Times,* August 26, 1969.
65. Lemon, "How to Succeed in Interviewing Elaine May (Try, Really Try)."
66. Abramowitz, *Is That a Gun in Your Pocket?,* 61.
67. "Nobody told me [about coverage] because they didn't want me on the movie and they wanted me fired," May, interview by Nichols.
68. Thompson, "Elaine May Spends Her Summer Knee-Deep in Film."
69. May, interview by Rosenthal, *Naked Lunch.*
70. May, interview by Rosenthal, *Naked Lunch.*
71. May, interview by Rosenthal, *Naked Lunch.*
72. Joyce Haber, "Walter Matthau Proves Nice Guys Do Finish Last," *Los Angeles Times,* March 21, 1971.
73. Marilyn Beck, "Editors Had Tough Time to Cut 'Leaf,'" *Long Island Press,* September 21, 1970.
74. Matthau to Sandra Shevey, unpublished audio interview for *Hearst's Sunday Woman,* date unknown, YouTube, https://www.youtube.com/watch?v=gjJL6 _1tw5g.
75. Thompson, "Elaine May Spends Her Summer Knee-Deep in Film."
76. Betty Baer, "If Mike Can, Elaine May," *Look,* February 10, 1970.
77. May, interview by Rosenthal, *Naked Lunch.*
78. Baer, "If Mike Can, Elaine May."
79. May, interview by Nichols.
80. Baer, "If Mike Can, Elaine May."
81. May, interview by Nichols.
82. Data of Bulletin of Screen Achievement Records, *A New Leaf* clippings (digitized fiche), Margaret Herrick Library.
83. Abramowitz, *Is That a Gun in Your Pocket?,* 62.
84. "Inter-Communication from Stanley Jaffe to Paramount-Charles Bluhdorn, Martin Davis, Robert Evans, Bernard Donnenfeld," October 7, 1969, *A New Leaf,* Production Records, Paramount Pictures Special Collection, File 180, Margaret Herrick Library.

85. "Inter-Communication from Stanley Jaffe to Paramount-Charles Bluhdorn, Martin Davis, Robert Evans, Bernard Donnenfeld," October, 7, 1969.

86. Lemon, "How to Succeed in Interviewing Elaine May (Try, Really Try)."

87. Contractually, she was entitled to ten weeks for a first cut and six weeks after that for a second cut ("Inter-Communication from Norman Flicker to Stanley Jaffe," February 16, 1970, *A New Leaf,* Production Records, Paramount Pictures Special Collection, File 180, Margaret Herrick Library).

88. "Inter-Communication from Bernard Donnenfeld to Charles Bluhdorn and Martin Davis," May 16, 1969, *A New Leaf,* Production Records, Paramount Pictures Special Collection, File 180, Margaret Herrick Library.

89. "Inter-Communication from A. N. Ryan," September 17, 1970, *A New Leaf,* Production Records, Paramount Pictures Special Collection, File 180, Margaret Herrick Library.

90. "Cable from A. N. Ryan to Arthur Klein," September 17, 1970, *A New Leaf,* Production Records, Paramount Pictures Special Collection, File 180, Margaret Herrick Library.

91. "Cutting-And-Editing Process Crucial to Direction; Penn Supports Elaine May," *Variety,* February 3, 1971. Although *A New Leaf* production records in the Paramount Pictures Special Collection contain a file entirely full of audience feedback and polling after a screening in New Rochelle, New York, on February 1, 1971, it was likely the Paramount cut.

92. "Inter-Communication from Norman Flicker to Stanley Jaffe," February 16, 1970, *A New Leaf,* Production Records, Paramount Pictures Special Collection, File 180, Margaret Herrick Library.

93. The murder scenes were shot and printed, one of which Elaine said in 2013 "was one of the funniest scenes I've ever seen because Walter watched Jack Weston drink poisoned scotch for just like 10 minutes." (May interviewed by Rosenthal, Austin Film Festival, Moveable Feast excerpts). Whether or not "The May Cut" actually exists—and more important, *where* it exists—has been a point of debate for decades. Elaine remains characteristically mum, though it seems unlikely that she would have refrained from putting out her version by now if she owned the print and rights to it. Realistically, it's likely that the film continues to be in Paramount's possession and was stored somewhere in their vast archive. An email inquiry with archivist Andrea Kalas, Paramount's SVP of asset management, in January 2022 resulted in an extensive search into Paramount's off-site storage facilities. ("It has come up in the past, but this time we're digging even deeper," she noted.) As of July 2022, nothing has turned up. "I hate to assume total loss and/or destruction, as we sometimes come across things—but I'm not optimistic, sadly," she says.

94. May, interview by Probst, *Millimeter* excerpts.

95. Tobias, "Elaine May: A New Film, but Not a New Leaf."

96. May, interview by Rosenthal, Austin Film Festival, Moveable Feast excerpts.

97. Stefan Kanfer, "Anthology of Gaffes," *Time,* March 29, 1971.

98. "Elaine May Denied Injunction vs. 'A New Leaf,'" *Variety,* March 10, 1971.

99. "Elaine May Sues Par," *Variety,* January 20, 1971.

100. Mike Marth, "Paramount Sued for Turning Over 'New Leaf,'" *Valley News,* February 5, 1971.

101. "Elaine May Suing to Halt New Film," *New York Times,* January 19, 1971.

102. Abramowitz, *Is That a Gun in Your Pocket?,* 63.

103. May, interview by Nichols.

104. May, interview by Rosenthal, *Naked Lunch.*

105. May, interview by Rosenthal, *Naked Lunch.*

106. May, interview by Rosenthal, *Naked Lunch.*

107. May, interview by Nichols.

108. Two major holdouts: Stanley Kauffmann at *The New Republic,* who wrote that

Elaine was "devoid of light-hearted comic feeling and nearly devoid of instinct for the camera," and Pauline Kael at *The New Yorker,* who called it "commercial in a rather bizarre way, . . . almost implausibly bad—and it's an unusually ugly major-studio production—yet it isn't offensively bad."

109. Vincent Canby, "W. C. Fields and Elaine May—Two of a Kind?" *New York Times,* March 14, 1971.
110. "Big Rental Films of 1971," *Variety,* January 5, 1972, from Smukler, *Liberating Hollywood,* 84.
111. Lemon, "How to Succeed in Interviewing Elaine May (Try, Really Try)."

CHAPTER 6: LAUGH AND LAUGH AND LAUGH AND SHUDDER LATER

1. Charles Grodin, interview by Jenni Matz and Bill Dana, American Comedy Archives, February 23, 2005.
2. Charles Grodin, *It Would Be So Nice If You Weren't Here* (New York: William Morrow, 1989), 185.
3. A. H. Weiler, "Now It's Simon and May," *New York Times,* November 21, 1971.
4. Weiler, "Now It's Simon and May."
5. Neil Simon, interviewed by John Joseph Brady; John Joseph Brady, *The Craft of the Screenwriter: Interviews with Six Celebrated Screenwriters* (New York: Simon & Schuster, 1981), 329.
6. May, interview by Phil Rosenthal, *Naked Lunch* July 21, 2022, https://open .spotify.com/episode/30cveCd824JIcwDRe5bnUf?si=3f1a9b54cd3f431e.
7. Grodin, *It Would Be So Nice If You Weren't Here,* 189.
8. Grodin, *It Would Be So Nice If You Weren't Here,* 163–64.
9. Grodin, *It Would Be So Nice If You Weren't Here,* 188.
10. John Gruen, "More Than Elaine May's Daughter," *New York Times,* January 7, 1973.
11. Gruen, "More Than Elaine May's Daughter."
12. Carol Kramer, "Jeannie Berlin: It Runs in the Family," *Chicago Tribune,* December 31, 1972.
13. "Meet Jeannie Berlin," New York *Daily News,* February 24, 1973.
14. Kramer, "Jeannie Berlin: It Runs in the Family."
15. "Meet Jeannie Berlin."
16. Joseph P. Boon, "Will Jeannie Berlin Win an Oscar Too?" *Bucks County Courier Times,* January 26, 1973.
17. Boon, "Will Jeannie Berlin Win an Oscar Too?"
18. Gruen, "More Than Elaine May's Daughter."
19. Erik Lee Preminger, author interview, January 15, 2021.
20. John Knott, "'Dealing' Has 3 Candidates for Stars of Tomorrow," Memphis *Commercial Appeal,* February 10, 1972.
21. Grodin, *It Would Be So Nice If You Weren't Here,* 190.
22. Simon to Brady, *The Craft of the Screenwriter,* 330.
23. Grodin, *It Would Be So Nice If You Weren't Here,* 190.
24. Simon to Brady, *The Craft of the Screenwriter,* 330–31.
25. May, interview by Rosenthal, *Naked Lunch.*
26. Simon to Brady, *The Craft of the Screenwriter,* 331.
27. Rachel Abramowitz, *Is That a Gun in Your Pocket?: Women's Experience of Power in Hollywood* (New York: Random House, 2000), 64.
28. Preminger, author interview.
29. Cybill Shepherd, *Cybill Disobedience* (New York: HarperCollins, 2000), 109–110.
30. Cybill Shepherd, author interview, April 16, 2021.
31. Abramowitz, *Is That a Gun in Your Pocket?* 64.
32. Preminger, author interview.
33. Grodin, *It Would Be So Nice If You Weren't Here,* 190–91.

34. Simon to Brady, *The Craft of the Screenwriter,* 329–30.
35. Simon to Brady, *The Craft of the Screenwriter,* 330.
36. Simon to Brady, *The Craft of the Screenwriter,* 331.
37. May, interview by Rosenthal, *Naked Lunch.*
38. Sidney Fields, "The Face Is Familiar, but . . . ," New York *Daily News,* April 26, 1972.
39. Grodin, *It Would Be So Nice If You Weren't Here,* 192.
40. Fields, "The Face Is Familiar."
41. David Streit, author interview, February 17, 2022.
42. Will Jones, "Elaine May Runs Her Movie Set with an Unobtrusive Hand," *Minneapolis Tribune,* April 2, 1972.
43. Streit, author interview.
44. Preminger, author interview.
45. Michael Hausman, author interview, September 22, 2020.
46. Jones, "Elaine May Runs Her Movie Set with an Unobtrusive Hand."
47. Shepherd, *Cybill Disobedience,* 112.
48. Sam Wasson, *Improv Nation: How We Made a Great American Art* (Boston: Houghton Mifflin Harcourt, 2017), 159.
49. Hausman, author interview.
50. Preminger, author interview.
51. Grodin, *It Would Be So Nice If You Weren't Here,* 191–92.
52. Shepherd, author interview.
53. Shepherd, *Cybill Disobedience,* 111.
54. Preminger, author interview.
55. Boon, "Will Jeannie Berlin Win an Oscar Too?"
56. Gruen, "More Than Elaine May's Daughter."
57. Like, in 1971, a direct request from Gregory Peck to appear at a gala fundraiser for the Motion Picture & Television Fund ("Letter from Mike Nichols to Gregory Peck," February 10, 1971, Gregory Peck Papers–Motion Picture and Television Fund–50th Anniversary Celebration, Margaret Herrick Library).
58. Val Adams, "Best of Nichols & May," New York *Daily News,* May 26, 1972. See also Norma Lee Browning, "Hollywood Today," *Chicago Tribune,* May 26, 1972.
59. Norma Lee Browning, "Hollywood Today," *Chicago Tribune,* June 5, 1972. An ad appearing in the *Chicago Tribune* on June 12, 1972, apologizing for the cancellation, indicated that they would be rescheduled at a future date, which never happened.
60. Will Jones, "After Last Night," *Minneapolis Tribune,* June 12, 1972.
61. Joyce Haber, "Nichols and May Do Benefit," *Los Angeles Times,* June 17, 1972.
62. McCandlish Phillips, "Rock 'n' Rhetoric Rally in the Garden Aids McGovern," *New York Times,* June 15, 1972.
63. Ken Wallace, "Nichols and May May Team Again," *Hackensack Record,* June 8, 1972.
64. Mel Gussow, "Nichols, Fortune Made, Looks to the Future," *New York Times,* June 3, 1975.
65. Gussow, "Nichols, Fortune Made, Looks to the Future."
66. For *The Heartbreak Kid,* Elaine sought out director of photography Owen Roizman, known at the time for his Academy Award–nominated work on *The French Connection.* "I don't want it to look like a comedy," she told him, although the extent of her technical vocabulary amounted to "I want New York to be gray and Florida to be golden and I want, when they get to the end, where there's snow, to be white" (May, interview by Rosenthal, *Naked Lunch*).
67. May, interview by Leonard Probst. Appears in Probst, *Off Camera: Leveling About Themselves* (New York: Stein and Day, 1975), 135.
68. Vincent Canby, "Film: 'Heartbreak Kid,'" *New York Times,* December 18, 1972.
69. Roger Ebert, "Heartbreak Kid," *Chicago Sun-Times,* January 1, 1972.

70. Pauline Kael, "The Current Cinema," *New Yorker,* December 8, 1972.

71. Daniel Bernardi, Murray Pomerance, and Hava Tirosh-Samuelson, eds., *Hollywood's Chosen People: The Jewish Experience in American Cinema* (Detroit: Wayne State University Press, 2013), 5–7.

72. Steven J. Ross, ed., *From Shtetl to Stardom: Jews and Hollywood* (West Lafayette, IN: Purdue University Press, 2017), 7.

73. Ross, *From Shtetl to Stardom,* 9.

74. Robert F. Moss, "'Blume' and 'Heartbreak Kid'—What Kind of Jews Are They?" *New York Times,* September 9, 1973.

75. Henry Bial, *Acting Jewish: Negotiating Ethnicity on the American Stage & Screen* (Ann Arbor: University of Michigan Press, 2005), 3–4.

76. Actress and comedian Sarah Silverman refers to the problem as "Jewface": "There's this long tradition of non-Jews playing Jews, and not just playing people who happen to be Jewish but people whose Jewishness is their whole being. It's defined as when a non-Jew portrays a Jew with the Jewishness front and center, often with makeup or changing of features, big fake nose, all the New York-y or Yiddish-y inflection. And in a time when the importance of representation is seen as so essential and so front and center, why does ours constantly get breached even today in the thick of it?" (Sarah Silverman, "Jewface, Iron Dome, Mr. Mom," *The Sarah Silverman Podcast,* September 30, 2021).

77. Henry Kellerman, *Greedy, Cowardly, and Weak: Hollywood Jewish Stereotypes* (Fort Lee, NJ: Barricade Books, 2009), 65.

78. Moss, "'Blume' and 'Heartbreak Kid'—What Kind of Jews Are They?"

79. Moss, "'Blume' and 'Heartbreak Kid'—What Kind of Jews Are They?"

80. May, interview by Rosenthal, *Naked Lunch.*

81. Gruen, "More Than Elaine May's Daughter."

82. Boon, "Will Jeannie Berlin Win an Oscar Too?"

83. May, interview by Rosenthal, *Naked Lunch.*

84. May, interview by Rosenthal, *Naked Lunch.*

85. May, interview by Leonard Probst. Appears in excerpts published in Michael Rivlin, "Elaine May: Too Tough for Hollywood?" *Millimeter* 3, no. 10 (1975).

86. May, interview by Probst, *Millimeter* excerpts.

87. See Marion Meade, "Lights! Camera! Women!" *New York Times*, April 25, 1971.

88. Barbara Koenig Quart, *Women Directors: The Emergence of a New Cinema* (New York: Praeger, 1988), 42.

89. Molly Haskell, *From Reverence to Rape: The Treatment of Women in the Movies* (Harmondsworth, UK: Penguin Books, 1974), 353.

90. Joan Mellen, *Women and Their Sexuality in the New Film* (New York: Horizon Press, 1973), 42.

91. Marjorie Rosen, *Popcorn Venus: Women, Movies & the American Dream* (New York: Coward, McCann & Geoghegan, 1973), 363–64.

92. May, interview by Probst, *Off Camera* excerpts, 133.

CHAPTER 7: TWO STOLEN REELS AND A CLOWN CAR

1. Stephen Farer, "You See Yourself in 'Heartbreak,'" *New York Times,* February 18, 1973.

2. Andrew Tobias, "Elaine May: A New Film, but Not a New Leaf," *New York,* December 6, 1976.

3. Rachel Abramowitz, *Is That a Gun in Your Pocket? Women's Experience of Power in Hollywood* (New York: Random House, 2000), 67. This story is backed up by Todd McCarthy, author interview, September 18, 2022.

4. May, interview by Leonard Probst. Appears in excerpts published in Michael Rivlin, "Elaine May: Too Tough for Hollywood?" *Millimeter* 3, no. 10 (1975).

5. May, interview by Probst, *Millimeter* excerpts.

6. Janet Coleman, *The Compass: The Improvisational Theatre That Revolutionized American Comedy* (Chicago: University of Chicago Press, 1990), 65. It also shows up as one of five May-authored productions Shepherd wanted to stage at the Compass in a list in his journal from 1956 (journal entry, undated between November–December 1956, page 80 in 1956–1959 journal, David Shepherd Papers, University of Chicago, Box 1, Folder 9).

7. Elaine May, interview with Haden Guest, Harvard Film Archive, November 12, 2010.

8. D. D. Ryan, "Peter Falk," *Interview*, November 1976.

9. May, interview by Guest.

10. May, interview by Guest.

11. May, interview by Guest.

12. Shipping, or the act of rooting for two fictional characters to be romantically involved, has been a fixture in TV and internet fandom for decades. Originating with fans of *The X-Files* who couldn't get over the sexual tension between Mulder and Scully, it's only grown in prevalence since the nineties. Today it is often applied to real people, too—not just characters—to uncomfortable effect.

13. Tom Miller papers, *Mikey and Nicky*, publicity, File 108, Margaret Herrick Library.

14. A. B. Weiler, "Movies," *New York Times*, November 21, 1971.

15. Julian Schlossberg, "Joyce Van Patten and Julian Schlossberg," *Mikey and Nicky—Bonus Materials,* produced by Kim Hendrickson (Criterion, 2019).

16. Tom Canford (Miller), *A Fever of the Mad* (Sawyerville: Hollow Square Press, 2013), 81.

17. Michael Hausman, author interview, September 22, 2020.

18. May, interview by Guest.

19. Canford, *A Fever of the Mad,* 74.

20. May, interview by Guest.

21. Peter Falk, *Just One More Thing: Stories from My Life* (New York: Carroll & Graf, 2006), 228.

22. May, interview by Guest.

23. "Peter Falk on pitching Elaine May's 'Mikey and Nicky' to John Cassavetes," YouTube, https://www.youtube.com/watch?v=6AKEaH2qWl0. Source host unkown.

24. Tom Miller papers, *Mikey and Nicky*, publicity.

25. Tom Miller papers, *Mikey and Nicky*, publicity.

26. Hausman, author interview.

27. Abramowitz, *Is That a Gun in Your Pocket?*, 66.

28. May, interview by Probst, *Millimeter* excerpts.

29. May, interview by Guest.

30. Hausman, author interview.

31. Tom Miller papers, *Mikey and Nicky*, publicity. See also Canford, *A Fever of the Mad,* 68.

32. "Nola [Saffro, Elaine's assistant] is tired, hungry, eats all the wrong kind of food—never gets enough rest, no time for herself, is getting very tired of it all" (Tom Miller papers, *Mikey and Nicky*, publicity).

33. One she claims was so bad she fired him four times, though she doesn't account for the fact that she brought him back three times (May, interview by Phil Rosenthal, *Naked Lunch* July 21, 2022, https://open.spotify.com/episode/30cveCd824JIcwDRe5bnUf?si=3f1a9b54cd3f431e).

34. May, interview by Rosenthal, *Naked Lunch.*

35. Hausman, author interview. A similar version of this incident was recounted by Victor Kemper, "Interviews," *Mikey and Nicky Bonus Materials,* DVD produced by Sonia Rosario (Home Vision Entertainment, 2004).

36. Canford, *A Fever of the Mad,* 44.
37. "Letter from Tom Miller to Larry Fields," June 9, 1973, Tom Miller Papers, Margaret Herrick Library.
38. Dan Rottenberg, "Elaine May . . . or She May Not," *Chicago Tribune,* October 21, 1973, 55.
39. Hausman, author interview.
40. Kemper, "Interviews." *Mikey and Nicky Bonus Materials.*
41. May, interview by Guest.
42. Abramowitz, *Is That a Gun in Your Pocket?,* 66–67; backed up by Sheldon Kahn, author interview, March 11, 2022.
43. Todd McCarthy, author interview, September 18, 2022.
44. McCarthy, author interview.
45. Kahn, author interview.
46. Kahn, author interview.
47. Kahn, author interview.
48. Kahn, author interview.
49. McCarthy, author interview.
50. Kahn, author interview.
51. McCarthy, author interview.
52. McCarthy, author interview; Tobias, "Elaine May: A New Film, but Not a New Leaf."
53. McCarthy, author interview.
54. Tobias, "Elaine May: A New Film, but Not a New Leaf."
55. Tobias, "Elaine May: A New Film, but Not a New Leaf."
56. May, interview by Probst, *Millimeter* excerpts.
57. Barry Diller, author interview, September 26, 2022.
58. May, interview by Probst, *Millimeter* excerpts.
59. Diller, author interview.
60. Hausman, author interview.
61. McCarthy, author interview.
62. McCarthy, author interview.
63. Why might Diller not remember the incident—which has been reported in both Rachel Abramowitz's *Is That a Gun in Your Pocket?* and recounted by Todd McCarthy? The memory lapse can be explained, perhaps, by the fact that by all appearances, he got got by Elaine May, and she won more than one battle against him, including ones like this. The memory would be demoralizing, borderline dehumanizing, and *deeply* embarrassing. A reminder: It's not just what people remember that you should question, but what they do not.
64. Diller, author interview.
65. Abramowitz, *Is That a Gun in Your Pocket?,* 67.
66. Hausman, author interview.
67. Jim Harwood, "Suits Fly as Par, Elaine May Bicker Over 'Mikey' Pic," *Variety,* October 22, 1975.
68. McCarthy, author interview.
69. McCarthy, author interview.
70. Diller, author interview.
71. Coleman, *The Compass,* 295.
72. "Par, Elaine May Sue Each Other; Film Over-Budget and Incomplete," *Variety,* October 29, 1975.
73. Diller, author interview.
74. "Par, Elaine May Sue Each Other."
75. May, interview by Guest.
76. Ken Auletta, "Hollywood Ending," *New Yorker,* July 24, 2006.
77. "Par Seeks Contempt Action vs. May, Husband In 'Mikey' Battle," *Variety,* September 13, 1976.

78. "Par Seeks Contempt Action."
79. "Par Charges Criminal Conduct in 'Mikey' Suit Vs. Elaine May," *Variety*, September 15, 1976.
80. May, interview by Guest.
81. Auletta, "Hollywood Ending."
82. Peter Biskind, "Thunder on the Left: The Making of *Reds*." *Vanity Fair*, January 22, 2007.
83. Hausman, author interview.
84. Coleman, *The Compass*, 146.
85. McCarthy, author interview.
86. Coleman, *The Compass*, 147.
87. May, interview by Guest.
88. Tobias, "Elaine May: A New Film, but Not a New Leaf."
89. May, interview by Guest.
90. Tobias, "Elaine May: A New Film, but Not a New Leaf." In Diller's version of the story, "Elaine and I had a conversation, and agreed that someone would go to a street corner or somewhere in New York and there the film would be, and that's what happened" (author interview with Barry Diller).
91. May, interview by Guest.
92. May, interview by Guest.
93. Julian Schlossberg, author interview, March 18, 2021.
94. Aileen Mehle, "Everybody Out to the Slopes," New York *Daily News*, December 15, 1976.
95. Julian Schlossberg, "Joyce Van Patten and Julian Schlossberg," *Mikey and Nicky Bonus Materials*.
96. John Simon, "May, Bogdanovich, and Streisand: Varieties of Death Wish," *New York*, January 10, 1977, 55.
97. Vincent Canby, "'Mikey and Nicky,' Film on Amity," *New York Times*, December 22, 1976, 34.
98. Canby, "'Mikey and Nicky,' Film on Amity."
99. From 1974 to 1975, only 1.54 percent (46 total) of the DGA's members were women (Maya Montañez Smukler, *Liberating Hollywood: Women Directors and the Feminist Reform of 1970s American Cinema* [New Brunswick: Rutgers University Press, 2019], 239).
100. Smukler, *Liberating Hollywood*, 243–45.
101. Kirk Honeycutt, "Women Film Directors: Will They, Too, Be Allowed to Bomb?," *New York Times*, August 6, 1978.
102. Sally Ogle, "The Struggle of Women Directors," *New York Times*, January 11, 1981.
103. McCarthy, author interview.
104. Peter Biskind, *Easy Riders, Raging Bulls: How the Sex-Drugs-and-Rock'n'Roll Generation Saved Hollywood* (New York: Simon & Schuster, 1998), 325.
105. Elaine May, interview by Mike Nichols, Film Society of Lincoln Center, February 26, 2006.
106. May, interview by Probst, *Millimeter* excerpts.
107. May, interview by Probst, *Millimeter* excerpts.

CHAPTER 8: NOTHING WAS A STRAIGHT LINE

1. Liz Smith, "Elaine May and Mike Nichols Now Doing Radio Commercials," *Baltimore Sun*, January 17, 1977.
2. Author interview with Erik Lee Preminger
3. Chris Fujiwara, *The World and Its Double: The Life and Work of Otto Preminger* (New York: Faber and Faber, 2008), 428.
4. Preminger, author interview.

5. Preminger, author interview.
6. Erik Lee Preminger estimates that it was less than nine weeks; he thinks close to six. Otto Preminger's biographer Chris Fujiwara places the timeline at ten (Fujiwara, *The World and Its Double,* 428–29).
7. "Elaine May Again," *Variety,* December 8, 1971.
8. Preminger, author interview.
9. Elaine May, American Film Institute Life Achievement Award gala, Tribute to Warren Beatty, June 12, 2008.
10. Charles Champlin, "Warren Beatty: Two Sides to a Hollywood Story," *Los Angeles Times,* January 29, 1979.
11. Champlin, "Warren Beatty."
12. Champlin, "Warren Beatty."
13. Newspaper reports wouldn't announce her involvement until March 1977 (see Emery Wister, "'It's Alive' May Be Year's Shocker," *Charlotte News,* March 14, 1977), although AMPAS has a script credited to her name dated as early as October 1976.
14. "Paramount intercommunication from Edith Tolkin to Julian Powden, Subj: HEAVEN CAN WAIT," February 24, 1977, *Heaven Can Wait* credits, File H-233, Margaret Herrick Library, Academy of Motion Pictures Arts and Sciences.
15. "Memo: Notice of tentative writing credits to the Writers Guild of America," January 6, 1978, *Heaven Can Wait* credits, File H-233, Margaret Herrick Library, Academy of Motion Pictures Arts and Sciences. The final film would be credited as "Screenplay by Elaine May and Warren Beatty."
16. Warren Beatty, interview with Ben Mankiewicz, TCM Classic Film Festival, April 23, 2022.
17. Peter Biskind, *Star: How Warren Beatty Seduced America* (New York: Simon & Schuster, 2010), 237–38.
18. Vincent Canby, "Let's Hear It for the Belly Laugh," *New York Times,* July 9, 1978.
19. Elaine May, *Heaven Can Wait,* marked first draft, undated, Margaret Herrick Library, Academy of Motion Pictures Arts and Sciences.
20. Dyan Cannon, author interview, January 14, 2021.
21. Cannon, author interview.
22. Biskind, *Star,* 235.
23. Charles Grodin, *It Would Be So Nice If You Weren't Here: My Journey Through Show Business* (New York: Vintage Books, 1990), 250.
24. Biskind, *Star,* 240.
25. As for Henry's writer's credit, Beatty explains that the WGA would not allow him to receive credit, so as a consolation, he was offered co-director instead (Beatty, interview by Mankiewicz).
26. Elaine May, American Film Institute Life Achievement Award gala, Tribute to Warren Beatty, June 12, 2008.
27. Biskind, *Star,* 269.
28. Biskind, *Star,* 260.
29. Jeremy Pikser, author interview, June 23, 2021.
30. Pikser, author interview.
31. Biskind, *Star,* 296.
32. Pikser, author interview.
33. Pikser, author interview.
34. Pikser, author interview.
35. Pikser, author interview.
36. Pikser, author interview. See also Peter Biskind, "Thunder on the Left: The Making of *Reds,*" *Vanity Fair,* January 22, 2007.
37. Reports on exactly when the film wrapped vary; according to a March 26, 1980, *Variety* article (via https://catalog.afi.com/Film/56684-REDS) and an

April 1980 article (Desmond Ryan, "Beatty Directs, Stars, and Goes in the Red," *Philadelphia Inquirer,* April 6, 1980), production was only just coming to a close in Europe that spring. Meanwhile, a New York *Daily News* gossip column said it "has been shooting for more than a year" in July 1980 (Marilyn Beck, "Don't Blink, or Brenda's 'Sin,'" New York *Daily News,* July 10, 1980).

38. Cindy Kaplan Rooney, author interview, May 16, 2022.
39. "At one point, we had about seventy people on the crew all the way from top to bottom," per Cindy Rooney.
40. Biskind, *Star,* 289–91, supported by Rooney: "I don't want to belittle the idea of being in the army, but you knew that you were signing on to something, you know what I mean? We worked very, very long hours most of the time. . . . I felt under a lot of pressure. I think everybody did, but people were really on board with the project. It's just that it was so unwieldy."
41. Rooney, author interview.
42. Feibleman to Biskind, *Star,* 231.
43. Rooney, author interview.
44. Phillip Schopper, author interview, July 18, 2021.
45. Brad Fuller, author interview, August 11, 2021.
46. Rooney, author interview.
47. Anne Thompson, "Warren Beatty Talks Hollywood Legends, Humanizing Howard Hughes and More in Career-Spanning IndieWire Interview," *IndieWire,* November 16, 2016.
48. Pikser recalls Elaine saying, on the matter of payment: "'I don't get money from Warren. I get other things from him.' And she didn't mean sex. She meant power. Political power in Hollywood."
49. Rooney, author interview.
50. Biskind, *Star,* 308; anecdote also recalled by Rooney.
51. Biskind, *Star,* 311. Backed up by Rooney that they were "conferring right up to the end."
52. Pikser, author interview.
53. Pikser, author interview.
54. Pikser, author interview.
55. Warren Beatty, Fifty-Fourth Annual Academy Awards, March 29, 1982.
56. Guy Flatley, "Blood and Funny Are the Range of Mike Nichols' Remarkable Back-to-Back Hits on Broadway," *People,* January 10, 1977, via Mark Harris, *Mike Nichols: A Director's Life* (New York: Penguin Press, 2021), 314.
57. Robin Adams Sloan, "Frost's Problem: Keeping the Freeze on His Nixon Tapes," New York *Daily News*, October 12, 1975.
58. Carolyn Lawson, "Nichols Returning with 2 Shows," *New York Times,* June 20, 1979.
59. Harris, *Mike Nichols,* 347.
60. Brown to Harris, *Mike Nichols,* 345.
61. Swoosie Kurtz, author interview, July 1, 2021.
62. Kurtz, author interview.
63. Kurtz, author interview.
64. Harris, *Mike Nichols,* 119.
65. Kurtz, author interview.
66. James Naughton, author interview, August 6, 2021.
67. Kurtz, author interview.
68. Naughton, author interview.
69. Kurtz, author interview.
70. Naughton, author interview.
71. Kurtz, author interview.
72. Naughton, author interview.

73. Frank Rich, "Who's Afraid of Nichols and May?" *New York Times,* May 4, 1980.

74. Elaine May, Mike Nichols in conversation at MoMA, April 18, 2009.

75. Susan Dworkin, *Making Tootsie: A Film Study with Dustin Hoffman and Sydney Pollack* (New York: Newmarket Press, 1983), 6.

76. Dustin Hoffman to James Andrew Miller, *Powerhouse: The Untold Story of Hollywood's Creative Arts Agency* (New York: Custom House, 2016), 195–96.

77. Marilyn Beck, "Credit Where Credit Is Due Sometimes Escapes a Script," New York *Daily News,* August 31, 1980.

78. Elaine May, *Tootsie,* March 22, 1982, revisions, Sydney Pollack Papers, Margaret Herrick Library, Academy of Motion Pictures Arts and Sciences Library.

79. Dustin Hoffman, to Sam Wasson, *Improv Nation: How We Made a Great American Art* (Boston: Houghton Mifflin Harcourt, 2017), 264.

80. Dustin Hoffman to James Andrew Miller, *Powerhouse,* 196.

81. Sydney Pollack, DVD commentary, *Tootsie* (Criterion Collection, 2014).

82. Pollack, DVD commentary.

83. "Girl who has a son—No husband—drinks too much," Elaine May, handwritten note on *Tootsie,* February 8, 1982, revisions, Sydney Pollack Papers, Margaret Herrick Library, Academy of Motion Pictures Arts and Sciences Library.

84. Pollack, DVD commentary.

85. Pollack, DVD commentary.

86. Elaine May, Mike Nichols in conversation at MoMA.

87. Elaine May, *Tootsie,* March 22, 1982, revisions, Sydney Pollack Papers, Margaret Herrick Library, Academy of Motion Pictures Arts and Sciences Library.

88. Hoffman to Wasson, *Improv Nation,* 264.

89. Memo, "Revised copy of redlined contract from January 22, 1982," February 5, 1982, *Tootsie*—legal (writers credits), File 1769, Sydney Pollack Papers, Margaret Herrick Library, Academy of Motion Pictures Arts and Sciences Library. At the time, rumors swirled that Elaine picked up $450,000 for her work, though Pollack denied that exact amount. See Aljean Harmetz, "Is Columbia Facing End of a Long Cycle of Hits?" *New York Times,* May 20, 1982.

90. Memo, "Revised copy of redlined contract from January 22, 1982," February 5, 1982, *Tootsie*—legal (writers credits), File 1769, Sydney Pollack Papers, Margaret Herrick Library, Academy of Motion Pictures Arts and Sciences Library. As for how her name got out: "The Writers Guild resolved credits on 'Tootsie,' with screenplay going to Larry Gelbart and Murray Schisgal and story by Don McGuire and Gelbart. Elaine May wanted no credit" ("Just for Variety," *Variety,* November 15, 1982). This is backed up by a slew of frustrated communication between the WGA and Pollack's office as the WGA attempted to gather all versions of the script to sort out credits—Sydney Pollack Papers, Margaret Herrick Library.

91. Western Union Mailgram from Sydney Pollack to Elaine May, December 22, 1982, *Tootsie*—New York Film Critics, File 1781, Sydney Pollack Papers, Margaret Herrick Library, Academy of Motion Pictures Arts and Sciences Library.

92. Author interview with Julian Schlossberg, April 1, 2021.

93. David Blum, "The Road to Ishtar," *New York,* March 16, 1987.

94. "Townhouse Tussle Goes to Court," *New York Post,* October 6, 1988. She had owned the brownstone at 320 Riverside Drive since 1973. (Mortgage between 326 West 89 Realty Corp and Genie Productions, November 28, 1973; ACRIS file FT_18300008529883). By 1981, she was living in the San Remo. See Phil Roura and Tom Poster, "Elaine May Has a Neighborly Case," New York *Daily News,* October 12, 1983.

95. Marlo Thomas, *Growing Up Laughing: My Story and the Story of Funny* (New York: Hyperion, 2010), 328.

96. Don Shewey, "On the Go with David Geffen," *New York Times,* July 21, 1983.

97. Jules Fisher, author interview, April 1, 2021.

98. Suzy, "White House—A Home for the Holidays," New York *Daily News*, December 23, 1983.

99. For a great deal of the twenty-four years they knew each other, Lillian Hellman hated Elaine, "nurturing a grudge that started because Elaine was Mike Nichols' friend and continued because she was my friend," Peter Feibleman wrote in *Lilly: Reminiscences of Lillian Hellman* (New York: Morrow, 1988). But in the final years of Hellman's life, with a little matchmaker work over the span of a weekend in Martha's Vineyard from Feibleman, the two grew close. Elaine "knew when and how to argue with Lilly and for how long," he wrote. "Not since Dorothy Parker had Lilly sat down with a woman who could partner her in all the games she liked, silly and serious games not yet invented—someone she could count on to play fancy champion badminton with words and never drop the bird" (*Lilly*, 289–90). When Hellman died, Elaine found a letter from her that had gone unopened; Elaine had sent Hellman a box of cigars to encourage her to switch from cigarettes: "I don't know whether I can accept cigars from a woman I can't get on the phone" (*Lilly*, 346).

100. Liz Smith, "A True Confession for John Travolta," New York *Daily News*, July 11, 1982.

101. Author interview with Phillip Schopper, October 16, 2021, confirms she was asked by Bill to polish the film. Bill Murray quote source: Bill Murray, Governors Awards, March 25, 2022.

102. Nancy Mills, "Emergency Call," *Los Angeles Times,* June 22, 1986.

103. Adrian Wooton, "Jonathan Demme," *Guardian,* October 10, 1998.

104. Wasson, *Improv Nation*, 308.

105. Shewey, "On the Go with David Geffen."

106. Elaine May, Mike Nichols in conversation at MoMA.

107. Patrick Goldstein, "They All Have a Secret," *Los Angeles Times,* March 15, 1998. See also Mike Nichols, *The Birdcage: The Shooting Script* (New York: Newmarket Press, 1977).

108. Carrie Rickey, "A Working Woman's Will to Win," *Philadelphia Inquirer*, December 21, 1988.

109. Caroline Aaron, author interview, September 2, 2022.

110. John Gregory Dunne, *Monster: Living Off the Big Screen* (New York: Vintage Books, 1998), 51–52. Ultimately, though, the concept didn't pan out, despite excitement from its members and Hollywood agents: "Elaine, Peter, Joan, and I had a number of very funny meetings and even funnier lunches, but in the end nothing actually came of the DBA Company, because after each of us had exempted those picture-makers with whom we had long-term professional and personal relationships, there were very few people left to share."

111. Marilyn Beck, "Credit Where Credit Is Due Sometimes Escapes a Script."

112. May, interview by Rosenthal, *Naked Lunch.*

113. Julian Schlossberg, author interview, March 18, 2021. Corroborated by author interview with Schopper, October 16, 2021.

114. Kashner, "Who's Afraid of Nichols and May?"

115. May, interview by Rosenthal, *Naked Lunch.*

116. "You don't need the publicity for you to be able to get the work. You don't run around saying, 'This script I got was so terrible, I had to really work on that one,'" says Schopper. "That won't get you your next job" (author interview with Phillip Schopper, October 16, 2021).

117. "Par Charges Criminal Conduct in 'Mikey' Suit vs. Elaine May," *Variety,* September 15, 1976

118. Stephen Farber and Marc Green, *Hollywood on the Couch: A Candid Look at the Overheated Love Affair Between Psychiatrists and Moviemakers* (New York: William Morrow, 1993), 214.

119. Farber and Green, *Hollywood on the Couch*, 209–10.

120. Farber and Green, *Hollywood on the Couch*, 212.

121. Deborah Hautzig, author interview, September 14, 2022.

122. Bernadette Mayer, interview by Adam Fitzgerald, "Lives of the Poets: Bernadette Mayer," Poetry Foundation, September 2010, https://www.poetryfoundation.org/articles/69658/lives-of-the-poets-bernadette-mayer.

123. David Rubinfine, Introduction to *Memory* by Bernadette Mayer (Vermont: North Atlantic Books, 1975), 5.

124. David Rubinfine to Bernadette Mayer, Bernadette Mayer Papers, 1958–2017, University of California San Diego, Box 13, Folder 18.

125. Farber and Green, *Hollywood on the Couch*, 212.

126. Milton Wexler to Farber and Green, *Hollywood on the Couch*, 210.

127. Julian Schlossberg, author interview, April 1, 2021.

128. Per confidential source, corroborated by author interview with Deborah Hautzig. Additionally, Penny Rubinfine published a paper in which she cites the loss of her mother at a young age and the sudden death of her father causing her to struggle "to understand my now parentless life and the absences in and outside of me," suggesting the absence of the stepmother who raised her for a great deal of her adolescence (Penny Rubinfine, "In the Pursuit of Absence: Reimagining Early Loss Within the Psychotherapy Relationship," *Psychoanalytic Dialogues* 26, no. 5 [2016]: 549–63, doi: 10.1080/10481885.2016.1214466).

129. Author interview with Phillip Schopper, October 16, 2021. See also: "Jeannie isn't speaking to Mama. One reason: Elaine made her do like 37 takes of the crying scene in the movie, then made her come back to do more takes" (Joyce Haber, "Guessing Game: Who'll Play MacArthur?" *Los Angeles Times,* January 8, 1973).

130. Stanley Eichelbaum, "A Truce for Shooting," *San Francisco Examiner,* February 3, 1974.

131. Elaine May, "Hotline," *Death Defying Acts: 3 One-Act Comedies* (New York: Samuel French, 1995), 46.

132. Schlossberg, author interview.

133. Earl Wilson, "Marlo Won't Talk About Private Life," (Long Beach, CA) *Independent Press-Telegram,* February 20, 1977.

134. Marilyn Beck, "Marlo Thomas Makes Comeback in 'Lost Honor,'" New York *Daily News,* December 23, 1983. It was brought up again in 2004 as one of Thomas's upcoming projects (James Brady, "In Step with Marlo Thomas," *Parade,* November 21, 2004).

135. Liz Smith, "Merrill: Met Treated Me Badly," New York *Daily News,* March 13, 1979.

136. Marilyn Beck, "After These 5 Years, Vadim Does It Differently," New York *Daily News,* December 23, 1983.

137. Phil Roura and Tom Poster, "Here and There . . . ," New York *Daily News,* June 11, 1979.

138. Mel Gussow, "Theatre: The Past Is Present," *New York Times,* August 26, 1979.

139. "Reunion, Literarily Speaking," New York *Daily News,* July 31, 1984.

140. Liz Smith, "Diane Arbus Film Still Coming Into Focus," New York *Daily News,* June 20, 1984.

141. Trevor Thomas, "A Playwright's Humorous Tough Talk," *San Francisco Examiner,* July 22, 1984. Multiple clippings from 1984 include references to the pair working on a screenplay. An inventory of David Mamet's papers at the Harry Ransom Center, the University of Texas at Austin, indicates that the work in question were early drafts of *State and Main.*

142. Elaine May, *The False Inspector Dew,* Green Draft, February 9, 1984. Received via email from Joe Martino.

143. David Blum, "The Road to Ishtar: How Warren Beatty, Dustin Hoffman, and Elaine May Made a Farce in the Desert for Just $40 Million," *New York,* March 16, 1987.

CHAPTER 9: DANGEROUS BUSINESS

1. G. Mac Brown, author interview, June 3, 2022. See also photo from set included in spread for Peter Biskind, "Madness in Morocco: The Road to *Ishtar,*" *Vanity Fair,* February 2010.
2. "Listen," *Los Angeles Times,* June 12, 1987.
3. Elaine May, interview by Haden Guest, Harvard Film Archive, November 13, 2010.
4. May, interview by Guest.
5. Elaine May, interview by David Schwartz, 92nd Street Y, May 17, 2011, from S. T. VanAirsdale, "Blind Camels, Idiot Execs, and 5 Other *Ishtar* Revelations from Director Elaine May," *Movieline,* May 18, 2011.
6. May, interview by Guest.
7. Pat H. Broeske, "The High Cost of 'Ishtar,'" *Los Angeles Times,* May 24, 1987.
8. May, interview by Guest.
9. Peter Biskind, *Star: How Warren Beatty Seduced America* (New York: Simon & Schuster, 2010), 326.
10. Bob Strauss, "On the Road to 'Ishtar' with Beatty and Hoffman," *Chicago Sun-Times,* May 10, 1987.
11. Mary Ellin Barrett, "50 Beatty / 50 Hoffman," *USA Weekend,* May 15–17, 1987.
12. Broeske, "The High Cost of 'Ishtar.'"
13. Broeske, "The High Cost of 'Ishtar.'"
14. "You have to be very careful if you're going to say no to something of Warren's, because his record as a producer-star is almost 1,000 percent. It probably *is* 1,000 percent in terms of just recouping on a per-picture basis, cash" (Guy McElwaine to David Blum, "The Road to Ishtar: How Warren Beatty, Dustin Hoffman, and Elaine May Made a Farce in the Desert for Just $40 Million," *New York,* March 16, 1987).
15. Biskind, *Star,* 335.
16. Biskind, *Star,* 335.
17. Biskind, *Star,* 335–36.
18. Paul Williams, author interview, September 2, 2021.
19. Williams, author interview.
20. Williams, author interview.
21. The final breakdown: five songs with lyrics and music by Paul Williams; four songs with lyrics by Elaine May, music by others; four songs with lyrics by Elaine May, music by Paul Williams; two songs with lyrics by Elaine May and Paul Williams, music by Paul Williams (all ten of Elaine's penned songs appear in at least partial form in the October 11, 1985, revised copy of the script).
22. Army Archerd, "Just for Variety," *Variety,* November 1, 1985.
23. "Columbia Pictures Revised Its HBO deal," *Los Angeles Times,* April 19, 1985.
24. Michael C. Jensen, "Coca-Cola Is Pressing Efforts to Uncork Arab Markets," *New York Times,* March 29, 1978.
25. "Zingers," *Los Angeles Herald Examiner,* May 13, 1987.
26. In Coca-Cola's 1985 annual report, the company's corporate assets (principally marketable securities, investments, and fixed assets) accounted for $873.1 million at the end of 1984, and $942.3 million at the end of 1985 (the Coca-Cola Company Annual Report 1985, https://pdfslide.net/documents/the-coca-cola-company-1985-annual-report.html?page=5).
27. May, interview by Nichols, Film Society of Lincoln Center, February 26, 2006.

28. Camel meat may be a delicacy, but camels also often carry syphilis, so there's a fair chance that last part was thrown in for dramatic effect (Peter Biskind, "Inside Ishtar," *American Film,* May 1, 1987. Story also told in Biskind, "Madness in Morocco: The Road to Ishtar").

29. "Paralysis descended on the set," Hoffman to Biskind, *Star,* 351.

30. Blum, "The Road to Ishtar."

31. Broeske, "The High Cost of 'Ishtar.'"

32. Biskind, *Star,* 354.

33. Stephen Rotter, author interview, July 27, 2021.

34. Biskind, *Star,* 349.

35. Biskind, *Star,* 349.

36. Phillip Schopper, author interview, July 18, 2021.

37. May, interview by Nichols.

38. Schopper, author interview, July 18, 2021.

39. Schopper, author interview, July 18, 2021.

40. Biskind, *Star,* 351.

41. Brown, author interview.

42. Williams, author interview.

43. May, interview by Schwartz.

44. Ida died around 1972; Tom Miller notes talking to her cousin Jackie and gathering biographical information about Elaine: "Elaine's mother was fat. Died last year of cancer. Came on suddenly; she was gone suddenly. A heavy smoker" (Tom Miller papers, Academy Library).

45. Schopper, author interview, October 16, 2021.

46. Blum, "The Road to Ishtar."

47. Rotter, author interview.

48. Brown, author interview.

49. Brown, author interview.

50. Brown, author interview.

51. Blum, "The Road to Ishtar."

52. Brown, author interview.

53. Brown, author interview.

54. "[Warren Beatty] is strong-willed and I liked him a lot, but I don't know, she just had this way of waiting everybody out," (Rotter, to author).

55. Brown, author interview.

56. Wasson, *Improv Nation,* 297.

57. Schopper, author interview, October 16, 2021.

58. Williams, author interview.

59. Blum, "The Road to Ishtar."

60. Peter Biskind, "Inside Ishtar," *American Film* 12 (May 1987).

61. Biskind, "Inside Ishtar."

62. Biskind, "Inside Ishtar."

63. Biskind, "Inside Ishtar."

64. Williams, author interview.

65. Williams, author interview.

66. Broeske, "The High Cost of 'Ishtar.'"

67. Williams, author interview.

68. Rotter, author interview.

69. *Hollywood Reporter,* March 28, 1986.

70. Blum, "The Road to Ishtar." Although he cites it as ending at ten p.m. the night before.

71. *Hollywood Reporter,* December 12, 1986, reports "according to a Columbia vp, who's in a position to know, Elaine May shot no less than 650,000 feet of film for *Ishtar.*"

72. Rotter, author interview.
73. Schopper, author interview, October 16, 2021.
74. Brad Fuller, author interview, August 11, 2021.
75. Fuller, author interview.
76. Ira Spiegel, author interview, March 4, 2022.
77. Fuller, author interview.
78. Fuller, author interview.
79. Both Schopper and Fuller recall her consistently telling them, "Sound is more important than picture."
80. Schopper, author interview, July 2021.
81. Rotter, author interview.
82. Rotter, author interview.
83. David T. Friendly, "No 'Ishtar' Cheer for Columbia," *Los Angeles Times,* September 4, 1986.
84. Rotter, author interview.
85. Spiegel, author interview.
86. Rotter, author interview.
87. Fuller, author interview.
88. Rotter, author interview.
89. Spiegel, author interview.
90. Brown, author interview.
91. Brown, author interview.
92. Spiegel, author interview.
93. Rotter, author interview.
94. Schopper, author interview, October 16, 2021.
95. Rotter, author interview.
96. Elaine May, lecture at Literary Arts (Portland), 1997, https://literary-arts.org /archive/elaine-may-2/(audio recording).
97. Caroline Aaron, author interview, September 2, 2022.
98. Katherine Rosman, "The Last Resort? Canyon Ranch Succumbs to Botox," *New York Times,* December 2, 2017.
99. Spiegel, author interview.
100. Lillian Ross, "The Boards," *New Yorker,* June 8, 1998.
101. Doris Roberts with Danelle Morton, *Are You Hungry, Dear? Life, Laughs, and Lasagna* (New York: St. Martin's Press, 2003), 86.
102. Confidential source, corroborated by Doris Roberts: "I turned to her and asked what it was that salt did to her. 'Oh,' she said. 'It makes me puffy'" (Roberts and Morton, *Are You Hungry, Dear?,* 87)
103. Biskind, *Star,* 369–70; some accounts allege that there were three separate cuts made. Rotter and Schopper suggest there was a session where everyone reviewed one cut and there were disagreements, but it remained one cut. Spiegel recalls Beatty and Hoffman "were constantly there, and so the politics and the dynamics were palpable" and recalls Hoffman having his own editing room.
104. Biskind, *Star,* 371. Also corroborated by Schopper, author interview, July 2021.
105. Rotter, author interview.
106. Rotter, author interview.
107. Fuller, author interview.
108. Author interview with Stephen Rotter and Ira Spiegel; corroborated in additional features.
109. Philip Wuntch, "Film Producer Beatty Goes Out on a Limb with Lavish Comedy," *Dallas Morning News,* May 10, 1987.
110. May, interview by Schwartz.
111. In 1999, the executive claimed he still had not seen the film (Mel Gussow, "At

Lunch With: David Puttnam; A Political Lesson Proves Apt for Film, Too," *New York Times*, January 5, 1999).

112. Charles Champlin, "Separating Fact from Friction over *Ishtar*," *Los Angeles Times*, May 23, 1987.
113. Blum, "The Road to Ishtar."
114. Spiegel, author interview.
115. May, interview by Nichols.
116. Evan Chung, "*Ishtar* Didn't Die a Natural Death," *Slate*, June 7, 2019.
117. Therese L. Wells, "Coke Takes $25 Mil 'Ishtar' Write-off," *Hollywood Reporter*, July 16, 1987.
118. Greg Kilday, "Hold the Camels," *Los Angeles Herald Examiner*, August 22, 1986.
119. Marilyn Beck, "Dustin Hoffman, Warren Beatty to Team in Elaine May Comedy," New York *Daily News*, April 9, 1985.
120. Jack Matthews, "Beatty, May, Hoffman Sign for a Big-Bucks Comedy," *Los Angeles Times*, July 5, 1985.
121. Samir Hachem, "Outtakes," *Los Angeles Times*, August 11, 1985.
122. Matthews, "Beatty, May, Hoffman Sign for a Big-Bucks Comedy."
123. Champlin, "Separating Fact from Friction over *Ishtar*."
124. It appears that Biskind observed two days of shooting late in its New York run for "Inside Ishtar." His feature is the only with first-person reporting from set.
125. Blum, "The Road to Ishtar."
126. Pat H. Broeske, "Outtakes: The Road to Ishtar," *Los Angeles Times*, February 16, 1986
127. Robert Osborne, "Rambling Reporter," *Hollywood Reporter*, April 4, 1986.
128. "Morning Report," *Los Angeles Times*, April 22, 1987.
129. "Just for Variety," *Variety*, May 15, 1987.
130. John Powers, "*Ishtar*," *L.A. Weekly*, May 15, 1987.
131. Janet Maslin, "Film: Hoffman and Beatty in Elaine May's *Ishtar*," *New York Times*, May 15, 1987.
132. Hal Hinson, "Ishtar," *Washington Post*, May 15, 1987.
133. Kathleen Carroll, "Mini Reviews," New York *Daily News*, May 30, 1987.
134. Duane Byrge, "*Ishtar*," *Hollywood Reporter*, May 11, 1987.
135. Roger Ebert, "*Ishtar*," *Chicago Sun-Times*, May 15, 1987.
136. David Denby, "Humps," *New York*, May 25, 1987.
137. Peter Rainer, "*Ishtar* Sinks into the Sand," *Los Angeles Herald Examiner*, May 15, 1987.
138. May, interview by Guest.
139. Bruce Bennett, "Hope and Crosby They Were Not," *Wall Street Journal*, May 16, 2011.
140. Confidential source.
141. Brown, author interview.
142. Aljean Harmetz, "Elaine May's 'Ishtar': A $51 Million Film in Trouble," *New York Times*, May 19, 1987.
143. David Edelstein, "Let's Get Small," *Village Voice*, May 19, 1987.
144. Denby, "Humps."
145. Edelstein, "Let's Get Small."
146. Andrew Sarris, "The Buddy Syndrome," *Village Voice*, June 23, 1987.
147. Leonard Klady, "Outtakes," *Los Angeles Times*, May 24, 1987.
148. Williams, author interview.
149. Laura Landro, "It Was Such a Flop, the Plaintiffs Won't Even Name It in Their Suit," *Wall Street Journal*, March 16, 1989.
150. May, interview by Nichols.
151. May, interview by Guest.
152. Elaine May, lecture at Literary Arts.

153. May, interview by Guest.
154. Again with the revisionist history: Julian Schlossberg insists she was offered hired gun–type directing jobs (which, what's the point), while Phillip Schopper says that to his knowledge, for the next thirteen years at least, she was never offered anything.
155. May, interview by Guest.

CHAPTER 10: THERE'S NO PRIZE, JUST A SMALLER SIZE

1. Author interview with Phillip Schopper, March 7, 2022.
2. Phillip Schopper estimates they spent $3 million (October 2021 interview); Schlossberg echoes the "We wanted to see if we could do it" sentiment in his July 2021 interview.
3. Author interview with Brad Fuller, August 11, 2021.
4. Vernon Scott, "Danny's Girl," *Indianapolis Star,* May 13, 1990.
5. Schlossberg estimates eight weeks, maybe ten, per July 2021 interview.
6. "Everyone agreed that the movie needed to find its shape in post" (author interview with Phillip Schopper, October 2021).
7. "She turned down directing jobs. It wasn't as if she was never offered a directing job, there was nothing that was offered to her that you want them to do" (author interview with Julian Schlossberg, April 2021).
8. Schopper, author interview, July 2021.
9. Ira Spiegel, author interview, March 4, 2022.
10. Schlossberg, author interview, July 2021.
11. Schlossberg, author interview, July 2021.
12. Schlossberg, author interview, July 2021.
13. Michelle Gorchow Sobel, author interview, February 23, 2022.
14. Sobel, author interview; further clarified via email, December 14, 2022.
15. Confidential source.
16. Brad Fuller, author interview, August 11, 2021.
17. Spiegel, author interview.
18. Elaine, I'm sorry, I don't know how to tell you this, but it absolutely is.
19. Spiegel, author interview.
20. Fuller, author interview: "About two or three weeks into her coming into the edit room, I walked out with her one night. It's about nine o'clock at night and we get to the sidewalk and she goes, 'If you could just point me to where north is.' She would not know how to get home if I didn't tell her which direction was north. And this was New York! This was Seventh Avenue! This is Seventh Avenue and 49th Street, so this is not like a place you had not seen before."
21. Fuller, author interview.
22. Sobel, author interview.
23. "Elaine May Finishes Off New Age," *Interview,* April 1990. It reads like many other printed "conversations" that Elaine would have in the next thirty years, ones that are clearly satirical, all coming from the pen of the woman who interviewed herself for *The New York Times* all those years ago.
24. Elaine May, "She's a Beginner, but What Connections," *New York Times,* April 1, 1990.
25. Author interview with Julian Schlossberg, April 2021.
26. *In the Spirit* promo, clip can be found on YouTube: https://www.youtube.com /watch?v=r5GGOaWFZx4.
27. Scott, "Danny's Girl."
28. Carrie Rickey, "New Age Widow, Monied Wife Share Philosophies, Laughs," *Philadelphia Inquirer,* July 6, 1990.
29. Kathleen Carroll, "A Few Screws Are Loose," New York *Daily News,* July 6, 1990.

30. Janet Maslin, "A New-Age Comedy, Crystals and All," *New York Times*, April 6, 1990.
31. Maslin, "A New-Age Comedy, Crystals and All."
32. Schlossberg, author interview, July 2021.
33. Schopper, author interview, November 2021.
34. "The best show here Tuesday afternoon wasn't on a movie screen. It wasn't even on dry land. It was aboard the Sea Goddess II, a Cunard cruise ship anchored a mile offshore and under charter to a group of rich American executives and their families. For nearly two hours, Elaine May, microphone in hand, worked the lounge of the Sea Goddess, entertaining and instructing the passengers, who had paid $13,000 each to come to Cannes for a week to learn something of the mysteries of movie making and, maybe more important, movie financing" (Vincent Canby, "Old Favorites Are No More at Cannes," *New York Times*, May 18, 1989).
35. "*Mr. Gogol* Delays Opening," *New York Times*, May 23, 1991.
36. Mel Gussow, "Recluse and Salesman: A Parable on Loneliness," *New York Times*, June 10, 1991.
37. Malcolm L. Johnson, "Cast, Director Conspire with Weather to Make Exciting, Uneven 'Othello,'" *Hartford Courant*, July 7, 1991.
38. Gregory Mosher, author interview, July 11, 2022.
39. Mosher, author interview.
40. Author interview with David Saint.
41. Frank Rizzo, "May's Way Not Always Conventional," *Hartford Courant*, August 18, 1993.
42. "This is a woman who does all her shopping by catalog because she hates to shop for clothes. She pays no attention to appearance in terms of clothing. She won't bother with it. It's not important to her. And yet I don't know when I've worked with an actress who is so particular about every single bit of clothing. It's very important to her that every detail be right" (David Saint to Frank Rizzo, "May's Way Not Always Conventional").
43. Saint, author interview.
44. Saint, author interview.
45. Saint, author interview.
46. Jeffrey Borak, "Williamstown Season Ends with Some Self-Indulgent 'Forplay,'" *Berkshire Eagle*, August 24, 1993.
47. "New York is an unspoken hope. Williamstown, Saint said, seemed to offer the company the chance to develop the piece away from the normal New York pressures. . . . 'We are looking at this as the first leg of a journey'" (Jeffrey Borak, "WTF Partners in 'Forplay,'" *Berkshire Eagle*, August 20, 1993).
48. Borak, "Williamstown Season Ends with Some Self-Indulgent 'Forplay.'"
49. Alvin Klein, "The Private Wars of Men and Women," *New York Times*, September 4, 1994.
50. Elaine May, "Hotline," *Death Defying Acts: 3 One-Act Comedies* (New York: Samuel French, 1995), 46.
51. Elaine May, lecture at Literary Arts (Portland), 1997, https://literary-arts.org/archive/elaine-may-2/ (audio recording).
52. Michael Blakemore, "Death Defying Director," *New Yorker*, June 3, 1996.
53. Aasif Mandvi, who had a bit part in the play, recalls her one note to him: "Remember, he's the outside world coming into this woman's bubble . . . he represents the outside world, he represents the Upper West Side." His version of the script set the play in the Lower East Side (Aasif Mandvi, author interview, August 26, 2022).
54. Blakemore, "Death Defying Director."
55. Jan Stuart, "Three Little Plays from Three Big Names," *Newsday*, March 7, 1995.
56. Stuart, "Three Little Plays from Three Big Names."

57. Clifford A. Ridley, "One-Acters in the Aura of the City," *Philadelphia Inquirer,* March 8, 1995.
58. Margo Jefferson, "'Death Defying Acts' Is All Words; 'The Heiress' Is Worthy," *New York Times,* March 19, 1995.
59. Vincent Canby, "Really a Jungle Out There, a Jungle of Urban Neuroses," *New York Times,* March 7, 1995.
60. Howard Kissel, "'Death-Defying Acts' Rescued by Allen's Hilarious Farce," New York *Daily News,* March 7, 1995.
61. Liz Smith, "Garbo at Gotham," *Newsday,* March 19, 1995.

CHAPTER 11: DON'T CALL IT A COMEBACK

1. Robert Osborne, "Nichols-May Tribute Recalls the Way It Was," *Hollywood Reporter,* April 20, 1992.
2. Jane Hall, "Nichols, May Honored by TV, Radio Museum," *Los Angeles Times,* April 17, 1992.
3. Osborne, "Nichols-May Tribute Recalls the Way It Was."
4. Caryn James, "Mike Nichols Surveys the American Dream," *New York Times,* February 25, 1990.
5. "Groovy After All These Years," *Newsweek,* May 18, 1992.
6. "Benefits," *New York Times,* November 6, 1994.
7. Bob Morris, "Pins and Needles," *New York Times,* November 14, 1993.
8. See John Lahr, "Making It Real," *New Yorker*; Mark Harris, *Mike Nichols: A Director's Life* (New York: Penguin Press, 2021), 140; Gerald Nachman, *Seriously Funny: The Rebel Comedians of the 1950s and 1960s* (New York: Back Stage Books, 2004), 351.
9. Sam Kashner, "Who's Afraid of Nichols and May?" *Vanity Fair,* December 20, 2012.
10. "Once we got over being mad at one another, we would come together for this or that ratfuck, and that was fun. We enjoyed it, people enjoyed it," Mike Nichols to Gerald Nachman, *Seriously Funny,* 351.
11. Glenn Collins, "A Double Reunion, 2 Decades Later," *New York Times,* May 2, 1992.
12. Douglas J. Rowe, "Mike Nichols Embraces Reconciliation," *Albany Democrat-Herald,* March 22, 1996.
13. Author interview with Julian Schlossberg, April 1, 2021.
14. "Hollywood Squeezing Scripters," *Variety,* April 17, 1995.
15. Though reports of her involvement and subsequent denials of it have gone back and forth so many times over the years it's impossible to know for certain. See "Cinefile," *Los Angeles Times,* January 15, 1989, followed by a denial from Julian Schlossberg in "Outtakes," *Los Angeles Times,* February 5, 1989.
16. "Dish," *Variety,* October 13, 1994. By 1997, they were still talking about this, but with a possibility that it would star Diane Keaton and Steve Martin. See "Production Line," *Screen International,* June 13, 1997. Additionally, at some point in time, Nathan Lane approached me with the idea to do it as a play with him and Andrea Martin (author interview with Nathan Lane).
17. "Just for Variety," October 30, 1991, *Variety*. By 1999, after being let go by Robert Zemeckis due to scheduling conflicts with *Cast Away* and *What Lies Beneath,* it was passed on for a rewrite by Barra Grant to be directed by Damon Santostefano ("Dish," *Variety,* April 13, 1999).
18. "Hollywood Cinefile," *Screen International,* September 11, 1992. The extent of her rework—what was intended as a dialogue polish turned into a structural overhaul—set the film back to developmental ground zero. Elaine's rewrites

would circulate for years attracting interest from stars, but failed to attach a director, and eventually would go unused (Patrick Goldstein, "'Bride's' Long, Long Path to the Altar," *Los Angeles Times,* August 3, 1999).

19. Mike Nichols to Sam Wasson, *Improv Nation: How We Made a Great American Art* (Boston: Houghton Mifflin Harcourt, 2017), 335.
20. Author interview with Phillip Schopper, October 16, 2021.
21. Harris, *Mike Nichols,* 473.
22. "Jack Cries Wolf," *Newsweek,* June 19, 1994.
23. Seen in the scene where Nicholson visits a doctor, who explains his situation in a nonplussed manner and explains that "We've become used to these things that defy human nature" (Mike Haley, author interview, August 10, 2022).
24. Haley, author interview.
25. "Jack Cries Wolf."
26. Haley, author interview.
27. Michael Wilmington, "How Mike Nichols and Friends Created a 'Wolf,'" *Chicago Tribune,* July 4, 1994.
28. John N. Smith, author interview, June 30, 2022.
29. Martin A. Grove, "Caught Up in Humor of Nichols' 'Birdcage,'" *Hollywood Reporter,* March 1, 1996.
30. Elaine May, lecture at Literary Arts (Portland), 1997, https://literary-arts.org/archive/elaine-may-2/ (audio recording).
31. Anita M. Busch, "Nichols, May Head for 'Folles,'" *Variety,* August 5, 1994.
32. https://www.hiv.gov/hiv-basics/overview/history/hiv-and-aids-timeline.
33. Elaine May, lecture at Literary Arts.
34. *The Birdcage* Press Book, *The Birdcage* production files, Margaret Herrick Library, Academy of Motion Pictures Arts and Sciences.
35. Elaine May, lecture at Literary Arts.
36. *The Birdcage* Press Book, *The Birdcage* production files, Margaret Herrick Library, Academy of Motion Pictures Arts and Sciences.
37. "I think from Mike's point of view, he wanted to do that story, but he also wanted a commercial success and he wanted it to be embraced by everybody. So he didn't want to put that kind of stuff in that might turn off some parts of America" (Nathan Lane, author interview, September 19, 2022).
38. Bo Welch, author interview, June 7, 2022.
39. Elaine May, lecture at Literary Arts.
40. Elaine May, lecture at Literary Arts.
41. Elaine May, lecture at Literary Arts.
42. Lane, author interview.
43. *The Birdcage* Press Book, *The Birdcage* production files, Margaret Herrick Library, Academy of Motion Pictures Arts and Sciences.
44. Adrian Lester to Mark Harris, *Mike Nichols,* 480–81.
45. Will Harris, "Hank Azaria," *AV Club,* September 14, 2011, https://www.avclub.com/hank-azaria-1798227403.
46. Lane, author interview.
47. Lane, author interview.
48. It appears six times in the script (Elaine May, *The Birdcage,* April 1995 revisions, combined blue, pink, peach, and green pages).
49. Lane, author interview.
50. Welch, author interview.
51. Elaine May, lecture at Literary Arts.
52. Elaine May to Mark Harris, *Mike Nichols,* 483.
53. Elaine May, American Film Institute Life Achievement Award gala, Tribute to Mike Nichols, June 10, 2010.
54. Mary Bailey, author interview, July 1, 2022.

55. Wasson, *Improv Nation*, 336.
56. Welch, author interview.
57. Nathan Lane notes that one of the reasons he hadn't spoken up sooner about the "fag" issue was because "I was intimidated by [Mike] and I didn't want to upset him after he'd given me this tremendous opportunity and was so kind and gracious to me and supportive," (Lane, author interview)
58. Welch, author interview.
59. Bailey, author interview.
60. "He was very protective of her, and very protective of her script. Protective of her, in a way, that was like a big brother," Nathan Lane says. "There was one day she was eating something at catering, and there were crumbs on her sweater, and we were just talking and she was sort of oblivious. I just remember him noticing and brushing it off her sweater, in that way that was a subtle thing" (Lane, author interview) Mary Bailey (author interview) concurs: "She was also completely absent-minded about some things. Like when she was eating a bagel, a lot of it would be on her blouse or shirt or whatever and only when somebody like Mike would say, 'Just brush yourself off here.'" Mike Haley also speaks of Elaine's habit of eating like an absolute slob (author interview).
61. Wasson, *Improv Nation*, 337.
62. Lane, author interview.
63. *The Birdcage*, Box Office Mojo, https://www.boxofficemojo.com/release /rl1229424129/weekend/.
64. David Denby, "The Beach Boys," *New York,* March 11, 1996.
65. Todd McCarthy, "The Birdcage," *Variety,* March 3, 1996.
66. Janet Maslin, "*La Cage Aux Folles,* but in South Beach," *New York Times,* March 8, 1996.
67. "GLAAD Applauds 'The Birdcage,'" press release, March 5, 1996, http://www .qrd.org/qrd/orgs/GLAAD/general.information/1996/applauds.birdcage-03.05 .96.
68. Gene Siskel, "Slogans Over Substance," *TV Guide,* July 12–18, 1997.
69. Bruce Bawer, "Why Can't Hollywood Get Gay Life Right?" *New York Times,* March 10, 1996.
70. "Letters," *New York Times,* section 2, page 6, March 24, 1996, https://times-machine.nytimes.com/timesmachine/1996/03/24/issue.html.
71. Robert A. McNamara, "*The Birdcage*: Just Like True Parents," *New York Times,* March 24, 1996.
72. Nathan Lane to Matt Wilstein, "Nathan Lane Wishes He'd Been 'Brave' Enough to Come Out to Oprah After *The Birdcage*." Oprah's "The Birdcage" special can be viewed on YouTube, https://www.youtube.com/watch?v=dZwxysUwHCg. The moment starts around 15:55.
73. *The Birdcage*, Box Office Mojo.
74. Bernard Weinraub, "*Birdcage* Shows Growth in Older Audience's Power," *New York Times,* March 12, 1996.
75. Emma Thompson to Mark Harris, *Mike Nichols,* 493.
76. Douglas J. Rowe, "Mike Nichols Embraces Reconciliation," *Albany Democrat-Herald,* March 22, 1996.
77. "People," *Newsday,* August 13, 1996.
78. James Kaplan, "True Colors?" *New York,* March 2, 1998.
79. Jeffrey Ressner, "Tale of Two Bills," *Time,* March 16, 1998.
80. Harris, *Mike Nichols,* 492.
81. "We rehearsed it like it was a play," says Caroline Aaron. "We had all of these readings of the script and then Elaine would make adjustments because it was her script. It was so interesting to watch her and Mike collaborate on 'Is it telling the story? When does it work?' I saw this unbelievable rigor in her

that I had not seen before, about really trying to solve the problems, or not necessarily even problems, but how to really make this story, as Mike wanted to tell it, come across" (author interview).

82. Patrick Goldstein, "They All Have a Secret," *Los Angeles Times,* March 15, 1998.
83. Bailey, author interview.
84. Aaron, author interview.
85. Bailey, author interview.
86. Robert Klein, author interview.
87. Bailey, author interview: "We discovered that we both really liked dancing—and not ballroom dancing as much as just going somewhere and there are old rock and roll things or newer disco things that we had learned—that we really liked dancing and there was nowhere that either of us knew in the city where we could go and do that."
88. Aaron, author interview.
89. Bailey, author interview.
90. Bailey, author interview.
91. Goldstein, "They All Have a Secret."
92. Klein, author interview.
93. Goldstein, "They All Have a Secret."
94. Elaine May to Mark Harris, *Mike Nichols,* 497.
95. Todd S. Purdum, "The Way We Are in the Era of Clinton," *New York Times,* March 15, 1998.
96. Glenn Whipp, "'Primary' Comparisons," *Los Angeles Daily News,* March 17, 1998.
97. Elaine May, interview by Phil Rosenthal, *Naked Lunch,* July 21, 2022, https://open.spotify.com/episode/30cveCd824JIcwDRe5bnUf?si=3f1a9b54cd3f431e.
98. James Kaplan, "True Colors?"
99. Joseph A. Kirby, "Mike Nichols Sees Plenty of Gray in 'Primary Colors,'" *Chicago Tribune,* March 26, 1998.
100. Elaine Dutka, "Clinton Embraces 'Elite,'" *Los Angeles Times,* September 18, 1992.
101. At the time, it was speculated that "Mike Nichols didn't want to offend the president or cause him a lot of embarrassment," (Faye Fiore, "Just What He Didn't Need Right Now," *Los Angeles Times,* March 2, 1998).
102. Janet Maslin, "Portrait of a Candidate as Casanova," *New York Times,* March 20, 1998.
103. Duane Byrge, "Primary Colors," *Hollywood Reporter,* March 13, 1998.
104. Kenneth Turan, "Inspired Insinuation," *Los Angeles Times,* March 20, 1998.
105. "We avoided the red carpet. That was a stipulation, didn't want to go down the red carpet" (Phillip Schopper, author interview, March 7, 2022).

CHAPTER 12: WE ADAPT VERY QUICKLY

1. Susan Wloszczyna, "Wilson and Vaughn: Leaders of the 'Frat Pack,'" *USA Today,* June 15, 2004, https://usatoday30.usatoday.com/life/movies/news/2004–06–15-frat-pack_x.htm.
2. Jane Hall, "Nichols, May Honored by TV, Radio Museum," *Los Angeles Times,* April 17, 1992.
3. See also "Calendar," *The Olympian,* September 19, 1997, regarding a lecture in Seattle, as well as Neal Broverman, "A Session with Elaine May," *Hartford Courant,* October 21, 1999. None of the dates correspond to any kind of publicity or attempt at visibility for an upcoming project or awards consideration (not that Elaine would ever do *that* dog and pony show), so their purpose is unclear. It's as if she decided to dip her toe into the lecture circuit, only to get out of it just as quickly as she got in.

4. Elaine May, lecture at Literary Arts (Portland), 1997, https://literary-arts.org/archive/elaine-may-2/ (audio recording).
5. Julian Schlossberg, author interview, March 2021.
6. Rick Lyman, "On Stage and Off," *New York Times,* October 31, 1997.
7. Elaine May, interview by Phil Rosenthal, *Naked Lunch,* July 21, 2022, https://open.spotify.com/episode/30cveCd824JIcwDRe5bnUf?si=3f1a9b54cd3f431e.
8. Alan Arkin, *An Improvised Life* (Cambridge, MA: Da Capo Press, 2011), 133–34.
9. Arkin, *An Improvised Life,* 134.
10. Honorary Oscar tribute documentary, dir. Marina Zenovich, 2022.
11. Phil Rosenthal, author interview.
12. Elaine May, *The Way of All Fish,* in Elaine May and Alan Arkin, *Power Plays* (Garden City, NY: Stage and Screen, 1997), 14–15.
13. Lillian Ross, "The Boards," *New Yorker,* June 8, 1998.
14. Elaine May, *The Way of All Fish,* 16–17.
15. May, *The Way of All Fish,* 19.
16. Elaine May, *In and Out of the Light,* in *Power Plays,* 93.
17. May, *In and Out of the Light,* 104.
18. Jacques le Sourd, "Elaine May Plays the Clown, with Style," *Daily Item* (Port Chester, NY), May 22, 1998.
19. Vincent Canby, "'Power Plays,' Something More Than a Family Affair," *New York Times,* May 31, 1998.
20. Ben Brantley, "Old Iconoclasts in In New Territory," *New York Times,* May 22, 1998.
21. May, interview by Rosenthal, *Naked Lunch.*
22. Only ten new plays opened on Broadway in the 1998–1999 season, half as many as twenty years prior (Robin Pogrebin, "Nary a Drama on Broadway; Straight Plays Are Thriving, but Elsewhere in Manhattan," *New York Times,* December 28, 1999).
23. Ben Brantley, "The Year Broadway Became the Boonies," *New York Times,* June 6, 1999.
24. Bruce Weber, "Theater Review: Taller Than a Dwarf; Imagine Ralph Kramden in a Midlife Crisis," *New York Times,* April 25, 2000.
25. Robert Simonson, "Bway's *Taller Than a Dwarf* Readying for Boston Previews, March 7–19," *Playbill,* March 1, 2000.
26. Schlossberg, author interview.
27. Elaine May, *Taller Than a Dwarf* (New York: Samuel French, York, 1999). May's 1962 typescript for *A Matter of Position* can be viewed at the New York Public Library for the Performing Arts, Billy Rose Theatre Division.
28. Jerry Adler, author interview, August 30, 2022.
29. Cynthia Darlow, author interview, August 12, 2022.
30. Adler, author interview.
31. Schlossberg, author interview.
32. Adler, author interview.
33. Adler, author interview.
34. Adler, author interview.
35. Darlow, author interview.
36. Donald Lyons, "Grumpy, Dopey 'Dwarf,'" *New York Post,* April 25, 2000.
37. Markland Taylor, "Taller Than a Dwarf," *Variety,* March 13, 2000.
38. Weber, "Theater Review."
39. Taylor, "Taller Than a Dwarf."
40. Schlossberg, author interview.
41. Parker Posey to Don Shewey, "An Outsider Plays an Outsider, Blown on the Wind," *New York Times,* February 2, 2003.
42. "'Dwarf' Is Closing," *New York Times,* June 7, 2000.
43. Caroline Aaron, author interview.

44. Aaron, author interview.
45. Julian Schlossberg, email, November 1, 2022.
46. Liz Smith, "Twiggy Branches Out," *Newsday,* June 13, 1999.
47. Richard Johnson, "Young at Heart," *New York Post,* April 10, 2000.
48. John Heilpern, "Out to Lunch with Stanley Donen," *Vanity Fair,* February 22, 2013.
49. Mark Feeney, "He's the Guy Who Sent Him Soaring," *Boston Globe,* October 4, 2009.
50. Mark Feeney, "He's the Guy Who Sent Him Soaring."
51. Ben Odell, author interview, October 7, 2022.
52. Aaron, author interview.
53. "I feel like he was invited into her world and she was grateful for him being willing to be there. Because, mostly, I saw Stanley and Elaine at Marlo's. Marlo's a big entertainer and a big celebrator," (author interview with Aaron).
54. Liz Smith, "To Wed or Not to Wed?" September 12, 2003.
55. Joyce Wadler, "Boldface Names," *New York Times,* September 30, 2003.
56. Lorraine Boyle, Peter Boyle's wife, called New Year's 2002: "Crazy. The whole thing was crazy. Elaine started riffing, going on. We couldn't leave" (Nancy Hass, "A Night Out With: Peter Boyle; Drop a Cue, He Grabs It," *New York Times,* January 6, 2002).
57. Robert Klein, author interview.
58. Gordon Cox, "This Bunch Hopes a Star Is Porn," *Newday,* December 12, 2002.
59. Mark Kennedy, "Director Stanley Donen Turns His Talents to Porn Stars," *Herald-Palladium,* December 15, 2002.
60. Mary Birdsong, author interview, September 21, 2022.
61. Birdsong, author interview.
62. Birdsong, author interview.
63. Birdsong, author interview.
64. "Elaine May's *Adult Entertainment* Starts Off Bway Nov. 16; Opens Dec. 2," *Playbill,* September 26, 2002, https://playbill.com/article/elaine-mays-adult -entertainment-starts-off-bway-nov-16-opens-dec-2-com-108550.
65. Birdsong, author interview.
66. Markland Taylor, "Adult Entertainment," *Variety,* November 11, 2002.
67. Malcolm Joseph, "Elaine May's 'Adult' Play Needs to Grow Up," *Hartford Courant,* November 4, 2002.
68. Markland Taylor, "Adult Entertainment."
69. "Backstage Pass," New York *Daily News,* November 10, 2002.
70. Previews in New York began on November 16, with the intended opening night set to December 2 ("Theater Listings," *New York Times,* November 10, 2002). The date was pushed to December 9 the following week ("Theater Listings," *New York Times,* November 17, 2002), then finally two more days shortly after ("Theater Listings," *New York Times,* November 24, 2002).
71. "Lining Up for 'La Boheme,'" [White Plains, NY] *Journal News,* December 5, 2002.
72. "Side Dishes," New York *Daily News,* December 2, 2002.
73. "Side Dishes," New York *Daily News.*
74. Ben Brantley, "Is She a Serious Actress? XXXtremely," *New York Times,* December 12, 2002.
75. Robert Feldburg, "The Art of Bump and Grind," *The* [Hackensack] *Record,* December 15, 2002.
76. Charles Isherwood, "Adult Entertainment," *Variety,* December 11, 2002.
77. Brantley, "Is She a Serious Actress? XXXtremely."
78. Robert Dominguez and Lance Gould, "Strike Boosts Off-B'way," New York *Daily News,* March 13, 2003.
79. Roger Ebert, "Allen Tells What's Important in His Life, 'Small Time Crooks,'" [Palm Beach] *Daily News,* June 4, 2000.

80. "The best reason to catch *Small Time Crooks* is for the occasional actors' grace notes, most of them supplied by Elaine May, as Frenchy's addled cousin May," wrote Peter Rainer for *New York* (Peter Rainer, "Money Tawks," *New York*, May 29, 2000).
81. Jan Stuart, "'Crooks' Banks on May's Antics," *Newsday*, May 19, 2000.
82. Michael Fleming, "Universal, Nichols Will Play 'Hearts' in Remake," *Variety*, January 27, 2000.
83. Michael Fleming, "For Roth, it's 'Potter' or 'Planet'?" *Variety*, July 20, 2000. The news blurb notes that a reading was held at the CAA headquarters with Robin Williams in the multiple roles played by Alec Guinness, along with Will Smith, Connie Nielsen, and Jada Pinkett Smith.
84. Elaine May, *Kind Hearts*, August 2001. Received via email from Ted Griffin.
85. Michael Fleming, "Nichols Gets the 'Skinny,'" *Variety*, July 27, 2004.
86. Carl Hiaasen, author interview, September 8, 2022.
87. Mark Harris, *Mike Nichols: A Director's Life* (New York: Penguin Press, 2021), 554.
88. Samantha Gross, "Start Spreading the News," *Oberlin Alumni Magazine*, Fall 2003, https://www2.oberlin.edu/alummag/fall2003/feat_start.html.
89. Ben Odell, "Seamless Transitions: Remembering Stanley Donen," *Filmmaker Magazine*, June 19, 2019.
90. Ben Odell, author interview, October 7, 2022.
91. Odell, author interview.
92. Odell, author interview.
93. Odell, author interview.
94. Michael Sragow, "Hollywood Maverick Succeeded on His Own Terms," *Baltimore Sun*, November 22, 2006.
95. Odell, author interview.
96. Odell, author interview.
97. Liz Smith, "Bacall Makes a Whistle Stop," *Newsday*, March 4, 2005.
98. "*Frost/Nixon* . . . has yet to open. But it's already been enjoyed in previews by Graydon Carter, with his two sons; Elaine May, with partner Stanley Donen; James Cromwell, and Nathan Lane" (Ben Widdicombe, "Gatecrasher," New York *Daily News*, April 11, 2007).
99. Elaine May attends a special screening of "Fahrenheit 9/11 at the Ziegfeld Theater in New York," June 14, 2022, photo by Henry McGee/Media Punch, https://www.alamy.com/elaine-may-attends-a-special-screening-of-fahrenheit-911-at-the-ziegfeld-theater-in-new-york-city-on-june-14–2004-photo-credit-henry-mcgeemediapunch-image443875722.html.
100. At an after party for *Hairspray*, thrown by Bernadette Peters and Glenn Close, Elaine didn't hesitate to mention that she had a new screenplay (though this one was "about Jerusalem") for Mike to direct (Liz Smith, "Weinstein's Wedding, Peters' Party," *Variety*, December 19, 2007).
101. It's true! She was one of the hosts for a New York Tastemaker screening of *The Thing About My Folks* in 2005 (Robert Riddell, "'Folks' Gather in Gotham," *Variety*, September 14, 2005).
102. Elaine May, "Proust Questionnaire," *Vanity Fair*, March 2009.
103. Sam Kashner, "Who's Afraid of Nichols and May?" *Vanity Fair*, December 20, 2012.
104. Julie Hinds, "Low-Key Traverse City Awaits Madonna," *Detroit Free Press*, August 2, 2008.
105. Coming onstage to thundering applause after a screening of *Ishtar* at the 92nd Street Y, she remarked: "Either you like the movie or I'm very sick" (S. T. Vanairsdale, "Blind Camels, Idiot Execs, and 5 Other *Ishtar* Revelations from Director Elaine May," *Movieline*, May 18, 2011). Elaine also made two consecutive appearances at the Harvard Film Archive in November 2010.

106. Marjorie Baumgarten, "A Conversation with Elaine May," *Austin Chronicle,* October 25, 2013.
107. Kenneth Lonergan, author interview, October 21, 2022.
108. Bob Verini, "Vets Cast Dubious Eye on Rewriting," *Variety,* December 12, 2008.
109. Upon seeing *Closer,* for example, she said: "They don't make their case, these people. They don't say the things that people say when they're getting ready to give the bad news. They don't put any spin on it. They just tell the truth when they want to leave. But so do a lot of people" (Lynda Gorov, "Nichols Says the Beauty of 'Closer' Is the Plot," *Boston Globe,* November 28, 2004).
110. Rosenthal, author interview.
111. Phil Rosenthal to Christine Blackburn, "Frozen Yogurt with Elaine May with Writer/Producer Phil Rosenthal," *Story Worthy,* January 2018, https://open .spotify.com/episode/73rXAh5G0BurrlvjyGB3kL?si=f3bf2ce6cb59470b.
112. Lonergan, author interview.
113. Lonergan, author interview.
114. Randy Skinner, author interview.
115. David Rooney, "After the Night and the Music," *Variety,* June 1, 2005.
116. Jeremy McCarter, "Musical Squares," *New York,* June 2, 2005.
117. Kathleen Allen, "There's More to Marlo," *Arizona Daily Star,* October 16, 2009.
118. Emily Nussbaum, "76 Minutes with Marlo Thomas," *New York,* October 7, 2011.
119. Aaron, author interview.
120. Kerry Lengel, "Marlo Thomas Talks of Latest Role, Feminism, Dad's Advice," *Arizona Republic,* November 8, 2009.
121. Dennis Harvey, "Moving Right Along," *Variety,* November 2, 2006.
122. David Saint, author interview.
123. Saint, author interview.
124. Peter Filichia, "Jolly 'Roger,' Thanks to Elaine May," (Newark, NJ) *Star-Ledger,* April 14, 2008.
125. M. Scot Skinner, "Thomas Brings 'George' to Life," *Arizona Daily Star,* October 30, 2009.
126. Charles Isherwood, "Each Family, Tortured in Its Own Way," *New York Times,* October 20, 2011.
127. Isherwood, "Each Family, Tortured in Its Own Way."
128. Scott Brown, "O Brother," *New York,* October 21, 2011.
129. John Lahr, "Bluebird of Unhappiness," *New Yorker,* October 24, 2011.
130. Skinner, author interview.
131. Skinner recalls "Stanley started having knee problems," and believes he had knee surgery. "And then it just all kind of disappeared, as things often do at that age" (Skinner, author interview).
132. Odell, "Seamless Transitions."
133. Elaine May, interview by Mike Nichols, Film Society of Lincoln Center, February 26, 2006.
134. May, interview by Nichols.
135. May, interview by Nichols.
136. May, interview by Nichols.
137. Odell, author interview.
138. Odell, author interview.
139. Kashner, "Who's Afraid of Nichols and May?"

CHAPTER 13: WHAT IS IMPORTANT IN LIFE AND ART?

1. Sam Kashner, "Who's Afraid of Nichols and May?" *Vanity Fair,* December 20, 2012.
2. "Mike Nichols" on PBS's *American Masters* would premiere on January 29,

2016, just fourteen months after his death. Schlossberg estimates that the production and editing process lasted about "eight to nine months" (Julian Schlossberg, author interview, September 2022).

3. Schlossberg, author interview.
4. Richard Brody, "A Lovingly Obsessive Tribute to Mike Nichols, by Elaine May," *New Yorker*, January 29, 2016.
5. Mike Fleming Jr., "Woody Allen Amazon Series Sets Cast: He Stars with Elaine May & Miley Cyrus," *Deadline*, January 26, 2016, https://deadline.com/2016 /01/woody-allen-miley-cyrus-elaine-may-amazon-series-1201690130/.
6. Sonia Saraiya, "TV Review: Woody Allen's Amazon Comedy 'Crisis in Six Scenes,'" *Variety*, September 29, 2016.
7. James Wolcott, "Miley Cyrus Makes Woody Allen's Amazon Series Worth Watching," *Vanity Fair*, September 30, 2016.
8. Mike Hale, "Review: 'Crisis in Six Scenes,' a Mere Ghost of Woody Allen Past," *New York Times*, September 30, 2016.
9. Eric Deggans, "Woody Allen Presents First TV Series, 'Crisis in Six Scenes,' on Amazon," NPR, September 29, 2016.
10. Saraiya, "TV Review."
11. Really, though, she would probably make even *that* funny, interesting, and worth watching.
12. Robert Lloyd, "Making a Break for TV," *Los Angeles Times*, September 29, 2016.
13. Based on Getty, Alamy, and Shutterstock databases.
14. "The next thing I know, they broke off. She broke off with him" (Robert Klein, author interview).
15. Carol Kane, author interivew.
16. Kashner, "Who's Afraid of Nichols and May?"
17. Caroline Aaron, author interivew.
18. Elaine May, interviewed by Phil Rosenthal, Austin Film Festival, October 25, 2013. Excerpts published in "AFF Panel: A Conversation with Elaine May," *Austin American-Statesman*, September 23, 2018.
19. David Saint, author interivew.
20. Caryn James, "The Fireworks of Elaine May," *New York Times*, February 24, 2006.
21. Chuck Stephens, "Chronicle of a Disappearance," *Film Comment* 43, no. 2 (March/April 2006).
22. President Obama Awards the 2012 National Medals of Arts and Humanities, July 10, 2013, https://www.youtube.com/watch?v=EciDRwKHONk.
23. Elaine May, 68th Annual Writers Guild of America Awards, February 13, 2016, https://www.youtube.com/watch?v=ubypaJvPI0A.
24. Originally appearing in *Vulture*: Ross Kenneth Urken, "Alec Baldwin Says *30 Rock* Is Ending Next Season," *New York/Vulture*, April 6, 2011, https://www.vulture .com/2011/04/alec_baldwin_30_rock_ending.html. This was picked up by out-lets like MTV News, *The Daily Beast, Salon, Entertainment Weekly,* and *Complex,* among others.
25. Phil Rosenthal, author interview.
26. Kenneth Lonergan, author interview.
27. Lonergan, author interview.
28. Lonergan, author interview.
29. David Cromer, "The 'Dangerous, Unafraid' Brilliance of Elaine May on Stage," *Hollywood Reporter*, May 21, 2019.
30. Lonergan, author interview.
31. Joan Allen, unpublished transcript of author interview for *Glamour* profile, May 29, 2019.
32. Sarah Larson, "Michael Cera, Elaine May Superfan," *New Yorker*, November 12, 2018.

33. Larson, "Michael Cera, Elaine May Superfan."
34. Cromer, "The 'Dangerous, Unafraid' Brilliance of Elaine May on Stage."
35. Lonergan, author interview.
36. Lonergan, author interview.
37. Lonergan, author interview.
38. Lonergan, author interview.
39. Cromer, "The 'Dangerous, Unafraid' Brilliance of Elaine May on Stage."
40. Joan Allen, author interview.
41. Allen, author interview.
42. Allen, author interview.
43. Lonergan, author interview.
44. Lonergan, author interview.
45. Cromer, "The 'Dangerous, Unafraid' Brilliance of Elaine May on Stage."
46. Lonergan, author interview.
47. Ben Brantley, "Review: Elaine May Might Break Your Heart in 'Waverly Gallery,'" *New York Times,* October 25, 2018.
48. Chris Jones, "The Waverly Gallery: Elaine May, Falling Apart on Broadway and Showing Us Our Future," New York *Daily News,* October 25, 2018.
49. Michael Riedel, "The Hottest Ticket for Theater Lovers Is 86-Year-Old Elaine May," *New York Post,* September 20, 2018.
50. Lonergan, author interview.
51. Allen, author interview.
52. Lonergan, author interview.
53. Lonergan, author interview.
54. Allen, author interview.
55. Larson, "Michael Cera, Elaine May Superfan."
56. Chad Perman, "Kenneth Lonergan on the Genius of Elaine May," Bright Wall/Dark Room, Interviews Issue 75, https://www.brightwalldarkroom.com/2019/09/30/kenneth-lonergan-on-the-genius-of-elaine-may/.
57. Perman, "Kenneth Lonergan on the Genius of Elaine May."
58. Lonergan, author interview.
59. Lonergan, author interview.
60. Mary-Louise Parker, author interview, September 9, 2022.
61. Renée Taylor, author interview.
62. Lonergan, author interview; Schlossberg, author interview.
63. Lonergan, author interview.
64. Lonergan, author interview.
65. Lonergan, author interview.
66. Lonergan, author interview.
67. Nicholas White, "Jennifer Lopez, Mary Kay Place, Bong Joon Ho Accept Los Angeles Film Critics Association Awards," *Variety,* January 12, 2020.
68. Saint, author interview; Aaron, author interview.
69. Lonergan, author interview.
70. Saint; author interview with Phil Rosenthal.
71. Elaine May, interviewed by Phil Rosenthal, Austin Film Festival, *Austin-American Statesman* excerpts.
72. Peter Hedges, author interview, June 20, 2022.
73. Hedges, author interview.
74. Hedges, author interview.
75. Hedges, author interview.
76. Hedges, author interview.
77. Parker, author interview.
78. Parker, author interview.
79. Hedges, author interview.
80. Parker, author interview.

81. Hedges, author interview.
82. Parker, author interview.
83. Confidential source.
84. Confidential source.
85. Roger Friedman, "Oscars Give Lifetime Achievement Award to Elaine May, She Only Agreed to Come at the Very Last Minute," Showbiz411, March 26, 2022. Corroborated by confidential source.
86. Elaine May, 12th Governors Awards, March 25, 2022, https://www.youtube.com/watch?v=8U7XIu_cWTM.
87. Elaine May, 12th Governors Awards.
88. Elaine once claimed to have turned down an opportunity to host *Saturday Night Live*, saying: "It frightens me to be a host. It's very nervous-making to go on as yourself and have your sole chore to be funny. It's scary. I'm not really a stand-up comedian; I work inside a scene or as a character. It just seems terrifying to me. That's why I didn't. I was too scared" (Elaine May, lecture at Literary Arts [Portland], 1997, https://literary-arts.org/archive/elaine-may-2/[audio recording]).
89. Saint, author interview.
90. Kashner, "Who's Afraid of Nichols and May?"

INDEX

Aaron, Caroline, 204, 228, 270, 284–85, 286, 296, 303
Abbott and Costello, 34
Academy Awards, 127, 314
  The Heartbreak Kid, 145
  Heaven Can Wait, 187
  Honorary Award, 325–27
  Mike Nichols, 80
  Primary Colors, 272–75
  Reds, 193–94, 231
  Tootsie, 202
Achille Lauro hijacking, 216
Actors Studio, 68
Adaptation/Next, 117–20
Adjani, Isabelle, 214, 228
Adler, Jerry, 282, 283–84
Adolph's Tenderizer, 60
Adult Entertainment, 286, 287–91
affirmative action, 276
After the Night and the Music, 298
Albert, Eddie, 138, 145
Alfred Hitchcock's Mystery Magazine, 113–14
Ali, Muhammad, 183–84
Alice's Restaurant, 134
Allen, Dede, 190, 191–92
Allen, Gracie, 64
Allen, Herb, 229
Allen, Joan, 314, 316
Allen, Steve, 57
Allen, Woody, 251, 301
  Crisis in Six Scenes, 309–11
  Small Time Crooks, 291–92
Altman, Robert, 294
Alyce Films, 170–71
American Dream, 35, 117, 145, 282
American Film, 230
American Idol, 236
American Masters, 307–9
American Museum of the Moving Image, 256
Anderson, Paul Thomas, 294
Andrews, Julie, 75
anonymity, 1–2, 13, 173, 181, 193–94

anti-Semitism, 145–46, 148–49, 261
Apatow, Judd, 236
Apocalypse Now, 177
Apology of Socrates, The, 22
appearance, 22–23, 37
Argo Off-Beat Room, 44, 54
Arkin, Alan, 278–85
Arnaz, Desi, 42, 66
Arrick, Rose, 84, 122, 214
Arzner, Dorothy, 113
Asher, Aaron, 21
Asner, Ed, 29, 30–31
At Long Last Love, 177
Austin Film Festival, 297
Avedon, Richard, 61, 71, 72
Aykroyd, Dan, 203–4
Azaria, Hank, 262

Bacall, Lauren, 145
"Bach to Bach," 68
Back to the Future, 212
Bailey, Mary, 265, 269–70
Baker, Carroll, 68
Baldwin, Alec, 312
Ball, Lucille, 42, 63, 66, 95
Baranski, Christine, 262
Barefoot in the Park, 98
Bart, Peter, 112–13, 120–21, 124
Barth, Belle, 64
Bates, Kathy, 272–73
Bawer, Bruce, 267
Beakel, Walter, 35
Beatty, Warren, 173, 183–94, 241, 252, 277
  Bulworth, 272, 273
  Dick Tracy, 257
  Heaven Can Wait, 185–87, 211, 232, 252
  Ishtar, 4–5, 210–38
  Mermaid, 208
  Reds, 187–97, 210–11
Beck, Marilyn, 231
Becker, Gerry, 253
Beer, Jax, 70

Belafonte, Harry, 99
Berkshire Theatre Festival, 115–20
Berlin, Annie, 10–12
Berlin, Harold, 11–12
Berlin, Ida Aaron, 10–11, 13
  in Chicago, 14–16
  in Los Angeles, 17–18, 19
Berlin, Jack, 7–8, 10–12, 20
  death of, 12–13
  in Yiddish theater, 7, 9–11
Berlin, Jeannie
  birth and early life of, 17–19, 25, 48,
    61, 77, 92
  directing *On the Way,* 300
Berlin, Jeannie, acting career of, 134,
    166, 207–8, 240, 296–97, 298, 303
  The Heartbreak Kid, 133–37, 140–41,
    145, 147, 149, 150, 207, 296
  In and Out of the Light, 278, 280–81
  Rumpelstiltskin, 94
  In the Spirit, 240
Berman, Shelley, 44–45
Beverly Hills Cop, 212
Bial, Henry, 146
Birdcage, The, 259–68, 275, 276–77
Birdsong, Mary, 25, 286, 288, 289
Biskind, Peter, 230
Black Sunday, 175
Blaine, Vivian, 103
Blakemore, Michael, 252–53
Blame It on Rio, 285
Blue Angel, the, 52, 54, 56, 57, 59, 62,
    66
Bluhdorn, Charles, 114–15, 124
Bogdanovich, Peter, 140, 177
Bologna, Joseph, 209
Bonnie and Clyde, 112, 184
Boston Daily Record, 73
Boston Globe, 116, 119
Bowen, Roger, 36
Bowie, David, 165
Boyle, Peter, 96
Brandman, Michael, 95
Brando, Marlon, 68
Brantley, Ben, 281, 298, 317
Breaking Bad, 311
Brecht, Bertolt, 25, 29, 30, 31
Brenman-Gibson, Margaret, 91
Brickman, Marshall, 91
Broderick, Matthew, 282
Brody, Richard, 308, 313
Brooks, James L., 236
Brooks, Mel, 113
Brown, G. Mac, 222
Brown, Helen Gurley, 92

Bulworth, 272, 273
Burns, George, 64
Burton, Richard, 75–76
Bye Bye Blues, 292–96, 297–98, 301–2,
    303

Cabaret, 292
Caesar, Sid, 34
California Suite, 180, 187
Calley, John, 88, 307
Canby, Vincent, 130–31, 145, 175–76,
    186, 254, 281
Cannes Film Festival, 177, 241
Cannon, Dyan, 185–87
Cantor, Arthur, 86
Canyon Ranch, 228
Capone, Al, 14
Carlin, Joy, 30
Carroll, Jean, 64
Carter, Jimmy, 142
Cassavetes, John, 240
  Mikey and Nicky, 157–67, 169, 173,
    297
Caucasian Chalk Circle, The, 29
Cavett, Dick, 136
CBS, 66, 88, 109–10
celebrity and fame, 8, 59–62, 107–9,
    255, 286–87
Central Park West apartment, 1, 203,
    244, 322
Cera, Michael, 314–15, 318
Champlin, Charles, 232
Channing, Carol, 115
Chariots of Fire, 231
Charlie Wilson's War, 292
Chekhov, Anton, 54, 137
Chelsea Nights, 298
Chernow, Ron, 311
Chicago, 14–16, 20–22, 62
  first meetings with Mike, 24–27
  improv comedy, 33–34, 38–44
Chicago, 292
Chicago Daily News, 24
Chicago Tribune, 130, 163
childhood, 7–8, 9–16
civil rights movement, 97, 99
Clinton, Bill, 268–69, 271–72
Clooney, George, 292
Close, Del, 45–46, 47, 50–51, 95
Coca-Cola, 216, 231, 234
"Cocktail Piano," 68
Coco, James, 122
Coe, Fred, 71, 84–86, 87
Coen, Ethan, 301
Cohen, Alexander, 71–72, 73–74, 76–79

Cohn, Mollie, 10
Columbia Studios, 80–81, 103
　Ishtar, 213, 216, 229–32
Columbia University, 293
comedy compared with romance, 2
Como, Perry, 59–60
Compass Players, 8, 21
　in Chicago, 32–44
　improv, 38–44
　Mike and Elaine's firing, 47–49
　in New York, 50–57
　in St. Louis, 45–49, 95
"Concerning Humour in Comedy"
　(Congreve), 62
Congreve, William, 62
Coppola, Francis Ford, 177, 185
COVID-19 pandemic, 322, 324–25
Crisis in Six Scenes, 309–11
Criterion Collection, 312
Cromer, David, 314, 315
Crosby, Bing, 211, 234
Crystal, Billy, 279
Cyrus, Miley, 309, 310

Dancing in the Dark, 298–99
Dangerous Minds, 259
Darden, Severn, 23, 45
Darlow, Cynthia, 283–84
Davis, Geena, 257
Day, Doris, 112
DBA (short for Doing Business As)
　Company, 205–6
Death-Defying Acts, 251, 254
de Beauvoir, Simone, 65
DeGeneres, Ellen, 267
Demme, Jonathan, 203
Denby, David, 266
Dick Tracy, 257
Didion, Joan, 182, 205
Diller, Barry, 152, 153, 168–71, 173–74
Diller, Phyllis, 64–66
Diners Club, 61
Directors Guild of America, 131, 176
"Disc Jockey," 53, 54, 57–58, 103
Donahue, Phil, 243
Donen, Stanley, 285–91, 311
　Adult Entertainment, 286, 287–91
　Bye Bye Blues, 292–96
　ill health and death of, 302, 319
Donnenfeld, Bernard, 127–28
Donner, Clive, 102, 103, 104–5
Drama Desk Awards, 120
Dunham, Lena, 313
Dunne, John Gregory, 182, 205
Dybbuk, The, 29

Ebb, Fred, 292
Ebert, Roger, 145, 165, 234
education, 16–17
Eisenhower, Dwight D., 78–79
Elaine May Players, 303
Elaine May Renaissance, 311–13
Elkins, Hillard, 113–15
Enter Laughing, 102–4, 106, 121, 206
Ephron, Nora, 236, 277
Equal Rights Amendment, 276
Evans, Robert, 112–13, 120–21, 128–29,
　188
*Evening with Mike Nichols and Elaine
　May, An,* 71–79, 81
　conflicts, 76–77
　Elaine's resignation, 79
　opening, 73–75
　origins of, 71–72
　out-of-town tryouts, 72–73
　reviews, 74
Everybody Loves Raymond, 2, 297

Fairfax High School, 16, 17
Falk, Peter, 307
　death of David Rubinfine, 206
　Hotline, 252
　Luv, 102, 103–7, 154
　Mikey and Nicky, 153–54, 157–64,
　　166–67, 169, 171–72
　In the Spirit, 240, 244
False Inspector Dew, The, 209
Farrow, Dylan, 310
Farrow, Mia, 310
Far Side, The (comic), 235
Father Knows Best, 33, 34
Feibleman, Peter, 15, 200
　DBA Company, 205
　Heaven Can Wait, 185
　Ishtar, 212
　Reds, 188, 189, 191
Fellini, Federico, 88
Feminine Mystique, The (Friedan), 65
feminism, 65, 151, 178
Fey, Tina, 312
Fiddler on the Roof, 83, 100
Fields, Bert, 171, 172, 200, 211–13,
　228
Fields, Freddie, 135
Fields, Verna, 176
First Line/Last Line, 53–55, 75, 78
Fisher, Jules, 100, 101
Flicker, Theodore J., 45–49, 51, 95–96,
　307
"flop era," 89–90, 101–2
Ford, Harrison, 257

Ford Pinto, 152, 153, 169–70
Forman, Milos, 165
Fornés, María Irene, 100
Fosse, Bob, 264
Freud, Sigmund, 62
Friedan, Betty, 65
Friedman, Bruce Jay, 132, 148
Friedman, Maria, 287
Fuller, Brad, 226, 229, 240, 243–44

Gardner, Herb, 183, 203, 204, 214, 249
Garr, Teri, 201
Gay and Lesbian Alliance Against
    Defamation (GLAAD), 267
Gazzara, Ben, 68
Geffen, David, 203
Gelbart, Larry, 205–6
Gelber, Jack, 115
George Is Dead, 299–301
Georgina's First Date, 36, 120
Gerwig, Greta, 313, 321–22
Getting Straight, 134
Ghostbusters, 212
Ghostbusters II, 203–4
Gibson, William, 115
Giving Up Smoking, 298
Gleason, Jackie, 34
Glover, Danny, 326
Godfather, The, 158
Golden Globes, 131, 145
Goodbye People, The, 249
Goodwill, 22
Goodyear Playhouse, 68
Gordon, Bobbi, 32
Gordon, Lorraine, 54
Gordon, Mark, 35, 96, 97, 172–73
Gordon, Max, 52, 54
Gould, Elliott, 146
Gould, Lois, 182
Gover, Robert, 113
Graduate, The, 112, 309
Graham, Henry, 144
Grammy Awards, 68
Grand Hotel, 208–9
Grant, Cary, 114, 145
Great Depression, 10
Green Mill Cocktail Lounge, 14
Greenson, Ralph, 91
Griffiths, Trevor, 188, 189, 193
Grodin, Charles, 203, 303
    The Heartbreak Kid, 132–33, 135–38,
        140, 145, 148
    Heaven Can Wait, 186–87
    Ishtar, 214, 216–17, 223, 233, 234
Gussow, Mel, 248

Hackman, Gene, 260–63
Haley, Mike, 258
Hamilton, 311
Hankin, Annette, 15–16, 33, 36
Harnick, Sheldon, 82–83, 91
Harris, Barbara, 29–30, 34, 37, 38
Harris, Julie, 68
Harrison, Jim, 257, 258
Hausman, Michael
    The Heartbreak Kid, 139–40
    Mikey and Nicky, 159, 162–64,
        169–70, 172–73
Hautzig, Deborah, 94
Hays Code, 42
HB Studio, 71, 88
Headland, Leslye, 313
Heartbreak Kid, The, 132–53
    casting, 132–36, 296
    production, 137–41
    reviews and criticism, 144–51
    the script, 136–37
Heartburn, 204
Heaven Can Wait, 185–87, 188, 211,
    232
Hebrew Actors' Union, 10
Heckerling, Amy, 232
heckling, 65–66
Hedges, Lucas, 314
Hedges, Peter, 322–24
Hellman, Lillian, 75, 95, 188, 203
Henson, Jim, 203
Here Comes Mr. Jordan, 184
Hiaasen, Carl, 292
Hickey, William, 88–89
Hi-Hat Lounge, 32, 38, 44
Hirsch, Judd, 88–89
Hiss, Alger, 93
Hitchens, Christopher, 62–63
Hoffman, Dustin, 257
    Grodin casting in *The Heartbreak Kid,*
        140, 148
    Ishtar, 4–5, 212–16, 218–23, 228–29,
        231, 235–36
    Tootsie, 200–203, 214
Holliday, Judy, 104, 107
Hollywood, 16, 80–81, 112–13, 277.
    *See also specific persons and
    films*
    blacklist, 145–46
    Hays Code, 42
    sexism in, 101–2, 177–79, 232–33,
        236–37
Hollywood High School, 16
Homecoming, 36
Hope, Bob, 211, 234

Hotline, 251–54
Hudson River, 2
Humphrey, Hubert, 141

I'm Not Rappaport, 204
improv comedy, 33–34
  basic rules of, 4, 46–47
  First Line/Last Line, 53–55
  May as godmother of, 46–47
  of Nichols and May, 38–45, 53–56,
    67–71
Improvisations to Music, 67–69
In and Out of the Light, 278–79,
    280–81
Indecent Exposure, 209
Indiana Jones, 241
intellectual property, 4
Interview (magazine), 245
In the Spirit, 240, 242–47
"I Saw Mommy Kissing Santa Claus,"
    42
Isherwood, Charles, 290
Ishtar, 4–5, 210–38, 245
  casting, 212–14
  music, 214–16, 235–36
  plot, 211–12
  post-production, 225–29
  production, 216–25
  reviews and criticism, 229–38

Jackson, LaTanya Richardson, 319–20
Jackson, Samuel L., 319–20, 326
Jaffe, Stanley, 124, 127, 128
Jefferson, Margo, 253–54
Jewish mothers, 27, 55–56
Joffe, Charles, 51–52
John Burroughs Junior High, 16
Johnson, Kevin M., 108
Johnson, Lyndon, 96
*Jokes and Their Relation to the
    Unconscious* (Freud), 62
Jones, Laurie, 240

Kael, Pauline, 145
Kahn, Sheldon, 166–67
Kama Sutra, 42
Kander, John, 292
Kane, Carol, 214, 311
Kauffmann, Stanley, 175
Keaton, Buster, 71
Keaton, Diane, 135, 146, 188, 194
Kemper, Victor, 164
Kennedy, Jacqueline "Jackie," 61
Kennedy, John F., 78–79, 96–97
  birthday celebration, 84, 272

Kennedy Center Honors, 309
Kerr, Jean, 95
Kind Hearts and Coronets, 291
King, Martin Luther, Jr., 99
King Kong, 175
Klein, Joe, 268–69
Klein, Robert, 270, 271, 287
Knack, The, 98
Koch, Howard W., 115, 123, 124, 128,
    129
Kraft Theatre, 68
Kubrick, Stanley, 177
Kurtz, Swoosie, 194–99

L.A. Weekly, 233
Labyrinth, 203
La Cage aux Folles, 259–60
Lahr, John, 84
Lamarr, Hedy, 145
Lambert, Zohra, 29
Lane, Mark, 97
Lane, Nathan, 260–63
Lange, Jessica, 201, 202
Larson, Gary, 235
Lasser, Louise, 96, 99
Lebedeff, Aaron, 8
Lemmon, Jack, 102, 103–6
Lester, Adrian, 262, 270
Levinson, Barry, 272
Lewis, Joe E., 14
Life (magazine), 15, 102, 109
Lincoln Center, 248, 302, 311–12
Living Newspaper, 33
Lo Bianco, Tony, 100–101
Lonergan, Kenneth, 297, 322
  The Waverly Gallery, 313–21
Longacre Theatre, 282
Look Who's Talking, 232
Los Angeles City College, 17
Los Angeles Film Critics Association,
    321–22
Los Angeles Times, 229, 230, 232, 233,
    310–11
Loved One, The, 88
Lupino, Ida, 113
Luv, 102, 103–7, 109, 121, 123, 154
Lyonne, Natasha, 172, 313
Lysistrata, 45

Mabley, Moms, 63–64
McCabe & Mrs. Miller, 184
McCarthy, Cormac, 268
McCarthy, Todd, 266
  Mikey and Nicky, 165, 167, 169, 170,
    173, 177

McElwaine, Guy, 213, 231
McGovern, George, 141–42, 184
McKay, Craig, 190
MacLaine, Shirley, 107
MacLeod, David, 214
McNally, Terrence, 115, 117–18
McQueen, Steve, 113
Madison Square Garden, 84, 141
Madonna, 264
Mailer, Norman, 75
Mamet, David, 209, 251
Manchester by the Sea, 314
Marathon Man, 175
Margaret, 297
Marshall, Penny, 232
Martin, Dean, 112
Maslin, Janet, 233–34, 247, 266, 273, 313
Mathieu, Allaudin, 23
Matter of Position, A, 83–87, 88, 90, 116–17, 118, 279, 281–82
Matthau, Walter
    California Suite, 180, 187
    A New Leaf, 122–26, 129–30
    One Hundred Dollar Misunderstanding, 114, 115
May, Marvin, 17–18
Mayer, Bernadette, 207
MCA/Universal Pictures, 112
Men, 257
Mermaid, 208
Merrily We Go to Hell, 113
Method acting, 18, 41, 73
#MeToo movement, 310
Meyer, Russ, 165
MGM Pictures, 112
Midsummer Night's Dream, A, 31
Mike Nichols and Elaine May Examine Doctors, 87
Mikey and Nicky, 152–79, 180–81, 184, 208, 209, 297
    backstory, 153–57
    lawsuits, 170–74
    post-production, 165–71, 225
    production, 157–65
    release, 174–75
    reviews and criticism, 175–79
Miller, Tom, 161, 163
Million Dollar Baby, 208
Miracle Worker, The, 72
Mirochek, Jan, 300
Miss Julie, 24–25, 30–31, 305
Mr. Gogol and Mr. Preen, 248–49
Mister Kelly's Chicago, 62
Mister Roberts, 68

Mocambo Club, 61–62
Monitor, 70, 87
Monroe, Marilyn, 84
Moore, Michael, 311
Mosher, Gregory, 248–49, 251
Mostel, Zero, 146
"Mother and Son," 54–56, 142, 256
Moving Right Along, 300
Muppet Movie, The, 214–15
Murray, Bill, 203, 257, 326
Museum of Television and Radio, 255–56
"Mysterioso," 68

Name of a Soup, 88
Nation, The (magazine), 239
National Medal of Arts, 312
National Society of Film Critics Award, 145
National Women's Conference, 178
Naughton, James, 194–95, 197–99
Nazi Party, 10, 145
Nervous Set, The, 95
Neugebauer, Lila, 315, 316
New Leaf, A, 120–31, 137, 139, 144, 150, 152, 153, 178, 257, 296
Newman, Chris, 163–64
Newman, Paul, 246
New Republic, The, 175
New School, 168, 178–79
New York (magazine), 175, 230, 266
New York, New York, 177
New York City, 50–79
    Compass Players, 50–57
    nightlife, 52–53, 57
New York Daily News, 254, 317
New Yorker, 56–57, 252–53, 308
New York Film Critics Circle Awards, 145, 202
New York Herald Tribune, 59
New York Journal-American, 56
New York Post, 317
New York Psychoanalytic Society & Institute, 92
New York Public Library, 256
New York Times, 58, 65, 70, 74, 94, 106, 108, 110, 118, 127, 130–31, 146, 158, 175, 176, 199, 233–34, 245–48, 251, 253–54, 266, 267, 281, 284, 290, 298, 310, 317, 319
New York Town Hall, 70, 71–72, 324
New York University, 134
New York World's Fair (1964), 97
Nichols, Mike, 13, 302–3
    acting classes of, 30–31, 38, 39

American Masters, 307–9
celebrity and fame of, 8, 59–62, 75, 302–3
early life of, 27–28
Mikey and Nicky, 155–56
move to New York City, 38
at University of Chicago, 24–25, 28
Who's Afraid of Virginia Woolf?, 80, 99, 122, 180, 193
Wolf, 257–58
Nichols, Mike, and Elaine May, 255–74, 304–6
An Evening with Mike Nichols and Elaine May, 71–79, 81
The Birdcage, 259–68
break-up, 81, 86–88
era of choosiness, 66
firing from Compass, 47–49
first meeting, 24–27
improv, 37, 38–45, 53–56, 67–71
Improvisations to Music, 67–69
Kennedy's birthday party, 84, 272
lover question, 27
A Matter of Position, 83–87, 88, 90, 116–17, 118, 279
Mike Nichols and Elaine May Examine Doctors, 87
New York Compass, 50–57
Omnibus "The Suburban Review," 57–60
Primary Colors, 268–74
In Retrospect, 256
reunions, 98–101, 141–42, 194–200, 255–56
tour of 1958, 61–62
Who's Afraid of Virginia Woolf?, 194–200
Nicholson, Jack, 190, 194, 257–58
Nights of Cabiria, 88
No Exit, 108
Not Enough Rope, 81–82, 84, 88–89, 251, 253

Obama, Barack, 312
Obie Awards, 100
Odd Couple, The, 124, 248
Odell, Ben, 286, 293–95, 303
Office, The, 100–101
Omnibus "The Suburban Review," 57–60
One Flew Over the Cuckoo's Nest, 165
One Hundred Dollar Misunderstanding, 113–15, 120
O'Neill, Eugene, 190
On the Way, 300

Opener Killing Trotsky, 300
origin story, 7–8
Oswalt, Patton, 172
Ouspenskaya, Maria, 18
Outer Critics Circle Awards, 120
Out-of-Towners, The, 133
Ozzie and Harriet, 34

Paar, Jack, 57, 59–60
Palestine Liberation Organization, 216
Palomar Pictures, 132
Paramount Pictures, 112–15
Mikey and Nicky, 152–79
A New Leaf, 120–31, 152, 153
One Hundred Dollar Misunderstanding, 113–15, 120
Parker, Mary-Louise, 323
Patinkin, Sheldon, 33
Peer Gynt, 31
PEN America Lifetime Achievement Award, 324–25
Penn, Arthur, 68, 72, 92, 114, 207
An Evening with Mike Nichols and Elaine May, 72
A Matter of Position, 84, 85, 116, 284
People (magazine), 276
Perkins, Anthony, 93
Peschkowsky, Michael Igor, 27
Peter, Paul, and Mary, 99
Pfeiffer, Michelle, 258–59
Pikser, Jeremy, 9–10, 189–90, 193
Pilates, 228
"Pirandello," 54, 69–70, 72, 73, 74, 196
Pittsburgh, 11–12
Piven, Joyce, 31
Plato, 22
Playbill, 48, 317
Playboy, 48
Playboy Club, 140, 141
Playwrights Theatre Club, 21, 28–32, 97
Plaza Suite, 133, 199
political correctness, 263, 276–77
Pollack, Sydney, 200–203
Ponder, Nancy, 50–51
Posey, Parker, 282, 283–84
Power Plays, 282, 314
Powers, John, 233
Preminger, Erik Lee, 181–82
The Heartbreak Kid, 134–35, 136, 139, 140–41
Preminger, Otto, 181–83
Presley, Elvis, 42
Previn, Soon-Yi, 310
Primary Colors, 265, 268–74, 275

Prince, Hal, 71
Pritikin diet, 228
Production Code, 145–46
Prohibition, 14
Proust Questionnaire, 295
psychoanalysis, 71, 91–92, 207
Puttnam, David, 229–31

Quart, Barbara, 149–50

Radio City Music Hall, 319–20
Rain Man, 235
Rambo, 235
Ramis, Harold, 203–4
RCA Building, 70
Reagan, Ronald, 211
Real You, The, 36
Redford, Robert, 246
Red Mill, The, 66
Reds, 187–97, 210–11
Red Shoes, The, 285
Reed, John, 187–88
Reiner, Carl, 102–4, 106
Reiner, Rob, 236
Relatively Speaking, 297, 301
repression, 42, 146
Rich, Frank, 199
Rickey, Carrie, 313
Rifkin, Ron, 303
Riverside Drive apartment, 61, 92, 98.
    02, 203
Road to Ranchipur, 234
Robbins, Jerome, 100–101
Roberts, Doris, 228
Robin Byrd Show, The, 287
Roger Is Dead, 300–301
Rollins, Jack, 48, 50, 51–52, 54, 56, 57,
    59–60, 76, 86
romance compared with comedy, 3
Romancing the Stone, 212
Rooney, Cindy Kaplan, 191, 192
Rosen, Marjorie, 149
Rosenbaum, Jonathan, 313
Rosenberg, Julius and Ethel, 129
Rosenthal, Phil, 2, 9, 279, 297, 312
Rottenberg, Dan, 163
Rotter, Stephen, 218–19, 225–29
Rubinfine, David, 71
    death of, 206–8
    marriage to Elaine, 90–93, 98,
        166–67, 206–8
    Mikey and Nicky and, 171–72
Rubinfine, Rosa, 91–92
Rudin, Scott, 314
Rumpelstiltskin, 31, 94

Runaway Bride, 257
Russell, Rosalind, 107
Ryan, Meg, 257

Sahl, Mort, 52–53, 54, 110
Sahlins, Bernard, 307
Saint, David, 249, 300–301, 311
Saint, Eva Marie, 68
St. Jude's Children's Hospital, 299
Saks, Gene, 249–51
Same Storm, The, 322–24
Same Time, Next Year, 199
San Francisco, 25, 72
San Remo, the, 1, 203, 241
Santoni, Reni, 96
Sardi's, 73–74
Sartre, Jean-Paul, 108
Saturday Night Live, 33, 276
Saving Ryan's Privates, 287
Sawyer, Diane, 272
Saypol, Irving H., 129
Scherick, Edgar, 132, 133, 137
Schisgal, Murray, 213, 214
Schlafly, Phyllis, 178
Schlossberg, Julian, 203, 208, 240, 278,
    308, 319
    David and Elaine, 207
    Hotline, 251, 252
    Mikey and Nicky, 158, 174–75
    In and Out of the Light, 278, 280–81
    In the Spirit, 240, 242–46
    Stanley and Elaine, 286
    Taller Than a Dwarf, 281–84, 286
    Witnesses to the 20th Century, 303
Schopper, Phillip, 15, 191, 239–44
    David and Elaine, 207
    Ishtar, 214, 217, 219–20, 226
    In the Spirit, 240, 242–44, 247–48
    Wolf, 257
Schweitzer, Albert, 58
Scorsese, Martin, 177, 313
Scot, Pat, 45
Screen Actors Guild Award, 268
Screen Gems, 161
Seacat, Sandra, 240, 242, 243, 247
Second City, 21, 34, 270, 276
Second Sex, The (de Beauvoir), 65
Seinfeld, 269
self-mythologizing, 8, 14
Selma to Montgomery march, 99
sex, 21, 28, 42, 43, 47
Sex, Lies, and Videotape, 241
sexism, 62–64, 89–90, 101–2, 176,
    177–79, 232–33, 236–37
Shaber, David, 182

Shakespeare, William, 31, 35, 78
Shakespeare Festival, 31
Shampoo, 184
She Loves Me, 83
Shepherd, Cybill, 135–36, 138, 139, 140
Shepherd, David, 28–29, 32, 34–35, 37–38, 43, 44, 47–48
Shining, The, 177
Shore, Dinah, 66
Sills, Paul, 21, 23–24, 25, 37–38, 44, 307
　Playwrights Theatre Club, 21, 28–30
Silver, Joan Micklin, 182, 240
Silverstein, Shel, 174, 251
Simon, John, 175
Simon, Neil, 124, 299
　California Suite, 180, 187
　The Heartbreak Kid, 132–33, 135, 136–37, 142–47
　Plaza Suite, 133, 199
Simon & Garfunkel, 256
Singin' in the Rain, 293
Siskel, Gene, 130, 267
Skinner, Randy, 298, 302
Skinny Dip, 292
Slavitt, David, 182
Small Time Crooks, 291–92
Smith, John N., 259
Smith, Liz, 287
Smith, Will, 291
Smith-Cameron, J., 298
Smothers, Tom, 109–10
Smothers Brothers Comedy Hour, 109–10
Sobel, Michelle Gorchow, 243
social media, 59, 313
Social Security, 204
Soderbergh, Steven, 241
Somebody Feed Phil, 312
Sondheim, Stephen, 61, 71
Spiegel, Ira, 227, 230, 240, 244
Spielberg, Steven, 212, 302
Splash, 208
Spock, Benjamin, 19
Spolin, Viola, 23, 32
Stallone, Sylvester, 235
Stanwyck, Barbara, 106, 107
Star Is Born, A, 214
State and Main, 209
Steppenwolf Theatre, 314
Steve Allen Show, The, 57
Storaro, Vittorio, 214, 220, 221
Strasberg, Lee, 30, 38, 39
Streisand, Barbra, 94, 107, 146, 232
Streit, David, 138–39

Strindberg, August, 24–25, 30–31
Stritch, Elaine, 291–92
Such Good Friends, 182–83, 204
Sullivan, Ed, 8
Sundance Film Festival, 241, 293
Sunset Marquis, 165
Sweet Charity, 88
Swing Shift, 203
Sylbert, Anthea, 135–36
Sylbert, Paul, 162, 187, 214, 219, 224
Symposium (Plato), 22

Take My Wife, 298
Take the Money and Run, 291
Taller Than a Dwarf, 281–87, 289, 298
Tarantino, Quentin, 313
Taylor, Elizabeth, 88
Taylor, James, 236
Taylor, Renée, 96, 122–23, 209, 319
"Teenagers," 42, 53, 54, 58, 77, 304
"Telephone," 53–55, 58, 251
Ten Little Indians, 36
Tharp, Twyla, 264
Third Ear, the, 95–98
30 Rock, 312
Thomas, Marlo, 203, 204, 241, 286, 297
　George Is Dead, 299–301
　Million Dollar Baby, 208
　In the Spirit, 240, 241, 243, 245–46
Thompson, Emma, 268, 271, 273–74
Time (magazine), 59, 267
Tonight at 8:30, 24, 28
Tony Awards, 98, 319–20
Tootsie, 200–203, 205, 206, 214
Towne, Robert, 188, 208
Travolta, John, 270–71
Trouble with Angels, The, 113
truthfulness, 3, 32–33, 292, 315
Truth in Comedy (Close), 46
Tucker, Sophie, 63
Turturro, John, 301
Two for the Seesaw, 72
Two Wigs and a Wag and Two Cocksuckers, 44–45

Ufland, Harry, 176, 177
Ullman, Tracey, 291–92
Ullmann, Liv, 326
University of Chicago, 21–22, 24–25, 28, 29, 34, 275, 307
University of Minnesota, 138

Vanity Fair (magazine), 205, 295, 310
Van Patten, Joyce, 282, 283

Variety (magazine), 266, 290, 310, 319
Variety Arts Theater, 287, 289–90
Venice Film Festival Award, 287
Verdon, Gwen, 88
Vidal, Gore, 307
Vietnam War, 96, 141
Village Vanguard, 52–53
Village Voice, 106, 235
Virtual Reality, 278–79

Wag the Dog, 272, 273
Walken, Christopher, 303
Wallace, George, 99
Waters, John, 240
Waugh, Evelyn, 88
Waverly Gallery, The, 313–21, 322
Way of All Fish, The, 278–80
Weill, Claudia, 240
Weinstein, Harvey, 292–93
Weld, Tuesday, 93
Weston, Jack, 100, 214, 223
Wexler, Milton, 91
What About Bob?, 203
What Planet Are You From?, 291
What's New, Pussycat?, 104, 184
Who's Afraid of Virginia Woolf?, 80, 99,
    122, 180, 193, 194–200

"Why Women Aren't Funny"
    (Hitchens), 62–63
Wiest, Dianne, 260–63
Wilder, Billy, 122
Williams, Paul, 214–16, 220, 223–24,
    225
Williams, Robin, 260–63, 291
Williamson, Marianne, 246
Williamstown Theatre Festival, 249–51
Wilson, Edmund, 76
Witnesses to the 20th Century, 303
Wolf, 257–58
women in comedy, 62–66
Working Girl, 204
World War II, 16
Wranovics, Fred, 38
writer's block, 33
Writers Guild of America Awards, 131,
    187, 193, 268, 312

Yablans, Frank, 152–53, 171, 174
Yentl, 232
Yiddish theater, 7, 7n, 9–11, 14

Zabar's, 2
Zelensky, Volodymyr, 326
Zemeckis, Robert, 212